SHAME

Shame

THE POLITICS AND POWER OF AN EMOTION

DAVID KEEN

PRINCETON UNIVERSITY PRESS
PRINCETON & OXFORD

Copyright © 2023 by Princeton University Press

Princeton University Press is committed to the protection of copyright and the intellectual property our authors entrust to us. Copyright promotes the progress and integrity of knowledge. Thank you for supporting free speech and the global exchange of ideas by purchasing an authorized edition of this book. If you wish to reproduce or distribute any part of it in any form, please obtain permission.

Requests for permission to reproduce material from this work should be sent to permissions@press.princeton.edu

Published by Princeton University Press
41 William Street, Princeton, New Jersey 08540
99 Banbury Road, Oxford OX2 6JX

press.princeton.edu

All Rights Reserved
ISBN: 978-0-691-18375-6
ISBN (e-book): 978-0-691-24100-5

British Library Cataloging-in-Publication Data is available

Editorial: Hannah Paul and Josh Drake
Production Editorial: Jenny Wolkowicki
Jacket design: Chris Ferrante
Production: Erin Suydam
Publicity: Kate Hensley and Kathryn Stevens

This book has been composed in Arno Pro

Printed on acid-free paper. ∞

Printed in the United States of America

10 9 8 7 6 5 4 3 2 1

CONTENTS

Acknowledgments vii

1 Introduction — 1
2 Honor and Shame among America's Veterans — 13
3 The Scourge of Shame — 25
4 Shame and Shamelessness — 44
5 Gilligan's Criminals — 65
6 "Since I Am a Dog": Shame and Recognition in Sierra Leone's Civil War — 74
7 The Shamelessness—and Shame—of Adolf Eichmann — 92
8 Trump's Idea of Shame—and How to Ward It Off — 111
9 Trumpelstiltskin: Spinning Shame into Political Gold — 124
10 Brexit — 144
11 Shame and Colonialism — 163
12 Shame and the Economy — 180
13 Shame and Mass Violence — 208

14 Shame and the West   232

15 Conclusion   263

Notes   285
Bibliography   309
Index   333

ACKNOWLEDGMENTS

MY WARM thanks to Hannah Paul and Josh Drake at Princeton for guiding me with grace and gentle efficiency. I would also like to thank the excellent production and marketing team at Princeton, including Jenn Backer for her copy editing, Jenny Wolkowicki for steering through the proofs, Virginia Ling for the index, and Sydney Bartlett for publicity. My reviewers were sometimes tough and always insightful, and I thank them for that (especially the second part). Thanks also to Sarah Caro for her enthusiasm for the original project. I would like to express my gratitude to my friends, family, and colleagues for their invaluable support. Martin Ruhs played a key role in launching this project, and I am very grateful for his help and encouragement. I would also like to say a special thank-you to Thomas Brodie, Ali Ali, Mats Berdal, James Hall, Henry Bagenal, Rob Maidment, Paul Rutman, Adekeye Adebajo, Clare Fox-Ruhs, Cristina Vergara Lopez, Cindy Ferrara, David Dwan and Gopal Sreenivasan. Thanks also to my Cambridge and St Antony's friends more generally. I am grateful to Maya for her insightful comments and also to Emma Kemp, Heather Ebner and Pascale Lafeber in my writers' group. I will not try to name everyone, but Ruben Andersson has been amazingly and consistently helpful with his insights and encouragement and I am especially grateful to him. My daughter has been funny and kind and encouraged me on the Brexit chapter in particular. I dedicate this book to my lovely wife, Vivian, more patient than a thousand saints and unswerving in her support and kindness.

SHAME

1

Introduction

SHAME IS A PAINFUL EMOTION—something we try to ward off and try not to feel. It's also something we generally try not to talk about. In fact, we are often ashamed of shame.[1] But today we need to talk about shame more urgently than ever.

In an increasingly bitter political arena, "Shame on you!" has become a kind of reflex for rival political groups, with the echo chamber of social media amplifying the accusations. Whether in the personal or the political sphere, a fever of electronic finger-pointing has been encouraged by the internet's peculiar combination of visibility and anonymity.

The lure of public condemnation has surely never been stronger—from body-shaming and celebrity-shaming to politician-shaming. Then along came Donald Trump, and you could do all three at once.

Whether in politics or beyond it, a habit of instant condemnation appears increasingly to be choking off curiosity and narrowing the space for an understanding of others even as such understanding seems more desperately needed than ever.

Responding to some hurtful posts from people she'd helped and trusted, the novelist Chimamanda Ngozi Adichie highlighted a wider problem of shaming and in-group conformity: "We have a generation of young people on social media so terrified of having the wrong opinions that they have robbed themselves of the opportunity to think and to learn and grow," she argued. "We are now angels jostling to out-angel one another."[2] While there are clearly positive sides to social media, the

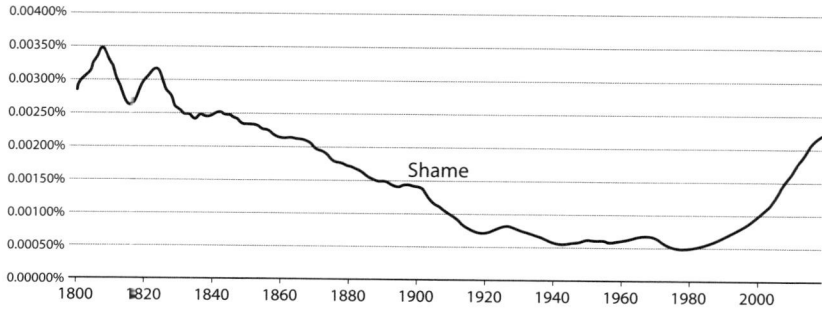

FIGURE 1. Trends in use of the word "shame."

digital pile-on is pervasive with online communities sometimes defining themselves in part by whom they shame.

We know, too, that mutual shaming has accompanied political polarization, notably in the United States. A key danger is that we are becoming trapped in some kind of *spiral of shame*. Shame begins to resemble a hot potato: we just can't wait to pass it on to someone else—or to pass it back the way it came.

According to Google Books' Ngram viewer, the use of the word "shame" declined pretty steadily (in Google's wide selection of English-language books) from the early 1800s to around 1940 and then stayed at a low level until around 1980. I remember shame as a pretty old-fashioned idea and the concept of a "shame society" even more so. But from the 1980s onward the use of the word "shame" rose pretty sharply.

Despite what appears to be a surge of both shaming itself and the use of the word "shame," few people seem actually to be changing their views. Very often, the shamed have dug in deeper. So if shame is supposed to be productive or transformative, it's not at all clear that this is working.

Why have shame and shaming become so much a part of the zeitgeist? What is it that lies behind our current surge of both shaming and talk of shaming? How can we guard against shame's damaging effects? And can we find a way to break out of the dangerous spiral of mutual shaming?

One major aim in this book is to explore the harm that shame and shaming can do. If we are going to address this damage, I argue, we need a good understanding of the many ways in which shame is manipulated. As part of this, we need to stop regarding shame as a relic of a distant past or as something that only prevails in so-called "shame cultures." More than this, we need to recognize that shame is being made to serve important political and economic functions in the Western world as well as elsewhere. Shame is not just a personal matter—a family dynamic, a legacy from a troubled childhood, or the currency of two people slugging it out on the street or online; it is also deeply political.

In particular, I am interested in the way that shame is *instrumentalized*. I want to explore its functions and its role in relation to large-scale human suffering. In part, this interest came out of my long-standing work on conflicts and humanitarian disasters. Since the 1980s, I've been investigating famines and civil wars, and I've had a special interest in the functions of phenomena (including famines and wars) that might at first glance seem only negative and dysfunctional. This evolving interest arose out of research in Sudan, Sierra Leone, Iraq, Guatemala, Serbia, Sri Lanka, and the Turkey/Syria border, and I've also researched disasters closer to my home in the UK (like the so-called "jungle" camp in France that was part of a "hostile environment" designed to deter migrants). I've found that these catastrophes generally serve important purposes, sometimes political, sometimes economic. No matter how much suffering has occurred, it has always been instructive to ask, "Who benefits?" (or in the Latin version, "Cui bono?"). Such practical benefits, moreover, have often been facilitated by a profound manipulation of shame.

Whether at a personal or political level, it would be a mistake to suppose that shame itself—for all its negative effects—is *purely dysfunctional*. For many influential actors, shame may be not so much a problem as an opportunity. Like other emotions, shame is not simply an escape or a retreat from "rational" projects like the pursuit of power and money; rather, shame has been integrated into the political economies that produce it and are in turn reinforced by it. While it would surely be difficult to find a time when shame *did not* play a major role in politics, today it does seem that shame is playing an especially important role in some very disturbing political processes.

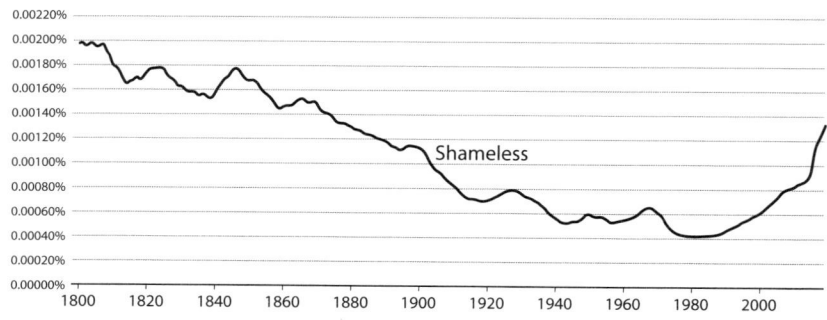

FIGURE 2. Trends in use of the word "shameless."

Even as we begin to realize the intimate connection between shame and major social and political problems, however, a contrasting—perhaps even an *opposite*—concern begins to loom into view. This is the problem of *shamelessness*. From Trump in the United States to Johnson in the UK, from Bolsonaro in Brazil to Duterte in the Philippines, from Modi in India to Salvini and Meloni in Italy, from Orbán in Hungary to Putin in Russia and many more, we have seen a series of leaders who seem to possess the quality of shamelessness in spades. Indeed, some of these leaders appear to be quite beyond shame or even embarrassment. The problem, from this perspective, is not that our politics exhibits too much shame but *too little*.

If we go back to Google Books, we find that the use of the word "shameless" follows a rather similar trajectory to the word "shame": it falls until around 1980 and then rises sharply.

What, then, is the relationship between these two apparently contradictory modern phenomena—on the one hand, what appears to be a destructive epidemic of shame and shaming and, on the other, a perhaps equally destructive epidemic of shamelessness? Why have these concepts become so salient and so prominent? How do shame and shamelessness relate to each other? And is it possible to move toward political habits that are more productive?

One factor that seems to be severely limiting our understanding of counterproductive and dangerous political processes (and the role of shame within them) is the so-called "rational actor" model—the assumption that people will rationally pursue their own interests. This assumption has been part of why many analysts have recoiled in horror and incomprehension when groups of people appear to act *against* their own interests: at times, it's as if a world of careful calculations has succumbed to "a world gone mad." A commonly cited puzzle here is support for Trump and for the UK's Brexit process from people who appear to have little to gain and much to lose.

But rather than concluding that people have "gone crazy," these phenomena should invite more careful attention to the emotions at play—and to the complex relationship between these emotions and the battle of interests that still lies at the heart of politics.

While there are plenty of important exceptions,[3] analysis of emotions has tended to be rather poorly integrated with analysis of interests. The division of academia into separate "disciplines" has often been unhelpful in this respect.

Of course, the picture is a complex one. The discipline of history lends itself to holistic approaches. And some subdisciplines—like political psychology—explicitly try to integrate politics and emotion. But while traditionally anthropologists have often sought to describe and explain the "strange" and "exotic" emotional and spiritual lives in societies far from their own, economists and political scientists have frequently focused on relatively wealthy societies (and often with a "rational actor" approach). Behavioral economists have added some useful complexity to the idea of a human being as a utility-maximizing organism but still routinely hold up emotion-free decision-making as a kind of ideal that is tainted in practice by errors and emotions. Part of the aim in this book is to contribute to the body of work that tries to integrate analysis of self-interest *and* emotion—and to do so by focusing on the interaction of self-interest and shame.

Crucially, understanding shame can help us greatly in comprehending the habit of buying—and selling—bogus or magical solutions for complex problems. Relatedly, it can help us understand how systems that yield rather substantial benefits for rather small numbers of people (and harm for a much larger number) are routinely considered somehow *acceptable*. Here, we need to investigate the process by which shame is loaded onto people as well as the varied strategies of those who offer to *relieve* this shame. Revealingly, the loading and the relieving have often come from the same source, so that we may discern here something of a *double game*.[4] At the extreme, this may even resemble a *mafia tactic* since mafias are specialists at relieving what they have also been threatening.

Importantly, a reservoir of underlying shame creates abundant opportunities for manipulation. In so many diverse areas of modern life (from populist politics to consumerism, from terrorism to the war on terror), one of the most important methods of advancing your own agenda has been to offer people some kind of plausible "escape" from shame—however bogus, magical, harmful, or self-interested the proposed remedy may be. Many of us seem to be perennially attracted to solutions that promise to "restore respect"—even when these "solutions" offer no tangible benefits and even when the "solutions" are likely, on any reasonable view of the evidence, to make our everyday lives significantly *worse*. As shame and shaming escalate, the opportunities to profit from offering a "remedy" may increase correspondingly, so that a range of hacks, quacks, fixers, wheelers, dealers, and charlatans are able to do better than ever. And significantly, in a world of shame, shamelessness itself can be sold as an attractive spectacle—a symbolic escape from shame, a taste of freedom, and a flight from the constraints, disparagements, insults, self-doubt, and self-admonishments to which mere mortals are regularly subjected and subjecting themselves.

In the long term, the magical nature of many of our favored "solutions" may begin to reveal itself—not least when the underlying problems that gave rise to shame in the first place remain largely unaddressed. Unfortunately, there is always the possibility that additional magical "solutions" can be offered—perhaps modified or disguised versions of the old ones. A key reference point for this process turns out to be consumerism, which flourishes precisely on the failure to satisfy underlying needs and perhaps constitutes something of a model for much of our contemporary politics.

Meanwhile, whether in the political or the economic sphere, we tend to find that there is a remarkably *perverse* distribution of shame—

that is, one that has very little relationship to the distribution of responsibility. Sexual violence epitomizes this, since it frequently creates a profound shame in the victims and yet often prompts remarkably little in the perpetrators—an imbalance profoundly shaped by social and cultural factors.[5] Part of this is that the shame and silence of the victims shield the perpetrators.

Perverse distributions of shame can also be observed within profoundly unequal economic systems, with poorer people experiencing shame in relation to their own poverty while those who have actively shaped and benefited from these unequal economic systems frequently exhibit a remarkable shamelessness.

How can we challenge destructive ways of thinking and behaving, including extreme inequality, violent politics, and outright war? One obvious way is by denouncing these things, and I have myself spent much of my professional career trying to uncover and document human rights abuses in a variety of civil wars and repressive postwar situations in many parts of the world. Of course, it's crucial to call out abuse and to call a spade a spade. Such denunciations would seem to be especially needed at a time when a conspicuous shamelessness attaches to abusive and neglectful politicians. The role of academics, journalists, outspoken aid workers, and organizations like Amnesty and Human Rights Watch is hugely important.

At the same time, I have also become aware that certain kinds of condemnation can themselves become part of the problem, and at least three points here are worth emphasizing.

First, condemnation tends to choke off understanding. One thing I have learned is that when people do bad things—and at the extreme this may involve creating a famine—they generally have *reasons for doing so*, whether these are military, political, economic, psychological, or some combination of these. Recognizing the existence of these reasons does not mean we have to approve or excuse the behavior. But they are reasons nonetheless. Linked to the existence of these reasons is the fact that perpetrators of human rights abuses frequently display some sense of *self-righteousness*, attaching at least some degree of approval to their own actions. So here we may again be entering the territory of shamelessness. Crucially, we get more and better ideas about how to prevent abuses when we take seriously the complex and often very human reasons why they happen—and when we explore the means by which they are legitimized. By contrast, where condemnation becomes the overwhelming focus, attempts at explanation get squeezed out—and may even feel like *excusing*.

A second problem with condemnation is that there are plenty of circumstances in which the shaming and condemnation of abuses may actually *fuel* the abuses in question. Angry individuals who are dismissed as "fanatical," "racist," "mad," "irrational," or "greedy" may be further enraged by such labels and may even end up conforming more closely to them.[6] Of course, this does not mean that they are *not* racist or greedy or fanatical. Nor does it mean we should keep silent or somehow "excuse" such behavior or attitudes. But assuming that shaming will lead to a productive shame turns out to be a huge leap of faith. In fact, shaming is very often *provocative*. One of the perils of diagnosing "irrational behavior" is that labeling people as "irrational" can quickly become part of an underlying shaming and an ongoing provocation—a shaming, perhaps, of "backward" or "ignorant" peoples or people. The backlash against Hillary Clinton's notorious claim that half of Trump supporters were a "basket of deplorables" should remind us that derogatory labels can even be adopted as a "badge of honor." In international politics, meanwhile, abusive leaders have sometimes profited from the perceived hostility of "the international community" (including measures like economic sanctions)—for example, by proposing themselves as protectors of what they proclaim to be an oppressed and unjustly punished or derided population.

A third problem with condemnation is that the process of shaming often feeds into a high degree of blindness to *the abuses of those who are doing the shaming*. In the context of local or international conflict, the shamed party may be a rebel group, a terrorist organization, an authoritarian leader, or a vilified individual such as a "drug lord" or a "human smuggler." But in my experience, those who sign up to the shaming and weakening of a widely condemned entity tend to have their own agendas, which frequently depart significantly from this loudly declared endeavor. Indeed, those who denounce "evil" most vociferously are frequently pushing various kinds of violence and exploitation—and these self-interested agendas (including international agendas) tend to acquire valuable "cover" precisely from the existence of what is being denounced. This—to a very large extent—is how impunity is constructed. And there is a further problem that has been little recognized: in large part because of the way impunity is constructed, those who condemn a demonized group may actually have an interest in the persistence or growth of this "enemy" group and may even take actions that strengthen the demonized group, including forms of active collaboration and provocation. In this context, shaming "the bad guys" acquires new meaning and new functions.[7]

In such circumstances, there is likely to be both shaming and blaming. While both activities involve the criticism of particular parties, they are also analytically distinct. Notably, an act of shaming will usually involve an attempt to make someone feel shame (though, as we shall see, there may be other aims); blaming on the other hand involves attributing responsibility for some harmful (or allegedly harmful) action or process. We shall see how shaming frequently adds "something extra" for those who are pointing the finger—not least when they are looking for some kind of impunity. It may also be even more provocative than blaming.

In chapter 2, I try to illuminate shame with a very specific example, looking at the politics of shame-distribution in relation to wars that have been waged by the United States (with a focus on the war in Iraq). Here, we encounter the strange case of Captain Rick Duncan, which illuminates shame dynamics in unexpected ways. It's a story that helps us see how a flight from shame—whether at the individual or societal level—can sometimes be more damaging than shame itself.

The next two chapters explore some important literature on shame, highlighting both a positive and a negative side. Chapter 3 shows how damaging shame and shaming can be, with some types of shame being *especially* destructive. Bringing in perspectives from anthropology, psychology, sociology, theology, politics, and history, the chapter shows how those who have been shamed en masse may be ripe for manipulation by those who offer some kind of "exit"—an escape from shame that often turns out to be temporary, illusory, and damaging in its own right.

Chapter 4 shifts the focus and looks at some of the more *positive* aspects of shame and shaming—and conversely at the problem of *shamelessness*. Can it be that both shame *and* shamelessness are driving social problems, including war itself? How are they related? What types of shame are we talking about—and what difference does this make? How is shamelessness constructed and maintained? More specifically, when policies prolong or exacerbate social problems, how are these failings accommodated? While chapters 3 and 4 cover important ground for the subsequent case studies, some readers might prefer to skip them and come back to them later.

Chapter 5 discusses the insights of someone who has strongly influenced my own thinking about shame: the American psychiatrist and prison reformer James Gilligan. Gilligan has worked extensively with violent criminals in U.S. prisons. He found that while inmates exhibited an extreme shamelessness in relation to their violent behavior, a formidable underlying shame had almost always fueled their violence, while shame in the present was a further provocation. Gilligan's perspectives offer tools that are potentially useful for understanding violence in a variety of contexts *outside* the prison system.

In chapter 6, I look at the vicious civil war in Sierra Leone in the 1990s, relating this to Gilligan's insights in particular. Conducting research in Sierra Leone in 1995 and again in 2001, I was struck by the very strong role that shame was playing in driving and shaping the violence. Yet shamelessness was also a significant cause of violence, with shame and shamelessness interacting in ways that it's important to understand.

Chapter 7 looks at a famously shameless individual, Adolf Eichmann, a man who expressed almost no misgivings or regret in relation to his key role in transporting Jewish men, women, and children to their deaths during the Nazi Holocaust. Yet it turns out that Eichmann *did* have a certain sense of shame (particularly shame around weakness).

Understanding the precise and peculiar nature of this shame can help us to understand Eichmann's behavior and, more generally, the complicated relationship between shame and shamelessness.

The next two chapters look at Donald Trump. Chapter 8 concentrates on Trump as an individual. It examines the relationship between his remarkable shamelessness and his personal ideas around what is—and isn't—shameful. As with Eichmann, Trump's extreme shamelessness in some respects has masked an acute (and peculiar) sense of shame; again, much of this is shame around weakness rather than shame around bad behavior. Chapter 9 broadens the discussion to look at the production of shame within American society and the way Trump was able to tap into this reservoir of shame. The chapter also examines the dangers of condemning and shaming Trump and his supporters while not paying significant attention to underlying socioeconomic processes or indeed to *the causes of Trump.*

Chapter 10 shifts the focus across the Atlantic, examining shame and shamelessness in relation to Boris Johnson and the UK's Brexit process. Again, the chapter looks at important underlying sources of shame and at the process of offering immediate (and largely magical) solutions such as Brexit itself and a more general *theater of shamelessness.* Chapter 11 brings empire and racism more explicitly into the frame, with a focus on the United States, France, and the UK in particular. The chapter suggests that a good deal of contemporary politics is constructed around warding off shame that centers on both empire and loss of empire, on harm done and loss of dominance.

Chapter 12 turns to the economy and examines shame, poverty, wealth, and consumerism. In particular, the chapter shows how consumerism has fed off shame and how highly inequitable and unforgiving economic systems have encouraged and distributed shame. It shows how shame keeps us working and buying. And it looks at how attempts to throw off shame have often fueled a concerted *re-shaming.*

The next two chapters focus on conflict. Chapter 13 looks at shame and mass violence, focusing on contexts outside Western democracies. The chapter highlights the perverse distributions of shame that have tended to accompany, fuel, and legitimize such disasters. Chapter 14 turns to the role of shame in wars directly involving Western countries and focuses on three contrasting cases: Germany after World War I; the Cold War; and the "war on terror" from 2001. Finally, the conclusion sums up and suggests ways of breaking out of our habit—and very frequently our vicious circle—of shaming.

2

Honor and Shame among America's Veterans

WE MIGHT THINK we know what shame is and how it works—not least because we have experienced it many times ourselves. But shame is a many-headed monster, and sometimes it is actually the *flight from shame* that does most of the damage. In this chapter, I begin with a story that underlines the strength of the impulse to flee from shame as well as the dangers in so doing. It's the story of a prominent and eloquent spokesman within the Colorado branch of Iraq Veterans Against the War. Drawing on a range of interviews with U.S. veterans, the chapter also highlights the way that both honor and shame have been deployed in relation to modern wars, and it shows how this has been done in ways that tend to perpetuate and legitimize violence.

"I'm coming over whether you like it or not," Rick yelled as he steered his pickup truck toward the latest hapless car in the lane next door, bringing a chorus of hooting horns. "I hate to be boxed in," he told me while I tried not to look too nervous. "And I hate driving behind a truck in case something falls off the back!"

Captain Rick Duncan—a keen bodybuilder with close-cropped hair and the staring, slightly distant eyes that are so common among those who have experienced war firsthand—was a passionate and articulate member of Iraq Veterans Against the War. He'd confided in me earlier about the brain injury he suffered as a result of an IED (improvised explosive device) that went off during his third military "tour" of Iraq; four of Rick's fellow marines in the same vehicle had been killed, and Rick had been awarded a Purple Heart.

The scar on Rick's forehead was the only visible sign of that explosion. But inside Rick's head was a metal plate, he revealed, which expanded when the weather hit 90 degrees or over—and caused him terrible migraines. Rick acknowledged that he had lost some temporal lobe function in the explosion; as a result, he had difficulty with distances.

Like when driving.

The good news, Rick added as we hurtled toward downtown Colorado Springs, was that he'd found a way to compensate. By counting the lines at the center of the road and by constantly factoring in readings from the speedometer, he could get a passable sense of distance.

The method was ingenious—and I was really hoping it was effective.

For those who know something about PTSD (post-traumatic stress disorder), Rick's driving style will not come as a big surprise. Aggression, jumpiness, excessive risk-taking—these are all common features of war-induced trauma.

Apart from his enterprising "line counting" Rick had adapted in other ways—timing his medication intake, for example, so that he could come off his bipolar drugs when he needed to get things done. Such adaptations were also not unusual among veterans.

But Rick was something else. Not only did he have this incredible energy and humor; he also had an amazing ability to position his own suffering within the wider context of the abuse and chronic shame that veterans were suffering on returning from a war that many people—soldiers as well as civilians—saw as essentially pointless. Earlier, over coffee, Rick said the war in Iraq had been a pointless waste of American and Iraqi lives. He talked so loudly and so excitedly that I figured half of Starbucks must have been tuning in:

> Are you familiar with whack-a-mole? They play it at carnivals. We're playing whack-an-insurgent! They just keep popping up! . . . There

were so many reasons given [for the war]. Mostly, they wanted a war in Iraq because they wanted a war in Iraq! I've traveled a lot. There *are* people out there that want to kill us, but it doesn't mean we have to go out and bomb people into submission!

Rick also stressed the shame of mental illnesses arising from combat, something he plausibly saw as being fostered by military culture. As we talked, his speech gathered pace, and it was littered with brackets and exclamation marks, while I struggled to keep up:

There's a saying, "You can never get over it, you can only get used to it." If you get over it, you're probably a psychopath! (I'm kidding!). Many don't feel comfortable with talking about these things, it's a machismo thing. I'm a third-generation marine. The idea is you deal with a problem yourself.

Alongside this loading of shame was a kind of systemic shamelessness. For example, Rick also emphasized that veterans were being shamefully deprived of the proper benefits, with the military tradition of deference to authority being systematically exploited: "The system trains you to obey and defend your country. Now the bureaucracy is using that same training to screw them out of the benefits they deserve. That's a betrayal!"

In many cases, the shame of war-induced trauma has been compounded when soldiers returned home, and Rick highlighted how the shame that in his view ought to have arisen from American policy was often redirected toward soldiers and veterans: "Abu Ghraib was a classic example. The euphemism was 'hicks with sticks.' They blamed it on a National Guard element from West Virginia. Since then, we know information and policy was promulgated from the top down." We may notice that here the boundaries between blaming and shaming become a little blurred. But for many of those who had been invited into the honor of serving their country, to be suddenly blamed felt like a shaming. At least with the Abu Ghraib example, language like "hicks with sticks" added an obvious layer of shaming in the sense of "This is what we expect from people like this." Rick saw himself as part of an effort to push back toward respect and recognition. as well as an effort to get the public to assume more responsibility for the war:

> With IVAW [Iraq Veterans Against the War], we want to reconnect the military with the American public. We take over a bar and listen to the marines and soldiers tell their stories of war ... I'm trying to re-bridge that divide, saying "This war is being fought in your name!" ... Most people are not being asked to sacrifice. President Bush said "Shop more!"[1] It leads to resentment from the veterans. There are very few indications that we're at war. ... When was the last time the American people were exposed to the casket of a dead marine? ... Where are the flags at half-mast?

Rick also stressed that veterans in IVAW were turning the shame and isolation of return and mental disturbance into something more positive, including an organized protest against the "war on terror" itself. He'd launched his own nonprofit organization to help his fellow veterans. This was around five years after the invasion of Iraq, and Rick was insightful on a certain kind of shamelessness in society at large—including a desire to look away.

I have to say that, as a researcher, it is characters like Rick that you really want to meet. For here was someone who had been part of important historical events, someone passionate, someone who was more than ready to share, and someone—importantly—who had the ability to extract valuable and insightful lessons. I could feel some kind of outrage rising inside me as Rick spoke, and I learned a great deal from him.

But there was one small problem.

Rick was a complete and utter fraud.

He had never been in the marines. He had never been in the military. He had never been to Iraq. He had never experienced a roadside explosion. He had never suffered a brain injury. He had no plate in his head. He had never received the Purple Heart. And his name was not Rick Duncan.

Apart from that, his story was pretty watertight.

Later, Rick (real name Rick Strandlof) described himself as "Colorado's second most stupid impersonator" (trailing, in his own estimation, a Denver man who pretended to be a firefighter and allegedly stole fire equipment while real firefighters were battling a real fire). Rick's self-awarded silver medal prompted one of his Facebook friends to respond drily, "Don't sell yourself short."[2] In truth, Rick was never afraid of the big lie. He even claimed to have been inside the Pentagon during the attack on 9/11—another total fabrication.

Ironically, it was Rick's rather manic (and apparently PTSD-influenced) driving that helped, belatedly, to raise suspicions among the IVAW veterans in Colorado. One day at a protest rally, Rick backed his red Toyota pickup truck into a gas main. Instead of waiting to talk to the police, Rick hastily fled the scene as gas leaked into the air. Veteran Mike Flaherty understood why Rick wanted to avoid the police: "What was he going to do when they took his ID in front of all of us and called him Mr. Strandlof?"[3] In retrospect, Rick's habit of talking incessantly about his PTSD also struck some IVAW veterans as odd since most guys wanted to keep these things quiet.

When Rick was eventually rumbled and it was discovered that no "Rick Duncan" had attended the Naval Academy in decades, the FBI tracked Rick back to his criminal records in Montana and Nevada.[4] The game was up, and a painful process of public shaming began.

As part of this, Rick was hauled onto CNN and subjected to a grim interview with Anderson Cooper. He was also charged with violating the 2005 Stolen Valor Act, which made it a crime falsely to claim receipt of military honors—a surprisingly common phenomenon. (The Stolen Valor Act was subsequently rejected by the Supreme Court on the grounds that it violated the First Amendment's guarantee of free speech, and the charges against Rick were dropped.)[5]

Rick was not simply stealing honor but also stealing—or at least buying into—the veterans' collective shame around a pointless war, as well as buying into the sense of community that they were building around their shared suffering. Before his cover was blown, he had said to me, "It's a question of what do you have that's attractive. IVAW does offer the camaraderie and knowing you're not alone." Rick certainly seems to have had an instinctive understanding and even empathy for veterans' suffering and shame. He was a good fundraiser and one veteran remembered Rick helped him a lot with depression.

Incidentally, I should also claim my own small portion of shame here. After all, despite years of investigating and writing about conflicts around the world, my many hours with Rick did not lead me to spot—or even, frankly, *suspect*—that he was an imposter. Rick's "fellow" IVAW veterans were certainly embarrassed (you may notice how quickly I flee from my own shame!). Rick had a high public profile as a "veteran" and had managed to fool his colleagues at close quarters during his IVAW membership of almost two years despite their direct experience of the environment in Iraq that Rick kept talking about. IVAW veterans later reported that Rick could move both his audience and himself to tears when he was talking about his experiences in Iraq.[6] One veteran suggested that to doubt such a man would have been heartless in the extreme.

Rick's experiences before and after his "radical veteran" persona are also revealing. Rick Strandlof was born in Montana in 1977 and his father seems to have abandoned the family early on. When Rick later came out as gay, his mother and her new husband rejected him.[7] When Rick was twenty, he was convicted of forgery and writing bad checks.[8] When he came out of prison, Rick moved to Reno, Nevada, but was soon found guilty of stealing a rental car. By mid-2007, he was in Colorado, where his boyfriend had a job.[9] He bulked up and emerged into the limelight as ex-marine and fledgling media star "Captain Rick Duncan."[10] Rick had earlier been diagnosed with schizophrenia and bipolar disorder, and the persona of Rick Duncan not only allowed an entry to the revered category of "veterans" but also may have permitted an escape from the stigmatized category of the mentally ill. Rather neatly, in Rick's case, any signs of mental illness could now be interpreted as PTSD—perhaps putting them squarely within a framework of pride rather than shame.

After his stint as a "radical veteran," our hero's creative streak did not desert him. He quickly fled from the shame of being a fake veteran, reinventing himself in a new social circle as Rick Gold, a Jewish oil-and-gas attorney, a passionate defender of Israel and Israeli culture, and a former soldier with both the Israeli Defense Forces and (once again) the U.S. Marines.[11] Embracing his new(ish) role with hutzpah, Rick quickly made new friends among Denver's young Jewish professionals. He mastered convincing details of Israeli history and culture, right down to the local beaches. His brain injury made a reappearance, and Rick's new friends sometimes attributed inconsistencies in his story to the explosion. Rebecca Saltzman, a psychotherapist familiar with PTSD among veterans, said later: "That was genius. He couldn't have picked a better excuse."[12] Eventually, Rick was rumbled once more (spotted at a gay pride festival by a politician who'd known him as "Rick Duncan"), and Rick wrote to a Jewish friend, "What I saw was a warm, inclusive community that I wished in some way I could be a part of."[13]

In Rick's blog entry for April 16, 2012, he noted: "After my latest sad attempt to find acceptance through deceit and dishonesty, I found myself drawn to a church in Denver called House for All Sinners and Saints." Rick said he was attracted to the idea that the invitation to the Lord's Table was between Christ and the individual, with no human—and no member of the clergy—able to stand in the way. Devoted to his new mission, Rick became the most helpful steward in the congregation, reportedly telling his minister, "It hurts a little, being loved for who I really am."[14] At around this time, Rick also became involved in cooking for protestors with Occupy Denver (inspired by Occupy Wall Street), and he explained with characteristic vim and humor, "I'm a whore for a cause."

Naturally, members of Iraq Veterans Against the War were generally livid when Rick's lies came out.[15] Most importantly, he was seen as damaging the anti-war cause by taking away from the credibility of anti-war veterans more generally and IVAW in particular.

But looking back, I cannot get away from the feeling that "Captain Rick Duncan," despite being a spectacular fraud and a serial liar who never went near the conflict zone he "knew" so much about, also showed himself to be an unusually sensitive, insightful, and in many ways caring individual—and someone who had valuable things to tell us about the American way of war. Could it be that it takes a schizophrenic individual to see through a schizophrenic society, a gifted liar finally to tell the truth, and a "fool on the hill" (in the Beatles' phrase) to "see the world spinning round"?

That idea has a certain poetic appeal. But I also encountered many real veterans who helped illuminate the peculiar distribution of shame that surrounds—and sustains—America's many wars. From these veterans' accounts, one could see how the possibility of productive shame around these wars tended to be closed down by a variety of techniques. Shame has been perversely distributed, with a great deal being loaded onto America's own soldiers and veterans. Soldiers and veterans have actually been *simultaneously* shamed and honored—and both reflexes have tended to feed a habit of war that has seen America participate in some thirty-eight foreign wars since the beginning of the twentieth century.[16]

In Iraq and Afghanistan, the absence of a general draft meant that a relatively small group of recruits was being sent repeatedly into the war zone—a practice known officially as "stop-loss" and unofficially as "churning." Each "tour" (itself a telling euphemism) could reinforce the trauma from the last, yet trauma was often downplayed in the interests of having individuals who could be deemed sufficiently healthy for future deployment. Part of the problem, veterans reported, was that war trauma was routinely relabeled as "personality disorder," effectively loading shame onto the individual while conveniently reducing the benefits payable.[17]

Whether in the "war on terror" or earlier, the moral pain of veterans has routinely been relabeled as pathology, making it harder to learn about the vicious realities of war.[18] Vietnam veteran Tim O'Brien commented in relation to a long-standing Hollywood obsession with deranged veterans: "The nation seems too comfortable with—even dependent on—the image of a suffering and deeply troubled veteran. Rather than face our own culpabilities, we shove them off onto ex-GIs and let them suffer for us."[19] Many IVAW veterans stressed that, between being idolized and stigmatized, it had become very difficult to speak. "Deadening" drug treatments were seen as an additional obstacle to articulating the horrors of war. Many IVAW veterans also emphasized that "churning" was dangerously insulating American society from the human costs of war and effectively reducing political pressure for withdrawal from Iraq. Meanwhile, the cost of the war to taxpayers was being kept well below what it would have been if soldiers and veterans were cared for properly.[20]

As is common with warfare more generally, an orchestrated reverence for soldiers' "sacrifice" seems to have played a major part in legitimizing and even sanctifying America's many foreign wars. In fact, many anti-war veterans complained that soldiers' deaths and injuries were being used to protect a pointless and unwinnable war from shame and scrutiny. One example of this maneuver came in 2005 as violence escalated in Iraq and the total number of U.S. troops killed rose relentlessly. Supporting continued war, leading self-styled liberal commentator Michael Ignatieff observed in the *New York Times* magazine:

> There is nothing worse than believing your son or daughter, brother or sister, father or mother died in vain. . . . Thomas Jefferson's dream [of freedom for all nations] must work. Its ultimate task in American life is to redeem loss, to rescue sacrifice from oblivion and futility and to give it shining purpose.[21]

Yet when I mentioned the argument that pulling out of Iraq might mean soldiers died in vain, one Iraq veteran replied angrily: "It's a complete crock! That's just a way to perpetuate war. They already did die for nothing! They did die in vain because we're in a bullshit war!" In the context of "churning" and neglect of veterans' welfare, many anti-war veterans had come to see conspicuous respect and gratitude for their "sacrifices" as a kind of cover for a deeper contempt or even a process of scapegoating.

Reflecting on the elements of deception during recruitment, on the fact that many recruits are under eighteen, on the scarcity of other alternatives for many teenagers and young men, on the practice of "churning," and on an egregious neglect of veterans' mental health, I began to wonder whether soldiers and veterans were not only *sacrificing* but also *being sacrificed*. It may even be that in the context of a major national disaster like 9/11 (and, in that case, a president saying America needed to show commitment to its own values), society feels the need for some kind of sacrifice or "blood offering"—and the objects of violence are not simply foreigners (who tend to bear the brunt of it) but also *one's own soldiers*. Carolyn Marvin and David Ingle have gone so far as to argue that "society depends on the death of its own members . . . the nation is the shared memory of blood sacrifice, periodically renewed."[22] The conspicuous honoring of soldiers does not necessarily preclude such a process: in a religious context, after all, the scapegoat is not simply killed but also revered.

Garett Reppenhagen, a former sniper and an influential member of IVAW, said many soldiers kill themselves because they felt they were fighting an unjustified war. He remembered:

> I killed civilians. That's part of what I'm dealing with.... In the war you have fully automated grenade launchers and weaponry that goes through walls, across the street, and into the building behind. You don't know what you're hitting. Someone sees a flash and fires and the guys around you fire. You can't see much.... You go to the building and you don't find a single person with an AK-47, but you find some dead civilians. That's kind of hard to swallow.

Reppenhagen described a process of brutalization that went well beyond guilt around individual incidents and involved an emerging sense of shame around *the person that one was becoming*. In home-raiding in Iraq:

> We'd act on information, someone saying someone was a rebel.... We may have sent a lot of innocent men to jail or to the grave. My small part in that is something I'm gonna always have to live with. I still had my senses and sense of decency. I was afraid that after a second or third time, those senses would go. Your anger at the [U.S.] government would spill over into anger at civilians.... It's like, "We're here for them. They don't want us, so why should I help them?" Some snap sooner than others. But we all have a point where we will snap.[23]

Yet Reppenhagen also emphasized that soldiers' violence and soldiers' suffering often reinforced the idea of a just war:

> Soldiers call it collateral damage or they say "You gotta break eggs to make an omelet," all these justifications. That's why everybody holds onto the noble cause idea, most of the soldiers do. They're thinking, "Why did I lose my buddy, or my arm, it had to be a damn good reason. If the president says it's a just war, then it is, so just shut the fuck up!"

In this way, violence itself may become a means of generating shamelessness around war—a profoundly disturbing phenomenon that we shall return to in the discussion of civil wars, genocides, and the "war on terror." For all the insights of the IVAW veterans, perhaps the most eloquent critic of this system remained the phantasmagoric "Captain Rick." In 2011—when Rick was inhabiting his real name, impoverished, and comprehensively shamed—he asked himself why he had adopted such far-fetched disguises:

> So here I sit—in this Starbucks . . . homeless, unemployed, mentally ill, addicted, reputation ruined by my own misdeeds. . . . What process in my mind determined that the best way to handle the situation was to construct a parallel reality and attempt to inhabit that reality? Perhaps it was done in an attempt to make up for what I felt was an inadequacy in my life, that I did not measure up to others in some way. Maybe it was done to protect myself from something I was threatened by, that was going to somehow hurt me. Maybe someday this will be revealed to me. Maybe someday it will not.[24]

The comment perhaps suggests a fragile awareness that shame around inadequacy was driving the dishonest embrace of honor, but it also suggests that the links between shame, delusion, and deception may remain obscure even to those most intimately involved. For Rick, each shaming does seem to have spurred some kind of flight from reality and some kind of flight from *himself*. Shamed for what he was, he repeatedly reinvented himself so that he was honored for what he wasn't—until he was shamed for that too.

While extraordinary in many ways, Rick's narcissistic flight into fantasy is not as rare as we might think. Military service has often been faked. And revealingly, a major habit of social shaming has emerged around the exposure of phony veterans. An investigation in the *New Yorker* found that "confrontations between service members and potential imposters became wildly popular on YouTube. They amass millions of views and are re-aired on Fox News."[25]

This media circus illustrates that the wheel of shame and shaming tends to keep on turning—and, more often than not, there is money to be made.

In the end, "Captain Rick" is interesting partly because he took deception to such ridiculous—and in many ways *brilliant*—extremes. But more than this, his move away from categories (mentally ill, convict, poor) that are routinely shamed and toward America's most conspicuously revered category illustrates the lengths people will go to when seeking to avoid both shame and isolation (which itself is a major incubator of shame). Rick's story—taken together with the insights of real veterans—also tells us something important about the peculiar mix of shame and honor that America (like many societies) imposes on its veterans. Certainly, Rick was "buying into" soldiers' honor, and many could never forgive him for that. But he also had an unusual sensitivity to soldiers' shame and its role in keeping people quiet and sustaining a system of serial warfare.

3

The Scourge of Shame

SO WHAT EXACTLY is shame anyway? What role does it play in political and economic affairs more generally? And just how harmful is it?

This chapter gives a sense of how damaging shame can be. It shows how shame, painful in itself, also has numerous bad effects beyond this immediate feeling. Shame can be intensely demoralizing and isolating. It has routinely cemented and legitimized unjust political systems, not least when people blame themselves for their own suffering. Whether at the individual or societal level, moreover, shame has repeatedly encouraged a dangerous flight into delusion.

Before proceeding further, it's important to say something about shame and guilt. While both shame and guilt are painful feelings that arise from a perception that one has done something wrong, two substantial differences stand out. First, while guilt tends to center on *particular actions* that one has carried out (or omitted to carry out), shame tends to center on *the whole person*: it suggests not just a *bad action* but a *bad person*.[1] As psychologists Ronda Dearing and June Tangney put it, "People experiencing shame evaluate the eliciting mistake or transgression as being indicative of a self that is fundamentally flawed."[2] Faced with a bad grade, for example, a shame-prone person may say "I'm so stupid!" while a guilt-prone person may say "I should have worked harder on that project!"[3] We may say that while shame is "a painful emotion caused by the belief that one is, or is perceived by others to be, *inferior or unworthy of affection or respect* because of one's actions, thoughts, circumstances, or experiences,"[4] guilt is "a painful feeling of self-reproach resulting from a belief that one *has done something wrong or immoral*."[5] A second key difference is that shame centers on how society views—or is imagined to view—a person. It implies the existence of an *audience* of some kind, whereas guilt centers largely on how one sees one's own actions.[6]

Shame is often seen as something that infuses "distant lands" and "distant eras," something that "modern" and "enlightened" people have collectively outgrown. Dov Cohen, an American social psychologist at the University of Illinois, noted in 2003:

> Shame is something we want to distance ourselves from ... it is something that cultures on the other side of the world do when they cloak their women head to toe and punish violations of chastity by killing. In the modern world, shame is something that we left behind and that surely other cultures will leave behind when they modernize and become just like us.[7]

Also contributing to an aura of backwardness around "shame cultures" has been the idea that they flourish when and where the rule of law has not yet been properly established. In these circumstances, as Cohen goes on to suggest, "the logic of deterrence takes over, and guarding one's reputation for toughness means that even the small slights and insults that might be encountered in everyday life have to be answered."[8]

But rumors of the death of shame have been greatly exaggerated. Shame cannot usefully be seen solely as the province of "shame-based" cultures or societies that are far from contemporary Western societies in time and space. Even as we run from shame, it seems to find a thousand ways to haunt us. Sometimes it seems that we might as well try to flee from our own shadow.

Condemning the "shame cultures" of others, moreover, can easily play a part in obscuring manipulations of shame in the here and now. It can also legitimize violence. One justification given for colonialism in relation to Islamic societies was the ostensible need to liberate women from their veils—an argument made by Lord Cromer, British

Consul-General in Egypt, for example.[9] This argument recurred in the "war on terror."[10]

When Western societies see themselves as separate from "shame societies," this seems to be part of a more general tendency to see oneself as "rational" and not excessively swayed by emotion. Within this framework, policymaking is routinely presented as "evidence-based." A common and related assumption has been that voters are rational and will vote in their own interests, so that something is going very wrong—Trump! Brexit!—when they don't. But rather than fixing only on the "startling exceptions" to a norm that we assume to be rational, it would be wiser to investigate the complex role that emotions (including shame) have long played in politics, including the politics that preceded (and gave birth to) characters like Trump.

Of course, the benefits of moving away from a number of shame-based practices are not to be underestimated. Shame has often been mobilized to control women and girls, and at the extreme this has included so-called "honor killings," often of young women seen to have tarnished a family's honor.[11] Historically, shame has been a major tool of patriarchy, a way of keeping people (especially women and girls) "in their place." But those who condemn "shame cultures" generally turn out to have *their own* shame cultures—and this is a major part of what we will be investigating.

Analysts have often been happy to highlight the prominence of shame dynamics in the Far East, the Middle East, and the Mediterranean. Ruth Benedict's *The Chrysanthemum and the Sword* stressed that Japanese soldiers often killed themselves rather than suffer the permanent disgrace of capture.[12] Writing on Cambodia, Alex Hinton argued that Buddhism and a "warrior heritage" had combined to nurture the idea that it was shameful if one endured an insult or slight without engaging in some form of retaliation or revenge. Hinton argued that the cultural context encouraged politeness and an avoidance of conflict right up until the moment of extreme violence. It also helped foster a major fear of revenge, and Hinton suggested that the Khmer Rouge's killings were strongly fueled by the fear that the relatives of those murdered would take revenge if they too were not killed.[13]

On one interpretation, Christianity tended to encourage a "guilt culture" and an emphasis on individual conscience in contrast to the "shame culture" of ancient Greece and Rome with their emphasis on respect.[14] But even in predominantly Christian societies, "shame cultures" persisted. In Greece, Roman Gerodimos notes that well into the twentieth century, violence was seen as "a legitimate means of restoring pride and honor in familial contexts."[15] In an essay originally published in 1977, Julian Pitt-Rivers said of Andalusia in Spain that "a woman is dishonored, loses her *verguenza* (shame in the sense of modesty), with the tainting of her sexual purity, but a man does not,"[16] while anthropologist Nancy Lindisfarne has pointed to the Spanish saying: "If all Spanish women are virtuous and chaste and all Spanish men are great seducers and lovers, someone has to be lying."[17]

In Ireland, a kind of alliance between Christianity and institutionalized shaming was exemplified in the infamous Magdalen laundries or asylums, a system that began in the eighteenth century (with the last laundry closing in 1996). Run by Catholic nuns, the Magdalen laundries were part of a patriarchal system in which women and girls were forcibly confined and scapegoated for sexual "transgressions" while men generally escaped such sanction. Inmates, often referred to as "fallen women," were put under strict surveillance, and many were subjected to physical and psychological abuse. In her careful study, Clara Fischer notes, "The alleged sins committed by women and girls confined in Magdalen laundries were read as stains upon their very characters and bodies, stains that could be removed (though never quite) through repentance and the backbreaking work of washing away stains from dirty laundry."[18]

Importantly, the process of shaming the "less enlightened" and "less modern" may take place not only across international borders but also *within* countries (including within Western democracies). "Other people" are positioned as emotional and irrational while those doing the labeling tend to position themselves as cool-headed and rational. Whether the shaming is within a particular country or between countries, words like "backward," "uneducated," "traditional," and "underdeveloped" may invite among the targets a vehement and even an aggressive rejection of this shame—and also, perhaps, of the "modernity" that is being promised but not delivered. That backlash may in turn redouble the original shaming.

Intriguingly, some elements of "shame culture" in the US—and regional differences—were highlighted in a 1996 study by Dov Cohen and his colleagues. Male students at the University of Michigan were divided into those who grew up in the North and the South.[19] Subjects had to walk down a corridor, where they were bumped into by a fellow student who called them an "asshole." On average, southerners responded significantly more aggressively with cortisol and testosterone levels rising higher.[20]

In an experiment that also involved a category of those from the western United States, various employers were sent a bogus job application letter listing qualifications and admitting that the candidate had previously killed someone who had insulted and attacked him in a bar fight. Southern and western employers reacted significantly more favorably than northern employers, and one southern employer was kind enough to write back, "As for your problem in the past, anyone could probably be in the situation you were in. It was just an unfortunate incident that shouldn't be held against you. . . . Once you get settled, if you are near here, please stop in and see us."[21] Of course, one has to be wary of stereotypes, including the shaming of "shame societies". But cultural differences in how shame is understood and mobilized—even differences within a country—would seem to be very real.

Trapped in Shame

Across the globe, we have grown up in worlds that seek to inform us that we are somehow inadequate—not rich enough, not sane enough or smart enough, not pretty or fit or cool or thin enough, not Christian enough, not Muslim enough, not secular or modern enough, not British or American or Indian or Korean or Nigerian enough, not cosmopolitan enough, not kind or nurturing enough, not heterosexual enough, not manly or womanly enough, and even not tough or violent enough. Basically, *not enough*. This is not primarily a matter of guilt or even of encouraging regret for one's actions. It's more about a perception of our whole self as falling short in the eyes of others. Psychoanalyst Paul

Hoggett notes that "in a moment of shame, the individual feels 'seen through', as if all their usual defences and their narcissism have evaporated."[22] As the book proceeds, we will see how diverse and far-reaching processes of shaming have often put the recipients into an extremely painful place from which an equally diverse cast of advertisers, warmongers, terrorists, tyrants, and charlatans have offered an escape. Routinely, we are ripe for their "remedies."

In looking more closely at the nature and effects of shame, one important point of reference is Brené Brown, a professor of social work in Houston, Texas, who has probably done more than anyone to raise awareness of the damage that shame inflicts. Brown defines shame as "the intensely painful feeling or experience of believing we are flawed and therefore unworthy of acceptance and belonging."[23] She emphasizes that a key characteristic of shameful feelings is that the individual tends to imagine that there is something *peculiarly or particularly* bad about themselves as an individual—perhaps even something that *merits* whatever misfortunes have befallen them.[24] In line with this, one of Brown's informants said shame was like "a prison that you deserve to be in because there's something wrong with you."[25] If shame is a scourge (and the word "scourge" originally means a whip), then shame is to a large extent a scourge that we wield ourselves—a self-flagellation.

Brown clearly struck a chord with her argument that large numbers of people are demoralized, made thoroughly miserable, and sometimes propelled into mental illness by a critical inner voice that is constantly trying to shame them. In her punchy style, Brown gives a sense of the often contradictory demands of modern society, many of them pressing down especially heavily on women and girls:

> If we can't pull it all off—lose the weight, bake and eat the cake, smoke the cigarettes and look cool, stay healthy and fit, buy all the products and, at the same time, love ourselves for who we are—GOTCHA! We get trapped in the shame web. That's when our fear starts to turn to blame and disconnection.[26]

That element of being *trapped in shame* comes out strongly in Brown's writing. Someone who feels they are "no good" will find it very hard to change their behavior, she emphasized, and that person may even be tempted to fulfill this negative label.[27] Meanwhile, "The less we understand shame and how it affects our feelings, thoughts and behaviors, the more power it exerts over our lives."[28]

A wide range of therapists, psychologists, and social workers have also emphasized the very negative effects of shame. A landmark publication was John Bradshaw's 1988 book *Healing the Shame That Binds You*. Importantly, Bradshaw noted that "once shame is transformed into an identity, it becomes toxic and dehumanizing."[29] Further, "There is shame about shame. People will readily admit guilt, hurt or fear before they will admit shame."[30] In his own childhood, John Bradshaw was stalked and sexually abused by a Catholic priest. He later acknowledged that shame "ruled me like an addiction ... I transferred it to my family, my clients and the people I taught."[31] More generally, he noted that family secrets could pass shame through the generations. Since shame was often not overtly or consciously felt but rather pushed aside, the damage effected by shame was especially difficult to heal. Bradshaw observed that "by defeating and humiliating the victim, the perpetrator is momentarily freed of shame," and he stressed that any sense of relief through abuse or through indulging in addictions was usually fleeting.[32] Fleeing from shame into violence or addictions (such as alcoholism) tended to precipitate more shame in a vicious circle.

More recently, there have been many psychological studies suggesting that shame-proneness is associated with increased risk of depression, anxiety, suicide and other forms of self-injury, obsessions and compulsions, narcissism, eating disorders, post-traumatic stress disorder, and substance abuse; such associations do not seem to be present with guilt-proneness.[33]

Crucially, shame tends to be profoundly *isolating*.[34] We tend to be silent about our own shame—and in these murky waters, shame flourishes like a weed, entangling us even as we try to present a brave face on the surface.[35] This is one area where shame departs sharply from its close and more mild-mannered cousin, embarrassment. Philosopher Krista Thomason noted that "we rarely look back and chuckle over moments of shame. ... While we can find sympathy in moments of embarrassment, shame distances us from others such that sympathy is unavailable."[36]

A key problem arising from abuse is that the victims often blame themselves. Psychologist Nancy Talbot notes that "shame is a core emotion for sexually abused women."[37] For example, one woman who had suffered from depression and had been repeatedly beaten by her father as a child said of her physically abusive husband: "I thought it was my fault because he told me it was. I believed everything he said—that I was bad, not fit to be a mother."[38] Christine Park notes that "children who are abused take responsibility for the abuse, concluding their pain is deserved because something is wrong in who they are. Self-blame allows children to maintain an image of their caregivers as good and caring."[39] In the 1994 BBC documentary *The Making of Them*, Nick Duffell, a former private school boarder, noted that boarders often wonder if their parents sent them away because they didn't love them; at the same time displays of weakness tend to be seen as shameful, encouraging boarders to "shut down" their feelings.[40] Summing up a range of literature in psychology and social work, Park comments: "At the heart of chronic shame is a sense of unlovability. . . . Shame is about fear of disconnection, because a shamed person senses something unacceptable about himself has been exposed, thereby making him deserving of abandonment."[41]

A therapist will often try to address the way responsibility for shame has been allocated by the client. Leslie Greenberg and Shigeru Iwakabe suggest that helpful therapeutic interventions involve "appropriately externalizing the blame, or 'putting the blame where it belongs.'"[42] It seems pretty clear that blaming an "appropriate" party will correspondingly reduce shame. In cognitive behavioral therapy, the client may be encouraged not to draw sweeping negative conclusions about themselves (a form of shame) from incidents that do not merit it.[43]

Psychiatrist and psychoanalyst Carlos Sluzki has explained the therapeutic process in terms of the difference between a "hostile" and a "friendly" witness.[44] Suppose you trip up while leaving a supermarket and spill all the groceries. This is embarrassing in itself, perhaps you even feel a little shame (as for example in asking, "Why do I never look where I'm going?!"). At the same time, the way people react will make a big difference. A "friendly witness" may help you to your feet, help you collect the spilled groceries, and perhaps point out that the pavement is broken or even that they recently had a similar stumble. Here, they are helping you escape from shame. By contrast, a "hostile witness" may laugh at you—in effect heightening the emotion of shame and even perhaps pushing it toward its more virulent and provocative cousin, humiliation. Within this schema, we can see that a good therapist represents a kind of friendly witness—listening, echoing, reframing stories, and eventually allowing a more realistic attribution of responsibility so that self-blame recedes and due weight is given to other people and wider circumstances.[45] Sluzki suggests that in the political sphere an ethnic nationalist of some kind may serve as a hostile witness, ramping up some underlying sense of shame. This figure may also propose some form of violence to *reverse* the shame. The ways in which collective shame is framed, hyped, and exploited will be a key theme in the current book—and there will be no shortage of hostile witnesses.

Punished for Who You Are

When it comes to politics, perverse distributions of shame echo the perverse distributions that have often been observed in situations of individual abuse. Again, the distribution of shame has tended to be drastically out of line with the distribution of responsibility.

In his book *States of Denial*, Stanley Cohen helpfully highlighted the existence of "just world thinking"—the belief that the world is fundamentally just—and he showed how quickly this could feed into the idea that victims "get what they deserve."[46] We have already noted how victims of sexual violence very often acquire a sense of shame.[47] Since a child learns the difference between "right" and "wrong" in part from the regime of punishments and rewards to which that child is subjected, it also seems logical that humans would to some extent infer what is right from what is punished, thereby inviting self-blame for violence suffered.

Both colonialism and totalitarianism tended to load a huge burden of shame onto the victims. In effect, people were punished not for what they had done but for who they were—the injustice of which is inherently shaming and indeed humiliating. In the practices of colonial and totalitarian governments, the very notion of guilt—which pertains specifically to people's actions—was radically set aside. In *The Origins of Totalitarianism*, Hannah Arendt noted that once the link between punishment and crime was severed, no one was safe.

Martinique-born psychiatrist and political philosopher Frantz Fanon showed how those on the receiving end of colonial violence routinely came to bear a very heavy burden of shame *and* guilt, and he tended to use the words interchangeably. Addressing the emotions instilled by colonialism, Fanon wrote in *Black Skin, White Masks*, "A feeling of inferiority? No, a feeling of non-existence. Sin is Negro as virtue is white. All those white men in a group, guns in their hands, cannot be wrong." Fanon added, "I am guilty. I do not know of what, but I know that I am no good."[48]

Fanon also referred to the "inferiority complex" of colonized people, a complex that he said was created by physical domination and by the subordination of local culture to that of the colonizing power. A colonized people were a "people in whose soul an inferiority complex has been created by the death and burial of its local cultural creativity."[49] Here, we are clearly in the realm of shame, and Fanon emphasized that an inferiority complex was strongly manifest in sexual relations, where "every woman in the Antilles, whether in a casual flirtation or in a serious affair, is determined to select the least black of the men."[50] For Fanon, it was resistance and ultimately rebellion that could free people from "this shackled life caught in the noose of shame."[51]

In one key passage in *The Origins of Totalitarianism*, Arendt observed that "common sense reacted to the horrors of Buchenwald and Auschwitz with the plausible argument: 'What crime must these people have committed that such things were done to them!'"[52] This was part of what Arendt meant by "action as propaganda"—the use of violent action to make ludicrous propaganda seem more plausible as time went by. Within this upside-down world, the link between crime and punishment that had been established in non-totalitarian times may well have been perversely "useful" for the Nazis (even as they abolished this link) in encouraging people to infer guilt from punishment.

Like the victims of colonialism, the victims of Nazism frequently felt a sense of shame. In his recollection of internment at Auschwitz, *The Drowned and the Saved*, Primo Levi explicitly equated shame and guilt, observing that "many (including me) experienced 'shame', that is, a feeling of guilt during the imprisonment and afterward."[53] Such feelings tended to increase among those who were eventually liberated from the camps: Levi suggests this was because suffering in the camps had the effect of temporarily expiating guilt and shame.

Levi wrote about the so-called *Sonderkommando*, concentration camp inmates who were instructed to maintain order among those arriving at the gas chambers but also to extract the corpses after people were killed and to pull out any gold teeth. Coercing cooperation was meant to be "an additional, crushing humiliation," Levi wrote, while "delegating part of the work to the victims themselves, and indeed the most filthy part, was meant to alleviate (and probably did) a few consciences here and there."[54] Levi also suggested that the Nazis' attitude toward the *Sonderkommando* (with whom they played a football match) was that "We have embraced you, corrupted you, dragged you to the bottom with us. You are like us, you proud people, dirtied with your own blood, as we are."[55]

The Flight from Shame

Much of the psychoanalytical and psychological literature on shame underlines the point that setbacks and suffering very often lead to feelings of shame, even in circumstances where the affected individual is in no way responsible. A second key conclusion—underlining some of Bradshaw's insights, for example—is that people tend to flee from (painful) feelings of shame into other things that may themselves be sources of suffering and shame. These include illusions, mental illness, and violence. Psychological and psychoanalytic writings have also illuminated shame—and flights from shame—in ways that will be helpful when we come to consider the politics of shame. We saw in the chapter on "Captain Rick" and (real) war veterans that the urge to flee from shame can be both strong and destructive. Whether at the individual or collective level, a flight from shame-around-violence will often reinvent the violence.

Aristotle observed that shame was a powerful emotion that could feed into both anger and violence, adding that "the persons with whom we get angry are those who laugh, mock, or jeer at us,"[56] while retaliatory violence reduced feelings of shame.[57] Suzanne Retzinger and Thomas Scheff drew on therapeutic experience with couples and noted that shame cues tended to lead to an escalation of anger and more shame.[58] Scheff argued that anger was a defense against painful and unacknowledged feelings of shame and that shame could powerfully fuel violence; yet taboos around shame made it "usually invisible in modern societies."[59] In her excellent 2018 book *Naked*, Krista Thomason suggested that "people either prefer being violent to feeling shame, or their feelings of shame are alleviated by acts of aggression."[60]

In psychoanalytical writings, the word "shame" has often been surprisingly *neglected*, although there have been crucial insights that address shame directly as well as a wide range of useful discussions of related concepts like guilt and the superego.[61] In Freud's work, notably, the punitive "superego" often pushed aside his important concept of the "ego ideal" (the self one would wish to be, seen as arising from a positive identification with a loved one)—and shame correspondingly took a back seat.[62] Freud's attitude toward the superego was ambivalent: it could usefully rein in desires but could also be a "tyrant" exerting "merciless violence."[63] Notwithstanding this general emphasis on the superego, Freud's early interpretations did put shame close to the heart of what is repressed into the unconscious. Noting the existence of "ideas that were pathogenic, and had been forgotten and put out of consciousness,"[64] Freud and Breuer's study of hysteria observed:

> they were all of a distressing nature, calculated to arouse the affects of shame, of self-reproach and of psychical pain, and the feeling of being harmed; they were all of a kind that one would prefer not to have experienced, that one would rather forget.[65]

In this account, repression pushes feelings of shame out of consciousness—often at the cost of serious mental illness. Paradoxically (and importantly when we come to consider political dysfunctions including political paranoia), a psychoanalytical framework suggests that mental illness and associated delusions are not *purely* negative phenomena but actually offer a way of "coping"—notably through warding off the most painful and terrifying feelings and memories. As Freud noted in *The Unconscious*, "The neurotic turns away from reality because he finds either the whole or parts of it unbearable."[66] In terms of flights from reality more generally, Freud observed, "We call a belief an illusion when a wish-fulfilment is prominent in its motivation, and in doing so we disregard its relations to reality."[67]

Freud saw the illusions or delusions informing depression and paranoia (for example) as hard to shift in part *because* they performed certain functions and because they protected the individual from deeply threatening thoughts, feelings, and memories. Psychiatrist and psychoanalyst Norman Cameron, an expert on paranoia, observed of the therapeutic process that the primary consideration "is not the character of the delusional structure but *what makes it necessary*."[68]

One topic that will recur often in our discussion of politics is shame around powerlessness. Swiss psychoanalyst Léon Wurmser, author of *The Mask of Shame*, noted that when a small child experiences some kind of traumatic event, the child will tend to recoil from the feeling of powerlessness that this induces. The traumatic experience might be very dramatic (such as abandonment by parents) or it might be more subtle (for example, a child's prolonged experience of not having feelings or desires acknowledged or respected). In either case, rather than accepting the powerlessness of its situation or facing its own feelings of helplessness and abandonment, the child will often attribute to itself great power, resorting to what Wurmser called "the omnipotence of responsibility."[69] This includes the belief that catastrophe can be warded off through behaviors that are essentially magical in nature—for example, through perfectionism, obsessive compulsive behavior, or various kinds of self-harm. (This might be compared, incidentally, with the common belief in the face of major disasters—going back at least as far as the

Black Death—that humans are not powerless and the right kind of ritualistic behavior can bring relief.)[70]

A key point in Wurmser's work is that self-blame and magical thinking arise in tandem, with the infant essentially attributing to itself a set of magical abilities that defend against the terror of powerlessness at the cost of ramping up shame and feeding a hypercritical superego.[71] But this system of magic sooner or later comes into some kind of drastic conflict with reality, leading to what Wurmser called a "narcissistic crisis" in which illusions sustaining a feeling of omnipotence are shattered.[72]

If we look at Freud's *Totem and Taboo*, we get a better grasp of how a magical sense of omnipotence can appeal at a collective level too. In what Freud called the "animistic" and "religious" stages of human history, people ascribed to themselves some significant ability to influence spirits or gods. But in the "scientific" age, according to Freud, any sense of human omnipotence was generally pushed aside, so that humans "acknowledged their smallness and submitted resignedly to death and to the other necessities of nature."[73] For Freud, contemporary flights into magical omnipotence were mostly the province of the mentally ill and those he called "primitives." But logically, it is not clear why *anyone* would rush to embrace the painful mindset that Freud identifies with the "scientific" age—and of course religion has not disappeared. Much of the analysis in the current book will suggest a more *universal* aspect to the flight to omnipotence. Whether we are thinking about flights to omnipotence or delusions more generally, we cannot assume that "science" has somehow banished them; indeed, it has in many ways *facilitated* them. The need to find ways of making collective delusions *unnecessary* (to use the framework applied by Norman Cameron to individual delusions) has rarely been more urgent.

Another important element in the embrace of delusions, of course, is Freud's idea of *projection*—essentially, the process by which desires or drives that are considered (for whatever reason) shameful or socially unacceptable are propelled or projected outward onto others so that the individual engaging in this process does not have to acknowledge these desires, drives, or shame.[74] In *projective identification*, the individual takes this a step further and acts in such a way as to *induce* the projected feelings in others.[75]

From a psychoanalytic perspective, projection is rather central to paranoia since the paranoid person flees from an awareness of their own (unacceptable) aggression by imagining that others have aggressive intent.[76] Melanie Klein followed Freud in attributing huge importance to the ever-critical voice of the superego, and she further illuminated the relationship between unease with one's own feelings and drives, on the one hand, and the development of paranoia on the other. Klein emphasized that an infant projects intolerable hostile feelings onto the mother (for example, when the mother withdraws or withholds the breast).[77] Because of the infant's hostile thoughts, the infant also fears revenge from the mother and thus experiences a kind of terror that gives the superego its persecutory quality.

Particularly in our discussion of empire, we will have cause to revisit this idea. More specifically, we will look at the tendency to take flight from one's own aggression into the assumption or fantasy that others are planning *revenge*. In this way, victims may be damagingly repositioned as perpetrators, helping to limit shame and legitimize both past and present violence.

One of the first psychoanalysts to address shame itself in a sustained manner was Helen Lewis, who published her book *Shame and Guilt in Neurosis* in 1974. From her own practice and her study of transcripts from other psychoanalysts' sessions, Lewis concluded that "unanalyzed shame" was a major hurdle to successful therapy.[78] She saw shame as "a relatively wordless state" that was deeply infused by denial.[79] Of course, the relationship of shame to anger and other emotions is complex, and we should be careful not to assume that shame is driving other emotions (as Paul Gilbert has wisely cautioned).[80] But Lewis convincingly linked extreme shaming to a kind of fury, suggesting that it was common for patients to want to "turn the tables" after experiences that they found humiliating.

Further exploring the distinction between shame and guilt, others have found empirical evidence that shame has significantly more damaging effects than guilt. In one important long-term study, a team of researchers in the United States assessed ten- to twelve-year-olds for guilt-proneness and shame-proneness and then interviewed most of them after they turned eighteen. Shame-proneness predicted drug use, risky sexual behavior, and some kind of embroilment in the criminal justice system, while guilt-proneness predicted the reverse.[81] Psychologists Stuevig, Dearing, Tangney, and the rest of the team suggested:

> Feelings of guilt about specific behaviors are less likely to invoke the defensiveness, denial, and *externalization of blame* that is so characteristic of shame. There is less risk in realistically assessing one's failures and transgressions [as in guilt] because at issue is a *bad behavior not a bad self*.[82]

Shame, Religion, and Violence

While religion can inspire and give hope, it can also instill a profound sense of shame and unworthiness. In many religions, moreover, shame at not being sufficiently devout has sometimes fed strongly into aggression, whether against co-religionists or others. The greatest shame and hostility has often been directed at those who are seen as lapsing from the category of "true believers" into the category of non-believers or idolators.

We have noted that Christianity is sometimes held to have encouraged an emphasis on guilt and conscience rather than shame, particularly in comparison to the emphasis on respect in the Roman Empire from which Christianity emerged. But Christianity also brought a substantial emphasis on shame. There was shame around the body and sex, with women (like Eve) generally being first in line for control and criticism.[83] In the Christian doctrine of Original Sin, even the newborn infant was sinful in nature, a belief that takes us rather far from the notion of guilt-for-things-done. Humankind *as a whole* was seen to have "fallen" when Adam and Eve tasted the forbidden fruit, taking us even further from the idea of individual guilt. And since Adam and Eve did not at this point know the difference between good and evil, having not yet tasted "the tree of the knowledge of good and evil," even *their* "guilt" was not exactly clear.[84]

Part of Nietzsche's scathing critique of Christianity was that it loaded a painful sense of shame onto already-existing suffering. In Christianity, according to Nietzsche, every pain was deserved, and the Christian priest or minister would always urge that suffering be understood "as a *state of punishment.*"[85] Certainly, disasters in predominantly Christian countries were repeatedly held to indicate that there had been sinning on a massive scale (though this reflex is hardly exclusive to Christianity). The old idea that disaster was a punishment calling for moral reform (as at the time of the Black Death) was later given a particular slant by Protestantism; and the underlying anxiety was especially high in the Calvinist version of Protestantism since you were predestined for either heaven or hell (and there might be certain "signs" of what awaited you).[86] In Britain at the end of the eighteenth century, the Anglican clergyman Thomas Malthus famously suggested that disasters like famine and plague were a natural corrective to overpopulation, having the advantage of discouraging laziness and promiscuity.[87] In his book *Chosen People*, Clifford Longley argued that the Protestants' self-image as a "Chosen People" (a template taken from the Israelites in the Old Testament) lent itself in Britain and the United States to a cycle of shame (around laxity and idolatry) and moral reform; when God sent punishment for lapsing by removing his protection, the cyclical process of reform would begin.[88] We may remember also that in the Old Testament, the fear that the Israelites would lapse into idolatry was so great that God commanded the massacre of many "idolatrous" ethnic groups whose very existence was presented as an intolerable temptation.[89] Even today, while there are various ways to escape from the shame and anxiety of sin and unworthiness, some of these are violent—as we shall see in the case of the "war on terror."

Especially in the context of 9/11 and the "war on terror," Muslim "fundamentalists" have routinely been painted as threatening and irredeemably *other*. But it's notable how much "fundamentalists" in different religions have in common. In the more insecure and purist versions of both Christianity and Islam, we get a strong sense that basic human desires are shameful and tempting. While such desires might be kept at bay through strict sanctions and disciplined religious observance, another defense has sometimes been violence against those who *lapse*. In a passage that brings out important resemblances between the Wahhabist version of Islam, on the one hand, and Protestantism on the other, Malise Ruthven notes, for example, that the eighteenth-century Islamist reformer Muhammad ibn Abd al-Wahhab

> preached a return to the purity of the early Islam of the Prophet Muhammad and the "rightly guided" caliphs, an Islam free from the accretions and practices, such as the custom of worshipping at the tombs of Muslim saints and asking for intercessions [from the saints], adopted during more than a millennium of "cumulative tradition."[90]

In practice, religious movements rejecting such "intercessions" have often proven to be a "tough ask," so that the danger of lapsing is ever present. In the case of Wahhabism, insecurities and intolerances have sometimes lent themselves to violence—not least in the movement's influence on al Qaida. We can see this fear of lapsing in the memoirs of Sayyid Qutb, a leading member of Egypt's Muslim Brotherhood and a key influence on al Qaeda. Qutb wrote vividly of the sexual temptations in the United States in particular.

In Hinduism, too, violence has sometimes been used to keep a shameful world of temptation at bay. The idea that violence may spring from temptation is underlined by Vinay Lal's insightful analysis of Hindutva, India's Hindu fundamentalist movement, and its targeting of "soft" Hindus. Lal refers to the pogrom directed at Muslims in Gujarat in 2002, which killed at least 2,000 people and left 150,000 homeless. Many human rights activists have called this a genocide and Lal notes that the killings were carried out "with the active participation of functionaries of the state charged with checking the violence."[91] Among the most prominent targets were not only mosques but also *dargahs*, burial sites of Sufi saints that are visited by Muslim and Hindu worshippers. In a key passage, Lal observes:

> Fear of oneself is often greater than the fear of the other.[92] Hindus who worship at *dargahs* are not only, from the perspective of militant Hindus, apostates, traitors and friends of Pakistan; they are

palpable reminders of the syncretism that has historically characterized what later assumed the corporate identity of Hinduism, uncomfortable reminders indeed of everything that advocates of a masculinist (and often genocidal) faith masquerading as Hinduism have disowned in their own past. The genocide perpetrated against Muslims masks Hindutva's genocidal impulses towards Hinduism.[93]

Conclusion

We have seen in this chapter that shame is painful in itself. It frequently undermines confidence and happiness. It routinely contributes to anxiety, mental illness, and delusions. And it's a very common cause of violence—for example when individuals respond aggressively to being shamed, when shame centers on religious "lapsing," when shame is manipulated by those stirring up violence, and when shame among the victims of violence feeds into silence and impunity. Many of the perspectives in this chapter suggest that we need to look very carefully, in politics as in personal life, at the way shame is manipulated. Alongside the instilling and reinforcing of shame, there are often powerful people who benefit from promising to relieve this shame.

4

Shame and Shamelessness

IT'S CLEAR FROM THE DISCUSSION so far that shame can do enormous damage. Shame is painful and disabling; and shame has often been systematically loaded onto people, with some kind of "escape" from shame being routinely and often simultaneously peddled. This frequently involves a major and damaging political, economic, or even religious manipulation. It's tempting to conclude from all this that shame is something we would be much better off without.

But let us imagine that, one fine day, we were to succeed in banishing the scourge of shame from the planet. Would this really be a better world? Perhaps this brave new "shame-free" world would not be so wonderful after all but would instead be full of shameless individuals wreaking havoc with hardly a thought for the consequences.

Perhaps shame is like rain or toilet paper—you don't miss it until it's gone.

When we look closely at *shamelessness* and all the damage it can do, our attention is drawn to the possibility that shame has a positive side. In the *Oxford English Dictionary*, "shameless" means "characterized by or showing a lack of shame; bare-faced or brazen."[1] Immediately, this doesn't sound good. In ancient Greece, Plato explicitly emphasized the dangers of shamelessness, and a strong whiff of contemporary relevance attaches to his observation that a man without shame is one who lets his passions run wild and becomes thereby a kind of tyrant.[2] The same goes for Plato's warning that shamelessness has sometimes been dangerously recast as bravery, insolence as good breeding, and disorder as freedom.[3] The problem of shameless individuals was also noted by Saint Thomas Aquinas in his publication *Summa Theologica* (believed to have been written between 1265 and 1274). "Those who are steeped in sin are without shame," he wrote, "for instead of disapproving of their sins, they boast of them."[4] The ancient Chinese philosopher Mencius noted pithily that "the shamefulness of being without a sense of shame is shameful indeed."[5] Bongrae Seok suggests that within the Confucian tradition shame is not just "a positive prosocial disposition" but also "an ideal character trait and a mark of moral excellence."[6]

In recent years, the perils of shamelessness have been highlighted by political developments in a number of prominent democracies (discussed further in chapters 8–11 in particular). Several leaders have gained a strong following despite some remarkably shameless behavior, with Trump only the most obvious example. In looking at the rise of right-wing populism in many parts of the world, we should consider that a significant degree of shamelessness has arguably been a major *asset* when it comes to attracting popular support—for example in the United States, the UK, Italy, Brazil, France, India, and the Philippines.[7] Indeed, while some people may see particular public figures as dangerously shameless, others may regard them as *thrillingly* shameless.

For at least part of the watching public, some combination of a *theater of shaming* and a *theater of shamelessness* seems to be strongly attractive. Both spectacles appear to offer an alluring and vicarious *escape from shame*, including shame around one's identity and shame around "not making it" (perhaps as a successful worker or consumer). We see this today with far-right Italian prime minister Giorgia Meloni, for whom a core message is that she should not be ashamed to proclaim that she is a woman, an Italian, and a family person; Meloni suggests, further, that being ashamed of one's identity turns people into "consumer slaves" who are at the mercy of "financial speculators." While this particular critique of consumerism seems notably half-baked, what is very clear is that understanding contemporary politics demands an analysis of who is mobilizing shame and shamelessness for what kinds of purposes.

Alongside the celebration of a "shameless" leader, we have sometimes seen a tendency to denounce some kind of "dangerous shamelessness" in other quarters. A strand of right-wing politics has routinely expressed alarm when oppressed or stigmatized groups are seen as discarding the shame that historically attached to certain relatively fixed characteristics such as race, gender, and sexual orientation. The message, very often, is that "they" have been able to assert their pride but "we" (the silent majority) are not only blocked from doing so but also told repeatedly that feelings of shame would be more appropriate. The sense of alarm may escalate when someone with a characteristic that has been strongly stigmatized ascends to a conspicuously high office (like president). In this vein, we have seen many conservative political pundits recently calling for a "return to shame"—not least in the United States.[8] In many countries, we have also seen what we might call a "counter-pride" movement—notably when people (explicitly or implicitly) assert their pride in being white, Christian, heterosexual, American, Italian, and so forth. Since structures of oppression and exploitation have been supported by perverse distributions of shame (not least when oppressed groups internalize responsibility and blame), it is not surprising that attempts to change the distribution of shame are often seen as threatening and subversive. Another problem is that those who feel under attack for their "white privilege" or other advantages may not *feel* (or in some case *be*) very privileged, particularly in a struggling economy, while their very whiteness may attach an extra dose of shame if they have not flourished despite this widely noted advantage.[9]

Some Positive Aspects of Shame

From a biological or evolutionary perspective, emotions *of any kind* are usually held to serve some kind of survival or reproductive function—and shame is no exception here. As part of this tendency, shame has sometimes been presented as promoting unselfish behavior that helps the group, while also strengthening social cohesion and kinship ties.[10]

One element of this is the function that shame is seen to have in reducing aggression. The "naturalistic" view of shame portrays it as a kind of submissive gesture whose functions echo those in an animal world where displays of shame signal a kind of "apology" for social transgressions, indicating compliance with social norms.[11] Among animals, displays of appeasement and submission—such as lowering the head, avoiding the gaze of another animal, or simply hiding—have been shown to reduce aggression in potential rivals. (I have experienced a hint of this myself when our family dog—Milo the maltipoo—studiously avoids my gaze and flips his head from side to side if caught climbing too high in the garden. He seems to know he's been "naughty"—it's cute, and it feels hard to tell him off for long.)[12] At the level of human interaction, Dacher Keltner and Lee Anne Harker note that "to remedy social relations following transgression of social rules, humans rely on apologies and appeasement gestures, which, like similar displays in other species, involve submissive and affiliative displays."[13] There is some evidence that a defendant's display of shame within a court of law, for example, encourages more lenient sentences.[14]

While submissive gestures may play a significant role in "conflict prevention," that may come at a huge price. Notably, a dominant group may require gestures of shame and submission—for example, showing one "knows one's place" or hiding one's sexual preferences—if it is not to escalate the violence that ultimately underpins its dominance. Pointing to the perceived threats of declining moral values, of gay pride, of a Black president, and of the growing voting power of African American and Latino constituencies, Myra Mendible notes in *American Shame* that "national decline is here imagined as the loss of control over those who now refuse to bow their heads in shame."[15]

The high stakes here are suggested even when it's an *individual* that is stepping out of historically approved behaviors. A novelist friend noted that in the village in the Spanish Pyrenees where some of her family comes from, describing someone's behavior as "shameful" conveys strong disapproval but describing them as "shameless" is actually a much *greater* condemnation; for a shameless individual has in a sense stepped boldly outside community values rather than simply breaching them and then perhaps showing remorse.[16]

Such perspectives underline that shame may be an important *social glue* but also that shame may be gluing together some pretty oppressive social practices. In further illustrating the possible social functions of shame, Dov Cohen and his colleagues note that where the writ of central government does not run, a quick defense of one's honor may serve to deter further violence. Here he cites the traditionally "herder" societies of the southern United States (and the Britain from which many southern settlers came).[17] Intriguingly, Cohen et al. also note that "in many societies with very high rates of violence, there is a considerable emphasis on congeniality, politeness and 'good company.'"[18] Cohen and his colleagues suggest that "because anger means violence in many cultures of honor, it becomes a very dangerous thing to express"[19]—a comment that may recall Alex Hinton's analysis of politeness-turning-suddenly-to-violence in Cambodia. In Cohen's University of Michigan experiments, while insulted southerners were notably more aggressive than any other group, un-insulted southerners tended to be significantly *more polite* than northerners.[20] Cohen et al. noted: "Numerous observers have argued that southern culture is indeed more polite than northern culture (perhaps as a way of avoiding conflict)."[21] (For what it's worth, I found people in Houston, Texas, enormously friendly and polite when I studied there in the 1980s, even though I was aware that Houston was a fairly violent place at the time.)

Among philosophers, positive accounts of shame tend to stress that it arises from moral choices (and more specifically from moral *breaches*). From this perspective, shame has often been seen as encouraging better behavior as we strive to be the kind of person that we—and others—would hope that we can be (something close to Freud's "ego ideal"). Freud himself, notwithstanding his description of the superego as a "tyrant," pointed to some more positive functions of the superego, as when he noted that "civilization . . . obtains mastery over the individual's dangerous desire for aggression by weakening and disarming it and by setting up an agency within him to watch over it, like a garrison in a conquered city."[22]

Philosopher Krista Thomason stresses that shame's painful qualities do not mean it cannot be helpful: "We do not always have to feel good in order to be good."[23] More specifically, Thomason suggests that "if we feel shame when we fail to live up to our values, we can use those painful feelings as a warning and a reminder."[24] Crucially, Thomason adds that "a liability to shame also shows that we are open to moral criticism and that we recognize the moral standing of others,"[25] whereas by contrast "the shameless person takes her own self-conception to be the *authority* on who she is. . . . [Shamelessness] is a failure to entertain other points of view about who we are."[26] Thomason's position is further clarified in her discussion of shame-versus-guilt. Guilt relies on a person's self-conception, and:

> the more focussed we are on our self-conception, the more unlikely it is that we will be open to views that undermine it. We may fall into the trap of trusting our judgement too much. We need a liability to shame in order to be open to challenges about who we think we are.[27]

We can see here that shame might usefully inject the views of others so as to shake up the self in a way that guilt cannot.

In his own generally positive account of shame, philosopher Owen Flanagan departs from the understanding of shame promoted by Brené Brown and others. He suggests that "shame does not in any way require a negative evaluation (by self or others) of a whole person. I can be ashamed that I did something shameful, or ashamed that I have certain recurring shameful desires, without thinking I am a bad or unworthy human being."[28] Flanagan argues that, in practice, shaming usually involves shaming people for very specific behaviors, rather than shaming their whole person: "When parents tell a child that they ought to feel ashamed because they lied, or hit their sibling, or behaved badly in school, they are not calling upon the child to think 'I am a failure.'"[29] Flanagan adds that while shame is often accused of taking "the global self" to be deficient and a failure, this (destructive) emotion is actually better understood as *self-loathing*.[30] By contrast, shaming for specific behaviors can be very productive, Flanagan suggests. Shaming has higher expectations for the self of the person shamed in comparison to simply trying to induce guilt for specific behaviors: "It asks that you *be* good, not just *act* good."[31]

Flanagan also wants to emphasize the potential moral problems arising from a secularization of society and he argues that when conscience loses some of its theological underpinnings, shame (and valuing the esteem of others) may helpfully step into the breach.[32] On a more personal note Flanagan suggests that while shame is often said to be especially painful, in a Catholic upbringing it was actually sin and guilt that put the fear of hell into him; by contrast, "God sees you naked and doing socially graceless things all the time, but he is not going to bring those things up on Judgement Day."[33] The really key point, for Flanagan, is that shame is not bad *in itself*:

> Shame's bad rap has to do with appalling values that result in people being taught or encouraged to be ashamed of things that no one should ever be ashamed about—the color of their skin, their sexual orientation, their gender, their whole self. The badness of these kinds of shame has to do with their terrible content, not with shame itself.[34]

In general, positive accounts of shame tend to stress that shame is useful both in prompting a degree of *self-reform* and in encouraging behavior that allows the avoidance of shame in the first place.[35] Philosophers Julien Deonna and Fabrice Teroni argue that much of the "bad press" that shame has received may be due to a focus on individuals who have experienced shame *in an extreme form*. They call this *humiliation*, which they acknowledge to be a significant cause of anger and aggression. They also suggest that evidence on the damaging effects of shame tends to relate to individuals who are especially *prone to shame* (because of their low self-esteem), rather than to the general population.[36] However, it seems more helpful to keep the notion of shame intact (in this case with humiliation at the extreme end of the spectrum), a point that will be developed further in our discussion of Gilligan and violent crime in chapter 5

Before looking in more detail at whether there is "good" and "bad" shame, it's important to mention an influential *historical* account of shame that paints the emotion in a generally positive light. In his

1939 book *The Civilizing Process*, Norbert Elias argued that violent appetites and passions were progressively reined in over many centuries of European history as bourgeois notions of shame gained ascendancy. In medieval society "the pleasure in killing and torturing others was great, and it was a socially permitted pleasure."[37] But over time such "pleasures" came to be severely frowned upon. The use of force was increasingly monopolized by the state; violence was gradually excluded from the public sphere; and "bourgeois" values like self-control and foresight increasingly held sway. On this account, societies were learning to be civilized and were suppressing unacceptable drives, rather as Freud had posited for individuals.[38] Indeed, on this view, the modern individual in some sense had to condense centuries of historical development into a single childhood.

Elias's analysis usefully highlighted not only the positive role that shame can play in society but also the importance of what it is (at various points and in various societies) that people are ashamed *about*.

But Elias's account also rather unhelpfully marginalized the extreme violence that European elites were meting out both in the form of colonialism and in the form of vicious punishments for the "lower classes" at home.[39] One also has to wonder why such a long and far-reaching "civilizing" process (with helpful versions of shame apparently being widely internalized) did not prevent such catastrophes as World War I or the Nazi Holocaust. In their useful critique, Sinisa Malesevic and Kevin Ryan suggest that Elias relies too heavily on a Hobbesian model that sees violence as *natural* for humans, a state of nature that only "civilization"—or a "civilizing process"—could rein in.[40] A radically different perspective posits that human inhibitions around violence are actually very strong and that the orchestration of mass violence requires a major effort to *erode* these inhibitions—for example through "breaking people down" during military training or through the bureaucratic compartmentalization highlighted by Zygmunt Bauman in his book *Modernity and the Holocaust*.[41] From this perspective, "civilization" is not the solution to violence but actually a *precondition* for mass slaughter: it erodes inhibitions against violence, thereby contributing to a dangerous shamelessness; it also adds greatly to the machinery available for destruction. There is certainly a need to explore the social and political processes through which people's shame around the infliction of harm has been overcome—sometimes by insisting that it would be shameful *not* to inflict harm. In chapter 7 on Eichmann and chapter 11 on empire and its aftermath, for example, we will see how shamelessness around violence can indeed be constructed in modern societies and how a self-conception as civilized can itself be extremely dangerous and a cause of great shamelessness.

Good and Bad Shame?

Our brief survey of some positive aspects of shame underlines the possibility that shamelessness can do great damage. It also suggests a need to ask *what kinds of shame are in operation*, whether there are certain kinds of shame that are *actively helpful*, and whether certain kinds are especially *harmful*.

Here, the concept of "moral shame" is particularly useful. It's the type of shame most commonly discussed in philosophy and moral psychology, and Thomason helpfully describes "moral shame" as shame that occurs when we fail to live up to norms, standards or ideals that we care about.[42] Moral shame generally relates to *what someone has done (or failed to do)*. Arguably, society could not *exist* without this kind of shaming. Thomason also makes a useful distinction between moral shame on the one hand and, on the other hand, shame about things that have either little or nothing to do with our moral character but center instead on threats to our social standing and reputation. In the latter category, Thomason mentions nakedness, being from a lower class, mental illness, appearance, and disabilities; she observes that many of these are things that children might tease each other about on the playground.[43]

Of course, hard-and-fast distinctions will generally bring problems, and one difficulty with Thomason's distinction is that when we fail to live up to ideals that we care about, that is something that will itself threaten our reputation and social standing. In some ways, moral shame may also be argued to move the concept of shame closer to guilt (though differences remain insofar as bad things done result in disapproval of the whole self, especially if there is a public element to this).

When we look at Thomason's list of things about which we are likely to feel *something other than moral shame*, we may notice that these center on *given characteristics*. Shaming people for these characteristics does seem to be something quite different from shaming people for bad or immoral decisions. It has different causes, different functions, and different consequences. So perhaps—in a slightly modified version of Thomason's binary—we should be emphasizing the distinction between *moral shame* (shame when we fail to live up to norms) and shame arising from *given characteristics*. Again, this distinction is not without problems. For example, many characteristics are somewhat fixed but not *entirely* (poverty, obesity, even gender); nakedness itself is hard to allocate between the two categories, moreover, since we are born naked but we also may choose to be naked.

A very important advantage of distinguishing moral shame and shame for (relatively) fixed characteristics is that it helps to highlight the inherent injustice in being shamed for such characteristics—in other words, in being shamed for something that we have *not actually done*.[44] As Owen Flanagan puts it, "The demand to change an unalterable trait is straightforwardly cruel."[45] A particularly pernicious type of shaming is shaming people for their body, their race, their gender, or their sexual preferences. Again, we may notice that when politicians (especially right-wing populist politicians) engage in conspicuous acts of shaming, this has frequently involved the shaming of an individual or group for given characteristics such as race, nationality, gender, sexuality, disability, and so on.

The grave unfairness of this kind of shaming implies a dangerous kind of authority and one in which crime is being recklessly separated from punishment (to go back to Arendt). This is likely to produce notable anxiety and outrage, particularly among those being directly targeted. At the same time—and perhaps *because* it is so unfair—this kind of public and theatrical shaming may also appear to some members of the public as an exhilarating break with convention, a daring breach of the rules, an impressive demonstration of personal charisma, and/or a restoration of pride for those who are *not* being targeted. We will see in chapter 9 how Hannah Arendt can help us to understand these diverse public reactions.

Thomason notes that one way of defending shame has been to define it, in effect, as moral shame, so that the rather obviously pernicious quality of shaming people for fixed characteristics does not contaminate the notion of shame itself. But Thomason herself suggests that we should *keep the category of shame intact*, and I follow her in this. It would seem very odd to argue that shame around one's color or sexuality, say, is not actually shame or that shaming people for fixed characteristics is not actually shaming. And, as Thomason points out, we do not generally try to split the emotion of fear (fear of spiders, fear of losing loved ones) even when fear has diverse manifestations and effects.

In the current book, we are primarily concerned with the *politics* of shame—and this means shame in all of its manifestations (not just the bits we "like" or "don't like"). Whether we are looking at moral shame or at shame for given characteristics, it's important to distance ourselves a little from trying to label shame itself as "good" or "bad." It's important to investigate how exactly shame of various kinds has been instrumentalized and politicized, with what purposes, and with what results. This is a large part of what I attempt in the book.

Finally, we should be careful to ensure that the glaring unfairness of shaming people for relatively fixed characteristics does not allow an excessively rosy view of moral shame. There is plenty of evidence, for example, that even shame for one's moral choices can be extremely damaging—not least when the values being encouraged by the shamers are themselves destructive. An example here might be shaming someone for choosing a path that is insufficiently belligerent.

Shame and Shaming

Insofar as shame can be plausibly depicted as a positive force, this would seem to imply that *shaming* is also positive. But does this necessarily follow? To deepen our understanding of shame, we also need to explore the complicated relationship between shame and shaming.

To some extent at least, shame and shaming can usefully be *de-linked*. For one thing, shame may be possible without shaming. For another, shaming may not necessarily lead to shame.

It's revealing that while both Thomason and Flanagan give considerable credit to (certain kinds of) shame, they are both extremely wary of shaming. Flanagan states, "I do not intend to advocate for shaming but for a mature sense of shame,"[46] while Thomason argues that "holding up the flaws of others for public scorn" is "unjustified even when it is done for noble reasons."[47] In shaming, she adds, "we take ourselves to be moral educators who are immune to the flaws that we point out in others."[48] We are also assuming, she suggests, that we are permitted to try to enforce virtue in others.[49]

But can we reasonably claim, for example, that shame is productive while shaming is not? Is not some degree of shaming necessary for shame to exist at all? There are reasons to think that shaming might *not* be a necessary condition for shame. Here, we should consider that shame might arise, for instance, from the existence or practice of a *good example* (perhaps a parental one) and from a person's perception that they have failed to follow this good example. No active shaming might be necessary here (though we might imagine that a fair amount of subtle or implied shaming may nevertheless occur). We should consider also that an *intentional* act of shaming may not be necessary for a feeling of shame to arise: for example, a child might feel shame if another child is praised for some achievement (even where the praiser has no intention of shaming the first child). It may be that shaming works best when it *is* subtle and is not recognized—or even perhaps intended—as an act of shaming.

If we turn to the question of whether shaming *leads to* shame, we might note, first of all, that the *Oxford English Dictionary* defines "to shame" as "to make (someone) feel ashamed." This clearly assumes that shaming *will* lead to shame. But in reality, while shaming *may* induce feelings of shame in the recipient, it may also lead to anger, defiance, indifference, and so on. And if shaming *does* lead to a feeling of shame, even this feeling may turn rather quickly into something else (like anger). While shaming can conceivably be productive, shaming often brings out the *unproductive* side of shame.

The following discussion explores some of the circumstances that seem to influence whether shaming leads to shame.

One important factor centers on "**buy-in**." Specifically, shaming appears to be much more likely to induce shame when the person or group being shamed actually subscribes to the collective or community values that they have breached.[50] If they do subscribe, it means in effect that these values have been temporarily set aside in the errant behavior. In these circumstances, the shaming may well be seen by the recipient as *justified* or *deserved*. Here we might think, for example, of the shaming of a government for an abuse of human rights. Where a government has signed up to international norms, there is at least the *possibility* of holding it to account for values it (says it) shares; again, such a government may (on an optimistic reading) have temporarily set aside its better self.

Aristotle also invoked "buy-in" when he said that "people before whom we feel shame are those whose opinion of us matters to us."[51] Broadly in line with this, Deonna and Teroni suggest that when we find that someone is making a negative judgment of us, we will often react not with shame but with *anger*; however, if the negative judgment threatens something *we value* (like the opinion of a group or membership of that group), then we are likely to feel shame. In this way, shame may be said to show our participation in group values—again, potentially a positive thing and arguably an essential foundation for any society. On somewhat similar lines, Sara Ahmed observes, "If we feel shame, *we feel shame because we have failed to approximate "an ideal" that has been given to us through the practices of love*."[52]

A second (related) factor influencing whether shaming leads to shame would appear to be **whether the person or group being shamed has respect for whoever is doing the shaming**. If there is only contempt, it is likely to make a big difference. This clearly relates to whether the target of shaming shares the values of the shamer but more specifically centers on the target's view of the shamers themselves: are they "respect-able" people or organizations?

Again, where there is no such respect, shaming may easily lead to anger. In *The Merchant of Venice*, Shakespeare shows the enraging quality of shaming when the shamers are themselves despised. In pushing the

Venetian court to honor his right to a "pound of flesh" from his debtor, the Jewish anti-hero Shylock broils at the hypocrisy of his accusers, saying they praise the law only when it suits them while denying him his legal right:

> You have among you many a purchased slave
> Which like your asses and your dogs and mules
> You use in abject and in slavish parts,
> Because you bought them. Shall I say to you,
> "Let them be free! Marry them to your heirs!"[53]

Those who are shamed may be shielded from *feeling* shame when they see themselves as outsiders who are in effect being stoned by people in glass houses. The Trump supporters rejecting (but sometimes embracing) the label "deplorables" come to mind here. More generally, political polarization seems to have a pretty inhibiting impact on the effectiveness of shaming. Indeed, compared with shaming within in a reasonably loving family (for example), shaming in politics seems only rarely to induce shame in its targets. In fact, if your opponents are shaming you, you may feel you are doing something right! An example of this—and an illustration of how politicians may even "pre-construct" a shameless space for their own abuses—came when UK home secretary Suella Braverman (who has been notably cruel in her attitude to asylum seekers) said, "It's got to this point where if I get trolled and I provoke a bad response on Twitter, I know I'm doing the right thing. Twitter is a sewer of left-wing bile."[54]

Part of our attitude toward the shamer will depend on their *tone*. In general, people don't like to be preached at; and correspondingly, if the shamer can somehow show some humility, it may help. In her insightful book *Is Shame Necessary?* Jennifer Jacquet highlights the interesting case of Antanas Mockus, intermittently mayor of Bogotá, Colombia, from 1995 to 2003. Mockus's creative and often effective ways of shaming bad behavior included getting pedestrians to hold up soccer-style red cards to bad drivers. Significantly, Mockus (perhaps appropriately named, at least for English-language readers) knew how to make fun of himself. Alongside his shaming campaigns he would humble himself before the public with shameless gestures like mooning his audience (to stop student disorder) and being filmed naked in the shower (as part of a water-conservation campaign).[55]

A third factor influencing whether shaming turns into shame is **the type of shame** that the shamer is attempting to invoke. Notably, when we are shamed for some aspect of ourselves that is a given characteristic or part of our identity rather than a moral choice, the inherent injustice and cruelty of this maneuver may easily result in anger rather than shame (or perhaps in shame that quickly *turns* to anger). That cruelty may also undermine more reasonable shaming: having been subjected to shame for being Jewish (and a moneylender), Shylock was hardly ready to respond positively to shame-for-cruelty.

Related to being shamed for given characteristics is the possibility that we will be shamed for something we didn't do (like a crime we didn't commit).[56] Again such shaming would be cruel or at least very unfair, and we will probably feel less shame than if we did carry out a crime (though we might still feel *some*).

A fourth significant factor influencing whether shaming induces feelings of shame seems to be **the sense of self-worth in the recipient**. Aristotle himself noted that confidence can insulate against jeers. And we've noted Deonna and Teroni's argument that low self-esteem makes people prone to feelings of intense shame and humiliation, a point that finds some support in Gilligan's work on violent criminals (as we shall see in chapter 5).

Fifth, the **age** of the person being shamed may also influence whether shaming turns to shame. A young child's values are being shaped by people around it and being (mildly) shamed may be an important part of this process. With an older person, values are likely to be more rigidly established, and using shame to shape or change behavior may not be easy: as the saying goes, you can't teach an old dog new tricks. At the extreme, a young child recruited to a rebel group might relatively easily embrace the idea that sympathy is shameful and cruelty praiseworthy (as did happen in Sierra Leone). At the same time, we should note that adults may also embrace some very perverse definitions of what is shameful, and that in special circumstances the values even of an adult may be turned around with terrifying rapidity (including through the use of shame). Noting the value of those who retained the ability to think and to doubt in the face of totalitarianism, Arendt emphasized how quickly "respectable society" could succumb to the destructive and delusional mindset of fascism: "we now know that moral norms and standards can be changed overnight, and all that then will be left is the mere habit of holding fast to something."[57]

Shamelessness and Underlying Shame

If we consider individuals who exhibit shamelessness, we may be tempted to imagine that theirs is a happy, stable, and untroubled situation (albeit often a destructive one) in which shame has somehow been permanently banished. But *are* such characters really without shame? Or would it be more accurate to say that they entertain and act upon some very perverse and dangerous definitions of what is shameful and what isn't? Perhaps they also expend a great deal of effort and energy in *warding off* various kinds of shame? Much of the relevant literature— and psychoanalytical literature in particular—suggests that an apparent state of shamelessness may conceal a constant struggle against shame. At times, this may approach a state of war within the mind.

Nietzsche criticized a general neglect of philosophers, novelists, and composers. (You can find his accomplished piano compositions on YouTube.) In a helpful summary, Ronald Speirs notes that, for Nietzsche (who lived from 1844 to 1900), shamelessness

> was an unsuccessful attempt to hide, both from themselves and from others, a deeply buried but ineradicable awareness among Nietzsche's contemporaries that they ought to be ashamed of their conduct of life. The Germans' lack of respect for the finer spirits of their own literature stemmed from their need to avoid any reminders of the standards that would bring their suppressed shame to the surface.[58]

Today we might think of the popular enthusiasm for trivia of all kinds and for so-called trash TV, which frequently involves at least some degree of humiliation (and as a queasy fan of *X Factor*, I should know).

Reality TV may similarly protect us from reminders of the more substantial cultural contributions that we have either ignored or failed to understand.

Nietzsche also noted that the German term *Scham* "can be positively charged, conveying a sense of modesty, reticence or propriety," including the ability to acknowledge greatness in another human being without any resentment.[59] While Nietzsche himself had many faults, excessive modesty was not one of them, and he felt that the lives of a few great individuals such as himself were worth more than the mass of ordinary people.

While Nietzsche gives us one interpretation of the origins of a certain kind of shamelessness, it is of course not easy to know what lies behind a shameless exterior. Anna Freud's work can give us some important pointers, however. Picking up on her father's work, she explored a number of defense mechanisms that prevent full awareness of unwelcome memories and feelings, and she remarked that certain emotional states within children are to be expected in specific circumstances. For example, a reward can reasonably be expected to elicit joy while an awareness of impending punishment may be expected to make a child anxious. But observation of children often revealed a very different picture:

> For instance, a child may exhibit indifference when we should have looked for disappointment, exuberant high spirits instead of mortification, excessive tenderness instead of jealousy. In all these cases something has happened to disturb the normal process; the ego has intervened and has caused the affect to be transformed.[60]

This suggested to Anna Freud that certain emotions were being pushed away or pushed out of consciousness, perhaps even replaced by very surprising emotions that were inappropriate in the circumstances. This was related to the suppression of drives and of awareness of these drives. In a "reaction formation," an unwanted feeling is replaced by its opposite, and Anna Freud suggested that this "secures the ego against the return of repressed impulses from within."[61] While shame was not the primary focus of her discussion, her framework (and particularly the idea of a "reaction formation") would seem to suggest that outwardly shameless behavior may conceal—and potentially reveal—some rather deep-seated and underlying feelings of shame.

There were strong hints of this during my research in Sierra Leone. On occasions, you could see that shame had been kept bizarrely at bay, with shamelessness persisting after leaving a military faction. For example, at a home for recovering child soldiers in Freetown, an eleven-year-old boy told me how he was recruited into the government army some three years earlier, how he was taught to fire an AK-47 machine gun, and given gin and gunpowder for "courage." As the boy spoke about his many acts of violence against rebels and civilians, he was smiling winningly, often laughing and then periodically pretending to fall asleep. It was sad to witness a child describe the terrible things he had done, and doubly sad to see him laughing about it. Of course this behavior was very far from the sense of shame or guilt or even regret that one might have expected or hoped for. At the same time, a sudden and total acknowledgment of shame would surely have been completely overwhelming. Staff at the home said a core aim was to get the children *gradually* to acknowledge the bad things they had done without making them feel that they were irredeemably awful as people. This can plausibly be seen as an attempt to avoid shaming the child while gradually nurturing a sense of guilt. In the short term and on the surface, it was shamelessness that was most in evidence.

Drawing on his clinical practice, the psychoanalyst Léon Wurmser offered a sustained focus on shamelessness as well as shame, and he came to see shamelessness as a defense against the *shame associated with weakness*. In a passage with strong contemporary resonance, he noted:

> Shamelessness is no simple regression to a stage before the establishment of a shame barrier. It is rather, like sadism, the outcome of a complex layering of defenses. Superficial shamelessness about betrayal, sexual provocation, and exhibitionism, coupled with brazen abuse of another person, undaunted by fear of ridicule and mockery, constitutes a defiant display of "power" in displaced form. The weakness about which the person is ashamed refers to tender feelings, to kindness, to warmth; these emotions represent subjugation and must be avoided at all costs.[62]

Thus, the shameless person is not actually free from shame but in some ways quite the reverse: he or she resorts to shameless behavior in a desperate attempt to keep feelings of shame at bay. This individual may exhibit shame around behavior that might reasonably be seen as praiseworthy (for example, gentleness, kindness, restraint, holding back from killing) while exhibiting little or no shame in relation to harm done (including violence). An outsider might see here a kind of upside-down morality, while the individual concerned may not be experiencing themselves as immoral but as exhibiting (their kind of) virtue.

But *why* would someone be so averse to feelings of weakness? In Wurmser's view:

> Since shame is contempt against oneself, the "shameless" cynic may in his core very well be a traumatically humiliated, cruelly shamed person who originally suffered a profound disregard for the self in its autonomy and now contemptuousness defends against a fatal brittleness and woundedness.[63]

In these circumstances, "the 'shameless' person, like the 'frozen' or ruthless person, acts to avoid the psychotic or near-psychotic terror of showing any of his feelings, because anyone who perceived them would gain power over him."[64]

Again, we should stress that in this case shame is not so much banished as *reversed*. Shame around bad behavior may still lurk in the background, and may feed a conspicuous shamelessness. But in notably shameless individuals, if Wurmser is right, shame tends to center more on *feelings of weakness* than on antisocial behavior. This perspective will be helpful when we come to look at Eichmann—and Trump.

Going back to Shakespeare, a famously shameless character is his Richard III. But again, we do not find in Richard a total *absence* of shame so much as an underlying shame around his body and his "unlovability" along with substantial shame around weakness or what we might call *good behavior*. As Melvin Lansky notes, "Richard's sense of shame at his unlovability has given rise to relentless destructive rage and to boundless ambition and shame at any inhibition of the destructiveness necessary to achieve his goal."[65] Again, Richard has not banished shame but turned it on its head. Within this upside-down world, it is not being a child-killer and a serial killer that brings feelings of shame, but rather it is any hint of conscience—interpreted by Richard as weakness—that might divert him from the ruthless pursuit of the ultimate power, the Crown. When Richard complains "O coward conscience, how does thou afflict me?" he makes explicit that he equates conscience with cowardice (and we might think back to Plato's warning that shamelessness may be dangerously recast as bravery). Even in such a killer as Richard, conscience and a more conventional sense of shame could not be *completely* banished. Just before his death on the battlefield, for example, Richard was haunted by the ghosts of his victims. Yet there were ways of keeping conscience at bay, and labeling it as weakness and cowardice was paramount.

When we turn to the psychiatrist James Gilligan in the next chapter, we will see more evidence of shame around weakness. Gilligan also showed how a strong underlying sense of shame tended to produce a remarkable outward shamelessness. For Gilligan, this shamelessness—sometimes including extreme violence without any apparent remorse—represented a *warding off* of potentially devastating feelings of shame.

Conclusion

In this chapter we have highlighted some important positive features of shame—not least the possibility that it holds us to a higher standard of being and doing. Could this then be a case of "Come back, shame, all is forgiven!"?

Not exactly. The arguments against shame and shaming have not gone away. And rather than lurching from shame-as-the-problem to shamelessness-as-the-problem, it seems much more productive to consider what it is that particular individuals, groups, and societies consider to be shameful, how they try to keep shame at bay, how they deploy shame within political and economic systems, and at what cost.

The chapter has explored the paradox that both shame and shamelessness can be extremely damaging. It would seem very odd, on the face of it, to attribute major social ills—or indeed anything—to *something and its opposite*. But several ways of resolving, or at least addressing, the paradox have been suggested here.

First, since there are different kinds of shame (with some being harmful and some at least potentially helpful), it makes sense that both shamelessness and shame can be damaging.

Second, the problem is not so much shame or shamelessness as the way that societies define what is shameful and what is not. As part of our understanding here, we will need to inquire how an individual's shame or shamelessness relates to the mores of the wider society.

Third, shamelessness and shame may *coexist*. They may coexist within the same social system and even within the same individual. We need to understand how shame and shamelessness *interact*. At the individual level, shamelessness may conceal—and may even be produced by—an underlying shame.

Whether in relation to individuals or social systems, we need to look, first, at the methods through which shame is warded off and, second, at the ways in which shame is actively stirred and manipulated. Where abusive systems acquire a shameless quality, the shamelessness does not arise naturally or easily; rather, it has to be constantly generated and regenerated. Part of the problem in such situations is that potentially helpful feelings of shame have been pushed aside. Conceptualizing rationality as the *eradication* of emotion can feed into this dangerous process; indeed, it increases the risk that shame (like other emotions) will be seen as shameful.[66]

In the chapters that follow, I emphasize that the key problem is not so much shame itself but the various ways in which shame is manipulated, the things that people are made to feel shame about, and the bogus or actively harmful solutions for shame that people are encouraged to buy into. Again, the type of shame makes a difference. But shame-for-choices and shame-for-given-characteristics have both been subject to extreme manipulation at the level of politics. The destructive ways in which people escape from shame—and are encouraged to do so—are a key theme; and again people may choose escapes from shame-for-choices as well as escapes from shame-for-given-characteristics.

5

Gilligan's Criminals

OVER SEVERAL DECADES, the American psychiatrist James Gilligan worked with violent criminals in U.S. prisons, nearly all of them men. He found that in almost all cases these individuals had suffered significant abuse in the past, usually in childhood and often repeatedly. Many had been physically abused (including sexual abuse) or subjected to life-threatening neglect. Crucially, Gilligan (who is not one of those who want to draw a line between shame and humiliation) observed:

> The basic psychological motive, or cause, of violent behavior is the wish to ward off or eliminate the feeling of shame and humiliation—a feeling that is painful and can even be intolerable and overwhelming—and replace it with its opposite, the feeling of pride.[1]

Stressing that violence could give a (rather short-lived) feeling of pride and respect, Gilligan said of those he worked with: "Such people experience the fear that they provoke in their victims as a kind of ersatz form of respect, the only type they are capable of achieving."[2] These prisoners were liable to react to any present-day threat of shame (sometimes very slight) with extreme violence. They had very short fuses.

Initially, Gilligan had assumed that a crime like armed robbery would be motivated by the desire to get money and material goods. He noted that this was indeed the "superficial explanation" that the armed robbers preferred to give—both to themselves and to Gilligan's team.[3] But when Gilligan sat down and talked at length with these men, they made comments like, "I never got so much respect before in my life as I did when

I pointed a gun at some dude's face."[4] The pursuit of respect through fear and violence was matched by the frequency with which violence was provoked by some perceived disrespect (or "dissing"). To be shamed was to be disrespected and the perception of respect-for-being-violent offered an escape.

One especially violent prisoner was placed in solitary confinement without possessions or privileges, and he would assault the prison officers every time they opened his door. Gilligan was invited to speak with this man and asked him, "What do you want so badly that you are willing to give up everything else in order to get it?" The prisoner, usually extremely inarticulate, replied, "Pride. Dignity. Self-esteem. And I'll kill every motherfucker in that cell block if I have to in order to get it."[5] More generally, Gilligan noted:

> I have yet to see a serious act of violence that was not provoked by the experience of being shamed and humiliated, disrespected and ridiculed, and that did not represent the attempt to prevent or undo this "loss of face"—no matter how severe the punishment, even if it includes death.[6]

Gilligan pointed out, too, that the word for overwhelming humiliation—"mortification"—comes from Latin roots that mean "made dead." Some of Gilligan's prisoners would describe the fantasy of going to their deaths in a hail of gunfire. Many reported having "died inside" long before they began killing other people. They felt empty and numb; or if we put it another way, they lacked the capacity to feel anything, including sometimes physical pain as well as emotions, such as empathy. That was part of what made them appear so shameless. Yet Gilligan observed that prisoners actually seemed to find the feeling of deadness and numbness to be more intolerable than anything. Many were just hoping to feel *something*, and one way of doing so was through mutilating themselves horribly.[7]

Gilligan came to see extreme criminal violence as the work of individuals with a heightened sensitivity to shame (because they themselves had been shamed in extreme ways). These individuals were desperate to keep at bay a reactivation or intensification of this underlying state. For these prisoners, a feeling of shame was potentially so overwhelming that it was warded off through extreme measures—including that sense of numbness but also a propensity for imposing shame on others through violence. In a chilling phrase that has notable political overtones, Gilligan refers to "the overbearing need to prevent others from laughing at oneself by making them weep instead."[8] In line with some of psychoanalyst Hanna Segal's work, Gilligan said we need "to interpret action as *symbolic language*."[9] In one case study, he interprets a truly horrific murder involving gouging out of the eyes and tongue as an assault on shame itself, on eyes that see and tongues that talk, as if the murderer were saying, "If I kill this person in this way, I will kill shame."[10]

There is some ambiguity in Gilligan on whether the harm done by shaming arises from *inducing* shame or whether it actually arises from a *failure* to induce shame (instead inducing anger). Gilligan tends to skate over this difficulty, referring, for example, to the violent person's "wish to *ward off or eliminate* the feeling of shame" (emphasis added). But if shame is being successfully *warded off*, it is presumably not being *felt*, whereas if shame is being *eliminated*, it *is* being felt—and then pushed aside as anger and violence take over.

At any rate, we may safely say that Gilligan's violent criminals were not taking shame on board in a helpful way. Rather, they were taking shame on board in the way a fragile ship might take on board a tidal wave or a torpedo. Indeed, for these individuals, even a small wave—or a small act of shaming—could be overwhelming, obliterating, and existentially threatening.

In Deonna and Teroni's terms, these were "shame-prone" individuals with unusually low self-esteem. At the same time, Deonna and Teroni's attempt to paint shame in a positive light (by saying that shame's violence-promoting effects are confined to a relatively small group of unusually shame-prone individuals) begs the question of how people got to be "shame-prone" in the first place. As we shall see in relation to Gilligan's experience with violent criminals, it is generally an intense process of shaming (usually in childhood) that *makes* people shame-prone; there is little reason to suppose that these individuals were especially "shame-prone" when this traumatic process *began*.

Gilligan's work can also help us think about whether shame is fundamentally different from humiliation or just a milder version. As noted, Gilligan tends to lump shame and humiliation together. But Julien Deonna, Raffaele Rodogno, and Fabrice Teroni, who distinguish shame sharply from humiliation in their book *In Defense of Shame*, suggest that humiliation is distinct, first, in being *demeaning* and, second, in being *seen by the recipient as undeserved*.

To my mind, that quality of being "demeaning" would actually seem to fit well with a large proportion of the varied shamings we are describing in the current book. Shaming seems to become more and more demeaning as the shaming gains in intensity. The more promising distinction may be the idea that humiliation centers on shame that is felt to be *undeserved*. But I think shaming often feels undeserved; and even in cases where it feels undeserved (perhaps a middle-aged man is being shamed for wearing a sweater that does not match his trousers), it may not be experienced as humiliation. On the whole, it seems to me more sensible to say that shame may be felt to be either more or less demeaning and either more or less deserved than to resort to splitting it off from humiliation (with which it has so much in common). The *Oxford English Dictionary* includes humiliation in its definition of shame, and vice versa, which is not very helpful in distinguishing them but does suggest that they have a lot in common. Like water turning into gas, shame may begin to look and feel like humiliation when it becomes sufficiently intense (and when the quality of being demeaning and feeling undeserved gets stronger). In line with my preferred definition of shame as *a feeling that one is or is perceived to be unworthy of respect or affection*, I would suggest that shame is best seen as an overarching concept that includes disrespect (often at the milder end) and humiliation (at the stronger end).

Going back to Gilligan's criminals, it's important to note that feelings of *guilt* appear to have been remarkably absent—and that punishment did nothing to instill such feelings.[11] Gilligan notes, "The person who is overwhelmed by feelings of shame is by definition experiencing a psychically life-threatening lack of love, and someone in that condition has no love left for anyone else."[12] This in turn makes guilt virtually impossible. Yet at the same time, Gilligan emphasizes, punishment was actually *escalating* shame. While conventional wisdom—and a "rational actor" model—suggests that severe crimes call for severe punishments that will deter the targeted individual in the future (as well as deterring others). Gilligan found that the more severely these men were punished, the more violent they became.[13]

Another thing we should notice in Gilligan's seminal studies of shame and violence is that the people causing the prisoners' original and underlying humiliation were usually entirely distinct from the present-day targets of violence. In other words, there was a radical—and in a sense, a magical—disconnect between "problem" and "solution," with the problem of humiliation in the past (normally by someone much more powerful than a child) generally being dealt with by targeting someone entirely different who happened to be "available" in the present. French philosopher René Girard once made a closely related observation, noting, "When unappeased, violence seeks and always finds a surrogate victim. The creature that excited its fury is abruptly replaced by another, chosen only because it is vulnerable and close at hand."[14] This kind of sharp disjuncture between "problem" and "solution"—and between "cause" and eventual "target"—will be highly relevant when we consider the process of political shaming and scapegoating. Again, the targets tend to have little or no connection to those who have contributed to underlying problems.[15]

Gilligan also wanted to stress that shame does not *necessarily* cause violence. Several things make it significantly more likely, though, that shaming someone will make them violent. The first is the intensity of the shaming itself: violence is usually produced by a degree of shame that is overwhelming and threatens the viability of the self; a strong experience of being shamed early in life means that violence could be provoked by just a small act of shaming in the present. For Gilligan, a second factor helping to turn shame into violence is a low level of guilt around bad actions; again, guilt inhibits violence while shame encourages it. A third circumstance in which shame is likely to lead to violence, Gilligan argues, is where the shamed individual lacks sufficient means to restore self-respect through *nonviolent* processes (through skills, achievements, standing in the community, esteem in the eyes of friends, family and colleagues as well as material status symbols and so on).

Gilligan found that the single biggest predictor of not reoffending was acquiring a college degree while in prison; over a twenty-five-year period, two hundred inmates in Massachusetts acquired a college degree and none returned for a new crime.[16] In emphasizing this factor, Gilligan noted that most of the violent criminals he worked with were poorly educated, unskilled or unemployed, and poor. Importantly, he suggested that when poverty and inequality stoke violent crime, this is not just because of people's grievances and frustrations but because these underlying conditions are removing nonviolent paths to self-respect.[17]

A fourth factor making it more likely that shaming would provoke violence, according to Gilligan, was a particular conception of masculinity. Gilligan emphasized that men commit much more life-threatening violence than women. And he highlighted the common idea that violence was often considered necessary for maintaining one's self-image as a "true man," while nonviolence (particularly in the face of some kind of challenge) was routinely seen as cowardly, wimpish, and lacking in "balls." This last of Gilligan's "preconditions" illustrates the importance of cultural context in setting the overall framework for what is considered shameful and not shameful. While Gilligan's prisoners undoubtedly had a distorted idea of morality, their ideas around shame and violence had a strong connection to more widespread ideas about masculinity and the shame of "showing weakness." Gilligan helps clarify the ways that culture can determine what we see as shameful.

In general, Gilligan helps us see that in some circumstances even a small act of shaming can constitute a catastrophic threat of shame, while in other circumstances even a substantial shaming may not undermine a person's self-esteem and sense of self to the point where they resort to violence. Gilligan also helps with the enterprise of "reading" violence and discovering its symbolic or even magical significance for the perpetrator.

A number of other studies have also suggested that shame plays a major role in violent crime. For example, criminologist David Luckenbill looked at the seventy murders in one California county over the period 1963–72 and found that in all of them the murderer interpreted the violence as the only way to save "face."[18]

Gilligan's focus on shame and respect found ethnographic counterpoints in work by Philippe Bourgois and Elijah Anderson, for example. Bourgois's book *In Search of Respect* documented his life among Puerto Rican street-level drug dealers in East Harlem,[19] and Bourgois suggested that "inner city Puerto Rican men, who are confined to the margins of a nation that is explicitly hostile to their culture and no longer requires their labor power, reconstruct their notions of masculine dignity around interpersonal violence, economic parasitism, and sexual domination."[20] For his part, Anderson highlighted what he called "the code of the street" after more than two decades studying poor parts of inner-city Philadelphia, an area that included a large African American population. Respect in inner-city Philadelphia had a dangerously "zero-sum" quality, Anderson emphasized:

> The extent to which one person can raise himself up depends on his ability to put another person down. This underscores the alienation that permeates the inner-city ghetto community. There is a generalized sense that very little respect is to be had, and therefore everyone competes to get what affirmation he can of the little that is available. The craving for respect that results gives people thin skins.... Many inner-city young men in particular crave respect to such a degree that they will risk their lives to attain and maintain it.[21]

In this context, manhood "implies physicality and a certain ruthlessness," Anderson noted, while prison itself was sometimes seen as bolstering a useful image of toughness. It was important to respond strongly to any disrespect.[22] Anderson noted further: "Many of the forms that dissing can take might seem petty to middle-class people (maintaining eye contact for too long, for example), but to those invested in the street code, these actions become serious indications of the other person's intentions."[23] Importantly, Anderson put this sensitivity into the context of wider social and racial inequalities:

> The code of the streets is actually a cultural adaptation to a profound lack of faith in the police and the judicial system. The police are most often seen as representing the dominant white society and not caring

to protect inner-city residents. When called, they may not respond, which is one reason many residents feel they must be prepared to take extraordinary measures to defend themselves and their loved ones against those who are inclined to aggression.[24]

We may notice here an echo of Cohen et al.'s suggestion that "honor cultures" seem to thrive in circumstances where state protection is scarce. One implication of Anderson's work is the need for the kind of employment that puts respect into greater abundance; also needed is a level of physical security that reduces the felt need to provide one's own "security."

An important implication of Gilligan's work, meanwhile, is that punishment regimes can play strongly into violent crime. In work that complements Gilligan's, John Braithwaite has highlighted the importance of what he calls "reintegrative shaming" in rehabilitating prisoners. Treating people only as "criminals" drives out other possible identities, Braithwaite suggested, whereas reintegrative shaming "is disapproval dispensed within an ongoing relationship with the offender based on respect, shaming which focuses on the evil of the deed rather than on the offender as an irredeemably evil person."[25] This is a definition that seems to encapsulate the approach at that home for recovering child soldiers in Sierra Leone.

For Braithwaite, stigmatization pushes the criminal toward what is, in important respects, a shameless community, and he notes that while murder for most people is unthinkable, "What criminal subcultures do is provide symbolic resources that render the unthinkable thinkable."[26] In line with both Braithwaite and Gilligan, John Pratt notes that in the Anglophone world the public fears criminals and prisoners more intensely than in Scandinavia, with those heightened fears fueling much harsher prison conditions and reducing the emphasis on rehabilitation.[27]

Gilligan's work should also remind us that many of the dynamics that might seem somehow "alien" or "exotic" (and some of these will be highlighted in relation to the war in Sierra Leone) are actually profoundly important and influential within Western countries too. Far from Western societies having somehow moved away from shame and shaming, we can actually observe a very intimate relationship between shame and violent crime in the United States. That provides crucial context for understanding the reproduction of America's system of mass incarceration and the protests that this system has helped fuel.

Some of Gilligan's insights can also be usefully extended to the "war on terror" and Islamist terrorism (as we shall see in chapter 14)—and indeed to right-wing extremism. When George Packer investigated violent jihadism in Paris, he found that recruitment in prison was a key channel with recruiters targeting the *fragiles*—psychologically vulnerable prison inmates who rarely received visits. Those recruited were "offered solace, a new identity, and a political vision inverting the social order that places them at the bottom."[28] One jihadist commented (in an echo of Gilligan's criminals), "Once they fear you, they cannot be contemptuous towards you anymore."[29] After interviewing active and former right-wing extremists in the United States, Sweden, and Germany, Michael Kimmel noted the importance of Gilligan's work and added, "I have found time and time again that [the extremists] have experienced that sense of humiliation and shame." Many had been abused as children and many were lonely at school, but "that just made them better targets, and the far right drew them in. The camaraderie of the community validates their masculinity, and—even more importantly than that—gives them a sacred mission. That is really powerful for these guys."[30]

While Gilligan convincingly portrays shame as driving the violence of his American prisoners, he is also stressing that shame (for them) attaches primarily to weakness and not to inflicting harm. When we turn to Adolf Eichmann (in chapter 7) and Donald Trump (in chapters 8 and 9), we will see how shame was defined to a large extent as weakness—and how damaging this was. In the following chapter, we look at the war in Sierra Leone—and Gilligan's insights will prove extremely valuable in interpreting the violence there.

6

"Since I Am a Dog"

SHAME AND RECOGNITION IN SIERRA LEONE'S CIVIL WAR

WHEN I MET IDRISS—a slightly built and pleasantly serene Sierra Leonean student in his mid-twenties—he explained the advantages of sitting down and sharing a meal with the rapists, child-killers, and limb-hackers who were rampaging through his country.[1]

"By running away from a rebel," Idriss began, "this is going to make things worse for us and exacerbate more cruelty. Hence the rebel slogan: 'Why are you running away from us, and you don't run away from ECOMOG [the West African military force that was fighting the rebels]? What do you see in us that you don't see in them?'"

We were sitting over drinks in the strangely tranquil setting of the Horse and Jockey pub in North Oxford, and Idriss—just as patient with my slightly awkward questions as he'd apparently been with the rebels—seemed like the perfect person to make sense of a senseless war.

I had by this time conducted two periods of research in Sierra Leone, one in 1995 and one in 2001 (research that was eventually published as the book *Conflict and Collusion in Sierra Leone*). But there were still many things I didn't understand about the rebels. Did they have a political ideology, for example? Did they want to convert civilians to their cause? And if they did, how did this square with the extremity of their abuses *against* civilians?

"They want some kind of recognition from the civilians," Idriss told me, "because they have some kind of ideology and beliefs.... You have to say 'OK, I'm with you, I support you. There's nothing wrong with you.'... I was able to use this tool to survive."

That emphasis on the need for recognition—and rebels' fear that civilians would see something bad in them—seemed bizarre, given that the rebels were also carrying out unimaginable atrocities. But Idriss spoke with the authority of someone who *had* in fact survived.

In Sierra Leone concern with recognition and respect was so prevalent among the various fighting groups that it strongly implied an underlying deficit of respect. And the frequency with which rebels and rogue soldiers inflicted some kind of humiliation on their victims itself seemed to speak of an underlying humiliation that they had experienced and were looking to reverse. Without "mutual recognition," Axel Honneth has suggested in a more general discussion, there is "an experience of disrespect or humiliation."[2]

Idriss had been living with his wife and their young child when rebels occupied their town of Waterloo in December 1998:

> They told civilians they didn't have to be afraid. I think they meant it. Most civilians stayed in the rebel area. It was a risk to go to Freetown [the capital, about eighteen miles way] but if there had been total madness in the rebel area, we would have tried to go.... They had cross-checked us. We became a makeshift community. They even shared food with us in the evenings.

Lists of atrocities in a war like Sierra Leone's can become a little numbing as one excess is piled onto another. This particular war became a byword for madness, for drug-fueled massacres, and even for evil itself. The relentless accumulation of atrocities helped create an image of an incomprehensible, despicable "other." It is just a small step (and one letter in the English language) from portraying the atrocities as "inhumane" to portraying the perpetrators as "inhuman," and the commonly used word "brutal" implies (if we take it literally) that perpetrators are themselves less than human.

Idriss's stories, on the other hand, suggested that even in the midst of the madness and viciousness that was Sierra Leone's war, fighters' strong desire for recognition was sometimes matched by a strong sense of justice (bizarrely warped though this was) along with a strong sense of what was shameful and not shameful. Certainly, the rebels defined shame in very particular—and often very perverse—ways.

Idriss was soon onto another story, and began by noting that some rebels attributed mystical powers to the African peacekeeping jets that thundered over their heads. One day, some rebels were sitting on Idriss's veranda and they became afraid because a local woman, who was mentally disturbed, was talking loudly to herself while jets flew by. The rebels were shouting at her to be quiet (though the pilots would clearly not have heard her), and eventually one soldier-turned-rebel called J. J. Blood became so agitated that he shot the woman in the jaw and then killed her outright. What made this even more horrific was that the woman was pregnant. Idriss recalled:

> I can never forget it, exactly three hours later, there was going to be a huge problem. . . . Some other "brigadiers" wanted to court-martial J. J. Blood. For them the rationale was that this woman was not normal but inadequate, so it was a gross violation according to their own idea of human rights.

According to their own idea of human rights?! It seemed such a strange phrase to apply to one of the most reviled armed groups in the world. The rebels were known for giving their innocent victims a macabre "choice" about whether they wanted "long" or "short sleeves"— amputation above or below the elbow. They also used forced labor on a large scale and did not hesitate to kill many of their more educated comrades at an early stage in the war. It was hard to find "the idea of human rights" in all that.

But I did not interrupt.

A group of would-be executioners—around twelve years of age— were lined up as a firing squad to punish Commander Blood, who argued his case strongly, saying it was better that the woman was killed than that everyone be killed by the jets. He was allowed to live, but the rebels insisted, "He ought to have known better." Idriss summed up the incident: "There's a belief in justice and of a welfare state ... but they define it differently."

Oddly, this apparent belief in "justice" was by no means an isolated example. For instance, when I was in Sierra Leone, a local aid worker told me about a rebel "court" he'd witnessed in the east of the country in 2000: "People's courts are how the rebels try people—I've seen it. Even if one small boy objects to a decision to sentence someone, the objection will stand. He cannot be overridden. There's a genuine belief in a new Sierra Leone." This practice emerged in the context of many young people feeling their voices had not been heard. When another researcher expressed surprise at this deference to children, adding that youths in the country always seemed so deferential themselves, the aid worker replied, "But this is a completely different world."

Back in the Oxford pub, I pushed Idriss a little further on how he saw the rebels, and he told me a story about his family.

At the time of the rebels' occupation, Idriss's baby had malaria and the family had no pills to control the fever. "We were afraid to ask the rebels," Idriss remembered. "We didn't know how they would react."

At one point, a young rebel—aged thirteen—was passing by and he saw that the baby was sick. "Haven't you got medicine or money?" the boy asked. He said he would go and try to find some medicine. But Idriss didn't take the boy seriously. Quite apart from the notorious callousness of the rebels, Idriss knew that medicines were always very scarce: "Drugs are very essential—they're like diamonds."

But then the young fighter returned. Idriss recalled that the boy's eyes looked like they were popping out. He seemed to be high on marijuana—hardly a good sign. But it turned out the boy was carrying some pills. "I was so delighted when he came back with two dozen Panadol," Idriss remembered, smiling. Idriss and his wife substituted local herbs to make the pills last longer, mixing the herbs with local water even though the water was unsafe. Somehow the baby pulled through. Idriss believed it was the boy's act of kindness that had made the difference: "That saved my baby's life!"

In a world that likes to divide people into "goodies" and "baddies," it is hard to get one's head around Idriss's further reflections on this incident:

> There are amputations of four- to six-month-old babies, killings of pregnant women. But despite all the destruction of people's lives and amputations, I can see two sides. They can sometimes really understand the situation of someone vulnerable—*even more than in a normal community* [my emphasis]. I was really touched by this thirteen-year-old. There are ideas of fairness and welfare, as opposed to simply being drug-crazed. There is sometimes a high quality of fairness. If someone has looted so much and not shared, they will go back and say, "You still have a lot and should share it around!" There is some concern with the welfare of the most vulnerable—among themselves and among civilians.

In many ways, the rebels were turning upside down a world that they perceived as corrupt and unjust. The rich and educated were to be humbled, the healthy were to be crippled, and the sane driven insane. At the same time, there was sometimes sympathy for the sick or the crazy, for the poor and uneducated, the forgotten and the young.

Idriss stressed that the rebels' sensitivity to shame was mirrored by their desperation for respect and recognition. But this led them quickly to an impasse:

> On the one hand, there's pressures [on the rebels] from commanders, from colleagues' expectations, and sometimes drugs. On the other hand, they face pressure from civilians. A lot of the rebels were outsiders initially. Success was not a question of manpower but how much people were prepared to follow their ideology. They still don't want to accept that their philosophy does not appeal, so they want to do it by force.... They unleash punishment, which makes the civilians shy away or treat them as enemies. At the same time, *they want some kind of recognition from the civilians because they have some kind of ideology and beliefs.* ... They would tell me, "If we don't 'perform'—a common word for atrocities against civilians—we can get killed or persecuted, or it makes us vulnerable to our enemies. But by that

performance, we unleash punishment on the people we should be defending." They are left feeling, who really gives us the recognition? They won't get it from civilians—understandably.

Idriss knew the survival of his family was literally on a knife-edge. One wrong move would have meant death or amputation for him, his wife, and even his baby. But Idriss said his ability to offer respect and recognition gave him "a little bit of power."

When Idriss heard that rebels were threatening a neighbor, it must have been tempting to steer well clear. But Idriss wanted to help. He rushed round to the neighbor's house and found that rebels were about to beat a young mother in front of her three-year-old child. Under the instruction of a sixteen- to seventeen-year-old "commander," a young rebel was about to flog the woman. The boy himself was only seven.

So how exactly do you intervene in such volatile and terrifying circumstances?

The first thing that Idriss did was to ask what was going on. The rebels told him they were punishing the woman for beating such a small child. They had come to the house a little earlier, looking for rice, and the woman had given them some. But then the three-year-old had blurted out that there was more rice hidden in a store, which the rebels also took. Food was scarce in wartime and, after the rebels left, they heard that the young woman had beaten her toddler in frustration. So now they had returned to exact what they presented as "justice" on behalf of the child. Idriss remembered how he engaged with the teenage commander:

> I addressed him, being very careful to show respect. I called him "Young soldier," saying, "I am just a civilian," and stressing "I am a bit daft." I said, "I mean no disrespect at all. It was wrong to beat the child, but I think maybe the woman does not need to be beaten too." It's very dangerous to come across as educated, very dangerous to challenge their authority.

Idriss also knew that becoming a rebel in Sierra Leone meant passing through a process of initiation that was a variation—and perversion—of traditional initiations within the country's secret societies known as Poro. Rebel initiations included being forced to carry out atrocities, sometimes against one's own community or even one's own family.

But Idriss, unusually inquisitive and empathetic, tried to see beyond the madness and the viciousness of this "upside-down" world:

> I became convinced there was some humanity there too, that there was a way of addressing the rebels. They have been through an initiation and want respect. I can understand it, as I went through the Poro initiation myself and afterward you feel that someone who has not been initiated is not on the same level.

Again, it is striking how much the views of civilians seemed to matter (in some sense) to people who were ready to conduct unimaginable cruelty against them.

By acknowledging the injustice of beating the child, by addressing the rebels in a calm and respectful way, and by denigrating himself, Idriss somehow managed to convince them not to beat the young mother. Looking back, he felt his background helped him deal with the rebels—not just in this incident but also during the rebel occupation as a whole. Idriss had been working at the time for Catholic Relief Services, helping poor communities and people who had been displaced by the war. Whether at work or face-to-face with angry rebels, he was very conscious of projecting the right image:

> I don't go around the camp with a briefcase. Neither do I go in tatters—they know I earn a salary. I go in clean jeans—not too poor. The moment they sense a link—in the camps, or among the rebels—to the people who are exploiting them, you're in trouble. You don't want to treat these people like animals. There has to be some respect. I think that was one of the reasons I survived [the rebel occupation of Waterloo] for all that time.

I did not go to Sierra Leone to investigate shame; I went there to try to understand the war and to look in particular at the role of economic agendas (including the soon-to-be-famous "blood diamonds") in shaping the violence. But I quickly ran into shame nonetheless.

My first research in Sierra Leone in 1995 had been during one of the peaks in the violence. In camps and makeshift schools and hospitals, many impoverished and traumatized civilians were telling me not to believe the professed enmity between rebels and government soldiers. They described how rebels and government soldiers were focusing on exploiting civilians through looting and forcing them to work in illegal diamond-mining, and how government soldiers were sometimes cooperating with rebels and sometimes even selling arms to the rebels. As a result, civilians were "between the deep blue sea and the devil."[3]

Attacks on civilians had actually become the norm in this war, and pitched battles were rare. If this was a war-to-win, then the fighters—whether rebels, government soldiers, or some faction in between—seemed bizarrely gifted at "losing hearts and minds." Commonsense ideas about what a war actually *is* were rapidly breaking down in Sierra Leone. For a war is normally considered to be a contest that two sides aim to win. But the aims in Sierra Leone were much more complicated—and fighters' behavior routinely made winning *less likely*.

The counterinsurgency was undermined by government soldiers' failure to confront the rebels and by their apparent preference for abusing civilians and exploiting the illegal or informal economy. Loyalty to a recently ousted president (Joseph Momoh) was one factor. Another was the disgruntlement (reflecting social and political grievances) among young soldiers whose background was often not dissimilar to that of the rebels. A third was the poor treatment routinely meted out to young soldiers. And a fourth was the presence of economic opportunities (notably from diamond trading) that poor pay and conditions made hard to resist. In many respects, this war seemed best understood as a kind of "rational" system of exploitation and repression in which the enemy was sometimes politically and economically *useful*. Cooperation between "enemies" came into the open in 1997 when government soldiers and Revolutionary United Front (RUF) rebels (ostensibly fighting each other for the previous six years) staged a joint coup d'état in Freetown, a sprawling, chaotic capital city where thousands of displaced people were crammed into old buildings and the houses of relatives. So now a kind of informal understanding or alliance that had long been brewing upcountry became much more visible.

Sierra Leone's rebellion, in combination with its lucrative natural resources, proved to be a quagmire that sucked in a succession of forces sent in to defeat the rebellion—government soldiers, some of the civil defense fighters who had stood up to rebels and rogue soldiers, and even some members of the West African peacekeeping force.

But if this war had elements of "rational" economic exploitation, the role of shame and humiliation was also extremely significant. Indeed, interests and emotions interacted in complex ways that were important to understand.

Before the war, Sierra Leoneans had been subjected to several strong undercurrents of shame: shame around poverty; shame around humiliation by neglectful national politicians and by village chiefs who dispensed a corrupt version of "justice"; and shame around the nonprovision of rights to health, education, and employment that all human beings were sometimes proclaimed to have. Rebel groups were offering to reverse some of the shame of powerlessness and neglect—whether through their (blurred and bloody) vision of a more just society or through the more immediate exertion of physical dominance over elders and civilians more generally. As part of the war, village chiefs were humiliated by rebels and even made to dance or plant rice in front of their communities. Meanwhile, the process of inducting and indoctrinating new recruits often included the offer of respect and status within this alternative community (particularly if they themselves engaged in extreme violence). Revealingly, when RUF rebels attacked villages, they often compelled applause for their atrocities from the victim communities, an extreme form of humiliation that seemed to underline how important "respect" actually was to the rebels (albeit that this "respect" was a fantasy and cruelly coerced).

At the same time, the rebels also *promoted* feelings of shame among recruits, using this to cement their own power and violence. They did this, for example, when they forced new recruits into atrocities against their own families and communities. Tattoos were also used to "mark" people as rebels and to make it impossible to return to one's village, with the tattoo being in effect an emblem of respect among the rebels but a source of shame as soon as an individual tried to go home. In effect, violence was used to compel a transition from the young person's normal community—in which violence would attract a normal amount of shame and shaming—and into an exceptional community where entirely different rules applied. Sexual violence was also used to drive a wedge between young female recruits and their communities, with Human Rights Watch reporting, "The rebels instilled fear in their 'wives' by telling them that their families would not accept them back."[4]

Exerting violence offered a (fleeting) escape not only from peacetime powerlessness and neglect but also from the powerlessness and humiliation of abuse within the fighting groups themselves. Fighting factions offered an escape into a kind of shame-free community of "fellow believers," and both rebels and rogue soldiers routinely used force to construct an emotional landscape in which shame was kept at bay and civilian suffering was either ignored or justified. If compelling applause was one element here, another (in relation to both civilians and fellow rebels) was punishing any sign of grief or sympathy in relation to atrocities. As Kieran Mitton comments, "what was shameful was often shame itself."[5] One woman reported that her baby was killed by a rebel captain in the north of the country, adding, "I was told not to cry as otherwise I would be killed as well." Human Rights Watch even called one of its main reports "We'll Kill You If You Cry." Rebels or civilians who stirred up feelings of shame around the rebels' atrocities could be killed on the spot. One thirty-year-old woman, who was raped by two rebels, said many rubbed coal onto their own faces and if you looked at them they would say, "What are you staring at?"[6] Eyes and tongues were sometimes assaulted. While preserving anonymity and impunity was sometimes a motive, shame-avoidance was another.

Mitton helpfully brings *disgust* into the picture. The *Oxford English Dictionary* defines disgust as "a feeling of revulsion or strong disapproval aroused by something unpleasant of offensive."[7] In line with this, disgust seems in Sierra Leone to have added an extra layer of energy and cruelty to rebels' tendency to "punish" those who showed normal feelings of human sympathy. Stressing that the rebels were an enclave society that saw the wider society as *rotten*, Mitton notes:

> Viewing shame as a dangerous social contaminant, the RUF acted to immunize itself against those who carried its deadly pathogen. Those showing symptoms of shame, such as objecting or crying during abuses, became objects of disgust. They were violently prevented from communicating their moral disease.[8]

In his excellent book *Rebels in a Rotten State*, Mitton shows how notions of disgust with a rotten and corrupt "other" infused violence both *by* and *against* the rebel RUF. He also shows how a language of disgust was used to portray various reviled parties as polluting and contaminating—and therefore all the more threatening. A final instrumentalization of disgust came, Mitton argues, when the bodies of victims were mutilated in ways that made them appear just as "disgusting" as they had earlier been portrayed.

When fighters were shamed for their atrocities, this was in itself provocative. In Freetown, one of the January 1999 attackers tied up and beat a police officer, saying, "You think we should remain in the bush don't you, but the bush is made for animals."[9] Naturally, the rebels' brutal behavior made them look like "brutes"—or less than human. Going back to Shakespeare's *The Merchant of Venice*, the Jewish moneylender Shylock explained how shaming him for his religion and profession had fueled his desire for a "pound of flesh": "Thou call'dst me dog before thou hadst a cause; But since I am a dog, beware my fangs."

Often unable to return to communities they had abused, many recruits became locked into a mad, violent world where what should have been shameful (viciousness) was routinely defined as a source of honor and rewarded while what should have been honorable (kindness, empathy) was routinely defined as a source of shame—and punished accordingly. In Sierra Leone, the natural process of inferring moral frameworks from punishment was cynically harnessed to extreme violence. And crucially, once a community of fighters with some kind of "inverted morality" had been created, it was extremely difficult for those outside the group (notably civilians) to shame these violent groups into better behavior. A major obstacle here was the fact that shame was precisely *what many fighters were trying to reverse and keep at bay*. As we saw, such shaming by civilians could bring the possibility of death for the shamer. For a shameless fighting community trying to protect itself from shame, being shamed proved something like a red rag to a bull.

By staging the 1997 joint military coup, rebels and rogue soldiers were hitting back at a growing civil defense movement that had pushed back against their systems of abuse while also publicly denouncing them. The coup-makers were also blocking a planned rapid demobilization of the army, which they saw as a humiliation. As for the violence itself, the habit of resorting to extremely humiliating forms of abuse was ramped up in the January 1999 attack on Freetown. Atrocities included rapes that family members were forced to watch, gang rape of underaged girls, and mass killings of civilians who took shelter in churches. The attackers gave distinct names to units that specialized in particular atrocities, a practice that suggested atrocity had become a bizarre badge of honor—and even a marker of identity—rather than a source of shame. Thus, there was the Burn House Unit, the Cut Hands Commando, the Kill Man No Blood (beating people to death), and the Born Naked Squad (who stripped their victims before killing them).[10] Many attackers had a sense of righteousness, and Foday, a peace worker taken hostage by the rogue army faction known as the West Side Boys, described the atmosphere after they participated in the attack: "No remorse," he said. "For some, it was like an achievement."[11]

I had the chance to speak to one of the young men who had participated in the January 1999 attack. He was pointing his finger as he spoke and made it clear that no interruption would be tolerated. "I was the first into Freetown on January 6," he told me. "I don't mind who knows it!" He referred to the execution of twenty-four soldiers accused of perpetrating the 1997 military coup: "Those people they killed, the twenty-four, they are the nucleus of the army. They were wiped out! These so-called people [in the civilian regime that followed the military government] were barbaric! We have sacrificed our life for this nation!" Strikingly (and this carries resonance in politics well beyond Sierra Leone), the self-righteousness of the reviled seemed only to *increase* as the shame directed at these groups escalated.

Within the government army and rogue factions relating to it, the domination and disrespect of young government soldiers by their superiors was feeding into soldiers' domination and disrespect of civilians. When I spoke with Foday (the captured peace worker), he noted the anger among many youths at elites who amassed wealth and liked to use young people to win elections before rapidly abandoning them. Joining the government army was no escape from bullying injustice, however:

> They feel they are not treated fairly, not receiving sacks of rice, and feel they are being used or bullied. . . . When they find themselves in the bush, they inflict the same injustice on those under them that they are complaining about. . . . Without money, they don't have self-worth.

At this point, Foday echoed almost exactly the analysis of one of Gilligan's criminals, adding: "When they have the gun, whether you like it or not, you must respect them."

Eventually, improved conditions for government soldiers had a positive effect on the war, and one young man who had applied to join the army said, "Civilians have started praising the military. You can be naturally peaceful, but the situation can make you behave like an animal. People can change. The environment is the thing."

Revealingly, earlier cutbacks had had the *opposite* effect—and many of the notorious West Side Boys fighters had been made redundant from the national army as part of a plan to cut military spending, a plan that looked good in theory but in practice threated to set demobilized soldiers loose in a devastated economy. Perhaps more than anything, the West Side Boys fighters who attacked Freetown felt disrespected. One local aid worker stressed the desire for reinstatement in the national army. When I suggested that this could hardly explain the atrocities in January 1999, he replied:

> The extremity of the violence? Before they took to the jungle, we hear elements of the army were joining secretly with the RUF. They were calling them "sobels." So people never wanted them. Civilians were not respecting that presence anymore. Secondly, with the *kamajors*

[civil defense], so all those grudges were fermenting in their hearts. So they took over in [May] 1997. So civilians preferred to stay at home. We never went to work for nine months. They felt that the civilians had gone against them, so they started killing the civilians indiscriminately. They thought they were unimportant in the eyes of the civilians. So they were finding every way to find recognition.[12]

Revealingly, young men in the West Side Boys faction were in the habit of promoting themselves to the rank of colonel or even brigadier. The hunger for respect was also epitomized by the rebels' acting commander, Sam Bockarie, who was behind the rebel offensive that culminated in the January 1999 assault on Freetown. Before becoming a rebel fighter, Bockarie had toured the diamond-mining areas as a professional disco dancer (a vocation, oddly enough, that he shared with the head of the 1992–95 military government, Captain Valentine Strasser). Bockarie then became a women's hairdresser and had intended to get a job in the Ivory Coast city of Abidjan, where he planned to seduce and cajole his way to France. In the event, he joined the rebels, and after the Freetown attack he proclaimed, "I never wanted myself to be overlooked by my fellow men. I think I am at a stage where I am satisfied. I have heard my name all over. I have become famous."[13] It's no coincidence that Tupac's hit song "All Eyez on Me" became a favorite with some of the rebels and soldiers-turned-rebels. Again, part of the shame was the shame of invisibility—and violence rather directly addressed this deficit.

Most young fighters emerged from the war with a sense of having been profoundly misled: any "respect" had been forced and fleeting; the fighters had not benefited from an education; and the great majority had not become wealthy either. Instead, they were typically saddled with a heavy burden of trauma and shame, arising both from abuse they had inflicted and from the abuse inflicted on them. Part of the difficulty of being "reintegrated" into civilian society and civilian values (and here Sierra Leone presented a starker version of a much more general difficulty) was that this involved leaving a world where shame had been kept determinedly at bay through propaganda and violence and emerging into a new world where overwhelming shame threatened to intrude at any time. One aid worker with ActionAid, discussing the "Never Again" peace campaign, said:

> When you go to ex-combatants and say you must demonstrate remorse, they will kill you! You have to time it. As far as he is concerned, he has done the right thing. You have to gauge the mood before you go in. When they have evidence of their colleagues being reintegrated and their colleagues have not been in jail and have schools, jobs, they can use that as a basis to trust. So they can talk more openly and feel remorse.

This latter approach aligns rather closely with the "reintegrative shaming" that Braithwaite has advocated for prisoners. But the fact remains that unless circumstances were very favorable indeed, shaming Sierra Leone's fighters for their shameful behavior was a considerable act of bravery. As a Tupac song favored by the rebels put it, "Only God can judge me." Shameless fighting communities were determinedly resisting the threat of shame.

While we have seen that shame was a major driver of the violence in that country, it is also clear that levels of shamelessness among the fighters were often exceptionally high; moreover, this shamelessness was itself a major contributor to violence. Again, we are presented with a paradox: How can a war be fueled by shame *and* shamelessness, by something and its opposite? A big part of the answer lay in the precise nature of the shame that was operating. Strikingly, rebels and other rogue fighting groups tended to exhibit a remarkable lack of shame in relation to their own atrocities—and often an extreme self-righteousness and even pride. But shame around *weakness* was notable.

The role of shamelessness is also clarified if we focus for a moment on two particularly disturbing aspects of the war: the role of drugs and the role of child soldiers. Many of the fighters in Sierra Leone's war consumed intoxicating substances including alcohol, heroin, cocaine, and marijuana, and understandably this fed the image of "drug-fueled madness." But drug consumption very often reflected a set of calculations—frequently extremely cynical—about how to overcome normal human inhibitions around violence. Drugs were not only consumed by fighters but *made readily available* to them. Some rebel leaders used alcohol, cocaine, and even gunpowder to stir up their followers. A fifteen-year-old boy reported that his legs had been cut open and that cocaine had been rubbed into his wounds: "Afterwards I felt like a big person. I saw the other people like chickens and rats. I wanted to kill them."[14] Other fighters administered drugs to themselves to "psych" themselves up for violence, often using marijuana to calm themselves down afterward. In this way, shame could be overridden when it came to carrying out acts of violence—and then minimized in the aftermath. Foday, the man held captive by the West Side Boys, summed up this system:

> They take drugs, but I don't think the drugs were deranging them. They do come back to normal. You don't notice madness in them. When they want to do the evil, that's when they take the drugs so that they can have the boldness to do it. And after they do it, they do drugs to dampen their consciences.

Both the government and the rebels recruited child soldiers. As with drug consumption, the widespread use of underage fighters was frequently depicted as a manifestation of madness. But again it tended to represent a cynical—and indeed shameless—calculation aimed at obtaining a highly manipulable (and cheap) fighting population that could be readily indoctrinated into a relatively shame-free world. On the other side of the coin, the "availability" of children also reflected widespread anger and disillusionment, stemming in part from commonplace experiences of shame and exclusion before and during the war.

Many civilians observed that the apparent shamelessness of fighting groups had been fueled not only by drugs but by their extreme youth. For example, a forty-two-year-old woman said of the child rebels:

> We feared them. They were cruel and hard-hearted; even more than the adults. They don't know . . . what is good and bad. If you beg an older one you may convince him to spare you, but the younger ones, they don't know what is sympathy, what is mercy. Those who have been rebels for so long have never learned it.[15]

This was part of the process of turning morality radically upside down. The fact that many young rebels had had their parents killed—or had simply been taken away from their families—also fed the brutality. Revenge against the world—sometimes against *anybody*—was part of this. A kind of shameless impunity was another. One small boy in full combat dress shot a father in front of his children, grandchildren, and wife, telling his victims, "We don't have mothers, we don't have fathers. We can do anything we want to do."[16] It was as if, in wartime, all restraints had been thrillingly removed, almost in *Lord of the Flies* style—and any expression of frustration or will-to-power was possible and permissible.

In the short term at least, the perpetrators seem to have got something that they wanted: a turning of the tables and a reversal of shame. Violence was frequently exhilarating and very often it seems to have *felt good*. But on any reasonable view of the matter, the fighters were not going to win respect or recognition by pointing a gun at civilians—let alone by perpetrating massive violence against them. In very extreme form, Sierra Leone's war showed the self-defeating quality of pursuing respect and recognition through violent means.

In the event, an initial and rather limited public sympathy with the rebels' poorly articulated cause (including their denunciations of corruption) quickly evaporated amid the rebels' escalating atrocities. And while atrocity could win you some lasting respect *within the group*, it's hard to imagine that compelling applause at gunpoint would give more than a fleeting feeling of being respected by civilians. As the shaming and public denunciation of rebel and soldier-turned-rebel groups escalated in Sierra Leone, a desperate desire for respect and recognition from civilians seems to have increased correspondingly, often finding renewed expression in an escalating violence. Indeed, this vicious circle helps explain much of the most extreme violence that afflicted the country for a decade.

If fighting groups constructed a kind of shamelessness around their own violence, a second key element of shamelessness in Sierra Leone attached to the *war system* as a whole. This included the indifference of the military government in Freetown, which tended to turn a blind eye toward abuses by its own soldiers and toward abuses *within* the army, abuses that did so much to fuel soldiers' violence against civilians. When evidence of government soldiers' violence against civilians did come to light, government officials sometimes simply relabeled these individuals as rebels: within this rather convenient framework, abuse by government soldiers became, in a sense, *logically impossible.*

A kind of shamelessness within the *international community* was often in evidence too. It was exemplified when humanitarian aid for Sierra Leoneans was reduced even while needs were mounting, a move that was sometimes defended through a classic piece of victim-blaming—the ostensible need to "reduce dependency" among the recipients of aid. A second example of shamelessness was the praise that international financial institutions lavished on Sierra Leone's abusive military government for its financial orthodoxy—even as government soldiers were ransacking the country. In reality, the predations of government soldiers were actually facilitating this trumpeted "economic miracle" by helping the government to keep down military spending—and inflation—even in the midst of a war. While shocking, this kind of quiet tolerance for abuse is not uncommon in international diplomacy. Whether in return for balancing the books or pushing through favored reforms, or in return for opposing Cold War Communists, or fighting "terrorists," or controlling migration, a range of abusive governments have routinely been offered considerable impunity for attacks on their own or neighboring peoples. The apparent "righteousness" of the relevant global struggle has been key to generating the shamelessness and impunity in which local abuses have flourished.[17] Shaming a demon group of rebels has often served much the same purpose.

Meanwhile, such shaming was remarkably ineffective—and often counterproductive—when it came to the behavior of Sierra Leone's rebels and "sobels." Having constructed a shameless world in which shame was relentlessly kept at bay, these groups were in no mood to take any criticism or advice from anyone. Shockingly, these perpetrators of inhuman atrocities were still human, and in many ways it was their humanity that was driving much of the violence. It was through understanding this humanity—in all its diverse manifestations—that an unusually sensitive individual like Idriss was able to exert some minimal leverage.

7

The Shamelessness—and Shame—of Adolf Eichmann

WHEN HANNAH ARENDT published *Eichmann in Jerusalem,* her remarkable book about the life and trial of Adolf Eichmann, she immediately captured the public imagination. One thing that many readers found especially shocking was that someone could be in charge of transporting over two million people to places of mass annihilation and yet calmly recount that he was simply doing his job, exhibiting little in the way of human emotions. Many were also disoriented by the fact that Eichmann showed very little of the virulent racism that one would naturally assume to be part of such a mass killing—and Arendt's book was appropriately subtitled *A Report on the Banality of Evil.* In one key passage, Arendt observed, "The trouble with Eichmann was precisely that so many were like him, and that the many were neither perverted nor sadistic, that they were, and still are, terribly and terrifyingly normal."[1] The Jerusalem trial showed how mass killing was in many ways effectively redefined as a form of "work" to be accomplished as efficiently as possible. As Arendt's account was circulated and discussed, the predominant image of Eichmann was of some kind of human robot, someone who claimed only to be following orders, someone who wanted to do "a good job," the ultimate bureaucrat. "Evil in the Third Reich," Arendt noted, "had lost the quality by which most people recognize it—the quality of temptation."[2]

It is true that Eichmann exhibited an extraordinary lack of imagination and empathy—an astounding ability to distance himself from the human catastrophe that he played such a major role in bringing about. But the popular image of Eichmann-as-automaton obscures important elements of Eichmann's character. If we revisit Arendt's text in all its complexity, and if we draw also on other fine studies of Eichmann by Bettina Stangneth and David Cesarani, we find a figure who is much more *human* than the "human robot" image would suggest. The humanity that emerges, however, is not the kind that endears Eichmann to us; quite the reverse. Along with that remarkable "distancing" from the consequences of his own actions, we find an Eichmann who was sometimes surprisingly squeamish in the face of the human suffering he was helping to inflict. But he was also deeply narcissistic and profoundly racist. And he was willing and able to overcome the reservations that he had, turning himself into a mass killer.

Particularly in the context of our wider discussion of shame and shamelessness, it is tempting to say that Eichmann was *remarkably shameless*. In one telling outburst during the last days of World War II, Eichmann told his subordinates, "I will jump into my grave laughing, because the fact that I have the death of five million Jews on my conscience gives me extraordinary satisfaction."[3] If that is not a manifestation of shamelessness, then it is hard to imagine what *is*. Shameless bragging, moreover, was something of a specialty for Eichmann. And while Arendt calls boasting "a common vice,"[4] Eichmann's self-aggrandizement was remarkably extreme and repulsive. In particular, he was narcissistically attached to the idea that he was doing a good job—and subsequently that he *had done* a good job—in deporting the Jews and dispatching them efficiently to their deaths.

Eichmann's shameless bragging comes through in Stangneth's *Eichmann before Jerusalem*, which deals with Eichmann's time in Buenos Aires. This was after he escaped from the victorious Allies in Europe and before he was captured by Israeli intelligence officials in 1960 and taken to be tried in Jerusalem. Stangneth draws on conversations involving Eichmann and other Nazis or Nazi sympathizers. These were recorded at various venues in Buenos Aires including the house of Willem Sassen, a Dutch actor, journalist, and lothario with long-standing Nazi sympathies who had arrived in Argentina in 1950. In many ways, the regular group meetings constituted a remarkably shameless community in which Eichmann sought and often found respect. As Eichmann himself put it, "I knew that in this 'promised land' of South America I had a few good friends, to whom I could say openly, freely and proudly that I am Adolf Eichmann."[5] Stangneth shows that while many Nazis in Argentina were concerned to deny the Holocaust or any role in what happened, Eichmann went against the grain: he actively boasted, for example, that the deportation of more than four hundred thousand people from Hungary in a few weeks was "actually an achievement that was never matched before or since."[6] This was a different Eichmann from the reluctant, order-following pencil-pusher that he portrayed in Jerusalem. In Argentina, Eichmann also bragged that in the early stages of Jewish deportations, operations progressed "splendidly and without any difficulty" and that some operations were "particularly nice and neat, with all the bells and whistles."[7] Moreover, "Nobody else was such a household name in Jewish political life at home and abroad in Europe as little old me."[8] Ironically, it was self-glorification that eventually brought Eichmann to justice:

> What eventually led to his capture [in Argentina] was his compulsion to talk big—he was "fed up with being an anonymous wanderer between the worlds"—and this compulsion must have grown considerably stronger as time passed, not only because he had nothing to do that he could consider worth doing, but also because the postwar era had bestowed so much unexpected "fame" upon him.[9]

So Eichmann's shamelessness was extreme and repulsive—and it came out most strongly when he was surrounded by like-minded individuals. At the same time, this was not the shamelessness of a robot; and shamelessness was very far from being the whole story.

When we look closely, we may notice that Eichmann sometimes exhibited a *strong* sense of shame. For a while, this even included elements of what one might call "normal" shame—by which I mean the shame that one would *expect* a person to feel in relation to participation in killing. Equally striking, however, is the way that Eichmann was able to "*overcome*" his reservations—and in this process, his complex feelings of shame played a significant part. In crucial respects, Eichmann conceptualized shame in ways that pushed him *toward* participation in mass murder rather than away from it. In particular, he had strong feelings of shame around weakness, around not doing a good job, and even around the possibility that the Nazis' turn to outright genocide might sideline him from a prominent role in historic events. Avoiding *these kinds of shame* turned out to be much more important to him than any shame arising from the infliction of suffering.

Cesarani's book on Eichmann includes the observation that "there was nothing in his childhood or youth to suggest psychological damage."[10] There is little evidence of the kind of humiliation—or the resulting short fuse—that Gilligan found in his American criminals. As an adult, there is no suggestion Eichmann was physically abusive with his family. What *was* notable in Eichmann, even as a young man, was a very strong attachment to success and significance, though such traits were common enough in Germany (and perhaps in any society).[11] Arendt noted that Eichmann

> had been an ambitious young man who was fed up with his job as traveling salesman even before the Vacuum Oil Company was fed up with him. From a humdrum life without significance and consequence the wind had blown him into History, as he understood it, namely, into a Movement that always kept moving and in which somebody like him—already a failure in the eyes of his social class, of his family, and hence in his own eyes as well—could start from scratch and still make a career.[12]

Within the Nazi bureaucracy, Eichmann established himself as an expert on the Jews and on Jewish "emigration," even learning Hebrew. He was to gain a formidable reputation as an energetic organizer of the deportation (or so-called "emigration") of Jews, including from Austria and from Germany into occupied Poland. His career was very important to him, not least the business of moving up the ranks. Even when facing trial in Jerusalem, Eichmann complained repeatedly about not getting the promotions he deserved.[13] He clearly wanted respect. And again, his sense of shame mixed in with a sense of grievance or frustration.

Over the course of 1941, it was becoming increasingly clear to the Nazi hierarchy that plans for the systematic expulsion of the Jews were going to be thwarted. Hopes of expelling Jews to Madagascar were fading, and the idea of expelling them into Russia was beginning to look less feasible in the light of military reversals in the winter of 1941–42. The policy of confining Jewish people within ghettos had been adopted as a temporary "fix," but senior Nazis in the occupied territories were increasingly complaining of an intolerable public health crisis centering on these ghettos.[14]

In September 1941, Reinhard Heydrich, head of the Reich Security Main Office, told Eichmann that Hitler had ordered the "physical annihilation" of the Jews. Eichmann quickly adjusted. He tasked himself with making sure there would be no "hitches" when Jews arrived at the death camps that were being rapidly assembled.[15] In late 1941 and early 1942, Eichmann made a series of visits to confirm arrangements for the reception of deportees, traveling to Lublin, Lodz, Minsk and Lwow, Auschwitz and Treblinka.[16] These visits gave the lie to his attempts to suggest that he was only concerned with railways: at Eichmann's trial in Jerusalem, the prosecution succeeded in establishing that he knew very well the fate to which he was dispatching so many Jews when he zealously organized the trains that took people to the death camps.

What has been under-recognized is Eichmann's surprising sense of revulsion at the atrocities that were being planned and, in some cases, carried out. When Eichmann was taken to the Polish town of Lublin, he was driven through a forest where he found a series of small wooden bungalows. He was shown how gas could be pumped from a disused Russian submarine into the bungalows, where Jews would be poisoned. "For me," Eichmann recalled in Jerusalem, "this was monstrous. I am not so tough as to be able to endure something of this sort without any reaction. . . . If today I am shown a gaping wound, I can't possibly look at it. I am that type of person, so that very often I was told that I couldn't have become a doctor."[17]

When Eichmann went to Chelmno, a killing center in the western part of Poland, he saw Jews being told to strip and forced into trucks that were actually mobile gas chambers. He recalled to the Israeli police before his trial in Jerusalem:

> I cannot tell [how many Jews entered]. I hardly looked. I could not; I could not; I had had enough. The shrieking, and ... I was much too upset, and so on, as I later told [Gestapo boss Heinrich] Müller when I reported to him; he did not get much profit out of my report. I then drove along after the van, and then I saw the most horrible sight I had thus far seen in my life. The truck was making for an open ditch, the doors were opened, and the corpses were thrown out, as though they were still alive, so smooth were their limbs. They were hurled into the ditch, and I can still see a civilian extracting the teeth with tooth pliers. And then I was off—jumped into my car and did not open my mouth any more. After that time, I could sit for hours beside my driver without exchanging a word with him. There I got enough. I was finished. I only remember that a physician in white overalls told me to look through a hole into the truck while they were still in it. I refused to do that. I could not. I had to disappear.[18]

In Argentina, Eichmann recounted that when he reported back to Müller, Eichmann said, "This can't go on, one can't do this."[19] Again, in the (then) Polish city of Lwow, Eichmann told the local SS commander, "Well, it is horrible what is being done around here; I said young people are being made into sadists. How can one do that? Simply bang away at women and children? That is impossible. Our people will go mad or become insane, our own people."[20]

Was this dissimulation? One can certainly understand why Eichmann might want to play up his reservations when facing a possible death sentence in Jerusalem. Cesarani considers this carefully, but (like Arendt) he takes Eichmann's apparent revulsion seriously:

> In Israel, he naturally accentuated the dismay he felt when he was faced by the tasks of genocide. Yet there is a remarkable consistency to his versions of these events as recorded in conditions of freedom

and captivity, when he could afford to brag, and when he was pleading for his life. In all of them he expresses unease with the turn in policy towards "physical annihilation" and remarks on his initial, personal distress.... The most graphic and shocking accounts of what he saw came not from [Israel] but from his taped memoirs in Argentina.[21]

If Eichmann had some genuine revulsion at atrocities, there was another reason—and, in terms of its influence on his *behavior*, a much more important one—for his unease at the switch to a policy of annihilation. He saw this shift in policy as potentially disastrous for his career and his office (section IV B 4, Reich Security Main Office).[22] In handwritten notes on the tape recordings made in Argentina, Eichmann noted that the "physical annihilation" order meant that

> I, as well as the subordinates in my section in the Gestapo office of what was then the Head Office for Reich Security, were *therewith relegated to second rank* in all matters concerning the "Final Solution of the Jewish Question", for what was now being prepared was assigned to other units and nailed down by another Head Office under the jurisdiction of the Reichsführer-SS and the Chief of Police. (emphasis added)

At Eichmann's interrogation in Jerusalem, he went further and said that after hearing the order for "physical annihilation" in September 1941, "Everything was taken away from me. All the work, all the efforts, all the interest; I was as it were extinguished."[23]

But once Eichmann realized that a policy of mass killing was being pushed from the highest levels, he quickly shifted his efforts. In Cesarani's words, Eichmann "adapted to policy that was not of his making, that threw into reverse the machinery he had established."[24] Moreover:

> Any misgivings he may have had, and he did have them for a short time, were superseded by the satisfaction that he and his team were still in business. Whether he liked it or not, and there are indications of ambivalence, in order to preserve his position and his office Eichmann embarked on a career in genocide.[25]

More than this, Eichmann became an enthusiastic, cunning, and ruthless facilitator of mass murder. Cesarani notes that power itself had a major corrupting effect on Eichmann and that he would take almost any action to maintain or increase it. If we go back to the paradox of Eichmann's often-expressed revulsion at atrocities, one thing we may notice rather quickly is how remarkably *self-centered* his concerns actually were. Confronted with the reality or the plans for mass killing, Eichmann seemed principally concerned not about the victims but about himself. Here, he exhibited three main anxieties.

The first was that he should not have to go through the pain of witnessing these atrocities. We might say that this is a perversion of a normal sense of shame (with Eichmann injecting a strong dose of narcissism and self-pity into the mix). Stangneth notes that from Eichmann's point of view:

> The problem wasn't that children had been put to death; it was that he had been forced to watch—when, at that time, he had two children of his own. "I am one of those people who can't stand to see corpses," he confessed to the Sassen circle. His stories are full of horrendous self-pity, for the burden of having to watch other people suffer fates that he had set in motion. But Eichmann manages to play the witness in these accounts, a mere historian of the horror, persuading himself and the others that he had nothing to do with the extermination. He couldn't have changed anything, and these "business trips" made him "an unhappy man."[26]

Eichmann's second anxiety around witnessing atrocities was substantially different. This was his concern that he might not have the requisite "toughness" for the job at hand. His sense of shame around the lack of "toughness" seems to have been compounded—as shame is usually compounded—when he imagined the looks and words of others. In Argentina, Eichmann mentioned the fear that "there would be some low-ranking little prick standing behind us, who would have interpreted it as a sign of weakness, and it would have spread like wildfire."[27] This recalls psychoanalyst Léon Wurmser's observation that the "shameless" person acts to avoid the near-psychotic terror of showing feelings, "because anyone who perceived them would gain power over him."[28] Eichmann's fears here apparently were realized during a visit to Auschwitz when he said of Nazi officials there that "they laughed, naturally, when my nerves broke down and I couldn't keep my military dignity."[29]

A third anxiety around atrocities was the one Eichmann expressed at Lodz, for example: that carrying out and witnessing atrocities might drive the perpetrators mad or turn them into sadists. This was not a fear that he expressed explicitly in relation to himself, but given that he mentioned it several times and given Eichmann's strong reactions, it seems unlikely that Eichmann would have seen himself as exempt from such processes.

Revealingly, Eichmann was by no means the only Nazi to stress the dangers of feelings of sympathy; nor was he alone in registering some discomfort with the suffering that the Nazis were inflicting. Eichmann expressed admiration for what he called the "winged words" of SS commander Heinrich Himmler, described by Arendt as "the member of the Nazi hierarchy most gifted at solving problems of conscience."[30] Himmler also seems to have felt obliged to overcome feelings of pity that the Nazis had labeled as weakness; Arendt noted:

> The problem was how to overcome not so much their conscience as the animal pity by which all normal men are affected in the presence of physical suffering. The trick used by Himmler—who apparently was rather strongly afflicted with these instinctive reactions himself—was very simple and probably very effective; it consisted in turning these instincts around, as it were, in directing these toward the self. So that instead of saying: What horrible things I did to people!, the murderers would be able to say: What horrible things I had to watch in the pursuance of my duties, how heavily the task weighed upon my shoulders![31]

In a speech to commanders of the Einsatzgruppen militias and the SS, Himmler observed, "To have stuck it out and, apart from exceptions caused by human weakness, to have remained decent, that is what has made us hard. This is a page of glory in our history which has never been written and is never to be written."[32] Himmler gave the SS its watchword, "My Honor Is My Loyalty," which located shame not in the carrying out of a homicidal order but in refusing to carry it out. Eichmann also kept repeating Himmler's claim that "these are battles which future generations will not have to fight again."[33] The danger of being "too humane" was similarly stressed by Reinhard Heydrich in *Das Schwarze Korps* (1935): "Were we to fail to fulfil our historical duty through being too objective and too humane, then no one will make allowances for mitigating circumstances. They will merely say: they did not fulfil their duty to history."[34] In this upside-down world, it was precisely the lack of sympathy or mercy that was seen as worthy of pride.

If we look at Christopher Browning's work on Nazi massacres in Poland, we see again how shame around *not killing*—and in this case "letting one's colleagues down"—proved a powerful impetus for violence.[35] Nazi police battalion members who refrained from massacring Jews in Poland tended to say that they were "too weak" to kill, not that they were too good or too ethical.

As for Eichmann, his willingness to overcome his reservations and feelings of revulsion was not simply a reflection of his own character but also of the ideological milieu in which he was working. Eichmann's shamelessness was part of a much wider shamelessness and cannot be traced simply to his "underlying shame." When we focus on Eichmann as an individual (as we have here), it is important to think about how his perverse definitions of shame (including his vestigial feelings of shame-around-violence) relate to the wider picture. Nazi ideology took a certain side of human nature (the capacity for pity and sympathy) and systematically redefined it as weakness, while elevating "toughness" and "hardness" to a position of honor.[36]

Here, it's worth going back again to Wurmser. We may recall that Wurmser highlighted how individual shamelessness may mask—and protect from—an underlying sense of shame. He also drew attention to what he called "cultures of shamelessness"—the social contexts that encourage a kind of *collective* inversion of morality. Drawing on Sigmund and Anna Freud, Wurmser noted:

> The cultures of shamelessness simply shift their sense of shame (as typically occurs with reaction formations)—from violence and dishonor, from betrayal and sexual exhibition to feelings of kindness, of loyalty, of tender regard and tactful restraint. These now become viewed as signs of worthlessness and feebleness and have to be shunned.[37]

This analysis appears rather precisely to describe Eichmann's working definition of what was shameful, which itself reflected not only his personal inclinations but also more widespread attitudes among Nazi officials and sympathizers. Comments from Himmler, Heydrich, and Eichmann himself indicate a strong sense of shame around any sign of *weakness*, so that any hesitation when it came to the gruesome task at hand was conceived as intensely shameful.

We may say, then, that Eichmann gave every sign of being *very ashamed of his feelings of shame*, at least when it came to "normal" feelings of shame around the infliction of violence and suffering. We have noted Arendt's comment that with Eichmann evil had lost the quality of temptation. We might go a step further and say that in Eichmann and other prominent Nazis it was leniency (or goodness) that had *acquired* the quality of temptation. Indeed, Eichmann repeatedly presented himself as heroically overcoming the temptation to be lenient. On the whole, he was able to demonstrate to his own satisfaction that he had exhibited the toughness required for sticking to his "ideals" and for keeping his word by following his oath of obedience to the law and the German state even when his human inclinations pointed in another direction.

Particularly revealing here was Eichmann's perverse sense of shame—expressed to his fellow Nazis and Nazi sympathizers in Argentina about the *incompleteness* of the Holocaust:

> Of course, I must say to you, human emotion also plays a role here. I too am not free of this. I too was defeated by the same weakness. I know this! I too am partly to blame for the fact that the real,

complete elimination, perhaps foreseen by some authority, or the conception that I had in mind, could not be carried out. I gave you some small examples of this. I was an inadequate intellect and was placed in an office where in truth I could have done more, and *should have done more*. What I told you must serve as an apology: one, that I lacked a profound intellect. Second, that I lacked the necessary physical toughness. And third, that even against my will, so that while I myself already felt handicapped, I was then also curtailed in carrying out the other things that would have helped me to a breakthrough, because for many years I was bogged down in a struggle against the so-called interventionists [that is, those officials wishing to limit deportations, whether out of pity, for money, or for some other reason].[38]

Perhaps Eichmann here was masking or displacing a sense of shame at what he had done with a (bizarre) sense of shame at what he had not done (or not done enough). Or perhaps any hint of a "normal" sense of shame had long since disappeared. At any rate, Eichmann's bizarre framing meant that shame was being attached not to killing but to being deflected from killing.

If weakness was seen as one way to be deflected, avarice was another. Commenting on his own unwillingness to accept money in return for mercy, Eichmann said, "Thank God I did not become a swine."[39] At the same time, Eichmann expressed regret that not everyone had understood the priority of achieving a "respectable" Final Solution in the face of possible extortion: "And this is why there are still a lot of Jews enjoying life today who ought to have been gassed."[40] While many have long debated whether human behavior is motivated by emotions or self-interest, a key part of Eichmann's defense of his own behavior was that he had actually followed *neither*. Arendt noted: "The perfect 'idealist', like everybody else, had of course his personal feelings and emotions, but he could never permit them to interfere with his actions if they came into conflict with his 'idea.'"[41] Thus, emotion itself was positioned by Eichmann as shameful.[42] Arendt commented:

> This uncompromising attitude toward the performance of his murderous duties damned him in the eyes of the [Jerusalem] judges

more than anything else, which was comprehensible, but in his own eyes it was precisely what justified him, as it had once silenced whatever conscience he might have had left. No exceptions—that was the proof that he had always acted against his "inclinations," whether they were sentimental or inspired by interest, that he had always done his "duty."[43]

In effect, Eichmann gave himself credit for transcending his own humanity (both the good and the bad parts). Arendt mentions two incidents when Eichmann did actually help Jewish individuals: a Jewish couple in Vienna (on whose behalf Eichmann's uncle had initially intervened) and a half-Jewish cousin. Revealingly, these exceptions to Eichmann's habit of extreme ruthlessness troubled him greatly and prompted him to "confess his sins" to his superiors.[44]

There was also great shame around *not getting tasks accomplished*, however vicious those tasks might be. Eichmann took Danish resistance to Jewish deportations as a personal defeat,[45] and he remembered in Argentina: "I had to recall my transports. For me it was a deadly disgrace."[46] Again, Eichmann's sole expression of regret around sending more than two million Jews to their deaths was that he had not succeeded in sending more. Reflecting on himself during his exile in Argentina, Eichmann observed:

> This cautious bureaucrat was attended by . . . a fanatical warrior, fighting for the freedom of my blood, which is my birthright and I say here, just as I have said to you before: your louse that nips you, Comrade Sassen, does not interest me. My louse under my collar interests me. I will squash it . . . I have no regrets! I am certainly not going to bow down to that cross! . . . it would be too easy, and I could do it cheaply for the sake of current opinion . . . for me to deeply regret it, for me to pretend that a Saul has become a Paul . . . we are fighting an enemy who, through many, many thousands of years of schooling, is intellectually superior to us. . . . And you must understand that this is my motivation when I say, if 10.3 million of these enemies had been killed, then we would have fulfilled our duty. And because this did not happen, I will say to you that those who have not

yet been born will have to undergo the suffering and adversity. Perhaps they will curse us.[47]

In his prison memoir Auschwitz commander Rudolf Höss recalled that during meetings in 1942–43 (when "the drink had been flowing freely"), Eichmann had been "completely obsessed" with killing every single Jewish person and had been convinced that "any compromise, even the slightest, would have to be paid for bitterly at a later date."[48] For Eichmann, at least according to Höss's account, there was no going back because "this extermination action was necessary in order to preserve the German people in the future from the destructive intentions of the Jews."[49] Eichmann's precise thinking here is unknown, but it is hard to imagine that this perception about the "destructive intentions of the Jews" was not intensified by the unfolding Holocaust itself. In an insightful analysis, Omer Bartov notes that Nazi atrocities on the Eastern Front powerfully reinforced the view within the military that the Russians and Jews were planning to destroy Germany—if only in revenge for what the German military was doing to them.[50] Himmler himself told army generals in May 1944 that children had been included in the mass slaughter because "we as Germans, however deeply we may feel in our hearts, are not entitled to allow a generation of avengers filled with hatred to grow up with whom our children and grandchildren will have to deal because we, too weak and cowardly, left it to them."[51]

Significantly, Eichmann himself lacked experience when it came to serving on the battlefront (though he did for a few days participate in a military mission to evacuate German civilians from a Russian army advance on the Hungary-Romania border). In the context of the Nazis' militaristic culture, this scarcity of experience was a major potential source of shame (and, more widely, Michael Wildt has noted the insecurities of the generation of Nazis who did not get to "prove themselves" through combat in World War I).[52] Rather than inspiring any humility or deference, Eichmann's lack of combat experience seems to have reinforced his determination to appear strong and "tough." Stangneth notes that:

> Sassen [the habitual host in Argentina] had belonged to the Waffen-SS [the combat branch of the SS] and had the frontline experience

and the scars to show for it, while Eichmann was in the General SS, which the frontline soldiers looked upon with disdain. His only scar was from a motorcycle accident, and his broken hand had been caused by a slippery parquet floor. This lack of combat experience was still an obvious stigma among ex-SS comrades in exile, and Eichmann was painfully aware of it.[53]

Stangneth observed further, "All these labels he applied to himself in Israel actually fit National Socialist conceptions of the enemy, and 'the bureaucrat' was almost the antithesis of the SS man."[54] In these circumstances, Eichmann *simply redefined the front to fit what he had actually done*. More specifically, he tried to claim that organizing and witnessing the death camps counted as "fighting at the front."[55] At one point in the Buenos Aires tapes, Eichmann screamed at someone in Sassen's living room, "You ridiculous pipsqueak! Did you fight at the front?" prompting Stangneth to comment in her biography that Eichmann had "obviously come to believe in his own frontline experience."[56] "Just take a moment to think," Eichmann continued in his rant, "about how I told you that we had a total war, and the front and the hinterland had become completely blurred.... There is no difference between the annihilation of enemy powers when a total war has been declared."[57]

Stangneth observes that Sassen "granted Eichmann's wish for recognition, as he then dictated a trenchant sentence with which Eichmann could doubtless identify: 'The battlefields of this war were called death camps.'"[58] Stangneth notes in addition that Eichmann "wanted to prove that he had suffered for Germany. This desire goes a long way to explaining why Eichmann describes the horror so frankly," and further "Eichmann really had seen some terrible things, but he had clearly forgotten that his 'enemy powers' had been defenseless, frightened humans, and that he had been chauffeur-driven to their annihilation in a warm winter coat."[59]

Such "front-line" fantasies helped ward off the shame of weakness. And when it came to "normal" feelings of shame and revulsion around atrocity, these were overcome not just through redefining shame as weakness and through Eichmann's obvious obsession with "doing a good job" but also through a range of other techniques that Eichmann, along with other Nazis, employed. Some of this extended even more widely, as Arendt noted:

> German society of eighty million people had been shielded against reality and factuality by exactly the same means, the same self-deception, lies, and stupidity that had now become ingrained in Eichmann's mentality ... the practice of self-deception had become so common, almost a moral prerequisite for survival.[60]

A key thing for Eichmann was a kind of compartmentalization: in Jerusalem he repeatedly insisted that while he had organized *transportation*, he had not been involved in killing. This "line of defense" was unsurprisingly to the fore when Eichmann's life was on the line.

A second form of self-protection, for Eichmann as for many others, lay in the use of euphemisms, so that mass killing became "evacuation," "special treatment," and "the final solution." Arendt noted that Eichmann's fondness for stock phrases helped make him an "ideal subject" for such evasions. Euphemisms also played a role—often a significant one—in deceiving others, including the Jews themselves, about what was being planned and executed. Arendt referred to "language rules," a phrase that itself was deployed by the Nazis and that often served as a euphemism for lying; more specifically, Arendt noted that language rules "proved of enormous help in the maintenance of order and sanity,"[61] notably by separating events from the perpetrators' old, "normal" knowledge about the immorality of lying and murder.

A third technique that Eichmann exemplified was what we might call *drawing the line*. For example, Arendt noted that Eichmann's

> conscience rebelled not at the idea of murder but at the idea of German Jews being murdered. He made the following claim: "I never denied that I knew that the *Einsatzgruppen* had orders to kill but I did not know that Jews from the Reich evacuated to the East were subject to the same treatment. That is what I did not know."[62]

For the Jews themselves, such distinctions made little difference. But "drawing the line" was important to Eichmann, and part of this—in his eyes—was avoiding "unnecessary" cruelties. As Arendt noted:

> Eichmann, asked by the police examiner if the directive to avoid "unnecessary hardships" was not a bit ironic, in view of the fact that the destination of these people was certain death anyhow, did not even understand the question, so firmly was it still anchored in his mind that the unforgivable sin was not to kill people but to cause unnecessary pain. During the [Jerusalem] trial, he showed unmistakable signs of sincere outrage when witnesses told of cruelties and atrocities committed by SS men—though the court and much of the audience failed to see these signs, because his single-minded effort to keep his self-control had misled them into believing that he was "unmovable" and indifferent—and it was not the accusation of having sent millions of people to their death that ever caused him real agitation but only the accusation (dismissed by the court) of one witness that he had once beaten a Jewish boy to death.[63]

A fourth technique that helped Eichmann ward off shame-around-harm-done was the idea that the Nazis were simply *following historical laws* such as Social Darwinism—and accelerating the inevitable. Eichmann's self-image as someone "blown into history" has been noted, while Heydrich—on his deathbed—quoted one of his father's operas, "The world is just a barrel-organ which the Lord God turns Himself. We all have to dance to the tune which is already on the drum."[64]

A fifth way in which Eichmann—and many others—overcame any reservations about mass murder was through the commonplace practice of presenting genocide as a "lesser evil." Of course, it would be hard to imagine a *greater* evil than the Nazi Holocaust. But among the Nazis there was an extraordinary tendency to present the killing as relatively humane in comparison to the available "alternatives." Arendt showed how the idea that one should embrace a "lesser evil" (in comparison to the maximum horror possible) was a key mechanism in the Holocaust, helping the perpetrators to salve what was left of their own consciences.

Thus, in 1941 some Nazis were saying that mass killing of the Jews was a relatively "humane" solution compared with other "solutions" to "the Jewish problem." For example, in July 1941, Eichmann received a memo from an SS official stationed in Warthegau, stating that "Jews [outside the Reich] in the coming winter could no longer be fed" and submitting for his consideration a proposal as to "whether it would not be the most humane solution to kill those Jews who were incapable of work through some quicker means. This, at any rate, would be more agreeable than to let them die of starvation."[65] In an accompanying letter to Eichmann, the same official noted "these things sound sometimes fantastic, but they are quite feasible."[66] In some Nazi officials' eyes, moreover, disease-ridden ghettos were themselves a public health catastrophe in comparison to which genocide was, in effect, a lesser evil.[67]

Arendt also argued that the idea of working toward a "lesser evil" encouraged a degree of compliance with the Nazis among many people—not least the Jewish Councils in the ghettos—in the (related) hope that this might mitigate the horrors and allow some people to survive.[68] In her essay "Personal Responsibility under Dictatorship," Arendt noted, "The extermination of Jews was preceded by a very gradual sequence of anti-Jewish measures, each of which was accepted with the argument that refusal to cooperate would make things worse—until a stage was reached where nothing worse could possibly have happened."[69] Arendt's criticism of the Jewish Councils was itself severely criticized, though other analysts have made related points more diplomatically than she did. Commenting on the Jewish Councils in the Jewish ghettos under Nazism, for example, Raul Hilberg noted:

> It should be emphasized the councils were not the willful accomplices of the Germans. Within the German superstructure, however, they were its indispensable operatives. . . . It was German policy to transfer to Jewish middlemen a large part of the physical and psychological burdens of destroying millions of men, women and children.[70]

That included much of the financial cost.[71] In this context of coerced cooperation, tragic calculations around "the lesser evil" were routinely made, and Hilberg notes "the Germans would frequently ask for only a certain number of deportees. It is this request that ignited an internal Jewish argument to the effect that if 1,000 Jews were given up, 10,000 would be saved, that if none were sacrificed, all would be lost."[72] While there was some armed resistance (famously in the Warsaw ghetto in 1943), the scale of resistance was generally limited by a range of factors including massive intimidation, hunger, the hope of being spared, the hope that the Nazis needed Jewish labor, the hope of a quick Allied victory, and even the arrival of optimistic letters that the Nazis had coerced from some of those already deported.[73]

In the Nazis' routine use of the phrase "to grant a mercy death," the idea of choosing a "lesser evil" merged murderously with the predilection for euphemisms. Arendt suggested:

> None of the various "language rules", carefully contrived to deceive and camouflage, had a more decisive effect on the mentality of the killers than this first war decree of Hitler [the euthanasia program], in which the word for "murder" was replaced by the phrase "to grant a mercy death."[74]

Again, "normal" shame was not exactly banished but instead was constantly warded off through techniques that we can identify. Whether it was compartmentalization, or using euphemisms, or "drawing the line," or "following history," or invoking "the lesser evil," or simply redefining virtue as temptation, such techniques helped to enable the unfolding horror. They also implied the existence of—or at least the potential for—some semblance of shame around harm done, a shame that was very effectively warded off precisely through such techniques. The case of Eichmann may remind us that not all Nazis were immune from feelings of revulsion or inhibition around violence: but insofar as Eichmann had to overcome elements of his own humanity in order to participate in genocide, he was chillingly successful in doing so.

8

Trump's Idea of Shame—and How to Ward It Off

WHEN THE NOTORIOUS *Access Hollywood* tape revealed that Republican presidential candidate Donald Trump had boasted about aggressively groping women, the threat of shame was all too obvious. Many felt that this was the end of Trump's political career.

In a campaign debate with Hillary Clinton in the run-up to the 2016 U.S. presidential elections, Donald Trump was asked about the tape. "Yes, I'm very embarrassed by it. I hate it," he said. "But it's locker-room talk, and it's one of those things. I will knock the hell out of ISIS."[1] There was a hint of shame if we accept that embarrassment is a milder version.[2] But Trump pointedly steered clear of acknowledging shame itself, while invoking the idea that *it's what men do* ("locker-room talk") and quickly turning the shame (and planned violence) on a terrorist group.

After that, Trump moved on to asserting that no one in American politics had been "so abusive to women" as Bill Clinton and that Hillary "attacked those same women and attacked them viciously."[3] He then proceeded to claim that Hillary Clinton and President Obama had been responsible for the emergence of the ISIS terrorists in the first place.

Rambling and erratic, Trump's self-defense nevertheless illustrates one of his most fundamental and consistent political reflexes: *the solution to shame was to shame someone else.*

This "someone else" could be either the person shaming him or some third party, and often both. Trump proved gifted at "weaponizing shame," as Adam Haslett put it in *The Nation*.[4] And on top of this, the quick passing of shame to others appears to have been integral to another notable characteristic of Trump: his remarkable shamelessness. It was natural, too, that the more shameless Trump appeared, the more his opponents wanted to shame him. In turn, Trump found ways of redirecting this extra shame toward others. Hence, in part, the vortex of mutual shaming in which America became caught.

In the discussion of Eichmann, we suggested that simply labeling an individual as "shameless" may be less productive than investigating what they find shameful and how they escape from shame (as they conceive it). Of course, one has to be careful about sweeping comparisons between contemporary politicians and the Nazis. But it's striking that with both Eichmann and Trump the working definition of shame centered to a large extent on *weakness and failure,* while *shame-around-immorality* featured only mildly or not at all. For all their differences, both men displayed a narcissistic concern to demonstrate "success" that seemed to be quite consistent with engaging in actions that, on any sensible view, would be regarded as shameful. This is in line with Andrew Morrison's work suggesting a strong association between narcissism and certain kinds of shame. In particular, Morrison suggested that the narcissist tends to see weakness and failure as deeply shameful and will often defend against this with grandiosity (an unrealistic sense that one is superior to others).[5] More generally, as Flanagan has emphasized, the problem is not shame but shame around the wrong things.

In his *Access Hollywood* conversation with Billy Bush, Trump boasted, "Just kiss, I don't even wait. And when you're a star, they let you do it. You can do anything."[6] In Trump's eyes, evidently, this was not abuse; it was what his "star status" allowed. In other words, it was *winning,* and in Trump's world it is winning—and being seen to win—that serves best in *banishing* shame. It follows that boasting about such abuses later was not simply a postscript or an indiscretion but an integral part of the activity—and also an integral part of Trump's never-ending project of warding off shame through spectacular—and publicly recognized—acts of "winning."

We know that Trump relentlessly projected himself as a winner in business (except in his tax returns, where he emphasized *losing*).[7] When Trump entered politics, he again presented himself—and sold himself—as a winner. He projected himself as embodying the qualities America needed to become a winner again, and he presented himself as a winner in the masculinity stakes too (for example, when getting his "good" testosterone levels revealed on air or when denigrating Hillary Clinton in 2016 for lacking a "presidential look").[8] In the widespread outrage over the January 2021 Capitol invasion, it's easy to forget that before the 2016 presidential election Trump proclaimed, "I would like to promise and pledge to all of my voters and supporters and to all of the people of the United States that I will totally accept the results of this great and historic presidential election if I win."[9] Alleging in advance that both the 2016 and 2020 elections would be rigged, Trump seems to have been concerned to protect himself against the shame of *not winning*.

Trump's sensitivity to shame was noticed well before he ran for president. With Trump in the audience at the 2011 White House correspondents' dinner, President Obama made fun of Trump's repeated insistence that Obama should prove he was born in America. "No one is happier, no one is prouder to put this birth certificate matter to rest than The Donald and that's because he can finally get back to focusing on the issues that matter, like 'Did we fake the moon landing?'" The audience laughed loudly, with the video suggesting that Trump was quietly livid at this point. Roger Stone, one of Trump's key political advisors, noted, "I think that is the night he resolves to run for president . . . maybe I'll just run. Maybe I'll show them all."[10] In a documentary aired during the 2016 presidential campaign, Michael d'Antonio, author of the biography *The Truth about Trump*, said:

> Donald dreads humiliation and he dreads shame and this is why he often attempts to humiliate and shame other people, so in the case of the president ridiculing him, I think this was intolerable for Donald Trump . . . Donald Trump's fantasy is to be the guy who takes the

key to the Oval Office from Barack Obama's hand in 2017 and it's personal. This is a burning personal need that he has to redeem himself from being humiliated by the first black president.[11]

In 2017, Omarosa Manigault, at that time a Trump aide and former contestant on Trump's reality TV show *The Apprentice*, observed: "Every critic, every detractor will have to bow down to President Trump. It's everyone who's ever doubted Donald, whoever disagreed, whoever challenged him. It is the ultimate revenge to become the most powerful man in the universe."[12]

Trump's vulnerability to shame (and the link to his shamelessness) was underlined by Tony Schwarz, who spent many hours with Trump when they were coauthoring *The Art of the Deal*.[13] Interviewed by the BBC in October 2018, Schwarz highlighted Trump's difficult, if economically privileged, childhood—a "very brutal" father and an "incredibly neglectful" mother spending barely any time with the boy.[14] Trump, in Schwarz's opinion, was looking for the love and admiration he didn't get as a child. That may sound simplistic, but Schwarz gave a detailed analysis of Trump's relationship to shame (and one that resonates with Wurmser):

> In Trump's case, in order to defend himself, in order to make himself feel safe, he cut himself off from the kinds of things that we associate with a healthy or relatively mature adult—empathy, subtlety, rationality, and above all a conscience, an ability to distinguish and to care about the difference between right and wrong. The sociopath is a person who cannot feel a sense of shame or whose shame is so overwhelming that they have to push it away because the feeling is just too intolerable. To feel that shame is to feel obliterated, and that I believe is at the heart of Trump's character—or his lack of character—and his behavior.[15]

What was most remarkable about Trump's desire for respect, according to Schwarz, was that it could never be satisfied. Schwarz said that while being president brings attention and at least a degree of respect, Trump "feels aggrieved in every moment and . . . feels a kind of paranoid sense that the world is out to get him, that he's being treated unfairly.... He never will feel like he gets what he needs.... He is a black hole, and this I observed up very close numerous times."[16]

Trump's Binaries

Integral to Trump's association of shame with weakness has been a binary thinking that lumps together *"strong, homegrown, and male"* (a source of pride) and opposes them to *"weak, alien, and female"* (a source of shame). Anyone spanning these poles endangers Trump's mental map of shame and his carefully cultivated shamelessness. Trump's evident problems with the idea of a *Black American president* were obvious from his "birther" obsession. Trump seemed unable to accept the idea of a *strong woman*, and so we found him bizarrely attacking Hillary for lack of stamina (a claim she easily rebutted in the 2016 campaign debates).

A particularly revealing threat to Trump's binary world was the idea of a *weak soldier*, which became an obsession. Trump denigrated former Vietnam prisoner-of-war John McCain ("a war hero because he was captured ... I prefer people that weren't captured").[17] Referring to mental health problems among veterans, Trump told a veterans group, "You're strong and you can handle it. But a lot of people can't handle it."[18] In November 2018, Trump flew to Paris and then failed to turn up at a ceremony to commemorate those who died in World War II, blaming rain, saying "the helicopter couldn't fly" and claiming that the Secret Service wouldn't drive him. Jeffrey Goldberg reported in *The Atlantic* that the helicopter and driving claims were untrue, adding:

> Trump rejected the idea of the visit because he feared his hair would become disheveled in the rain, and because he did not believe it important to honor American war dead, according to four people with firsthand knowledge of the discussion that day. In a conversation with senior staff members on the morning of the scheduled visit, Trump said, "Why should I go to that cemetery? It's filled with losers." In a separate conversation on the same trip, Trump referred to the more than 1,800 marines who lost their lives at Belleau Wood as "suckers" for getting killed.[19]

This was clearly a very odd stance for a president to take toward those who had died for their country. But it spoke strongly to Trump's idea that weakness was shameful.

Trump's unease with "weak soldiers" also sat uncomfortably—but in a sense quite logically—with his own absence from the Vietnam War. An accomplished athlete, Trump played soccer, baseball, and football at military high school and then tennis, football, and squash at college. But after four deferments of military service for college study, a doctor's letter referring to "heel spurs" won Trump a fifth deferment; Trump told the *New York Times* that the heel spurs were never operated on but healed up "over a period of time."[20] Fortunately, Trump's absence from the carnage did not prevent him from serving heroically in his own way: during a 1998 radio show hosted by Howard Stern, Trump observed that avoiding sexually transmitted diseases while dating was "my personal Vietnam. I feel like a great and very brave soldier," adding with characteristic charm that women's vaginas were "potential landmines."[21] Like Eichmann, Trump was not beyond redefining his actions in terms that invoked service and sacrifice, but—as with Eichmann and his redefinition of the "front" so as to include attending the concentration camps—it was a quite a stretch. Unsurprisingly, Trump's "Vietnam" remarks were taken by many veterans as strongly disrespecting their service and sacrifice.[22]

Another threat to Trump's binary world was *the Muslim war hero*—hence his apparent compulsion to launch into a (politically hazardous) attack on the parents of Capt. Humayun Khan. At the 2016 Democratic Convention, Khizr Khan criticized Trump's proposed "Muslim ban," noting that Khan's own son, a Muslim, had died fighting for the United States in Iraq. He noted, too, that Trump "consistently smears the character of Muslims. He disrespects other minorities."[23] Khan then addressed Trump directly: "You have sacrificed nothing and no one!" It was certainly a blow to Trump, and for a brief time it looked like it might even be a defining moment of the 2016 presidential campaign. But Trump himself hardly seemed to blink: "I think I've made a lot of sacrifices," he responded. "I work very, very hard. I've created thousands and thousands of jobs, tens of thousands of jobs, built great structures.

I've had tremendous success. I think I've done a lot."[24] That of course missed the point that employing people and telling them to build things is not quite the same as losing your life in the service of your country. Yet Trump's state of shamelessness was apparently intact—just so long as he could claim to others and himself that (unlike those fallen soldiers) he was not a "loser."

Trump's reverence for masculine strength and his fear of the alien came together in his famous wall, which seems to have offered a magical solution for diverse sources of shame. In Trump's wall, the alien was positioned as a threat to ordinary Americans, especially women, while the wall was positioned as a (very masculine) protective response. Trump infamously said of Mexican immigrants, "They're bringing drugs, they're bringing crime. They're rapists. And some, I assume, are good people."[25] Trump's language was telling when he described the proposed wall between Mexico and the United States in his 2016 "immigration" speech in Phoenix: "On day one, we will begin working on an impenetrable, physical, tall, powerful, beautiful southern border wall."[26]

As Trump and his audience excited and emboldened each other, the crowd shouted "Build the wall! Build the wall!" and Trump delivered a thrilling additional shaming that was surely intense enough to qualify as a humiliation: "And Mexico will pay for the wall!" In a passage that might offer a field day for Freudian psychoanalysts, Trump went on to evoke a hypermasculine world that would destroy the tunnels that bring everything bad into America:

> We will use the best technology, including above and below ground sensors, that's the tunnels. Remember that, above and below. Above and below ground sensors. Towers, aerial surveillance and manpower to supplement the wall, find and dislocate tunnels and keep out criminal cartels.[27]

Of course Trump's positioning of himself as the great protector of American women was deeply ironic in view of his own record here, including numerous accusations of sexual harassment against him. But just as the wall implicitly positioned all the bad things outside of

America, it also implicitly positioned all the bad things outside Trump himself. Omer Bartov noted in another context that "the most nightmarish vision of the elusive enemy was to discover that he was none other than oneself."[28]

Significantly, one prominent public figure who failed to fit into Trump's binary framework was Trump himself—and not just because of the Vietnam deferments. Of course, Trump was not lacking in height and he retained a liking for sport (or at least golf). But with his famous oddly luxuriant and carefully positioned orange-to-blonde hair, his slightly mannered voice in the middle-to-high range,[29] his extreme vanity, his habit of waving his hands in the air, and his taste for elaborate furniture, Trump—already seventy when he became president—was not entirely convincing in his assumed role of manly man.

Perhaps this is not so odd if we remember that Trump's promise, like that of many gifted orators, is a promise of *transformation*. It's notable that Hitler, physically unprepossessing, often began his speeches hesitantly and built up to a roaring demon. Trump's style was different. But playing up the modesty of his (immodest) beginnings, he did insist that his ability to transform himself into a hugely successful businessman was a model for the transformation of America. His 2016 campaign story was part of his political pitch, as when he told a rally in Louisiana, "I started at 7 percent, and they thought I'd wipe out. Then I got 15 percent and then 25. . . . We're on the rise . . . America will be dominant, proud, rich."[30]

Along with all the macho talk, Trump sometimes projected a kind of personal fragility and a sense of hurt. On one reading, he gave you "Four Seasons in One Day." Mixing the musical references, he offered not only Posh Trump (the successful businessman), Sporty Trump (the golfer), Scary Trump (the threat-maker), and Ginger Trump (the famously orange complexion) but also Baby Trump: during the first presidential debate Trump complained about his opponent's negative ads, "It's not nice. And I don't deserve that!"[31] a plaintive note for someone so scathing. Even his struggles with the English language could be oddly endearing, challenging the common perception that politicians talk down to people.

The Fear of Being Wrong (Not *Doing* Wrong)

Trump's self-image as strong and as a winner was intimately bound up with his self-image as *getting things right*. While he consistently displayed a lack of shame when it came to *doing wrong*, he appears to have attached a great deal of shame to *being wrong*—a possibility so threatening that it could not even be acknowledged. As president, Trump projected himself as in touch with a reality that others could not see, and as part of this he attributed to himself great powers of *prediction*. In a March 2017 *Time* magazine interview, Trump proclaimed:

> I'm a very instinctual person, but my instinct turns out to be right. When everyone said I wasn't going to win the election, I said well I think I would. You know it is interesting, somebody came up to me and said the other day, gee whiz, the *New York Times* and other people, you know other groups, had you down at one percent, well, I said no I think I am going to win, and people smiled, George Stephanopoulos laughed, you remember. He thought it was very cute, and very funny. Other people smiled. And some people, the smart people or the people that know me didn't laugh at all. There are people that know me, like Carl Icahn and many others, that didn't laugh at all, they thought I was going to win . . . Brexit, I predicted Brexit, you remember that, the day before the event. I said, no, Brexit is going to happen, and everybody laughed, and Brexit happened . . . I was saying Brexit was going to pass, and everybody was laughing, and I turned out to be right on that.[32]

Here, Trump mentions laughing five times and smiling twice. The rather relentless message is that people laughed at me whenever I made a prediction, but I have always been right. Revealingly, Trump sometimes imagined or invented jeering even when there was none. Calling in November 2015 for greater surveillance of Muslims inside the United States and for a return of refugees, Trump said of the Twin Towers attack on 9/11: "I watched in Jersey City, New Jersey, where thousands and thousands of people were cheering as the building was coming down." Yet there was no evidence of such cheering.[33] After that, one of the first things Donald Trump did as president was to impose a notorious travel ban on seven Muslim-majority countries.

Defending this ban at a rally for supporters in Florida in February 2017, Trump mentioned terror attacks in Brussels, Nice, and Paris and noted, "You look at what's happening. We've got to keep our country safe. You look at what's happening in Germany, you look at what's happening last night in Sweden. Sweden! Who would believe this?!"[34] It turns out Trump's expression of incredulity here was entirely appropriate. For no one—least of all the Swedes—was aware of any major incident in Sweden (let alone a terrorist outrage). Perhaps the Swedes had carelessly slept through their own terror attack, possibly suffering from too much Swedish "burn-wine"? But rather than putting the Sweden gaffe behind him, Trump was keen to hold onto it. On March 23, 2017, *Time* magazine published an interview with Trump by Michael Scherer. When Trump was asked about his (baseless) accusation that President Obama had conducted wiretapping against him, Trump said:

> I predicted a lot of things, Michael. Some things that came to you a bit later. But, you know, we just rolled out a list. Sweden. I make the statement [implying a terror attack in Sweden], everyone goes crazy. The next day they have a massive riot, and death, and problems [a reference to the riots and car-burning in a suburb of Stockholm that took place two days after Trump's faux pas] . . . I predicted a lot of things that took a little bit of time.[35]

On April 7, 2017, there was an *actual* terrorist attack on Stockholm by an Uzbek citizen with ISIS sympathies. The UK's *Daily Mail* ran the headline "Was Trump Right about Sweden All Along?"[36]

Back in January 2016, Trump said Brussels was "like living in a hellhole."[37] March 22, 2016, saw terror attacks at a Brussels subway station and at Brussels's Zaventem airport, and a year later Trump congratulated himself:

> I said Brussels is not what it used to be, very sad what has happened to Brussels. I was absolutely lambasted. A short time later they had the major attack in Brussels. . . . And then people said you know

Trump was right. What am I going to tell you? I tend to be right. I'm an instinctual person, I happen to be a person that knows how life works.[38]

One might say that within President Trump's world there was actually *no such thing* as a lie that he spoke or a mistake that he made. For what might at first *appear to be* a lie or a mistake was actually (from his point of view) a far-sighted statement—or prediction—that, with the passage of time, would one day be proven to be true. In this way, Trump cleverly insulated himself from the shame of being wrong. In her book *The Origins of Totalitarianism*, Hannah Arendt noted that a totalitarian leader's statements "cannot be disproved by facts, but only by future success or failure"[39] and that "demagogically speaking, there is hardly a better way to avoid discussion than by saying that only the future can reveal its merits."[40]

Arendt also can help us understand some of the other dangers with Trump's claims to be always right and to be able to predict the future. She noted for example that "mass leaders in power have one concern which overrules all utilitarian considerations: to make their predictions come true."[41] In the case of the Nazis and the Soviet Communists, there was a drive to *create* the future that would reveal the merits of predictions about "dying classes" and "dying races." Arendt noted that the demagogue's "principal quality is that he 'was always right and will always be right.'"[42] In her insightful essay "Truth and Politics," Arendt quoted Hugo Grotius, a Dutch scholar who rose to prominence in the seventeenth century: "Even God cannot cause two times two not to make four." Arendt went on to observe:

> Seen from the viewpoint of politics, truth has a despotic character. It is therefore hated by tyrants, who rightly fear the competition of a coercive force they cannot monopolize, and it enjoys a rather precarious status in the eyes of governments that rest on consent and abhor coercion.[43]

Arendt also saw the lie and the fictional world as feeding the will to power—if only because some approximation to absolute power would be necessary to make an outrageous lie appear true.[44] That would also be a compelling reason not to *give up* power. Demagogues actually use inflammatory statements and inflammatory actions as a way of *making* their predictions come true (another form of "action as propaganda"), Arendt observed, and this included predictions about the "inevitability" of certain kinds of violence.

Of course, Trump was no Hitler. But the importance that Trump attached to those who *laughed* at his predictions had disturbing historical resonances. On becoming chancellor of Germany on January 30, 1939, Hitler proclaimed that "the Jewish race" had "only received my prophesies with laughter" when he had said he would become head of state and "settle the Jewish problem." Yet soon, he claimed, the Jews would be "laughing on the other side of their face." The format of Hitler's January 1939 pronouncement was essentially the following:

1. I made a prediction.
2. People laughed at me because of this prediction.
3. My prediction, nevertheless, is coming true.
4. I am *making* my prediction come true.

The narcissist always wants to be right. Before Trump won the Republican primaries, clinical psychologist Ramani Durvasula noted that a narcissist "lacks empathy" and is "very grandiose," prone to tantrums if they don't get their way. They dish out criticism but "absolutely can't take it." Craving validation, they are often attracted to social media.[45] If that is not ringing a sufficient number of bells, Durvasula added that a common behavior among narcissists is to "engage in something called gaslighting where they literally doubt your own reality, leaving you feeling like you've gone crazy." Often accused of gaslighting, Trump unwittingly summed up the technique when he claimed, "What you're seeing and what you're reading is not happening." If we go back to John Bradshaw's classic book on shame, we may note his observation that a narcissist will often have parents who overindulge the child's sense of greatness but offer little listening or emotional security.[46] We know too that, alongside the punishments and the repeated urgings to "Be a killer," Trump's father would also indulge his son, telling him, "You're a king," and even letting him deliver his papers from a hired limousine when there was rain or snow.[47]

Of course, we may never know *exactly* why Trump became Trump or why he always had to win and be right. Anecdotes about people's childhoods have their limits when analyzing national and international affairs. What we do know is the eccentric and dangerous—but hardly unique—way in which Trump conceptualized what was shameful (weakness and being wrong) and not shameful (*doing* wrong). This strange framing of shame provides not only a vital clue to his character but also (as we shall see in the chapter that follows) a vital clue to his *appeal*.

9

Trumpelstiltskin

SPINNING SHAME INTO POLITICAL GOLD

DESPITE HIS MANY CRUELTIES on the campaign trail including the public mocking of a disabled journalist, despite his boasting about aggressively groping women, and despite his innumerable and often extreme liberties with the truth, Donald Trump was elected to the presidency of the United States in November 2016. After four years in office in which he frequently exhibited a remarkable contempt for truth and for democratic institutions, an *increased* number of Americans voted for him in the (high turnout) 2020 elections.

For many observers, all this was shocking enough. But another possibility—even more disturbing—began to suggest itself: the possibility that many people were voting for Donald Trump not just *despite* his many transgressions but also, in some sense, *because of them*. Could it be that many supporters were not so much *forgiving* Trump's transgressions as *rewarding* them? One Vietnam veteran, Rick Lytton, age sixty-seven, hinted at this dynamic at a May 2016 Washington, D.C., bikers' rally: "We need to retake America. He [Trump] is an asshole, and that's what we need."[1]

Taken in the round, Trump's speeches and the audiences' reactions suggested a considerable appetite for illegality. In fact, Trump himself realized relatively early that—for millions of Americans—his bad behavior was not actually detracting from his popularity. Thus, at a January 2016 campaign meeting in Iowa, Trump proclaimed, "I could stand in the middle of Fifth Avenue and shoot someone [mimes shooting] and I wouldn't lose any voters, OK? It's like incredible!" a boast that prompted laughter from the crowd.[2] Here, the boast stands as a kind of proxy for the shooting—and the laughter is a kind of immediate "proof" that Trump can get away with anything!

After Christine Blasey Ford testified at the 2018 Senate hearing (saying Supreme Court nominee Brett Kavanaugh sexually assaulted her when they were teenagers), Trump mocked her testimony at a Mississippi rally and again drew laughter from the crowd.[3] And in the video of Trump's October 2018 Montana rally, almost every person in the crowd behind the president was smiling or laughing when Trump endorsed local congressman Greg Gianforte's May 2017 assault on *Guardian* reporter Ben Jacobs, who had asked a question about health-care reform.[4] Trump's performance came complete with a mime of the "body slam" that took Jacobs to the floor. At that Montana rally, Trump said he'd wondered if the body slam might hurt Gianforte's chances in the special congressional election that followed shortly after the attack. But then he'd reconsidered: "Well, wait a minute. I know Montana pretty well. I think it might help him—and it did!" (more laughter and applause).

A key message here seemed to be: I know your faults and I still love you; and conversely, you know my faults and you still love me! Such incidents recall Arendt's reference to the profound allure of "crimes committed in the spirit of play . . . the combination of horror and laughter."[5] We have noted that Trump's strong aversion to being laughed at was part of his aversion to shame. When large numbers were laughing together in a political rally (and often laughing at some kind of cruelty that he was embodying or encouraging), it was as if shame had magically evaporated for both Trump *and* his audience. In the act of ridiculing (subjecting someone to mockery and derision)[6] and in the act of laughing along, there was a kind of instant escape from being mocked or derided—a kind of playground reflex that Trump intuitively understood.

If Trump's bizarre and abusive behavior as presidential candidate and then as president revealed a dangerous appetite for illegality (and for freedom from restraint), the events of January 2021 showed how a collective appetite for illegality was taking on a more dangerous aspect. Trump was once more stirring up the crowd, this time to fight his defeat in the November 2020 presidential election, and members of the crowd promptly invaded the Capitol building just at the point when the Senate was ratifying Joe Biden's victory. For all the deadly seriousness of the incursion (which resulted in five deaths), there was also a kind of carnival atmosphere[7]—laughter, animal masks, Confederate flags, dramatic inversions of the norm as the invaders planted their feet on senators' desks, and so on—more "crimes committed in the spirit of play." Even after this, Trump retained a hold on the Republican Party; while the Senate voted 57–43 to impeach him for incitement to insurrection, the vote did not reach the two-thirds majority required for impeachment.

Trump's political appeal rested heavily on offering others the kind of escape from shame that he routinely provided for himself. This seems to have been key to his charisma. Psychoanalyst Heinz Kohut once observed that the "power of the gifted leader can be effectively engaged only in the area in which the fantasies and wishes of the masses are like his own."[8] Kohut argued that at certain historical moments, feelings of shame and powerlessness are ubiquitous and "individuals seek to melt into the body of a powerful nation (as symbolized by a grandiose leader) to cure their shame and provide them with a feeling of enormous strength, to which they react with relief and triumph."[9]

Trumpelstiltskin fit this template well, spinning the unpromising straw of shame into political gold. While Trump's privileged background was a far cry from that of millions of his supporters,[10] his aversion to shame and weakness—and his remedy of "winning"—struck a chord. He stirred up Americans' underlying sense of shame and promised an instant remedy.

As with the totalitarian fantasies that Arendt saw as so seductive, the magical nature of Trump's diagnosis and proposed "remedies" did not, for very large numbers of people, undermine their appeal. In one major survey, 50 percent of men and 34 percent of women agreed with the statement "Society as a whole has become too soft and feminine."[11] This was quite a lot, but among Trump supporters the figures were as high as 74 percent of men and 59 percent of women.[12] It was in this context that Trump promised a transformation from "weakness" to "strength" and "masculinity." Campaigning for Trump in January 2016, Sarah Palin hyped up and sexualized the "humiliation" that the Obama administration was allegedly heaping on America in the sphere of foreign affairs. Referring to the fifteen-hour holding of ten U.S. Navy personnel by Iranian authorities earlier that month, Palin proclaimed:

> We're watching our sailors suffer and be humiliated on a world stage ... because a weak-kneed capitulator-in-chief has decided that America will lead from behind ... they capture and we kowtow, and we apologize, and then, we bend over and say, "Thank you, enemy." ... No more pussy footin' around! ... [Are] you ready for a commander-in-chief who will let our warriors do their job and go kick ISIS ass? ... Ready to make America great again, are you ready to stump for Trump?[13]

As with the words used by Trump in describing his wall, such sexually loaded language chimed with Wendy Brown's suggestion in 2010 that fears around an emasculated state, around loss of sovereignty, and around "penetration" by immigrants mirrored wider fears around deindustrialization and the "demasculization" of the male population in particular.[14]

Trump's promised wall offered to ease these anxieties while minimizing shame through the implication that all the "bad things" lay outside rather than inside America. But while the wall was claimed to protect America from weapons and criminality, major weapons manufacture and legal imports continued.[15] While Trump claimed to offer protection from "Muslim terrorists," most terror attacks were coming from white supremacists.[16] While immigration was painted as a mortal threat, the economy was deeply dependent on it.[17] Somewhat similarly, during the coronavirus pandemic Trump railed against "the China virus" even as lax domestic controls and a run-down public health and social security system were promoting the spread of the virus. As the figures for Covid deaths escalated, it was not just the source of the problem that was being determinedly located *on the outside* but also the shame. The dangerous consequences of such maneuvers did not remove their psychological appeal.[18]

Trump understood that to sell the remedy for shame, you first have to sell the shame—and his strategy here was in line with received wisdom in advertising.[19] One template was the sales script for the ill-fated Trump University: "Do you enjoy seeing everyone else but yourself in their dream houses and driving their dream cars? . . . Your plan is BROKEN and WE WILL help you fix it."[20] On the campaign trail, Trump portrayed the United States as a place of desolation and shame from which he alone could deliver it. This message was exemplified in a 2016 campaign speech in Henderson, Nevada:

> Right now we owe 20 trillion dollars debt, 20 trillion dollars. It doubled under President Obama. Our infrastructure is like that of a third world country. . . . Our police are underfunded, understaffed and under-supported and Hillary Clinton basically accuses our police of all being racist.[21]

To ramp up the underlying shame even more, Trump again injected laughter into the mix: "Hillary's Korea deal, South Korea, cost us another 100,000 jobs . . . and South Korea, like almost every other country, is laughing at how stupid we are." Arguing that "drugs and criminal cartels are pouring into our country on an hourly basis," Trump said immigrants were getting welfare and health care while veterans were dying due to lack of medical assistance. On employment, he declared, "Our jobs are being stolen by countries with much smarter leadership than ours."[22]

Without controlled borders, "we don't have a country," Trump proclaimed,[23] adding that without major defense spending "we won't be respected at all . . . [and] we don't have a country."[24] In 2018, the broken record of his rhetoric proclaimed that without protective tariffs "you almost don't have much of a country."[25] Raising the specter of a shamed and even a disappearing country was the game here, and there was little felt need to argue why particular measures were needed—or how exactly they would help.

Shame and Trump's Supporters

Trump was more interested in tax cuts and dismantling structures—including civil service structures—that might challenge his personal power than in creating the infrastructure that could rebuild America.[26] But the promised escape from shame had real force when so many were struggling to realize the American Dream in the face of stalling social mobility and escalating inequality.

Americans had been told so often that "Anyone can make it if they try hard enough" that many had drawn the logical conclusion: "If I have not made it, it is my fault for not trying hard enough." Joe Bageant put this point very well in *Deer Hunting with Jesus*, a portrait of his hometown, Winchester, Virginia: "The American bootstrap myth is merely another strap that makes the working poor privately conclude that they must in some way be inferior, given that they cannot seem to apply that myth to their own lives."[27] Bageant also noted that this self-blame often had a racial dimension:

> To be white and poor or just making it is a paradox in America. Whites, especially white males, are supposed to have an advantage they exploit mercilessly. Yet slightly over half of all the poor people in the United States are white. . . . Still, the myth of the power of white skin endures, and so does the unspoken belief that if a white person does not succeed, his or her lack of success can be due only to laziness.[28]

Logically, the greater the emphasis that is placed on white privilege, the greater this shame becomes. For some at least, the drive to persecute and discriminate has offered some relief from underlying shame. Scott Huffman, a leading pollster in South Carolina, commented:

> The typical Trump supporter is going to be white. They're more likely to be male. . . . Not so much college educated, usually those with high school or lower education. People who think that whites are being discriminated against as much or more than African

Americans. These are people who feel that they are being marginalized, that they are now the underdogs. They're the ones who feel the most pinch. They're looking for someone to voice that anger. To return their efficacy, their sense that they matter, and feel that this billionaire, the person they aspire to be, is the one who speaks for them.[29]

One disgruntled Republican from South Carolina, James Porter, was asked why Trump had been able to get so much support among those that he himself would probably call "losers." Porter pointed to the denunciations of Mexican "criminals" and Muslim "terrorists" and noted, "Because he has made them [his supporters] believe that they are losers because of other people."[30] The public had already shown an appetite for Trump's theater of shaming, with millions tuning in to *The Apprentice* catchphrase—not "You've won!" but "You're fired!"

In *Strangers in Their Own Land*, Arlie Russell Hochschild's insightful study of the communities around Lake Charles in Louisiana, the author brought out just how difficult it had become to achieve the American Dream or anything resembling it. In a related article in *Mother Jones*, Hochschild wrote:

> Many blue-collar white men now face the same grim economic fate long endured by blacks. With jobs lost to automation or offshored to China, they have less security, lower wages, reduced benefits, more erratic work, and fewer jobs with full-time hours than before. Having been recruited to cheer on the contraction of government benefits and services—a trend that is particularly pronounced in Louisiana—many are unable to make ends meet without them.[31]

Hochschild's book showed the intensity of the current hunger for recognition and respect among the largely forgotten white working-class voters in Louisiana, a hunger that Trump skillfully tapped into by conspicuously conferring recognition and respect in the present moment, by promising a great-again America in the near future, and by finding scapegoats. After being elected president, Trump continued to offer conspicuous respect for many groups in America who felt somehow "under fire," including soldiers, military veterans, the police, and evangelicals.[32] Hochschild invoked the idea of a "deep story":

> The deep story of the right goes like this: You are patiently standing in the middle of a long line stretching toward the horizon, where the American Dream awaits. But as you wait, you see people cutting in line ahead of you. Many of these line-cutters are black—beneficiaries of affirmative action or welfare. Some are career-driven women pushing into jobs they never had before. Then you see immigrants, Mexicans, Somalis, the Syrian refugees yet to come. . . . As you wait your turn, Obama is using the money in your pocket to help the line-cutters.[33]

Hochschild explained the "deep story" in more detail:

> You are a stranger in your own land. You do not recognize yourself in how others see you. It is a struggle to feel seen and honored. And to feel honored you have to feel—and feel seen as—moving forward. But through no fault of your own, and in ways that are hidden, you are slipping backward. You turn to your workplace for respect—but wages are flat and jobs insecure. So you look to other sources of honor. You get no extra points for your race. You look to gender, but if you're a man, you get no extra points for that either. If you are straight you are proud to be a married, heterosexual male, but that pride is now seen as a potential sign of homophobia—a source of dishonor. Regional honor? Not that either. You are often disparaged for the place you call home. As for the church, many look down on it, and the proportion of Americans outside any denomination has risen. You are old, but in America, attention is trained on the young. People like you—white, Christian, working and middle class—suffer this sense of fading honor demographically too, as this very group has declined in numbers.[34]

Hochschild also notes a common feeling among white men in particular that expressing pride in one's identity was somehow only allowed to others. Meanwhile, resentment at alleged "line-cutters" helped deflect anger from those at the top of the pile, who were getting richer and richer. As psychologist and community worker Mary Watkins noted, "For those who hold economic power, it is advantageous to split less privileged Whites from communities of color and to ensure that they think the American Dream is possible to achieve if only it weren't for the interlopers."[35]

For someone like Republican senator Mitch McConnell, who had made a political career out of opposing restrictions on big business (and in particular on campaign financing), Trump's grassroots support was both an asset and a potential problem. McConnell's dependency on Trump was underlined when McConnell criticized Trump's remarks on the August 2017 protests in Charlottesville. Trump had said there were "very fine people on both sides" after white nationalists clashed with counterprotesters. The senator's criticism sent his ratings in Kentucky plummeting. At the same time, Trump needed McConnell—not least to help block impeachment.[36] History professor Timothy Snyder called this an alliance between "gamers" (who game the system) and "breakers" (who dream of breaking it):

> In the four decades since the election of Ronald Reagan, Republicans have overcome the tension between the gamers and the breakers by governing in opposition to government, or by calling elections a revolution (the Tea Party), or by claiming to oppose elites. The breakers, in this arrangement, provide cover for the gamers, putting forth an ideology that distracts from the basic reality that government under Republicans is not made smaller but simply diverted to serve a handful of interests.[37]

Hochschild shows how, with resentment directed at "interlopers" and Washington, the Tea Party was able to attract some of its strongest support in Louisiana, where neither state government reliance on federal funding nor ordinary voters' reliance on federal assistance undermined a strong antipathy to "big government."[38] Indeed, Hochschild also notes a common "dread at joining the parade of 'poor me's.'"[39] Hochschild observes, in addition, that Louisiana's high levels of pollution did not persuade voters to back environmental regulation just as the state's extreme vulnerability to rising sea levels did not prompt support for measures to address global warming or land-sinking.

Concerns about fairness and "line-jumping" are neither new nor confined to the South. After conducting research among Tea Party activists in Massachusetts, Vanessa Williamson, Theda Skocpol, and John Coggin noted such perceptions in 2011:

> Tea Party activists remain deeply concerned about this nonworking and perhaps criminal class of people, typified by young people and unauthorized immigrants, who have unduly profited from government programs [and] wrested control of the government from hardworking average Americans. It is this belief, rather than any absolutist commitment to free-market principles, that underlies Tea Party opposition to government programs.[40]

Hochschild concluded on the basis of her own investigations: "Those on the right I came to know felt two things. First, they felt the deep story was true. Second, they felt that liberals were saying it was not true, and that they themselves were *not feeling the right feelings*."[41] In these circumstances, Trump promised not just an escape from unemployment and underemployment but also an escape from the shame of poverty, from the shame of holding certain opinions and having certain feelings, and from the shame of being invisible and unheard.[42] In his study of Winchester, Virginia, Joe Bageant also notes the lure of recognition, whether by populist political or fundamentalist religious leaders, for "those who do the thankless work of this world and suffer the purest snub of all: invisibility."[43]

In these circumstances, the thrill and liberation of Trump was that he took something hidden and shameful and brought it shamelessly into the open. "We're not silent anymore; we're the loud, noisy majority," Trump told one Louisiana rally.[44] As the crowd left the meeting, fans were saying to one another, "See how *many* of us there are!"[45] Amid this euphoria of acceptance, Hochschild noted that "it was with joyous relief that many heard a Donald Trump who seemed to be wildly, omnipotently, magically free of all PC constraint."[46] Thoughts and feelings that had been partially hidden or a silent source of shame were now coming out into the public sphere and were being actively celebrated. Reading Hochschild's compelling account, you get a sense that the "shadow-side" highlighted by psychoanalyst Carl Jung was being brought joyously into the light, honored and indeed exemplified by a politician with a knack for making people feel good about their murkier instincts and emotions. In this forum, there would be no more apologies for "illiberal" beliefs, only acceptance.

In Trumpworld, love meant never having to say you're sorry.

Politics professor Jill Locke captured some of this dynamic when she noted:

> What fuels the Trump presidency is its ability to provide a device through which "the people" channels its own longing for unfettered speech and actions, sexual indiscretion, and other desires it feels have been unfairly regulated and censored by "political correctness," feminism, anti-racism, and so on. US voters and citizens who have supported Trump—both before and after the [2016] election—repeatedly praise him for saying what they are too afraid to say, for speaking his mind frankly and authentically.... They have transferred their own resentments about adulthood into him, and therefore the insult that he is a child is misplaced; his childishness is precisely the investment, and it will never be used to undo him.[47]

This is Trump not only as shame-slayer but also as superego-slayer. It takes us back not only to Baby Trump but to the strange allure of Trump's cruelty. At times, Trump seemed to fascinate his audience in rather the same way that the serial killer Villanelle fascinated her audience (and UK intelligence agent Eve) in the TV series *Killing Eve*: while part of us may want to condemn someone who seems to have no conscience and to be purely interested in their own pleasure, is there perhaps a part of all of us that would like to be that way too? Conscience may be a heavy bag to carry.

You would think that veterans would be especially suspicious of Trump after his avoidance of military service in Vietnam and after his disrespectful remarks about John McCain in particular. But veteran

Robert Gardner, age sixty-seven, said Trump's disparaging remarks about prisoners of war didn't bother him much. "I've got a mouth like that too," he added. "Shit comes out that shouldn't come out."[48] This illustrates a point that is brought out more systematically in Hochschild's ethnographic account: part of Trump's attraction for his supporters seems to have been that he makes them *look good by comparison*! Or, to put it another way: "Here, finally, is someone important who not only expresses respect for me and my opinions but will not look down on me because he is just as 'deplorable' as I am." This perverse dynamic begins to make sense if we take seriously the widespread shaming of people for "politically incorrect" attitudes and opinions (and sometimes for their poverty) that was highlighted by Hochschild. From this perspective, Trump was so bad he was good.

We have noted Trump's instinct for forcefully countering criticism, and this reflex seems to have extended to his supporters. Hochschild gave an interesting analysis of why this might be so when she discussed the aftermath of one Trump rally:

> Having once experienced the elation—the "high"—of being part of a powerful, like-minded majority, released from politically correct rules of feeling, many wanted to *hold on to that elation*. To do this, they fended off challenge. They sought affirmation. One woman with whom I spent six hours talked about Trump continually, countering possible criticisms, leaving no interstitial moments when skepticism might emerge. It occurred to me that the reason for this shield of talk was to protect her elation.[49]

To his supporters, Trump was offering not just respect (which may sound a little dry) but a sense of being *embraced*, even loved. That, too, is enticing when you feel a sense of shame, and psychoanalyst Léon Wurmser noted in *The Mask of Shame* that the core experience of shame is not simply a sense that the self is "weak, dirty and defective" but also, at a very deep level, a "conviction of one's *unlovability*."[50] While Trump's opponents often painted his supporters as prejudiced and poorly educated, Trump declared at a rally in Nevada, "I *love* the poorly educated!"[51]

In her Louisiana study, Hochschild made the important observation that, with economic crisis deepening, Trump was tending to depart from a Republican tradition of criticizing welfare recipients en masse:

> [Trump] has shamed virtually every line-cutting [or alleged line-cutting] group in the Deep Story—women, people of color, the disabled, immigrants, refugees. But he's hardly uttered a single bad word about unemployment insurance, food stamps, or Medicaid, or what the tea party calls "big government handouts" for anyone—including blue-collar white men.[52]

Hochschild noted that a distinction between "makers" and "takers"—broadly, those who are productive and those who take government "handouts"—had traditionally been a key maneuver on the political right as well as an important source of pride for many working people, however poor. More specifically, "Shaming the 'takers' below had been a precious mark of higher status."[53] But Hochschild also wanted to ask what happens to this system of shame-avoidance and pride-rescue when the loss of secure employment is so far-reaching that the perennially shamed category of "takers" becomes something closer to the rule than the exception. In other words, what happens when vulnerable blue-collar workers themselves become "takers"? Trump seems to have seen an opportunity here. In putting aside the normal anti-welfare rhetoric, Trump "offer[ed] blue-collar white men relief from a [welfare] taker's shame."[54] (We should note, though, that Trump still proved willing to *undermine* important benefits, most notably Obamacare.)

One way of thinking about these dynamics is to consider, at a more general level, some possible responses to disaster or misfortune. Human beings generally require an explanation and need to attribute responsibility—and one way of representing the options is displayed in figure 3. In this graphic, the types of blame that invoke some kind of shame have been represented by options 1, 2 and 3, with options 2 and 3 tending to invite some type of moral reform in the society and not just in the individual. Option 4, "blame your government", is often the most

1. Blame yourself
2. Blame God or Gods
3. Blame flaws in the society/'sins'
4. Blame your government
5. Blame a scapegoat
6. Blame a party with real responsibility but exaggerate it

FIGURE 3.

politically radical option (generally involving anger and perhaps a call for radical reform such as socialism). After that we move towards options 5 and 6. Option 5 involves the scapegoating of some party with no responsibility for the relevant disaster and option 6 (closely related) involves the blaming of some party that has a small responsibility that has been significantly exaggerated. These last two options will very often point policy in a more racist or even fascistic direction—reflexes that are clearly alive and well within many democracies—and these options may interact damagingly with options 2 and 3 that call for "moral reform" in society.

Now from a government's point of view or an elite's point of view, it may make sense to push explanations away from the most politically threatening zone (option 4) and towards explanations that involve members of the public shaming themselves individually or collectively (options 1, 2 and 3) or towards explanations that involve the shaming and targeting of scapegoats (broadly, options 5 and 6). From the point of view of an ordinary person, there may be an interest in pushing explanations into the blame-your-government zone (4) or the scapegoating zone (5 and 6); this sidelines explanations that are shaming—and Hochschild (like Arendt before her) shows how feelings of shame could feed strongly into the scapegoating zone.

The chart may also help in understanding why a politics-of-scapegoating is often seen as urgent or useful (as we saw in post-World War One Germany) at times when the threat of a radical or revolutionary politics is high. In times of crisis, the dividing line between radicals on "both sides" of the political spectrum may not be as sharp as we tend to imagine.

Commenting in January 2016 on a book tour in America's heartlands, Robert Reich said he

> kept hearing from people who said they were trying to make up their minds in the upcoming election between supporting Bernie Sanders or Donald Trump.... Most of these people said they were incensed by "crony capitalism," by which they meant political payoffs by big corporations and Wall Street banks that result in special favors such as the Wall Street bailout of 2008. They wanted to close tax loopholes for the rich.... They wanted to reduce the market power of pharmaceutical companies and big health insurers, which they thought resulted in exorbitant prices. They were angry about trade treaties that they characterized as selling-out American workers while rewarding corporate executives and big investors.[55]

In the run-up to the 2016 presidential elections, a key part of Trump's orchestrated relief from shame were the aggressions and denunciations that largely fell into zone 5. Revealingly, this broader process of shaming seems to have operated on a smaller scale in Trump's rallies, and this is well conveyed by Hochschild:

> In nearly every rally, Trump points out a protestor, sometimes demonizing them and calling for their expulsion.... Such scapegoating reinforces the joyous unity of the gathering. The act of casting out the "bad one" helps fans unite in a shared sense of being the "good ones," the majority, no longer strangers in their own land.[56]

In this drama (played out on the grander scale of Trump's xenophobia), the "bad ones" are targeted not just because they challenge Trump's rather dubious version of "the truth" but also because they provide a focus for collective shaming that helps give the majority a sense of belonging and respect.

Hochschild showed how even among the middle class in America, there has been a growing sense of precariousness. In fact, the fear of *losing* the American Dream has become a major preoccupation, and many now perceive that there is "little shelter from bad news." As Hochschild noted:

Being middle class didn't mean you felt secure, because that class was thinning out as a tiny elite shot up to great wealth and more people fell into a life of broken teeth, unpaid rent, and shame. . . . They resented all the labels "the liberals" had for them, especially "backward" or "ignorant Southerners" or, worse, "rednecks."[57]

Evangelicals like Jerry Falwell Jr. praised Trump for not looking down his nose at them.[58] Researcher Robert Jones found a huge nostalgia for the 1950s among white evangelical Protestants, which chimed with the Make America Great Again promise.[59] That promise also struck a chord in the Rust Belt; reporter Pema Levy said of the people in Youngstown, Ohio: "Trump's promise to take them back in time is alluring."[60]

Importantly, Trump's loading of shame onto outgroups was part of a much longer tradition, particularly in the Republican Party. In his 2004 book *What's the Matter with Kansas?* Thomas Frank highlighted an important paradox: the often vehement adherence to right-wing ideas—and right-wing definitions of "the enemy"—among huge numbers of Americans who had themselves been suffering economically from right-wing policies. In particular, Frank showed how millions of Americans had lost their economic security through liberalization, outsourcing, oligopolization, foreclosure, and the demise of unions.[61] In Kansas, five or six large agribusinesses had come to dominate, hitting the pockets of consumers and also forcing many farmers into debt and even foreclosure; unionized labor had been undermined, in part through the use of immigrant labor; and companies kept taxes low by playing off towns and states against each other. Yet reforming the economic and political system had been a surprisingly low priority for most of the people victimized or left behind by these policies. In fact, large numbers of poorer voters—whether in Kansas or the United States as a whole—seemed routinely to be voting against their own economic interests. While not everyone agreed with Frank,[62] he made a strong case that a tradition of hostility toward corporations had been displaced into a kind of "feel-good" politics that involved stirring hostility toward a range of "outgroups" and toward a set of forces (science, evolution, secularism, pluralism) that were associated with "liberal" and "urban"

America and that were held to be undermining some old and comfortable certainties.[63] (In *Phishing for Phools*, George Akerlof and Robert Shiller noticed something similar in terms of a heavy focus on "emotional" issues that tended to distract attention from complex and technical economic matters that need to be addressed if inequality is to be tackled.)[64] As for the Democratic Party, Frank said it reinvented itself as "the *other* pro-business party"[65] and rarely offered either a convincing alternative explanation for poverty and inequality or an effective remedy. From an anthropological point of view, it may also be that the Republicans were benefiting from promising to respect taboos (like those on gay marriage and abortion) that some associated with a lost "Golden Age."[66]

In his 2007 study, Bageant painted a grim picture of his hometown, Winchester, Virginia, asking—like Thomas Frank—why the working class there tended to vote Republican and apparently against their own interests. He noted in one neighborhood nearly everyone over fifty had serious health problems and two in five people didn't have a high school diploma.[67] Many of the jobs in Winchester had been outsourced abroad. Others were low-wage jobs offered by businesses that were attracted by low state taxes and minimal environmental regulation. Many in Winchester had no health insurance. Most would "rent until they die," with medical bills running up debts, no chance of passing a house to children, or even remortgaging it to pay for higher education.[68] Households with two people working would often have a joint income of $30,000–35,000, and yet many had convinced themselves that they were middle class. All this was *before* the 2007–8 crash, which Bageant saw coming because so many people had been lured into mortgages they could not afford. Meanwhile, patriotism and nationalism were if anything being invigorated by poverty. Joining the military was often the best hope. More generally, and as Bageant put it in his trenchant style:

> Even if we are one house payment away from homelessness, even if our kids can't read and our asses are getting so big they have their own zip codes, it's comforting to know we are at least in the best place on earth. There is America, and there is the rest of the world—envious and plotting to bring us down and "steal our freedom."[69]

From his own wide-ranging research in rural America, Robert Wuthnow noted a strong feeling that Washington and big corporations were helping themselves while the "small guy" suffered and was disrespected. He quoted Kentuckian Dee Davis of the Center for Rural Strategies: "A lot of us in rural areas, our ears are tuned to intonation. We think people are talking down to us. What ends up happening is that we don't focus on the policy—we focus on the tones, the references, the culture."[70]

We might also consider two takes on Wisconsin. In her study of rural Wisconsin, Katherine Cramer Walsh found a widespread resentment of urban officials and a feeling that rural residents were neglected and subject to negative stereotypes (which many fired right back at public officials via their own stereotypes like lack of common sense).[71] As part of a televised road trip on a garishly multicolored bike, the engaging British artist Grayson Perry did some much briefer, but also revealing, digging in Wisconsin. In Minocqua, a Republican area in the northern part of the state, he met a group of fairly elderly and comfortably off Republican women: "I am very much Republican," one woman declared. "I'll be out there [on the 2020 campaign trail] with my candidate signs and things, and someone I do not know will come right up into my face to give me some kind of reason why I'm terribly wrong."[72]

That made Perry curious. "What do they think you're like, what gets them so hot under the collar?" he asked. Another woman chimed in: "They probably think that we're uninformed, that we're backwoods maybe. We don't read newspapers, we don't get television." Then the first woman resumed: "The word that comes out and it's over and over is 'racist,' because every one of us, being white, living here in northern Wisconsin in a district that's very Republican, we're somehow racist, and I've never considered that a part of my fabric." This comment prompted a chorus of "Me neither!" Then the first speaker continued, "Right now the white man in America is just being pummeled. 'Oh, you're so awful, you're white privilege!'"

At this point, Perry asked, "Has anyone ever felt ashamed to be American?" eliciting another chorus, this time of "No, never!" Then a third woman spoke, to general approval: "That's one thing you disliked about

Obama. He acted like he was ashamed of us. He was ashamed of what this country stood for. He was ashamed of the people of this country. Obama went around the world and apologized for the United States."

Putting these many academic and more journalistic accounts together, we can get a sense of a landscape where many people feel fairly comprehensively shamed and sometimes neglected—and where they are sensitive to any further shaming for their views or their speech or whatever it might be. When Trump arrived on the political scene, he was a kind of *anti-apologist*—a trait exemplified when Trump condemned the practice of kneeling in the National Football League as part of the Black Lives Matter movement, telling a rally in Tulsa, Oklahoma: "We will never kneel to our great American national anthem, to our great American flag—we will stand proud and we will stand tall."[73] Trump's refusal to be shamed and his failure to apologize for things like his aggressive groping were fully in line with his anti-apologist persona.

While tapping into a great variety of discontents (and boosted by a cyclical economic recovery), there was very little evidence that Trump was fixing underlying problems in the American polity or economy. With the promised revival of American infrastructure never arriving, more than 80 percent of the benefit from Trump's 2017 taxation bill went straight to the wealthiest 1 percent.[74] Trump's health-care reforms made many people in rural areas even more vulnerable than they had been before—adding to their suffering when the coronavirus hit.

Yet it remained the case that any substantial criticism of either Trump or his supporters was fraught with difficulty. Given the central role of shame in fueling the rise of Trump, the common tendency to shame his supporters—as mad, ignorant, racist, or a "basket of deplorables" (in Hillary Clinton's notorious phrase)—risked fueling right-wing sentiments and consolidating his support. This dynamic is part of what made Trump so scary: criticism felt like pouring fuel on the fire. In North Carolina, Trump invited supporters onstage with him to ask the crowd if they looked deplorable.[75] After widespread outrage at Trump's referral to "very fine people on both sides" in Charlottesville, Trump told a rally in Phoenix, Arizona: "The media can attack me but where I draw the line is when they attack you, which is what they do when they attack the decency of our supporters."[76] In an important sense, Trump was *feeding off* criticism, which perhaps helps explain why so many of his critics felt so desperate (and turned up the heat). But shame not only bounced off Trump; he also knew how to turn it to his advantage.

There was considerable hypocrisy here too. During the Covid pandemic, Olivia Troye, a White House aide, reported that Trump had told one task force meeting that the pandemic was helping him in relation to his supporters because "I don't have to shake hands with those disgusting people." Ms. Troye added later: "He talked all the time about the people themselves being disgusting. It was clear that he wanted nothing to do with them."[77] In many ways, Trump fits the model of what Christopher Lasch—back in 1979—described as an increasingly widespread narcissistic personality who was "ravenous for admiration but contemptuous of those he manipulates into providing it."[78] How Trump—or anyone else—was going to be nourished by the adulation of those who were themselves despised remains unclear.[79]

Yet Trump's ability to entrance his audience remained. Even his rambling and sometimes ungrammatical style, so often mocked by well-educated critics, seemed to carry the message that he did not think he was any better than "ordinary folk." He also knew intuitively that if you can make people feel good—and in particular if you can take away people's sense of shame about how they live and what they think—then that puts you in a position of very considerable power. Through talking down and then talking up America, through serial scapegoating, through convincingly portraying himself as less politically correct and more objectionable than his audience, and above all perhaps through never apologizing, Trump displayed an almost unerring instinct for the political manipulation of both shamelessness and shame.

10

Brexit

SHORTLY AFTER THE UK'S 2016 "Brexit" vote, UK Independence Party leader Nigel Farage told the European Parliament, "When I came here 17 years ago and said I wanted to lead a campaign to get Britain to leave the European Union, you all laughed at me. Well, I have to say, you're not laughing now, are you?"[1] While Farage was probably underestimating European bemusement at the Brexit he'd helped to precipitate, it's remarkable how frequently this trope of "you're not laughing now" has recurred. From Brexit to Trump to civil wars and even genocides, shame has often been hyped through some reference to *ridicule*, a move that invites a *silencing of the ridicule*—perhaps through laughter, perhaps through violence, or perhaps through Arendt's "combination of horror and laughter."[2]

Farage's remarks reflected a wider process of hyping and then reversing shame that mirrors right-wing populism across the Atlantic. Both Farage and Boris Johnson claimed the Brexit vote reversed a shameful subordination of Britain to Brussels, and a narrow majority of voters backed Brexit. Farage explicitly referred to the day of the Brexit vote as "Independence Day," and later Johnson cranked up the hyperbole, claiming that under Prime Minister Theresa May (who was trying to push through a slightly "softer" version of Brexit) "we are truly headed for the status of colony."[3] Johnson had also proclaimed before the referendum that "Napoleon, Hitler, various people tried this [unifying Europe], and it ends tragically. The EU is an attempt to do this by different methods."[4] Showing an impressive grasp of history, Johnson added that the EU was "pursuing a similar goal to Hitler in trying to create a powerful superstate."[5]

The economic case for Brexit was always thin with the great majority of published papers suggesting that the impact would be negative—and strong negative impacts did in fact materialize.[6] A strong argument can be made that most Leave supporters were voting *against* their own interests. As a solution for poverty and inequality, cutting the UK out of Europe was at best tilting at windmills—no more logical, perhaps, than solving U.S. poverty by walling the country off from Mexico. The strong element of irrationality in Brexit recalls Thomas Frank's analysis of poorer people supporting the Republicans in the United States, particularly since those areas of the UK that voted most strongly in favor of leaving the EU were also the areas set to suffer most severely from the loss of European markets and subsidies.[7] Of the 65 most disadvantaged areas in Britain (indicated in the UK's 2017 *Social Mobility Commission*), fully 60 had voted Leave.[8] Moreover, many people appear to have *consciously* voted against their own interests (or at least appear to have been willing to embrace the damage): one survey in July 2017 suggested that fully 61 percent of Leave voters would accept "significant damage to the economy" from Brexit as a "price worth paying" for leaving the EU, while 39 percent went so far as to say that the loss of their own job or that of a family member would be a price they were willing to pay.[9]

Clearly something was at stake here beyond money and livelihoods, and sometimes the manipulation of emotion was openly acknowledged. Arron Banks, the main funder of the Leave campaign, said it had embraced "an American-style media approach. What they said early on was 'Facts don't work,' and that's it. The Remain campaign featured fact, fact, fact, fact, fact, fact. It just doesn't work. You have got to connect with people emotionally. It's the Trump success."[10]

As with Trump, the Brexiteers' emphasis on national shame and humiliation was a contentious interpretation that set up a particular "solution." In his excellent book *Heroic Failure*, Irish writer Fintan O'Toole referred to "the strange sense of imaginary oppression that underlies Brexit."[11] Tellingly, there were no Brussels prisons to empty or liberate. Even the many deprivations allegedly imposed by "Eurocrats" were largely phantom, and after Brexit "prawn cocktail flavor crisps could not be restored to the millions of children craving them for the simple reason that they had never ceased to be available."[12] Perhaps there was something reassuring in the trivial nature—and generally the phoniness—of many of the accusations that were leveled at the EU; at times, this was Brussels as scary movie, as if part of the pleasure lay in knowing the "bad guy" wasn't actually real.

Revealingly, when Johnson was working as a journalist in Brussels, he had boosted his profile by playing up the EU's alleged attempts to control the size or shape of British bananas, sausages, and condoms.[13] Johnson's obsession was matched in much of the popular press, and in 1994 *The Sun* led with the headline "Now They've Really Gone Bananas" and the more suggestive "Euro Bosses Ban Too Bendy Ones."[14] Of course, Sigmund Freud famously said that sometimes a cigar is just a cigar, and the same is presumably true of a banana. But if it's a banana *and* a sausage *and* a condom, we might want to think again. ("Sausage wars" subsequently reappeared in a dispute with the EU over chilled meats entering Northern Ireland.) We've seen how James Gilligan and others have noted that shame is often structured along gendered lines— and these obsessions suggest that Brexit was a notable example. The message seems to have been that a once proud and virile nation was being dragged down by the faceless bureaucrats of Brussels, so that even the famous British sausage was no longer safe. One is reminded of Arendt's observation that while reality itself is often unpalatable and hard to believe, lies have often been carefully crafted with a view to making them credible.[15]

Nor did the loaded symbolism stop at the bendy ones. Brussels bureaucrats wanted to force donkeys to wear nappies on British beaches, it was claimed. And those in peril on the sea, the public was told, included British trawlermen under threat from emasculating EU-imposed hairnets.[16] Of course, Johnson and the rest of the press—perhaps in a very British way—were half joking. But only half. The sense of endangered masculinity was a recurrent theme—and it mirrored some of Trump's erotic investment in his "impenetrable, physical, tall, powerful, beautiful" wall. In Brexit as in Trumpism, concerns around masculinity blended neatly and dangerously with a sense of hurt imperial pride. And as Johnson bemoaned the EU's fictional assault on crisps and sausages,[17] it was almost as if the British working man was arriving home after a long day only to find the EU telling him he couldn't eat his favorite foods or put his feet on the table. Somehow the target of Margaret Thatcher's concern with Britain's "nanny state" in the 1980s had migrated across the Channel to Brussels. If Britannia could no longer rule the waves, then perhaps it could at least waive the rules.

Alongside all this instrumentalization of shame with all its heavily gendered overtones, there was also a notable *shamelessness* around Brexit. In fact, Johnson—like Trump—seemed to *embody* an escape from shame, making a show of independence from haircuts, suits, and social conventions; at the extreme, he made a virtue out of vice. As with Trump's electoral success in the United States, a *theater of shamelessness* seems to have offered a kind of vicarious and symbolic escape from shame. Trump's sexual abusiveness found a distant and milder echo in Johnson's sexual irresponsibility.

At times, Johnson portrayed himself as *thrillingly* irresponsible, and on BBC radio he talked about his time as a journalist in Brussels where he was getting awards for attacking European bureaucracy. Noting how pressures for "a single polity" were generating "the most fantastic strains in the Conservative party," Johnson confided:

> So everything I wrote from Brussels, I found I was just chucking these rocks over the garden wall and I listened to this amazing crash from the greenhouse next door over in England as everything I wrote from Brussels was having this amazing, explosive effect on the Tory party, and it really gave me this I suppose rather weird sense of power.[18]

You would think such a confession would be damaging: it is hard to imagine that a sensible electorate would really want a leader who shamelessly boasted about his appetite for destruction. Yet Johnson not only helped steer through the Brexit referendum vote but also won the December 2019 elections with a comfortable majority.

Like Trump (with whom he shared that slightly rebellious hair), Johnson managed to position his "honesty" as an antidote to excessive "political correctness," striking a chord with many people. In September 2019, one newsagent in London, who had businesses in Yorkshire and family from Pakistan, told me that he was a strong supporter of Brexit and that he hoped Boris could "bulldoze" through the Brexit process and end the uncertainty hampering business decisions. "But don't you think he's a bit racist?" I asked, mentioning the time when Johnson compared women in hijabs to pillboxes. "*Everybody's* racist," the newsagent replied quickly. "He's just a bit more open and honest about it. That thing with the pillbox is just a joke. I call my friends 'Pakis.' Does that make me a racist? You can't say anything these days! You can't even give a sweet to a child."

The conversation was interesting to me partly because I share at least the frustration with over-caution and over-regulation. In academia, for example, students have to fill in a long "ethics" form if they want to ask someone a research question. Aggravating as such red tape can be, most of the UK's form-filling had been generated in London rather than Brussels. But bashing Brussels offered an exciting release.

Back in January 2019, at a time when Johnson was leading the criticism of Prime Minister May for being too soft on Brexit, I got talking with a middle-aged couple in a café in Witney, Oxfordshire (the constituency of former prime minister David Cameron until he resigned following the Leave referendum victory in June 2016). I mentioned Johnson's "crashing glass" confession, and the woman observed with some affection, "He's a naughty boy!" I said the greenhouse story reminded me of the Bullingdon Club at Oxford University, an expensive dining society (of which Cameron and Johnson were both members) that had a reputation for trashing student rooms and restaurants (sometimes offering on-the-spot compensation). "Yes," the man in the café chipped in with enthusiasm. "Boris and Cameron were at Eton together and they used to wind each other up. I'd vote for Boris!" In some ways, the conversation recalls Jill Locke's comment on Trump: "the insult that he is a child is misplaced; his childishness is precisely the investment." If a complicated sense of loss has been evident among the (disproportionately aged) supporters of Brexit, the boyish exuberance of a Boris may even have offered a glimpse of what was slipping away.

In *Heroic Failure*, O'Toole addresses the wider phenomenon of upper-class arrogance in the UK, observing that it was "easy to turn patrician languor into a sense that the whole thing is a jolly game. Each is a way of saying that none of it really matters, and of brushing off any real responsibility for the consequences."[19] In Brexit itself, the appetite for destruction does appear to have found an enjoyable outlet. A shameless, self-destructive, and even nihilistic element among the "Leavers" was encapsulated when Boris Johnson—at that time foreign secretary and a leading "Brexiteer" among the Conservatives, the UK's traditional party of business—responded to UK-based industrialists' fears about losing access to European markets with a less-than-diplomatic "Fuck business!"[20]

Another self-destructive strain revealed itself in Leavers' lack of concern for the strong possibility that Brexit—for all the trumpeting of British nationalism that infused it—would actually *break up* the UK, spurring Scottish succession and jeopardizing the Northern Ireland peace in the interests of what was often a very English nationalism.[21] Survey data showed a very strong link between those who identified as "English only" and hostility to the EU.[22]

Alongside such reckless appetites, the *details* of Brexit were frequently neglected. Cameron himself had no stomach for steering through the exit he had precipitated, and Johnson declined to put himself forward after Cameron's resignation. But the drama of the hunt was thrilling indeed. O'Toole noted:

> The idea of eccentricity—though closely hedged in by class and gender—has a long history as a signifier of English freedom. England's glorying in upper-class eccentrics, so the story went, contrasted favourably with the conformism of slavish continentals. . . . The harm*ful* eccentric is a construct to which the very English language seems resistant. But the harm is all too real: the indulgence of eccentricity brought clownish absurdity and self-centred recklessness into the heart of political power.[23]

Echoes of empire mixed in with the longing for lost freedoms. In *The Origins of Totalitarianism*, Arendt put her finger on some of this when she said British colonial officials found in the colonies a "conservation, or perhaps petrification, of boyhood noblesse."[24]

Brexit Britain saw a prominent role for men who did not quite want to grow out of their Oxford undergraduate gowns. The city of Oxford (where I live and have incidentally clung to my own illusion of eternal youth in the college football team) is what they call a "Remainer stronghold." Yet having earlier played no small part in grooming Arendt's manchild for empire, Oxford would also strongly shape Brexit. Some small portion of this was Oxford-as-provocation (as when the UK Independence Party's Douglas Carswell boasted that his party was "not the private property of a small clique in London who went to the same Oxbridge colleges").[25] Then there was Oxford-as-school-for-Brexiteers. Jacob Rees-Mogg, a key campaigner for Brexit, went to Oxford, as did Dan Hannan, an early opponent of European membership. Taking over as prime minister from Oxford-educated Cameron, the Oxford-educated Theresa May embraced the cause of "getting Brexit done" before resigning as Conservative Party leader in June 2019 when Oxford-educated Johnson took over. Of the seven men who survived the first round of the subsequent Tory leadership at the time, no less than six had studied at Oxford.[26]

Simon Kuper (who himself arrived at Oxford as a student in 1988) highlighted the culture in the Oxford Union society in particular: "You won debates not by boring the audience with detail, but with jokes and ad hominem jibes. Almost all aspiring Tory politicians passed through the Union . . . the Union favoured debating skills and ambition without a cause." When it came to Oxford, Johnson's shamelessness was exhibited not just in his actions but in his eagerness to boast about them. Kuper notes:

> In any essay for The Oxford Myth (1988), a book edited by his sister Rachel, Johnson advised aspiring student politicians to assemble "a disciplined and deluded collection of stooges" to get out the vote. "Lonely girls from the women's colleges" who "back their largely male candidates with a porky decisiveness" were particularly useful, he wrote. "For these young women, machine politics offers human friction and warmth." . . . Johnson added: "The tragedy of the stooge

is that . . . he wants so much to believe that his relationship with the candidate is special that he shuts out the truth. The terrible art of the candidate is to coddle the self-deception of the stooge."[27]

The passage captures the peculiar mix of ambition, misogyny, and secret contempt for one's supporters that has often been evident in right-wing populism, whether in the UK or other countries.[28] It might take us back to Trump, for example, and to Christopher Lasch's 1979 observation that the narcissist is "ravenous for admiration but contemptuous of those he manipulates into providing it." Johnson's shameless dissimulation—an honesty-about-dishonesty—was itself a demonstration of arrogance and power. Yet even when Johnson was revealed to have written two articles, one in favor of Brexit and one (unpublished) against,[29] this did not seem to hurt him much.

O'Toole brilliantly dissected the casual destructiveness and habits of self-harm in imperial and post-imperial Britain, citing Stephanie Barczewinski's comment that "the highest form of English heroism is stoicism in the face of failure,"[30] as well as George Orwell's observation that "the most stirring battle-poem in English [Tennyson's "The Charge of the Light Brigade"] is all about a brigade of cavalry which charged in the wrong direction," and the poet John Betjeman's gloomy invitation: "Come friendly bombs and fall on Slough! It isn't fit for humans now."[31] (One might add to this impressive list the words of British singer-songwriter Morrissey, whose inspired 1988 hymn to miserabilism *Every Day Is Like Sunday* has him mourning the seaside town "that they forgot to bomb," before upgrading Betjeman: "Come, come, nuclear war!") O'Toole noted further:

> In the imperial imagination, there are only two states: dominant and submissive, colonizer and colonized. . . . In reality, Britain went from being an imperial power to being a reasonably ordinary but privileged Western European country. In the apparition conjured by Brexit, it went straight from being the colonizer to being the colonized.[32]

O'Toole argued that as openly expressed racism became more taboo (and politicians distanced themselves, for example, from Enoch

Powell's notorious speech about the "rivers of blood" that immigration would bring to the UK), the EU stepped into the breach and offered an outlet for "sublimated or displaced rage at Them."[33]

This fusion was symbolized by the migrants/refugees in Calais, painted as an existential threat that (despite France's far-reaching role in British border control while Britain was *inside* the EU) would somehow be addressed by *leaving* the EU. Calais was a major focus of popular press coverage in the run-up to Brexit, and I had the chance to do some research in Calais's so-called "jungle" camp just after the Brexit vote in the summer of 2016.[34] Right-wing populism's instrumentalization of suffering in Calais depended on a number of stereotypes about the migrants—a highly contentious and shaming script in which migrants were some combination of *violent, terrorists, disease-ridden, desperate, crazy, lazy,* and *driven by the lure of welfare "benefits."* Yet it soon became clear that most of the problems presented as *emanating from* the migrants could actually be traced to *the shameful way they were treated.* In general, poor conditions for migrants and the destruction of part of the camp in February–March 2016 helped create the image of infighting, disease, and desperation that made Calais such a potent political symbol for the Brexiteers. This violence was part of a joint British and French attempt to deter migration and—in line with Arendt's concept of "action as propaganda"—helped create the sense of "threat" that was used to justify the violence. This in turn helped the construction of Brexit as a (magical) way of ending the threat and restoring Britain's proud history as a sovereign nation.

For many Leavers, Brexit was an escape from shame into pride. But Brexit also produced an additional layer of shame and shaming. As in the United States, part of this was highlighting the stupidity and intolerance of those who were said to be so possessed by xenophobia that they voted against their own interests.

Both shame and shamelessness were manipulated when Brexit was positioned as a solution for popular frustrations. Yet there was nothing in Brexit itself that could realistically address these frustrations or the socioeconomic conditions that gave rise to them. Britain is one of the most unequal societies in Europe; and after the 2007–8 financial crisis, wage inequality actually grew rapidly.[35] Popular anger at the financial sector was high, and a widespread disillusionment with politicians in London only grew worse with post–financial crisis policies of austerity that hit poorer people—and poorer local authorities—particularly hard. Yet over a long period, radical politicians committed to redressing the balance have generally struggled to gain power, and indeed the Conservatives have won all four general elections since the financial crisis occurred. While many people think of power as seesawing between Labour and Conservative, it is notable that at the time of going to press the Conservative Party has been in office for all but thirteen of the last forty-six years.

It is hard to escape the impression that the Europhobia and related "enemy definitions" informing Brexit offered to extend a long Tory tradition of using nationalism to distract people from underlying grievances. Part of this maneuver was tapping into some rather deep reservoirs of shame that had been imposed on millions of ordinary people through a combination of harsh policies and harsh words. Brexit fitted into a longer habit—in a way a kind of "double game"[36]—in which shame was imposed with one hand (for example, through unemployment, austerity, and the language of "skivers" and "scroungers") alongside promises to restore a sense of pride through some kind of belligerence in relation to external or internal "enemies." A significant part of the impetus for Brexit came from an alliance between the shameless and shamed, a toxic blend of calculation and desperation. In this, too, it resembled Trumpism.

Access to History—and the Shame of "Nonexistence"

In his insightful 2011 book *Chavs: The Demonization of the Working Class*, Owen Jones observed:

> Working-class identity was something that used to be central to the lives of people living in communities like [east London's] Barking

and Dagenham. It gave a sense of belonging and of self-worth, as well as a feeling of solidarity with other local people. When this pride was stripped away, it left a vacuum that the waking beast of English nationalism has partly filled.[37]

Both the right-wing British National Party (BNP) and the UK Independence Party (UKIP) (which rose as the BNP fell) had no plan for recovery beyond "the free market." Instead, they blamed foreigners for the shortage of housing and jobs—fears that were also whipped up in much of the media.[38] Jones noted further:

> The rise of the far right is a reaction to the marginalization of working-class people. It is a product of politicians' refusal to address working-class concerns, particularly affordable housing and a supply of decent, secure jobs. It has been fueled by a popular perception that Labour had abandoned the people it was created to represent.[39]

That perception was exemplified by one fairly elderly resident of Jaywick, Essex, who told the *Guardian*'s John Harris in 2014, "We're a backwater, ain't we, that nobody gives a shit about.... Bloody Blair, he went more bloody Tory than the bloody Tories." After this, the man declared that he was going to vote for Johnson in the upcoming elections and that "I want to get out of bloody Europe." When Harris asked what Johnson and Brexit were going to do for the country, the man replied, "Well, I don't know—as long as he gets us out of the mire."[40]

Adrift and abandoned, many people seemed to be clutching at anything vaguely resembling a lifeboat. When sociologist Lisa Mckenzie researched views on Brexit among relatively poor people in east London, she got to know one woman with two children, a woman who was made homeless in 2013 and had recently been told she would probably wait twelve to fifteen years for social housing. Disillusioned with normal party politics, the woman had been energized by the Leave campaign. Asked whether she wasn't worried that Brexit would make things worse, the young woman replied, "I can't see how it can get much worse for me, but at least it's a change, it's something."[41]

Fueled by neglect, an underlying anger and resentment were also stoked by disparagement. In a classic case of adding insult to injury, pronouncements by politicians and journalists loaded a heavy burden of shame onto those already experiencing the shame of poverty and abandonment. At least three elements to this can be distinguished.

First, there was the depiction of working-class people as lazy[42]— manifested in that focus by politicians and right-wing media pundits on so-called "skivers" and "scroungers." Such labels were widely resented, particularly when good jobs were scarce, as Mary O'Hara documented in her 2014 book *Austerity Bites*:

> That the government (and mainstream politicians generally) were guilty of a kind of "profound disconnect" was a sentiment shared by people at the sharp end of austerity all over the UK. Everywhere I went terms such as "they live on another planet" and "they have no idea what it's really like" were used by people genuinely baffled by why so much vitriol was being levelled at them while they were trying to find a job. The notion of unemployment as a "lifestyle choice," as the Chancellor George Osborne was so fond of referring to it, was laughable to the interviewees. And, they asked, when it was an international banking crisis and unprecedented recession that had wreaked havoc on the economy, how was it the fault of people who were out of work that they couldn't get a job? Were they merely convenient scapegoats for a failed system?[43]

A second kind of shaming had a more racial and cultural dimension. Particularly given the rise of the BNP and then UKIP (and to the extent that scapegoating was being done *by* working-class people rather than simply being directed *at them*), there was an increased opportunity for a kind of "secondary" shaming of the kind commonly directed at Trump supporters—notably a shaming for being racist. As Owen Jones noted:

> The BNP has thrived in traditionally white working-class areas with a long history of returning Labour candidates. Little wonder that the rise of the BNP has reinforced one of the popular "chav" caricatures

of the white working class: a beer-bellied skinhead on a council estate, moaning about hordes of immigrants "coming in and taking our jobs."[44]

Writer and academic John Rapley observed in the *Guardian* in 2017 that the narrative of a meritocratic society making scientific progress "made no room for the losers of this order, whose resentments were derided as being a reflection of their boorish and retrograde character—which is to say, their fundamental vice."[45] Jones also commented that while "ruling elites have made it clear that there is nothing of worth in working-class culture, we have been (rightly) urged to celebrate the identities of minority groups."[46] He argued that this encouraged many white working-class people to develop similar notions of ethnic pride.

A third element in the shaming discourse directed at working-class people, paradoxically, was the idea that they *did not exist*. In her studies of working-class communities in east London and ex-mining towns of Nottinghamshire, Lisa Mckenzie noted not just a sense of being "left behind" but a sense of "not existing."[47] This might remind us of Fanon's reference to "A feeling of inferiority? No, a feeling of non-existence," or perhaps Joe Bageant's reflection that invisibility in America was "the purest snub of all." Owen Jones quoted a 1994 *Times* column by Janet Daley: "I fear long after Britain has become a successful multi-racial society it will be plagued by this diminishing (but increasingly alienated) detritus of the Industrial Revolution."[48] He noted further, "Pretending that the working class is no more—'disappearing' it, if you like—has proved particularly politically useful."[49] Here as so often, action appears over the long term to have served as some of the best propaganda: for part of the force behind the idea of the disappearing working classes was precisely Thatcher's attack on the unions and the working class more generally in the 1980s. A sense of disappearing could easily feed into hostility toward immigrants, moreover. One woman in east London who had turned away from Labour told Mckenzie that a Leave vote would stop the inflow of migrants and that there was a "big plan ... to get rid of us ... and replace us with cheaper workers."[50]

Labour's Tony Blair, prime minister from 1997 to 2007, claimed to occupy the *moderate middle ground* in politics, sometimes pointing to reactionary forces who stood in the way of modernization and globalization.[51] From Blair's point of view, the ultimate and most extreme representative of these forces was the terrorist. Of course, the 1990s was also the period when Francis Fukuyama was famously invoking "The end of history," and many saw liberal democracy as the only option in a post–Cold War world.[52] Yet if all decent and reasonable people were held to agree on the (globalizing) status quo, it followed logically that anyone dissenting was neither decent nor reasonable—either that, or they did not actually *exist*. Chantal Mouffe's 2005 book *On the Political* seems to have anticipated some of the factors energizing Brexit as well as Trump: she argued presciently that "consensus" politics in which there was no meaningful clash of left and right tended only to suppress passions and antagonisms rather than abolishing them, raising the danger that "democratic confrontation" will be "replaced by a confrontation between essentialist forms of identification or non-negotiable moral values."[53]

Given the multiple layers of shame that were brewing, the allure of an escape from shame—an escape into power, sovereignty, and voice while passing on shame to a range of others—appears to have been very strong indeed.

Again, Arendt can help us here. Noting the "frustration, resentment, and blind hatred"[54] of those who embraced some kind of terror tactics (whether from the left or the right) in the aftermath of World War I, she discerned "a kind of political expressionism which used bombs to express oneself, which watched delightedly the publicity given to resounding deeds and was absolutely willing to pay the price of life for having succeeded in forcing *the recognition of one's existence* on the normal strata of society."[55] She added that many people wanted "access to history even at the price of destruction."[56] That phrase might make us think back to the Capitol invasion of January 2021 as well as Brexit. Of course, Brexit was a vote and not a "terror tactic," but the lure of "access to history"— even at a high price—remained considerable. Politics professor Tony Wright gave this assessment of Brexit:

> There is a sense of powerlessness that mocks the self-governing promise of democracy. The EU referendum seemed to offer an

opportunity to reclaim lost power—over our laws, over our rulers, over our borders—that was eagerly taken, despite the authoritative warnings about the dire economic consequences of doing so.[57]

In Stoke-on-Trent, the Midlands city registering the highest "Leave" majority,[58] Reverend Geoff Eze observed:

> The city now finds itself suffering from some of the highest unemployment rates in Britain. The decent jobs, which once gave people dignity, have trickled away—replaced by insecure, poorly paid work in services and distribution. The pubs, the labour clubs and the mutual societies that tethered these working communities together—that's gone too. For decade, after decade, after decade, the working men and women of Stoke-on-Trent felt forgotten. But Brexit changed all that.[59]

Stoke reporter Phil Corrigan pointed to the vague hope that voting Leave would somehow bring industry back to the city. Yet the Stoke-based British Ceramic Confederation was meanwhile pleading for tariff-free access to the European single market.[60]

Alongside these various complex manipulations of different types of shame was a shamelessness that was made up partly of the recklessness that we have already remarked upon and partly of a fairly naked pursuit of self-interest. Brexit served the political ambitions of Johnson and a range of followers who it helped to elevate, including the next prime minister, Liz Truss. Beyond this, there was the wider function of channeling popular grievances into jingoistic gestures. Then there was the hope that Brexit would allow the pursuit of a still-more-unfettered economy with relatively weak regulation of finance, labor, and the environment (a prospect made more attractive by the threat of tighter regulation of finance, including money laundering, from Europe). Revealingly, hedge fund specialists were particularly keen on Brexit, fearing increased EU regulation.[61] O'Toole commented:

> For the cynical leaders of the Brexit campaign, the freedom they desire is the freedom to dismantle the environmental, social and labour protections that they call "red tape." They want to sever the last restraints on the very market forces that have caused the pain. . . . On

the lunatic fringe of Brexit—a fringe long enough to get in the eyes of rational governance—there is a belief that England can find itself only when the remnants of socialism and liberalism are burned off in the crucible of pain. Suffering is not a side effect of the great project; it *is* the medicine.[62]

Another element of shamelessness resided in Brexiteers' attempts to insulate themselves from the looming costs of Brexit. In June 2018, Somerset Capital Management (co-owned by Jacob Rees-Mogg) launched a Dublin-based tax-efficient "collected asset vehicle" investment structure so that it could continue to operate within the EU regulations. Soon after, Rees-Mogg launched a second Dublin-based fund "to meet demand from international investors concerned about the effects of Brexit." In a typically pithy comment, O'Toole noted, "For all the talk of national sovereignty, in his [Rees-Mogg's] real world it is the super-rich individual who exerts a transnational sovereignty. For the gods, there is always an exit—even from Brexit."[63]

Once the Brexit vote was in, shaming took on new—and sometimes more frightening—dimensions. Several layers of shame were now piling on top of each other. In many ways, the Leave vote had the effect of reinforcing preexisting prejudices, with poorer Leave supporters often stereotyped (like Trump supporters) as ignorant, crazy, and racist.[64] In Oxford, it became common to hear well-to-do people refer in anger and frustration to the "idiots"—and sometimes the "racists"—who had voted to leave the European Union. Extreme surprise at the outcome fed into this. Those who had already been shamed and stereotyped were shamed for embracing magical solutions that themselves involved the shaming of various scapegoats. Meanwhile, the shame directed at Leavers offered a clue to the social gulf that helped create the referendum result in the first place.[65]

Any hint of such shaming, meanwhile, was eagerly seized on by Brexit hard-liners, mirroring Trump's pounce on Hillary Clinton's "basket of deplorables" comment. For example, when former Labour Party minister Peter Mandelson said that some Brexiteers "are nationalists in the sense that they hate other countries, and they hate foreigners," the populist *Daily Express* countered with the headline "How Dare He Insult 17m Brexit Voters!" Nikolay Mintchev noted that "the far right can articulate any critical association of Brexit with racism as a sweeping liberal accusation that 'the people' are racist."[66] A commonly expressed idea was that the metropolitan elite—the same people who had been out of touch with the public for decades—were trying to block the "will of the people" now that it had finally been expressed. This feverish political climate was further inflamed by press campaigns against "traitors," "saboteurs," and "enemies of the people."[67] Popular anger that had readily attached itself to Eurocrats and immigrants could turn with similar ease on troublesome judges and foot-dragging MPs.

Meanwhile, the fashion for positioning politics within a shame framework—something to which *both sides* resorted—only hardened the relevant fault lines. While polls did suggest a slight swing back to Remain (which later gathered pace as the effects of Brexit began to bite), remarkably few people changed their minds between the 2016 referendum vote and Britain's departure from the EU in January 2020.[68] In a shaming environment, it would seem, people *dig in*.

Meanwhile, we are seeing what Gordon MacLeod and Martin Jones have called 'a scandalous failure even to begin addressing the very economic and social inequities and the sources of discontent that generated the Brexit revolt in the first place."[69] Indeed, the situation would seem to be even worse than that: for the team that pushed through Brexit have also been pushing through a package of regressive measures—not only of further liberalizing markets and removing environmental and labor protections but also of cutting overseas aid, ramping up nuclear weapons spending, and criminalizing protest. When the coronavirus hit, a reverence for the free market and a sense of British exceptionalism both proved to be sources of vulnerability, with the government (insofar as it favored "herd immunity") sometimes appearing to *welcome infection* as a way to strengthen the immunity of the "herd." By

September 2022, the British economy was being plunged into a major crisis as even international markets rebelled at the Liz Truss government's plan for major tax cuts.

In *Moneyland*, an investigation into the huge volume of capital that is laundered (not least in London) and/or put into tax havens, Oliver Bullough observed that the Leave campaign's clever slogan "Take Back Control" was actually pointed at the wrong target. The EU had been helping a wide range of countries work together against unaccountable wealth, making it harder for crooks and thieves to keep their fortunes.[70] By distancing itself, Britain was only widening the loopholes. As Bullough noted:

> The real threat to the liberal order is not the poor immigrants, but unaccountable money. Offshore bandits are looting the world, and this looting is undermining democracy, driving inequality and sucking ever greater volumes of wealth into Moneyland, where we can't follow it. The solution is not to pull up the drawbridge, not to demonise foreigners who flee their collapsing countries in the hope of a better life in the lands where their nation's money has found a home.[71]

Meanwhile, important democratic norms were being eroded. Like the United States, the UK saw an attempt to construct a kind of "charismatic" authority: an emphasis on executive authority; a temporary suspension ("proroguing") of Parliament to push through "the will of the people"; a prime minister ready to tell Parliament that the best way to avoid further deaths like that of Labour MP Jo Cox (murdered by a far-right extremist) was to push through Brexit as quickly as possible; and a populist contempt for the truth that simultaneously purported to be a kind of "honesty." To some degree, the ruthless *means* adopted in the name of "getting Brexit done" may have become *an end in themselves*—or at least a means to *some ends other than Brexit*.

For "Remainers" like myself, there was the awkward but unalterable fact that a majority of those voting in the referendum had voted to leave the EU. After that vote, many opponents of Brexit voiced the hope of a second referendum that would take account of the *terms* of a proposed

Brexit deal. But much of the UK press was mobilizing against this idea—and the shaming of "Remoaners" was spilling over into warnings of violence.

To a degree, Brexit had channeled shame into anger. But this anger was volatile, and the search for internal enemies was widening. In December 2018, *The Sun* asked, "Do you think Brits are too reserved for civil disorder?" adding that a second vote would unleash a "tsunami of rage" and citing the "febrile atmosphere of the [2016] referendum, during which Jo Cox MP was heartbreakingly murdered."[72] In January 2019, Prime Minister May declared that a second referendum vote on the terms of a Brexit deal "could damage social cohesion by undermining faith in our democracy," a point immediately escalated in the *Daily Express* front-page headline: "Second Vote Will Lead to CIVIL UNREST."[73] In the combustible atmosphere of the time, such media interventions felt more like a threat than a prediction.

Back in that upmarket Witney café, I showed my friendly middle-aged couple a copy of the *Daily Express* with that "civil unrest" headline and asked what they thought. "Hopefully we're not like the French!" the woman said. "Probably the last time it happened was over the poll tax." I found this somewhat reassuring but then she added, "I don't know if there'll be civil unrest, but I think there *should be!* It's a democracy, we've had a vote. We're not yet doing Trumpism! It's true that people didn't know exactly what they were voting for, but still."

Of course, we know that support for Brexit was strong not just in poorer regions but also in many wealthier areas, particularly in the countryside.[74] Even so, amid the overpriced Black Forest gateaus and mille-feuille of the Cotswolds, that call for civil unrest felt deeply jarring. It also resonated with a major *Future of England* survey in 2019, which revealed that when Leave voters were asked if violence against MPs was "a risk but worth it to take back control," fully 71 percent agreed.[75]

When the couple left the café, it felt like a very British departure. "Nice talking with you!" the woman said. "When we see you next, there might be no windows left on the high-street!"

We laughed a little nervously.

More crashing glass.

11

Shame and Colonialism

THIS CHAPTER LOOKS at shame and shamelessness when it comes to colonialism, with a focus on the United States, France, and the UK. While a comprehensive survey would be a huge task, here I focus on a rather particular argument. To some degree, there has been shame around harm done. But this type of shame has often been treated as a grave threat that must be energetically warded off. One manifestation of this warding off has been the kind of "anti-apologist" politics that we saw with Trump. Along with shame—and potential shame—around harm done, there has been shame around *loss of* preeminence or *loss of* empire. This has often been stronger than shame around abuse. Indeed, the priority to shame-around-weakness that was manifest in prominent individuals like Trump seems to extend to the way that many countries deal with their colonial or imperial past. Meanwhile, like shame around colonial harm, shame around loss of imperial preeminence has often been instrumentalized in politics. These twin instrumentalizations of shame have tended to feed racism and violence in both the past and the present.

United States: Shame and Backlash

A little more than a year after Trump became president and some two years before widespread protests at police racism and violence erupted across the United States, I found myself talking with an amiable storekeeper in an old mining town in America's Midwest. A pale and well-preserved cowboy-hatted man of retirement age who had spent much of his career in a non-combat role in the military, he was now selling paintings, models, and other artifacts related in some way to Native Americans.

Business was slow, he said—and soon we were on to politics. The storekeeper quickly told me he regarded Trump as a very dangerous leader before launching into a surprising attack on the U.S. company Halliburton and all the lucrative and corrupt contracting that had taken place around the U.S.-led invasion and occupation of Iraq.[1]

The cowboy hat seemed perhaps an odd touch in a Native American artifacts store. But having myself written about the many downsides of the "war on terror," I was beginning to warm to this courteous and intelligent gentleman. I asked if Native Americans showed much interest in his merchandise. Only a little, he said, adding, "No American feels good about the way the Indians were treated. It's the same with the blacks. Bringing them over as slaves from Africa was so wrong!"

That seemed to suggest an appropriate—if rather abrupt—sense of shame. But soon our conversation took on a more disturbing aspect. Still on the theme of African Americans, the storekeeper noted:

> I don't think they'll ever forgive us. They are pretty much waiting to take their revenge. They're all on welfare now. The Mexicans will probably join in as well. I expect this country to be the shortest-living country in history! . . . There are so many guns around and that doesn't help.

My host (who turned out to be a former gun dealer himself) was now getting into his stride and pretty soon—via Trump and the danger of world war—we were on to World War II. Apparently, this could easily have been avoided: "Hitler was one crazy guy. His big mistake was that he should have taken Africa. Everyone would have been pretty happy with that! And that's some nice property for someone, great national parks."

It felt like we had traveled some distance from a comfortable condemnation of Trump and profiteering in Iraq to the fear of "revenge" for slavery and now the suggestion that Hitler should have been bought off with a slice of prize Africa. As the encounter became more and more unsettling, it reminded me that startling views on race and the wider world—and bizarre readings of history—are by no means confined to Trump supporters: sometimes it feels too convenient to take all the "bad" instincts and shove them onto Trump and his followers. More than this, the conversation illustrated the complexity of shame dynamics. Notably, it suggested that even *appropriate* feelings of shame can feed into fear and prejudice, with fear of backlash playing a key role.

Fear of backlash or revenge implies that some sense of shame is lurking somewhere. But it also tends quickly to squash any incipient sense of shame. In the imagination at least, the victim quickly becomes the perpetrator. Addressing the issue of "white fragility,"[2] clinical psychologist Jane Caflisch commented:

> When something we have said or done is described as "racist" we may feel attacked in a total way, to our core; and may perceive whoever was hurt by our words or actions—with their "accusing eyes" reflecting back an image of ourselves that we don't want to acknowledge as true—as the *actual* persecutor.[3]

Writers like Frantz Fanon and Joel Kovel have suggested that colonialism was informed by an attempt to keep at bay the shame of the "primitive" and disavowed self through projecting it onto those who were colonized.[4] More practical fears of revenge may come into play too. Fear of reprisals sometimes *accompanied* colonial violence, helping to legitimize the decimation of the Native American population (at least in the eyes of some perpetrators).[5] Commenting on militias' "policing" of the U.S. southern border in his 2019 book *The End of the Myth*, Greg Grandin notes, "Vigilantes often describe themselves as the rear guard of the Mexican American War of 1846–48, standing against an enemy they believe is intent on retaking land they lost at the end of that conflict."[6] In the contemporary fear of "replacement" expressed by white nationalists, we may again detect some element of repositioning the victim as the perpetrator.

We might also consider the United States' mass incarceration here. While there are many causes of this ongoing scandal, fear of revenge should not be discounted. In her book *The New Jim Crow*, Michelle Alexander has shown how a highly racialized system of mass imprisonment—itself involving a massive imposition of shame—has origins in slavery and in a widespread fear of Black rage and violence that persisted among white people long after slavery was abolished.[7] A complex mix of shame and fear seems to have coalesced in the image of the "criminalblackman," a bogeyman who spurred the rise of profitable prisons and proved to be a notable resource in numerous political campaigns including those of Richard Nixon and George H. W. Bush.[8]

In the run-up to the 2020 presidential elections, Trump made a strong appeal to perennial white anxiety—notably through painting Black Lives Matter protests as a threat to white suburbia.[9] While there was a good deal of public outrage and even shame at the death of George Floyd (and many others killed by the police), there was also a growing and sometimes orchestrated fear of protestors' violence, this time recast by President Trump as "terrorism." As Jonathan Metzl put it in the *Boston Review*, "White anxiety inverts traditional notions of aggressor and victim: How can 'we' be the purveyors of privilege or supremacy when we are the ones who are under attack?"[10] As part of the redefinition of victimhood, the slogan "Black Lives Matter" was sometimes refashioned into "Blue Lives Matter" (the police) and "White Lives Matter."

Alongside the flickers of remorse as colonists pushed forward, there was also the exhilaration of expansion and victory. But when this expansion ran into its limits, a different kind of shame became prominent—the shame around *loss of power* and *loss of preeminence*. We get a good sense of this from Richard Hofstadter's classic 1965 study *The Paranoid Style in American Politics*. Hofstadter argued that the endless "victories" of America's expanding frontier instilled a dangerous sense of omnipotence, a "belief that we have an almost magical capacity to have our way in the world."[11] When reversals occurred, a sense of omnipotence was in large part preserved, often via the conclusion that "We must have brought about our own demise!"—and not least via the cry of "*betrayal*."[12] In a reflex that was hardly confined to America but nevertheless was repeatedly manifest there, the shame of powerlessness was often pushed away by shaming and blaming internal enemies. In the

United States, these included the Japanese Americans interned after Pearl Harbor as well as the "reds" and what Republican senator Nixon called a "fifth column" after stalemate in Korea.

The Vietnam War crystallized a twin threat of shame: shame for suffering inflicted and, as time went by, shame for stalemate and then defeat. In October 1969, U.S. vice president Spiro Agnew tried to deflect shame around the conduct of the Vietnam War when he called anti-war leaders "an effete corps of impudent snobs who characterize themselves as intellectuals."[13] Nixon's anti-communism and extreme hostility to criticism was clearly lending itself to the pursuit of enemies at home as well as abroad, and defeat in Vietnam strengthened this reflex. On the domestic "front" the narrative of betrayal in Washington was subsequently picked up by extreme right-wing militia groups, in which many Vietnam veterans participated, sowing some of the seeds for subsequent militia militancy and some forms of right-wing terrorism.[14] We can see here how shame—whether over harm done or weakness—can be harnessed to some very toxic kinds of politics.

In the longer term, rather than prompting America to recoil from war per se (which might have been an example of shame working in a *positive* way), the experience of Vietnam encouraged forms of warfare in which U.S. casualties were low and aerial power was increasingly relied upon.[15] In the context of war in former Yugoslavia, Vinay Lal noted the habit of rejoicing "that not a single American life had been lost to enemy gunfire."[16] In these changed circumstances, war had arguably lost some of its heroism and some of its honor. But the shame of Vietnam had still been accommodated within a system of serial warfare.

While warfare was changing, America was still finding it difficult to impose its will. After 9/11 and U.S.-led military operations in Afghanistan and Iraq, Edward Said observed: "It is quite common to hear high officials in Washington and elsewhere speak of changing the map of the Middle East, as if ancient societies and myriad peoples can be shaken up like so many peanuts in a jar."[17] Such fantasies rarely survive the harsh tests of reality; and just as Saigon once fell to the Viet Cong, Kabul was eventually to fall to the Taliban. Under Trump, the enduring habit of finding a "fifth column" found expression in his notorious anti-Muslim ban. Critical of America's expensive and long wars abroad, Trump seems to have redirected a long-standing Islamophobia—one that both informed and fed off the "war on terror"—toward "the enemy within." Meanwhile, Trump was also denouncing the "deep state" that he said was undermining him from within the institutions of the U.S. government, a discourse that eventually helped feed the big lie that Trump had won the 2020 election. Timothy Snyder, observing pithily that "post-truth is pre-fascism," noted that such lies bring with them "of necessity, a conspiracy theory: Imagine all the people who must have been in on such a plot and all the people who would have had to work on the cover-up."[18] For those who cannot contemplate the shame of defeat (whether abroad or at home), a violent lurch into fantasy—and a proliferation of internal "enemies"—is a timeless way of trying to escape; and fantasy may invite violence to make it appear true.[19]

France: Falling from Grace?

In France, shame around bad actions seems to have blended with—and has often been swamped by—shame around loss of preeminence. Agnès Desarthe, author of *This Fickle Heart*, placed France's complicated feelings around colonialism and decolonization into a broader historical context. She pointed to

> the fact that it's impossible for France not to see itself as what it used to be. The heritage of the French Revolution when France was the champion of freedom, of liberty, and French was spoken everywhere. They cannot overcome this defeat. Everything started in 1870 [with losing the Franco-Prussian War] and since then it has been one defeat after another. This first one [1870], humiliation, and that led to the Dreyfus affair [when a French officer of Jewish descent, Captain Alfred Dreyfus, was falsely accused of spying for the Germans]. And then war [and the] French resistance—was it really French or was it resistance in France? And then decolonization, which was done in a crazy way. So it's one guilty feeling after another and a problem of self-image. When you walk around the streets here in France, you see

grim faces. People are sad, you don't know why, and it's because we think we're not as wonderful as we used to be and we cannot come to terms with this new image, and it's difficult for us.[20]

While "guilt" is referenced here, phrases like "a problem of self-image" imply a significant sense of shame. When it came to shame around the loss of France's preeminence, this appears to have been "compensated," to a degree, through the pursuit of *la gloire* in Africa in particular. But this hubristic and compensatory reflex tended only to reinforce the underlying shame (or at least the threat of shame) around bad actions, as when France was found to have supported genocidal elements in Rwanda.[21]

In France as in the United States, shame has sometimes fueled the search for *internal* enemies—and this takes us back to the Dreyfus affair. Anti-Semitism was a growing force in France in the late nineteenth century, and Dreyfus was of Jewish descent. He was also from Alsace, which had been lost to the Germans as a result of the 1870 defeat. Shortly after Dreyfus was falsely accused in 1894, Sigmund Freud himself commented:

> The purpose of paranoia is to ward off an idea that is incompatible with the ego, by projecting its substance into the external world. . . . The *grande nation* cannot face the idea that it could be defeated in war. Ergo it was not defeated; the victory does not count. It provides an example of mass paranoia and invents the delusion of betrayal.[22]

Later, a sense of "betrayal" at the loss of Algeria in 1962 fed the rise of the far right, with veterans like Jean-Marie Le Pen (accused of torture as a paratrooper in Algeria in a detailed investigation by the *Guardian* and *Le Monde*)[23] complaining that part of this betrayal was allowing Algerians and other Muslim immigrants to settle in France.[24]

France has seen a strong backlash against attempts to come to terms with its history of empire and with contemporary manifestations of racism more generally. On April 21, 2021, exactly sixty years after France's most senior generals staged a putsch in French Algiers to protest Algerian independence, twenty retired generals and hundreds of retired senior officers signed a letter to President Macron warning of a "disintegration" of French society, denouncing "anti-racist" values whose "sole aim is to create on our soil ill-feeling, even hatred between communities" and pointing an accusing finger at the *"banlieues* [Paris suburb] mobs" that were said to be creating no-go areas within France.[25] Some 40 percent of the French military stated that they intended to vote for the far-right National Rally party.[26]

France's version of right-wing populism has made great efforts to ward off shame around colonialism and racism, often pursuing this endeavor under the guise of "honesty." French political scientist Francoise Vergès notes of modern-day France, "The conservatives break 'taboos'... they dare to 'say loudly what people think privately.'" This includes highlighting the "internal enemy," claiming for themselves the status of victims, and proclaiming "the right to be 'proud' of one's country, one's flag, the right to say 'no' to repeated demands to revise the national myth."[27]

This "honesty," of course, is not honest about the past or the present. Noting the reluctance to remember slavery and other horrors in France's colonial past, Vergès observes that this "demonstrates again what Fanon saw as a form of narcissism deeply ingrained within the French political psyche, the idea that the French people is incapable of mass murder, crimes and massacres."[28] Vergès refers to the common idea that slavery "existed in lands where French ideals were betrayed and violated by adventurers who could not 'represent' France";[29] the idea was that those responsible "were not fully French ('uneducated' settlers or lost 'soldiers of fortune')."[30] In short, French colonial republicanism created a sharp break "between France (where universalism was born and where it was said to flourish) and its colonial territories (where the exception can *naturally* be the rule)."[31]

This distinction, always a rather creaking and self-serving attempt to ward off shame, today looks creakier than ever. For one thing, Vergès's "exception" has very visibly "come home." In 2016, when I interviewed residents in the so-called "jungle" camp at Calais before it was destroyed by police, there were numerous accounts of police violence. One could see how a "state of exception"—a situation in which human rights were violated in relation to a particular population and in which crimes did not count as crimes—had actually moved disastrously inside France itself.

Much of this was done with British encouragement and material support in the name of preventing migration to the UK. One could also see very clearly the contradiction between France's self-image as the origin of human rights, on the one hand, and on the other the manifest hostility toward—and shameful neglect of—migrants/refugees living there. At times, this contradiction has led to a search for a physical solution, as when the very destruction of the "jungle" camp was presented as a "humanitarian" act that would eliminate insanitary conditions while also erasing the highly visible "shame" of the camp itself. Yet conditions for the migrants in Calais deteriorated in the wake of this aggression, as the police were determined to uproot the migrants whenever they tried to settle or rest.

For a significant part of France's white population, the country's postcolonial shame and melancholia appear to have blended with an underlying fear of *replacement*, so that again the victim has to a large extent been repositioned as the perpetrator. In one study by the Paris-based Fondation Jean Jaurès, 59 percent of those who had participated in the *gilets jaunes*, a populist movement that highlights the difficulties of those on relatively low incomes, said they believed France's political elites were encouraging immigration in order to *replace* them.[32] Noting the fear of "replacement" within Paris in particular, Christophe Guilluy commented that "large global cities work on a dual dynamic: gentrification and immigration."[33]

As elsewhere, those fears relate to feelings of invisibility, fears that found a counterpoint in the trademark yellow vest designed to make workers *visible*.[34] When President Macron inaugurated Station F in Paris, a location for start-up businesses that is also a converted rail depot, Macron referred to the project's origins: "A train station—it's a place where we encounter those who are succeeding and those who are nothing,"[35] prompting journalist James McAuley to reflect:

> This was the moment when a large percentage of the French public learned that in the eyes of their president, they had no value. "Ceux qui ne sont rien" is a phrase that has lingered and festered. To don the yellow vest is thus to declare not only that one has value but also that one exists.[36]

Commenting on his own best-selling and autobiographic novel *The End of Eddy*, Édouard Louis recalled how the factories in his northern French village closed in the 1960s and 1970s, so that people were "hopeless, poor and subjected to an endless violence."[37] This in turn led to racism and homophobia, with the young Édouard being told that he was bringing shame on his family by being effeminate. At the time, Édouard hated books, and he remembered, "When I would see a book, I would think this is an aggression, this is an assault, because this book is telling me 'You will not read me. You are not the kind of people who read.'"[38] That may seem to take us some distance from the topic of empire. But when Marine Le Pen (daughter of Jean-Marie) emerged on the national political scene (becoming head of the far-right National Front in 2011), almost everyone in this village voted for her, Louis recalls. Le Pen went on to call for the "de-Islamization" of France, to claim that multiculturalism had failed, and to be runner-up to Macron in the 2022 presidential elections. According to Louis, Le Pen was the only politician who even recognized the *existence* of people in his village: "When I was a kid, my mother would say Marine Le Pen is the only one who talks about us. And to vote for Marine Le Pen was just a desperate attempt to exist in the eye of the other."[39]

United Kingdom: The Colonial Present

At a UN conference on racism that was held just a week before the terror attacks of September 2001, UK prime minister Blair issued a statement of "regret" about slavery, noting, "It would not be sensible for governments to accept responsibility for the actions of governments so long ago. What is important is what we do in the present."[40] But a key problem here is that "what we do in the present" is itself closely linked to a history that Britons do not, on the whole, wish to acknowledge. Commenting on Blair's statement, Sara Ahmed noted:

> Such a delimitation of responsibility . . . works precisely through forgetting that what happened "long ago" affects the injustices of international politics in the present, in which the world's resources are

unequally and unjustly divided between nations and continents.... Regret is named as a kind of disappointment, an almost polite sense of "What a shame" rather than "We are ashamed."[41]

Attempts to inject more shame into Britain's enduringly shameless approach to colonial violence have themselves been instrumentalized by politicians and journalists stirring up popular prejudices and appealing to so-called "traditional values." These right-wing populists seem to understand (or at least perceive) that if they can construct an invitation to examine history as a threat of shame, then they can—like Trump—turn shame into political gold. As part of this, they sell their own shamelessness, their instinct for not apologizing.

Andy Beckett notes that since the 2007–8 financial crisis in particular, "picking fights" has become a prominent part of UK politics—a reversion in some ways to the Thatcher government's obsession with "the enemy within" in the 1980s. Targets have ranged from the relatively powerful ("Eurocrats" in Brussels) to less powerful people like migrant/immigrant groups and so-called "scroungers" on benefits. Increasingly, targets have also come to include those seeking a clearer recognition of colonial violence and present-day racism. Rather central in the UK's contemporary "culture wars" has been the tactic, exemplified by the Johnson government, of telling voters, as Beckett put it, "that their country and values are being undermined by subversive forces."[42] As one government source put it, "Boris thinks that he and Munira [Mirza, head of Boris Johnson's policy unit] are in the same place on this as the vast majority of the public, and that every time there is another row about [colonial] statues or Churchill or white privilege, another Labour seat becomes winnable."[43] Beckett observed:

> Before Johnson, prime ministers such as Tony Blair and David Cameron often sought to play conflicts down—"We're all in this together," as Cameron liked to say—in order to appeal as widely as possible. Yet since 2015 the Conservatives have found that they can win elections with the strong support of only a few large sections of the population, principally older white voters and inhabitants of rural and smalltown England.[44]

(Incidentally, if this was true of general elections, it proved even more the case with internal Conservative leadership elections. Liz Truss became prime minister in 2022 on the basis of just over 80,000 votes from party members in the run-off with Rishi Sunak.)

In the UK, the extension of shamelessness into the present is reflected in monuments like the statues of the murderous entrepreneur Cecil Rhodes in Oxford. Attempts to reckon with colonial violence and its legacy have tended to promote a major backlash. Indeed, potential shame has routinely been warded off with great indignation—and with shaming the shamers. The habitual claim here is that legitimate pride in British values and history is under attack from the "woke" brigade. Shame is kept at bay—and political points are correspondingly scored—by going on the offensive. After the toppling of the statue of slave trader Edward Colston in Bristol, for example, Communities Secretary Robert Jenrick said "baying mobs" and "woke worthies" should not be allowed to erase part of the nation's history.[45] In May 2021, after Oriel College refused to remove its statue of Rhodes (citing "regulatory and financial challenges"), Education Minister Gavin Williamson rushed to endorse the decision, saying it was important to avoid "censoring history."[46] After students at Oxford's Magdalen College decided to take down a picture of the queen and argued that *she* had links to colonialism, the front-page *Daily Express* headline shouted, "How Dare They! Oxford Students Cancel Our Queen."[47] Reacting to attempts to diversify reading lists and "decolonize" the university curriculum, the *Daily Mail*—not normally known for its long discussions of philosophy—ran the headline "They Kant Be Serious!" adding, "PC students demand white philosophers including Plato and Descartes be dropped from university syllabus."[48]

Where there is shame around empire, a lot of it (as in France) is shame around *loss of* empire[49]—and again this can be instrumentalized politically. Even before 9/11 (and contradicting his emphasis on "long ago" imperialism), Blair was declaring in 1997: "Century upon century it has been the destiny of Britain to lead other nations. That should not be a destiny that is part of our history. It should be part of our future. We are a leader of nations or nothing."[50] After 9/11, Blair ramped up the neocolonial rhetoric, declaring, "Let us re-order this world around us!"

And all the while, of course, Britain has clung to its special status as a nuclear power and one of the permanent and veto-wielding members of the UN Security Council.

Part of Tony Blair's sense that "we are all in this together" rested on a high-profile belligerence toward *external* enemies, notably in the "war on terror." Here too, it was not difficult to see that the colonial past was hardly "over": in fact, it was being harnessed to contemporary hubris. Current manifestations of imperialism, in turn, have tended to contaminate the ability to feel shame around the past: as Paul Gilroy suggested in a comment on the "war on terror," colonial brutality tended to get overlooked "because a sanitized history of the imperial project is required by those who wish to bring it back to life."[51] Beyond this, the simple failure to commemorate colonial famines (including famines in India and the Great Famine in Ireland) encourages blind spots around Britain's *continuing* role in creating famine (notably in Yemen), as Alex de Waal has noted.[52] So the past, in many ways, is not even past. In a related observation, Gilroy suggests that strong elements of denial and amnesia around the British empire have encouraged many Britons to view postcolonial people as "unwanted alien intruders," as people lacking any historical connection to their fellow subjects.[53] Meanwhile, some of the shame around invasion and colonization has apparently been offloaded onto those seen as "occupying England's own streets" (in Fintan O'Toole's phrase)—perhaps reflecting fears around some kind of "reverse colonization."[54] This takes us back to the fear of replacement and, perhaps buried rather deeply, of *revenge*. In such framings, the victim (whether of past colonial violence or of present-day warring parties) is again being repositioned as a perpetrator. The political benefits of denouncing and shutting out these alleged "invaders" encourage—and depend upon—a warding off of shame around empire as well as a blindness to the continuing damage wrought by, for example, the "war on terror."

Perhaps the simplest solution to shame over colonialism and shame over colonial settlement has been to *deny the damage and talk up the* "*benefits.*" This was the approach of Theodore Roosevelt, U.S. president from 1901 to 1909, when he coolly observed that "the expansion of the peoples of white, or European, blood during the past four centuries . . . has been fraught with lasting benefit to most of the peoples already dwelling in the lands over which the expansion took place."[55] When the French government forced more than half of Algeria's rural population into "resettlement" camps as part of its vicious counterinsurgency in Algeria, the process was sometimes shamelessly laundered as "modernization" or "de-peasanting."[56] When it came to the British empire in India, famine mortality from 1876 to 1902 has been conservatively estimated at anywhere from twelve to twenty-nine million people. Yet "political economy" stressed the benefits of withholding relief (such as preserving people's work ethic and morals). Winston Churchill presided over the 1943 Bengal famine, and earlier, when he was part of General Kitchener's army in Sudan, he described the Maxim gun, mounted on a gunboat, as "a beautiful white devil" that floated "gracefully on the waters"; as the Dervishes were cut to pieces, Churchill noted that this was "the most signal triumph ever gained by the arms of science over barbarians."[57]

Such shameless violence is difficult to come to terms with for those who revere Britain and those who regard Churchill, who after all inspired the country to stand up to Nazism, as Britain's greatest national hero. More generally, a collective reluctance to take the shame of empire on board—or even to accept the shame of *losing* empire—has offered important opportunities for political actors who sell a sense of "pride in Britain," who make a virtue of not apologizing, and who project a kind of dominance in the present.

Somewhere in the zeitgeist—and extending well beyond the UK, United States, and France—is a sense of something slipping away, a sense of something being replaced and disrespected. Even the insistence that minorities sign up to national "values" hints at an underlying uncertainty around what these values actually are. In these circumstances, a call to violence is one way of demonstrating one's faith in these values—a dangerous way of looking at things that was especially prominent in the wake of 9/11 as we shall see in chapter 14. In the United

States after 9/11, it was also sometimes claimed (without much evidence) that terrorists were driven by envy—and in particular that they "envy our freedom." The message seemed to be that "they" want what "we" have (even though we may not). With Western citizens' faith in the future having acquired a distinctly fragile quality, many on the political right have exhibited a growing determination to insist on the envy of others—not just the terrorists but the millions of unfortunates said to be desperate for access to precisely this precarious future. Hence, in part, the perceived need for formidable barriers that will keep out the green-eyed multitude of would-be "economic migrants."[58] In this mode, British prime minister David Cameron announced, for example, that there was "a swarm of people coming across the Mediterranean seeking a better life, wanting to come to Britain."[59] This is not just nationalism but also narcissism. Of course, there are indeed a great many people who want, for various reasons, to move to richer countries, including the United States and Britain. But drifts toward intolerance in the West actually diminish the lure of "freedom" for would-be migrants.[60] And meanwhile walls are a message not only to "others" but also to *oneself*—namely that, while our shoes may be increasingly tattered, there are billions who would like to be in them.

In these diminished circumstances, it not just migrants' much-trumpeted desire but their suffering that may reassure. Back in 1996, Zygmunt Bauman pointed to the juxtaposition of "tourists" and "vagabonds," tourists being modern free-floating individuals who could move around but lacked a secure livelihood or future while vagabonds were those such as refugees who were *compelled* to move and would rather stay put. After noting that "the vagabond is the tourist's *alter ego*" into which "guilts too awesome to be thought of are dumped," Bauman added, "One can live with the ambiguities of uncertainty that saturate the tourist life only because the certainties of vagabondage are so unambiguously loathsome and repugnant."[61]

With more Americans looking south as well as north for more affordable health care, envy itself cannot necessarily be assumed. A detailed 2017 Amnesty International report highlighted "evidence of a sharp decline in economically motivated immigration [to the United States] from Latin America from 2000 onwards," noting also that the American Dream no longer had the same hold and that *forced* migration was increasingly dominant.[62] Of course, racism and intolerant political climates are also factors that put people off.[63] Meanwhile, the people who do populate Western democracies' "migration crisis" are often propelled by processes with important origins *within* those democracies. Most come from former colonies, from Latin American countries negatively affected by the "war on communism" and the "war on drugs," and from Middle Eastern countries that have borne the brunt of Western democracies' post-9/11 belligerence. The shame around these various root causes is warded off, very often, through shaming the migrants themselves.

Beyond the United States and the UK and France, countries that have experienced some kind of loss of dominance include Spain, Italy, Greece, Turkey, the Netherlands, Russia, and China. The list goes on. After Greece was humiliated by EU- and IMF-imposed austerity and labeled "the sick man of Europe," Roman Gerodimos observed:

> This residual inferiority complex—which is aggravated by widespread emphasis on the country's chronic ills—is complicated by a residual superiority complex regarding Greece's perceived role as a source of democracy, philosophy, and European culture, which only serves to maintain narcissistic feelings of aloneness and persecution.[64]

The drive to dominate tends to diminish the "great power" status of others. And while democracies in Western Europe and the United States seem sensitive to *their own feelings of shame* around lost dominance (or at least determined to ward them off), a little more sensitivity to *the shame of their rivals* would encourage a different and ultimately more constructive approach. In Russia, the aggressive liberalization of the post–Cold War period led to a sharp escalation of poverty, and this came on top of the humiliating "defeat" in the Cold War and the fall of communism.[65] Yet U.S. military expenditure remained close to Cold War levels, and NATO was not only retained but expanded eastward, contributing significantly to many Russians' sense of humiliation and renewed encirclement. In these circumstances, Russian national pride has several times been violently and indeed viciously asserted. Taking post–Cold War history seriously is not about "excusing" Putin, which would certainly be a fool's endeavor. At the same time, in international as well as national politics, there is always a pressing need to try to understand how things might be seen—and how shame might be experienced—by people other than yourself. In his more general discussion of foreign policy, Reinhard Wolf observes, "Just as with oxygen, being denied respect suddenly brings to the fore just how vital the 'stuff' actually is."[66] Putin's manipulation of shame is also important to understand, as is his apparent shamelessness. A striking paradox is that Putin has brought more shame on himself—and by extension Russia—through his actions over Ukraine in particular. But we have seen many times in this book that shame-for-abuse tends not to deter those who are pushing back against shame-for-loss-of-power.

12

Shame and the Economy

IF WE TURN now to shame and the economy, it's important to look at systems for dishing out, distributing, and relieving shame. In this chapter, we look first at shame and consumerism—not least at the business of selling shame and selling solutions for shame. After that, we examine the distribution of shame within society, focusing on shame around "underdevelopment," on shame around poverty, on shame around poor performance, and finally on the shamelessness of the rich. The relevant distributions of shame have been notably perverse and have also served identifiable political and economic functions.

Consumerism: Selling Shame and Salvation

In his remarkable 1961 essay "Advertising: The Magic System," Raymond Williams observed that in the early days of mass advertising there was an emphasis on the specific qualities of products (for example, soap might be said to clean well and to smell nice). But subsequently, consumer products were increasingly presented as possessing strangely *magical* powers: "You do not only buy an object: you buy social respect, discrimination, health, beauty, success."[1] Williams argued that the problem with our consumer society was not that we were too materialistic but rather that we were *not materialistic enough*; indeed, if we were sensibly materialistic (that is, if we confined our interest to the usefulness of objects), then we would find most advertising to be of insane irrelevance.[2]

By the end of the nineteenth century, advertisers were learning to stir up shame and anxiety around dirt, illness, and social status. In fact, the increasing taboo around exposing bodily functions highlighted by Elias as part of a "civilizing process" seems to have dovetailed neatly (and damagingly) with this development.[3] Cultural historian T. J. Jackson Lears observed:

> After the turn of the century, men's toiletries were no longer merely grooming aids: they became keys to success and barriers against embarrassment. Women as well were reminded repeatedly about the possibilities of giving offense through bad breath, yellow teeth, body odors, and shabby home furnishings. . . . Guests were everywhere in *Good Housekeeping* during the 1920s—evaluating food, furniture, children's behavior, even the bathroom drains. . . . Epitomizing the older therapeutic ideal of well-managed health, a spotless bathroom became a focus for female achievement. . . . To paraphrase Sartre: in the new consumer culture, hell was—truly—other people.[4]

We can see here that while guilt has some advantages for those who are pushing consumer products, shame will often serve much better. In particular, consumerism tends to depend on seeing oneself through the eyes of others—and then buying into things that offer to remove the shame of others' (imagined) disapproval. In the advertising analyzed by Jackson Lears, appearance was presented as an outward manifestation of one's inner sinfulness (laziness, overindulgence, even poverty), so that, at the extreme, dirtiness, illness, and not conforming to certain ideas of beauty were becoming markers of shame from which only a constant stream of purchases could bring redemption. As the efficiency of housework increased, so did the standards of cleanliness and domestic order that were expected.[5] On TV, advertisements took the invisible germs in your toilet and made them embarrassingly visible. A relatively recent advertisement for fabric freshener insisted that while your couch might smell OK *to you*, your guests are secretly horrified. Hell, in other words, was still other people.

It's interesting to place this emerging system alongside what some writers have portrayed as another "magic system": the historical excesses of the Catholic Church in offering forgiveness of sins via a (profitable) system of penances. This system included a trade in supposed religious "relics" to which magical powers were often attributed.[6] We might plausibly see this as a system that offered (at a price) an escape from a sense of sin and shame that it was simultaneously promoting; and many critics did in fact begin to see the system in this way. As the Reformation approached, growing numbers of people in Europe suggested that many of the touted solutions (including the rituals and rackets that centered on holy relics) were bogus, self-serving, or both.[7] Prevailing religious practices were increasingly attacked as a world of profit, superstition, and idolatry.

That was Nietzsche's view of Christianity *as a whole*. Even after the Reformation, Nietzsche portrayed Christianity as *exploiting* the crippling sense of shame that it was simultaneously promoting—in effect selling the sin and then selling (sometimes literally) the salvation. Nietzsche described the priest as "a parasitic kind of human being which prospers only at the expense of every healthy form of life," adding that "the priest *lives* on sins, he needs 'the commission of sins.'"[8] Of course, many will consider Nietzsche's views too harsh—or downright offensive. But his critique—which targeted Protestantism as well as Catholicism—serves again to highlight the possibility that the imposition of shame may be linked in some way to the extraction of benefits by those who promise to *remove* this shame.

This turns out to be a rather concise description of a central technique within consumer capitalism. Of course, there have been many rebellions against this particular system of profit and power—not least in left-wing revolutions. But in general the consumer system, like the Catholic Church, has proven remarkably resilient. Even manifestations of backlash have offered opportunities for renewal.

Part of what consumerism achieved in the first place was to "rescue" capitalism from a crisis of overproduction by stimulating demand. Max Weber had famously shown that what he called "the Protestant Ethic" played an important role in fostering the rise of capitalism—essentially through encouraging a combination of savings (because self-indulgence was frowned upon) and hard work (which brought some reassurance that one might be one of the "elect" or the "saved").[9] In line with this, Protestantism also seems to have reinforced shame around self-indulgence, laziness, and "failure." But how could the capitalist system maintain and actually boost levels of *consumption* so that there was enough demand for all the many goods that capitalism was now capable of producing?[10]

A restrictive society based on scarcity and discipline had found its counterpart in Freud's emphasis on controlling desires. In a more permissive society based on relative abundance, desire was increasingly *cultivated*.[11] At the same time, shame was still useful. Having been so effectively harnessed to boosting production, shame was now increasingly being harnessed to boost consumption.[12] Where impulses had previously been reined in, now they were being actively stimulated.[13] Increasingly, advertising did not so much extoll the product as manufacture a product of its own: the restless, anxious, and shame-prone consumer.[14]

That's where the imagined or dramatized disdain of others proved to be so useful. To the extent that products were now *status symbols*, the system depended on an underlying anxiety about status, and in effect it had to generate an enormous amount of shame in order to sustain itself. Even in city streets, you can see how this works: for however many clothes you buy and however expensive they are, the wafer-thin mannequins are still there in the shop—elegant, chin up, slightly disdainful of the real people walking by. The main target for such shaming has tended to be women. But today men and children are increasingly being invited to share in the opportunity to worry about their appearance and their bodies. Meanwhile, the value of a product is often related to the exclusion of those who cannot afford it. As Gore Vidal observed, "It is not enough to succeed. Others must fail."[15] In their study of shame and poverty in the UK, Elaine Chase and Robert Walker mention "not having the right trainers" as a marker of poverty,[16] and Larry Ray points out that more marginalized groups may be particularly reliant on access to consumer goods as a marker of respect.[17]

Within any status-conscious system, respect from one's "superior" cannot realistically be expected. And at the same time, recognition and admiration from those who are "below" you will hardly count: after all, the recognition that counts (to invoke Hegel on the master and the slave) is recognition from someone that you yourself respect.[18] Meanwhile, as Alain de Botton and John Armstrong observed in their 2013 book *Art as Therapy*,

> It's in the nature of media-dominated societies that they will, by definition, expose us to a great deal more glamour than most of us have the opportunity to participate in. Commercial images give us a ringside seat at the holidays, professional triumphs, love affairs, evenings out and birthdays of an elite we are condemned to know far better than they know us.[19]

If keeping up with the Joneses was not difficult enough, now we have to keep up with the Kardashians;[20] we may "like" their lifestyles, but they are unlikely to "like" ours.

The obvious unreachability of high-profile lifestyles for billions of people invites a rebellion against the consumerism and inaccessible glamor that is being foisted on us through traditional and social media—a barrage that is implicitly and sometimes explicitly shaming. With everyone presenting their "best face," shame is systematically ramped up. But disillusionment, too, can be instrumentalized, and the consumerist system has proven remarkably adept at preserving itself—and preserving its own immunity from shame—even as it relentlessly stirs up shame among would-be buyers. We may say, in fact, that the consumerist system has routinely warded off its own "Reformation."

In part, it has been precisely by *not* meeting our underlying psychological needs that consumerism has been able to renew itself. In this sense, the system *depends on failure*: as the band U2 once sang, "You can never have enough of what you don't really need." (Of course, this lyric acquires a certain irony in light of the band's well-publicized tax-avoidance strategies, but the point is taken nonetheless.)

Alongside the idolization of celebrities, we also have a flourishing shadow culture that centers on bringing celebrities down through various kinds of public shaming. Such shaming seems to offer a "safety valve"—a symbolic redress when public recognition is scarce and when far-reaching economic redistribution has been ruled out by various versions of neoliberalism. This shaming takes diverse forms: the carefully coaxed embarrassing behavior in *The Housewives of Orange County*; the grubby press campaign against Meghan Markle; the forced grub-eating of the UK's *I'm a Celebrity . . . Get Me Out of Here!*; and the joys of *10 Child Celebs Who Aged Badly* (eleven million views on YouTube). On a more individual level, British journalist Sali Hughes has spoken out about the extreme distress over several years that was caused by a group of women devoted to denouncing her and her family on a "trashing" site.[21]

Whether it is the shaming of celebrities or the shaming of one's political opponents, most of this energetic activity seems remarkably ineffective in changing behavior. Cathy O'Neil, author of *The Shame Machine*, gives the example of shaming "anti-vaxxers" in the context of Covid. At the same time, it's clear that a little shaming doesn't hurt the ratings; and if shaming tips over into humiliation, so much the better. O'Neil observes:

> Attempting to shame someone in a way that's obviously not going to work actually creates outrage spirals and that's the primary way that social media companies profit off our shame because they get us in these endless cycles where we spend all of our time on Facebook or Twitter clicking on ads.[22]

Even "trashing" sites bring in advertising, and in 2018 an internal Facebook study acknowledged: "Our algorithms exploit the human brain's attraction to divisiveness."[23] In addition to the profit motive and the background political function of offering a vicarious "leveling down," such shaming (and such spirals of shaming) may help to create a sense of community—perhaps also propping up fragile individual identities. We should note, too, that all this is happening in circumstances where traditional identities, including identities centering on employment, have been significantly eroded. In an important contribution, Myra Mendible observes:

> On any given day in America's twenty-four-hour news cycle shame is a hot commodity. Stories and images of disgraced politicians and

celebrities solicit our moral indignation, their misdeeds fueling a lucrative economy of shame and scandal.

Again, the purpose of shaming may not actually be to induce better behavior. As Mendible notes:

> Nothing fosters the illusion of solidarity like shared condemnation: joining the chorus of outrage that follows the exposure of the rich and famous, we play out a fantasy of community that otherwise eludes.... Duly disciplined, the exposed offender, egotist, or fool bolsters our faith in the notion that, in America, personal responsibility accounts for failures and everyone—even the rich and famous—get what they deserve.[24]

Miley Cyrus's "twerking" at the 2013 MTV awards was garnering over 300,000 tweets *per minute*, with outrage featuring prominently and *Politico*'s Keith Koffler saying not only that her performance heralded "our culture's destruction" but also that President Obama was "abetting our moral disintegration."[25] The shamed celebrity will sometimes be mercifully and profitably rehabilitated and rebranded, with the star perhaps making high-profile confessions and self-justifications on their road to a combination of recovery, best-selling memoirs, and appearance on reality shows.[26]

If capitalism harnessed shame around dirt and indolence to boost production and then tapped into shame around appearances to boost consumption, today what has been called the "attention economy" often flourishes on the visibility that shaming can bring. Commenting on the surprising popularity of QAnon among some members of California's "wellness" community, the *Los Angeles Times* noted that overabundant "wellness" teachers were finding that politically controversial positions (including opposition to the Covid vaccine) could be extremely profitable. One yoga teacher observed: "In behind-the-scenes marketing trainings, aspiring wellness influencers were told that 'being controversial, taking definitive positions that make people love you or hate you, is a great way to build your brand.'"[27] Trump himself claimed notoriety had real monetary value.[28]

So where is the Reformation? At various points, there have been hints of a limit to people's willingness to buy into advertising's magic system. And today, global warming in particular is casting a dark shadow of shame over this wasteful "magic system." Even back in the late 1980s, I remember watching an ad in the cinema in which glamorous people were swanning around the Caribbean on motorboats. What surprised me was not the ad's magical and slightly nauseating slogan "When you're drinking Bacardi" but the widespread booing in the cinema at this particular message.

It is striking, though, that skepticism about advertising has repeatedly been accommodated while shame has been regularly kept at bay. One factor here is the profitability of *not meeting* people's needs. A second is advertising's habit of proceeding at a symbolic and implicit level, so that very often there are no empirical claims to be disproved.

A third factor is that cynicism has repeatedly been harnessed to the consumerist system. For example, in a landmark 1987 ad, Volkswagen sold its Golf car not so much as a route to love but as *preferable to people*: a smartly dressed woman got into a car that bore the sign "Just Divorced" and the slogan followed: "If only everything in life were as reliable as a Volkswagen." In a sense, this was a rejection of Williams's "magic system" (in which the product is a means to another human being's approval); now the product was being presented as preferable to humans per se. In this posthuman dystopia, the more unreliable humans became within a corrupting capitalism system, the more alluring the products would become! In 2011, perhaps anticipating the politics of honesty-about-dishonesty, Cadbury promised a luxury yacht if you bought two of its "Squares" chocolate biscuits, adding with some humor, "It's all lies. They're not even square."

In the 1980s, with sales of cigarettes under threat from growing evidence that they kill, some advertisers shamelessly turned the problem around. In the successful UK advertising campaign for Silk Cut cigarettes, the ads actually seemed to *reinforce* compulsory government health warnings by associating cigarettes with a variety of sharp and violent objects like chainsaws (covered in purple silk) while Benson and Hedges picked a massive golden tomb (an Egyptian pyramid) to sell its brand. Marlboro gave us images of crocodiles in a swamp with the red caption "They come here for the tourists" above the government warning "Smoking when pregnant harms your baby."[29] Again, it was a system feeding bizarrely—and in this case hungrily—on its own shortcomings.

Like its nemesis "the Islamist terrorist," capitalism was not above turning even death and oblivion into a promise. More prosaically, the chronic stress of manic overwork (much of it to ward off the shame of "not having enough" or "not being enough") finds its fixes (its short-term and often magical remedies) in a range of expensive "escapes"—from holidays to gyms to spas to varied intoxications. Back in 1979, Christopher Lasch noted that "the propaganda of consumption turns alienation itself into a commodity."[30] Today, we are very much in that world.

The Distribution of Shame

As consumer capitalism has consolidated itself, the systemic loading of shame today includes not only the practice of shaming people for all the conditions that consumerism claims to address (ugliness, dirtiness, dowdiness) but also the practice of shaming people for poverty, for underdevelopment, and for underperformance.

Shame and Esteem

Today, perverse distributions of shame around the economy have helped create the context for right-wing populist politics, and we have looked at some of these dynamics in the United States and UK in particular. While the discipline of economics generally focuses on the production and distribution of goods and services, we also need to understand the production and distribution of shame, including shame around poverty or wealth. Part of this is understanding how an aura of shamelessness is constructed around unfair economic systems, and how this involves the loading of shame onto those who are most disadvantaged within these systems. From this point of view, the problem with neoliberal ideology has some resemblance to the problem that Nietzsche perceived with Christianity: it tends to load a heavy dose of shame onto a situation that is already very painful.[31] That in turn helps explain the success of politicians who know how to spin shame into votes.

We noted that shaming for given characteristics has an inherently cruel quality, notably in comparison to shaming for choices. Shaming someone for poverty has the cruel quality of shaming someone for what tends to be a relatively fixed characteristic. At the same time, the message of the American Dream is that poverty is *not* a fixed characteristic—as long as you work hard enough. But this message risks adding an *additional* layer of shame.

We've noted, too, that shaming may not necessarily lead to shame. As Frantz Fanon and Axel Honneth have both emphasized, shame around lack of recognition may lead to anger and may even create the possibility of throwing off oppression.[32] In Gandhi's hands, this rejection of oppression involved mobilizing the latent shame of the oppressors through nonviolent noncooperation. But many escapes from shame have been offered that *don't* involve resistance to oppressive systems; and while these may provide some temporary relief, they often have the effect of cementing the underlying abuse and the associated system of shaming. Such escapes include the political "solutions" of right-wing populism (generally involving the shaming of "outgroups"), the consumerist "solutions" offered by advertisers (generally involving the offer to eliminate shame with the right purchase), and the shaming of celebrities (generally offering the satisfaction of a symbolic "leveling down"). Since such "escapes" do not tackle underlying injustices and inequalities that powerfully fuel shame, they tend to feed into subsequent spirals of shame and shaming.

In their 2006 book *The Economy of Esteem*, Geoffrey Brennan and Philip Pettit drew on a range of famous novelists and philosophers to show that "people are deeply attached to the esteem of others."[33] Esteem is scarce, they emphasized: concern with esteem "grades people against each other on a more or less continuous scale";[34] and not everyone can be "above average." Within this general scarcity, those who are socially marginalized will have a *particular* concern with issues of esteem.[35]

Observing that esteem is the opposite of shame, Brennan and Pettit suggested that "esteem means more to those who have less of it. That is a result of the diminishing marginal utility property of all goods, which property we take to apply no less to esteem than to other things."[36] This makes sense if we reflect, for example, that we tend to get over our successes quite quickly and start hankering after the next one; our failures, on the other hand, may gnaw away at us for years.

Particularly where genuine respect is hard to find, people often look to their own micro-community or "echo chamber" for approval. The hunt for scarce recognition often means jointly embracing alternative values that are prized within a particular locality or marginalized group. This may involve a joint rejection of the culture that seems to be rejecting them.[37] Here, we might think of wartime Sierra Leone, of Gilligan's prisoners in the United States, or of inner-city Philadelphia where Elijah Anderson observed that there was such intense competition for the little respect that was to be had. Again, we can see that shame is not a relic from the past but something actively produced in the present. Douglas Cairns notes helpfully that Brennan and Pettit's model

> predicts that the violence and anti-social behaviour of inner-city gangs, far from representing the isolated survival of a concern for honour that no longer pervades the rest of society, are in fact a function of a wider economy of esteem in which all members of a society are implicated.[38]

Whether our focus is local, national, or global, we are again not looking at archaic "shame cultures" so much as environments being actively shaped by the contemporary distribution of shame (and esteem) in the wider society.

We have noted, moreover, that finding esteem within a subculture (as in Black pride or gay pride) can easily set off a political backlash. This then creates the context for a kind of mutual shaming that has distinctly mixed consequences for politics but is often profitable for those who control the media, especially social media. When the adherents of right-wing populism are themselves shamed, they may also go deeper into a kind of subculture that finds esteem from within itself—and reinforces a sense of community by collectively rejecting the values and credentials of those who shame it. This is part of the *politics of non-apology* that we discussed in relation to Trump and in relation to colonialism. While Brennan and Pettit do not directly address the *political economy* of shame, they do help us to understand the context in which a variety of subcultures may turn shame into pride. They also help us to understand the spirals of shaming within our current inequitable system, a system in which esteem as well as wealth is very unfairly distributed.

Shame and "Underdevelopment"

If hard work were really rewarded, it has been said, then African women would be the richest people on the planet. Yet poor people around the world—of whatever gender—have been regularly shamed for their poverty, illiteracy, laziness, underdevelopment, and (in the fashionable language of today) lack of "resilience."

During the civil war in Sierra Leone, the very frequency of acts of shaming and humiliation itself suggested a strong underlying shame that fighters were attempting to reverse. The relevant sources of underlying shame included abuses during the war itself, shortcomings in the development process, and negative messaging around this development process. In Freetown in 2001, I asked Amy Smythe (an activist and former government minister) how she explained the atrocities in the war. While one should be wary of overgeneralizing, she offered an important insight:

> People in the communities have a sense of justice and respect for life, but people have been so disempowered and being told they are useless, they are poor, they are illiterate, and they have lost their humanity and are behaving like animals. People are not poor—they are rich in potential. . . . Before, their self-perception was different.

While Smythe was very aware of the many adverse effects of poverty, she was also drawing attention to a rather fundamental problem with the idea of "development." This is the damage done when people (very often in countries trying to recover from the devastating impact of colonial rule) are defined in terms of what they are *not* (for example, through the use of terms like "backward," "underdeveloped," and "illiterate").

In Sierra Leone, as in so many countries around the world, shame had been ramped up when people were bombarded with images of "the good life." During the civil war, a Western aid worker with long experience in Sierra Leone told me: "People are exposed to what's possible. They see the expatriate standard of living, movies. You can't stop it.... In Kailahun [upcountry] so many people wanted to leave. Freetown [the capital] is the goal, and Freetown is the gateway to the West." In the major town of Bo, a teacher with long experience stressed that children had become very interested in the trappings of Western lifestyle without being able to afford it, creating a susceptibility to rebel recruitment.

Insofar as modernity was sold as *the* lifestyle, it seems to have felt shameful to be excluded.[39] Since only the elites could afford this lifestyle, shame around exclusion from modernity fed aggression toward those who were seen as acquiring it corruptly. Certainly, RUF rebels sometimes denounced corruption and conspicuous consumption, as when Charles Kamara (RUF representative on the country's peace commission) told me, "The elite will spend 7,000 dollars on a tie-pin, and then tell you this cost 7,000 dollars to impress you. But it doesn't impress anyone!... You get the same with big public spending projects to imitate and impress the white man."

Many Sierra Leoneans expressed a sense of being ignored, exploited, and disparaged by those who were relatively well-educated. Gaskin Kormor, a fairly successful farmer and a preacher, recalled that when he and vast numbers of other civilians were being pressed into portering duties by the rebels in eastern Sierra Leone, a small group of civilians had an emergency meeting (away from the rebel soldiers); here, the "uneducated" pointed at those like Kormor who were a little more educated, saying, "Oh you book-people—you want to ride vehicles, live in mansions, and travel around the world. You people are the cause of this war today." Kormor actually agreed, noting, "Almost everyone wanted to be fed with a silver spoon. People looked down on agriculture as a mean job."

In Sierra Leone, while education might just offer a route out of poverty, in practice desirable jobs were scarce and schools were severely underfunded. One local aid worker emphasized that violence could somehow reverse a loss of face:

> The educational system has increased rebel and soldier numbers. A lot drop out of school early and these do not have fair job opportunities and, having gone to [secondary] school, they do not want to go back to their villages and till the land. They feel they are a little too enlightened to go back and till the soil![40] They feel their friends will laugh at them, and say you're still farming even though you went off to school. They saw that being a rebel you can loot at will, then you have a sway over your former master, who used to lord it over you, or the others who might have laughed.

Somewhat similarly, Rajesh Venugopal notes that in Sri Lanka those who had gained status by graduating from secondary school would often remain unemployed rather than accept low-status employment or undergo the humiliation of a return to the family farm.[41] Related dynamics were also noted by U.S. general William Corson in relation to Vietnam; commenting on the Vietnamese education system in the run-up to the Communist rebellion there, Corson wrote:

> After achieving a certain social status through education—regardless to what level—it is extremely difficult for a Vietnamese to return to the rice fields as a shoulder-pole carrier. The peasant cannot understand why he has to—and the [Viet Cong] cadre is Johnny on-the-spot to tell him.[42]

A number of studies of poorer countries have argued that putting "development" and "modernity" on a pedestal is inherently shaming when people are only superficially invited to participate.[43] This is a key point to emerge, for example, from Peter Uvin's study of Rwanda before the 1994 genocide. Noting the strong desire to move to urban areas, Uvin wrote, "Little is left of the pride of the African farmer in his culture."[44] He observed that in Rwanda the project of development had the effect of humiliating people when it "acts in the name of the poor but excludes them from its benefits. . . . It is not surprising that there exists a strong need to scapegoat others and to direct aggression and frustration externally."[45] Government restrictions on migration to urban areas had also tended to lock people into agriculture in conditions of growing population and increasing land scarcity, with the army (as is often the case)[46] offering a way out and a route to "modernity." But the Rwandan genocide was immediately preceded by a peace process that threatened large parts of the army with redundancy. When the country's prime minister tried to reassure the troops that they would be employed in development projects, this seems to have provoked them all the more. Human Rights Watch noted, "It was just such menial labour that they thought they had left behind in their new military careers."[47] Government soldiers were subsequently to play a key role in the genocide, where the impulse to scapegoat others—referred to by Uvin—was given full rein.

Even the idea that education and other aspects of development are a "human right," laudable in many ways, can be a mixed blessing. For if these human rights exist and yet you, as an individual, still do not have access to these rights, what then are you supposed to conclude? It may be tempting—and even logical—to conclude that you are considered less than human. In Sierra Leone the RUF rebels' (half-hearted) "Apology to the Nation" stated, "We did not take to the bush because we wanted to be barbarians, not because we wanted to be inhuman, but because we wanted to state our *humanhood*."[48] But we have noted that atrocities do not in practice underline the humanity of the perpetrator; quite the reverse. So the need for recognition—including recognition through violence—seems to have been reinforced in what was often the most vicious of circles.

If people have sometimes rebelled at a humiliating exclusion from modernity, rebellion itself may be dismissed as a manifestation of greed and fanaticism,[49] so that the system as a whole ensures the continued shaming of those who are less privileged. Meanwhile, governments in poorer countries have been shamed for "corruption" that reflects in part the hollowing out of government structures via externally imposed programs of "structural adjustment."[50] When it comes to the "economy of esteem" at a global level, indeed, there seems to be an almost endless supply of techniques for ensuring that the bulk of shame remains among the poor while shamelessness attaches stubbornly to the more privileged.

Shame and the Poor in Richer Countries

The most striking characteristic of the American political economy since around the 1980s is that there has been massive and escalating inequality, along with a strange political consensus (challenged only sporadically) that this either cannot or should not be substantially addressed.

A careful study in the *Quarterly Journal of Economics* found that wealth concentration was high at the outset of the twentieth century but fell between 1929 and 1978. This fall was propelled in part by the New Deal that followed the 1929 Wall Street crash and subsequent Great Depression. Between 1978 and 2012, the wealth share of the richest 0.1 percent of population shot up from 7 percent to an incredible 22 percent, almost reaching the levels of 1929 again, while the wealth share of the top 1 percent had reached *fully 42 percent* by 2012.[51] Tax rates for the rich fell from an average of over 80 percent (in the years from the 1930s until 1980) to just 30–35 percent (from the 1980s).[52] In his 2014 book *Capital in the Twenty-First Century*, Thomas Piketty showed that the total stock of world capital was growing at 4–5 percent while economies were only growing at an average of 2–3 percent. That meant that big dynastic fortunes were taking a higher and higher share of the wealth. Moreover, wealth was being used—especially in the United States—to push for a legal framework in which wealth distribution was getting drastically more unequal.[53]

For the poor in America, inequality has been catastrophic. Philip Alston, the UN Special Rapporteur on extreme poverty and human rights, reported in 2017 that forty million people were living in poverty within the United States. Among the wealthier democracies, the United States had the highest infant mortality rate and the lowest rate of social mobility, and Americans were living on average "shorter and sicker lives." Yet at the same time, the United States has been spending more on national defense than China, Saudi Arabia, Russia, the United Kingdom, India, France, and Japan *put together*. In his research, Alston "saw sewage filled yards in states where governments don't consider sanitation facilities to be their responsibility"; he highlighted mass incarceration fueled by minor infractions followed by escalating fines and finally jail; and he noted "soaring death rates and family and community destruction wrought by prescription and other drug addiction."[54]

Alongside this extraordinary unnecessary poverty, there is a sense of being neglected, ignored, and excluded that has been widely remarked upon. Part of this is exclusion from Brennan and Pettit's "economy of esteem." Even looking at politicians' promises over a long period is salutary. In 1932, Franklin D. Roosevelt vowed to help "the forgotten man at the bottom of the economic pyramid," and in Roosevelt's case he actually did a great deal to make good on this pledge. Yet by the time Bill Clinton was accepting the Democratic Party's nomination for the presidency in 1992, he did so "in the name of the hardworking Americans who make up our forgotten middle class." Clinton immediately promised, "When I am president, you will be forgotten no more."[55] But inequality, which had widened sharply under Reagan, widened still further under Clinton. By the time Trump was standing for reelection, he vowed in May 2020 that "the forgotten men and women of our country will be forgotten no longer."[56] It seems there is no era in which American politicians forget to promise not to forget the forgotten masses.

Widening inequality helped fuel political tensions including perceptions that "elites in Washington" did not care about ordinary people, and some of this resentment was crystallized by the 2007–8 crisis and the bank bailouts. Although Trump talked winningly about "draining the swamp," under his administration welfare and public health programs were severely cut alongside a project of tax reform that increased the inequality between the richest 1 percent and the poorest 50 percent.[57]

To understand America's perversely unequal distribution of wealth, we need to understand its perversely unequal distribution of shame. While the poor have been severely shamed, the rich have been remarkably shameless.

As part of this, poverty has routinely been taken—by the poor and non-poor alike—as a manifestation of vice, while wealth has frequently been taken as a sign of enterprise, risk-taking, and virtue. Again, action as propaganda is relevant; and just as a punishment may be taken to imply a crime, so too success may be taken to imply some kind of virtue (or, within a religious framework, God's approval).

UN Special Rapporteur Alston noted that

> large numbers of welfare recipients are assumed to be living high on the hog. Some politicians and political appointees with whom I spoke were completely sold on the narrative of such scammers sitting on comfortable sofas, watching color TVs, while surfing on their smart phones, all paid for by welfare. . . . Revelations of food stamps being used for purposes other than staying alive draw howls of outrage from government officials and their media supporters.[58]

Yet this concerted shaming seemed to be strangely absent in relation to the wealthy. Alston observed, for example, that "revelations of widespread tax avoidance by companies and high-wealth individuals draw no rebuke, only acquiescence and the maintenance of the loopholes."[59]

Part of the problem here is racial. Alston found that when it came to the widespread condemnation of the poor as lazy, "racist stereotypes are usually not far beneath the surface. The poor are overwhelmingly assumed to be people of color."[60] Historically in the American South, the slavery-based plantation system saw poor whites often aspiring to the economic status of white planters but having little means of getting there since the big plantations had taken the best land, often pushing poor whites into uplands and other marginal areas—and of course requiring much less of their labor because of slavery.[61] Affluent whites suffered the shame of Civil War defeat.[62] But with agrarian depression in the 1880s and 1890s, a strong populist movement was beginning to erode racial barriers as poor people of whatever color responded to extreme inequality and pushed back against the railroads, banks, and other large corporations.[63] Yet this emerging radical politics proved fragile. As happened much later with the Black Lives Matter protests, the spectacle of black and white people cooperating politically was seen by many as a threat—and a racialized politics offered a way to defuse this incipient alliance.[64] As Michelle Alexander has observed:

> Segregation laws were proposed as part of a deliberate effort to drive a wedge between poor whites and African Americans. These discriminatory barriers were designed to encourage lower-class whites to retain a sense of superiority over blacks, making it far less likely that they would sustain interracial political alliances aimed at toppling the white elite.[65]

Or as Bob Dylan put it more briefly, "You've got more than the blacks, don't complain!"

Of course, shame could not be warded off entirely through passing it on to others, and the idea that "anyone can make it" persistently encouraged a degree of self-blame among a wide range of people who were struggling. Alexander noted:

> the key to our collective self-image is the assumption that [social] mobility is always possible, so failure to move up reflects on one's character. By extension, the failure of a race or ethnic group to move up reflects very poorly on the group as a whole.[66]

Shaming for "failure" has been escalated when derogatory labels for the poor have been widely embraced: from "rednecks" to "hillbillies" and "white trash" for white people to the slurs of "welfare queens" and "deadbeat dads" that have sometimes been loaded on Black Americans. We've seen, too, how the act of supporting Trump could usher in an additional layer of shaming, including shame for acting irrationally.

The UK too has been experiencing high levels of inequality (though less drastic than in the United States), with perverse distributions of shame helping to consolidate this. We have noted Owen Jones's work on the demonization of the working class; he observes further, "Smearing poorer working-class people as idle, bigoted, uncouth and dirty makes it more and more difficult to empathize with them."[67] Important work on the shaming of poorer people has also been done by Elaine

Chase and Robert Walker, who highlighted the felt shame of being in debt, of living on a "benefits" estate, of being subjected to an increasingly punitive and suspicious benefits system, of being treated by officials as a "sponger," and of withdrawing from social situations due to a lack of money or clothes or the ability to buy gifts or drinks. Chase and Walker noted, "The media portrayal of the archetypal 'benefit family', with numerous children and making large demands on taxpayers' money, was one which participants were acutely aware of."[68] At the same time, poorer people in the UK were tending to portray themselves as hardworking and were using benefits only as a last resort, distinguishing themselves sharply from those who didn't want to work and from young mothers allegedly having more babies to access benefits and housing. Some also focused on immigrant workers who "have taken all the jobs and housing."[69] These reflexes seemed to offer a sense of self-respect and moral standing, Chase and Walker suggested. But this was a zero-sum game in which solidarity was being undermined by a pernicious politics of shame and shaming.

Shame and the Rich

Alongside the shame of poverty, the shamelessness of the rich has routinely been spectacular. Increased inequality encourages the privileged to rationalize their privilege[70]—and shaming the poor has often been an important part of this. Yet continued belief in the idea of a meritocracy contrasts with a lack of social mobility in the real world, and this has helped fuel popular resentment at what philosopher Michael Sandel calls those "inhaling too deeply at their own success."[71]

Sometimes a crisis emerges that poses a significant challenge to a relatively shameless system of extreme inequality. The crisis brings the possibility of a radical shake-up not just in politics but also in Brennan and Pettit's "economy of esteem." Suddenly, and perhaps only for a brief period, the most wealthy may find shame directed *at them*. This happened with the crash of 1929 and again with the financial crisis of 2007–8. Yet shame for relatively powerful groups—and the possibility of corrective action—may also be warded off while shame is simultaneously redirected toward the most powerless.

Huge inequalities have been legitimized by the idea that financiers and entrepreneurs are the ultimate *risk-takers*—a position of honor that is said to merit corresponding rewards. Yet when we look at the *actual* distribution of risk (for example, in the United States and the UK), it appears to be heavily loaded against the poor and in favor of the alleged "risk-takers."[72] This comes out clearly in Thomas Piketty's work. In particular, by showing that *inheritance* had become an increasingly dominant route to wealth, Piketty makes a substantial challenge to the argument that wealth stems fundamentally from hard work and risk-taking.[73]

The idea of the rich as risk-takers was also challenged by responses to the 2007–8 financial crisis. That crisis was an invitation to examine very critically the policies and processes that helped create it. Financial deregulation from the 1980s had led to a growing concentration of business among the major banks alongside reckless lending practices and huge bonuses. Part of the financial crisis, moreover, stemmed from brokers luring clients into mortgages that they could not afford while bankers passed on the risks to others by packaging bad debts with good debts. Yet rather than prompting fundamental reform, the financial crisis—in both the United States and the UK—prompted a mass "bailout" of banks that were considered "too big to fail." The combination of "bailout" and austerity meant that shame ended up being very perversely distributed. Again, punishment implied a crime while rewards implied the absence of bad behavior. In practice, austerity loaded pain and shame onto the poor, the unemployed, and the disabled, and in the UK orchestrated fears of "another Greece" helped wed policymakers to damaging spending cuts even after other countries had realized that deficit spending could help recovery.[74]

In *Pity the Billionaire,* Thomas Frank noted:

> In the early months of 2009, it was mass public outrage against bankers that threatened to pull Americans out of their chairs and onto the streets. By the time a year had elapsed, however, the bonus boys' misbehavior had been pretty much forgotten. In no time at all, the public's rage had migrated from Wall Street to Washington. Before long the only populism available in the land was an uprising against

government and taxes and federal directives—in other words, it was now a movement in favor of the very conditions that had allowed Wall Street to loot the world.[75]

In the UK, popular ire turned quickly from bankers toward members of Parliament amid press revelations of unreasonable expense claims at the taxpayers' expense.[76] Also frequently condemned was the Labour government that had bailed out the bankers in an attempt to prevent financial collapse, running up a considerable debt in the process. As Clarke and Newman observed, a financial crisis was in effect being transformed into a *fiscal* crisis, bringing a rather similar focus on "the unwieldy and expensive welfare state and public sector, rather than high risk strategies of banks, as the root cause of the crisis."[77] And austerity was also presented as necessary to restore "market confidence."[78] Clarke and Newman added that "the rapid restoration of banking bonuses (and the accompanying lack of shame) has consistently dramatized the profound—and deepening—inequalities of sacrifice."[79]

What is striking, on both sides of the Atlantic, is just how shame-proof the dangerously under-regulated banking system proved to be. Thomas Frank sums up the renewed "market populism" in the United States very well:

> We were suffering, it held, because our leaders had broken faith with American tradition, meaning the laissez-faire system that prevailed before the dawn of organized labor and the regulatory state. . . . Our elected officials had never been pure enough. . . . Until the day free enterprise is totally unleashed, capitalism itself can be held responsible for nothing.[80]

A common response—notably, among the "Tea Party" groundswell of Republican support and sympathetic media outlets—was to blame even relatively poor people for borrowing "beyond their means," to insist that the "free market" ideology was never given a proper chance, and to argue that fundamental market principles were being dangerously set aside by recent attempts to bail out both banks and small lenders.[81] This was a perverse but in many ways brilliant maneuver. It also brings to mind Clifford Longley's analysis in *Chosen People*: for in Tea Party ideology, the breaking of a taboo (non-interference in the market) was held to call for stricter adherence, greater purity, and atonement-through-austerity.

But meanwhile disillusionment with the selfishness of what some called "metropolitan elites" was being fueled substantially by both the financial crisis itself and the official responses to it. As Mark Danner noted in the *New York Review of Books*, "Trumpism is partly the child of the 2008 Wall Street collapse and the vast sense of political corruption and self-dealing it brought in its wake."[82]

In the 1980s, President Ronald Reagan, while often credited with a ruthless devotion to "the free market," actually presided over a rapid *expansion* of state spending, much of it on defense and much of it lining the pockets of key supporters of the Republican Party. Gore Vidal observed, "We have free enterprise for the poor, and socialism for the rich."[83] Today, protection against oligopolies has been significantly eroded, and Robert Reich has highlighted the use of lobbying to construct laws that favor big businesses over small businesses.[84] My own experience in London as an oil and shipping reporter helped convince me that there is nothing very "natural"—or "moral"—about the way that markets work. With big profits and losses being made on deals linked to the prices I reported, I was offered incentives for moving these numbers up or down including an expensive holiday (declined) and having my neck broken (also declined). This was a remarkably shameless world in which intimidation and manipulation were commonplace. Liberal amounts of alcohol helped to lubricate the system and ease any twinges of conscience, while in general the watchword was Gordon Gekko's famous claim in the 1987 movie *Wall Street* that "greed is good."

Shame and Performance

We have noted the shaming of the "lazy poor." But today the shaming of people for not working hard arguably embraces *almost everyone*. As psychoanalyst Paul Hoggett has suggested, "Performativity is everything in a neo-liberal culture where 'safety nets', if they exist at all, are for the 'inadequates.' In a world full of risks, only the resilient survive."[85] Dependency, in these circumstances, becomes increasingly risky and increasingly shameful.[86] The "empowered self," as Hoggett puts it, goes about "making a difference" and yet "marches beneath the shadow of failure and humiliation."[87] At the same time, "'The outliers', 'underachievers', and 'under-performers' produced by performance measures become targets of manipulation, disapproval and anxious self-scrutiny.'"[88]

Education is one of the fields where all this has taken a firm grip. In the UK, schools became obsessed with obtaining the right exam "metrics," under pressure from governments that themselves wanted to show improved "performance." In the United States, some schoolteachers' pay was even linked to their pupils' performance, significantly adding to the pressure on everyone to make sure that grades were good.[89] Back in 2003, Stephen Ball, a sociology professor at London University, noted that both schoolteachers and academics were being subjected to a world of targets, monitoring, recording, comparisons, and League Tables, leading to "a sense of being constantly judged in different ways, by different means." Within such environments, staff were becoming chronically unsure as to whether they were "doing enough, doing the right thing, doing as much as others, or as well as others, constantly looking to improve."[90]

That analysis rings a cacophony of bells in terms of my own experience as an academic. In fact, the situation has deteriorated considerably since Ball's article was published. At my own university of the London School of Economics (LSE), pretty much everything is measured and monitored while shame waits patiently for anyone who falls short on teaching, research, or "citizenship." In such environments, the habit of constant judgment is often *internalized*—and fear of being judged sometimes seems to feed a desire to be one of the judges. Meanwhile, student evaluations are used to judge one's teaching, with graphs showing how you rate in comparison to colleagues across a wide range of criteria. Even departments in which the income has soared (from rising numbers of students paying rising levels of fees) can be labeled, after the relevant accounting work has been done, as "failing" or "problem" departments. This is not just LSE, of course, a university where academics are much more privileged and much better able to do their own research than in most universities. Such systems of surveillance-cum-shaming are now pretty much everywhere in UK and U.S. academia, and most of the academics I talk to are not (if I can put it mildly) happy about it. Yet in a cautious and even fearful climate, there is almost no culture of public complaint or even discussion: the closest you get to this are probably the "anonymous academics" in the pages of the *Guardian*. The precarity of public commitment to the universities (often seen as turning out graduates in "useless" subjects) has helped set the tone here. Also significant has been the trend toward employing more and more people on precarious short-term contracts, taking advantage of the huge numbers of people with qualifications appropriate for academia.

More generally, and on both sides of the Atlantic, the idea of a state that can protect people and contain their various anxieties has been to a large extent abandoned.[91] On top of the loss of traditional working-class jobs, there are also huge numbers of people who feel anxious, unprotected, and just plain poor amid hard-to-access services, escalating education and health-care costs, and minimal social security. With a fraying safety net, it can easily feel like a case of "everyone for themselves." It's tempting to resort to a kind of manic working in the search for financial security and in the hope that one will not be either discarded altogether or placed into a system of shaming that increasingly reserves its fiercest condemnations for "losers" and those with "bad metrics." In this increasingly anxious and shame-ridden world, as Lynne Layton puts it, "we daily run ourselves ragged."[92]

Of course, economic crisis just tightens the screws. Meanwhile, even leisure may not bring significant relief: revealingly, the habit of measuring performance is frequently internalized, and it often spills over into a person's private life and leisure time. At the extreme, there are the "self trackers" who constantly measure their vital signs (pulse, blood pressure, blood oxygen, sleep, and so on). In Hoggett's own clinical practice:

> Brief moments when the demand of the ideal is satisfied punctuate the background hum of performance anxiety, bringing mostly relief

rather than euphoria.... So many of the people I see believe themselves to be just "not... enough"—not slim enough, not manly enough, not clever enough, not successful enough, not sexual enough... the list goes on. It is as if they are measuring themselves against an imaginary ideal that can never be met.[93]

In Freud's terms, people are falling short of the "ego ideal" (the inner image of oneself as one wants to become).[94] But this ideal is established to a large extent by systems—including public and private institutions—that have enormous power as well as a vested interest in precisely the idea that we are constantly "falling short." A huge range of workers end up being tarred with this brush. So delivery workers have to meet stressful targets and find every move is being tracked, while railway workers are under pressure to bring in "efficiency" savings, with cuts to staff and overtime pay, and so on. On the UK railways, these pressures have helped to establish a bizarre trajectory of honor and shame: as Adil, a station employee, recently put it to me, "We were key workers and heroes in Covid, then 'lazy bastards' in the strike, then key workers again for the queen's funeral. They need to make up their minds!"

Of course, one might consider that it is better that we know how well people are doing in their work—and better to hold them to a certain standard. But things are getting out of hand. Everyone from police to health workers complains that bureaucracy, surveillance, form-filling, and fear of not measuring up are taking them away from the job they thought they were doing. It's getting harder to think clearly, and trust is eroding in the name of "transparency."[95] With more and more people feeling either replaced or monitored by machines of one kind or another, we are forced to become more and more machine-like—to keep up with the technology, to tick the right boxes, to calculate and measure but not to critique. Yet this process is not only deeply shaming in itself as humanity seeps away into the screen; it also smooths the path—as Arendt observed as long ago as 1958—for machines to replace us all the more.[96] Nobody, after all, can do machine-like work as well as a machine.

Conclusion

No matter which phase of capitalism we are in—and whether the emphasis is on production, consumption, attention, or surveillance—shame and shaming always seem to be around to lend a helping hand. This may make us *try harder*. But in practice the dream of "making good" has combined with a great deal of ideological blaming for poverty and with the structural difficulties of realizing some version of the American Dream. This in turn has created a giant reservoir of shame, from which huge numbers of people have been seeking different kinds of escape.

Again, shaming does not necessarily lead to shame: it may, for example, be enraging—and perhaps politically energizing in a constructive way. But shame has also been a resource that routinely fuels our most magical thinking, whether at a commercial or political level: it strongly informs our buying and our voting, and frequently leads us away from our best interests. Many of the most chronically shamed, moreover, are kept isolated from each other in struggling households or fearful workplaces. For those with internet, the main contact with "reality" may be an infosphere that itself offers purchases, pile-ons, and political fantasies as fleeting escapes from shame. Given this and given the extremely painful nature of shame itself, those who can make plausible offers to relieve our underlying shame, however temporarily, may rise (shamelessly) to the top. For them, shame is often a form of economic and political gold. Meanwhile, an emerging economy of mutual shaming and an emerging politics of mutual shaming serve as massive distractions from major social problems, tending only to solidify the inequality that does so much to generate shame in the first place.

Significantly, alongside all the (profitable) shaming of the rich and famous, there is a relative scarcity of the type of shame that might actually *challenge* their power and wealth. Catching a news report about elderly Americans being advised to stretch out their supplementary food rations by "watering down milk and soup," Mendible asked in 2016:

> Where is the flurry of outraged tweets at this shameful "solution" to hunger in the world's richest nation? Where are the outcries of moral

indignation at the incarceration of a generation of young Black men, the demonization of immigrants, the injustices committed in our name on "foreign" and "alien" bodies? This is the unacknowledged shame that binds us in silent resignation.[97]

While there is sometimes forgiveness and even profit for the mighty who have fallen (perhaps only to rise again), Mendible stresses that "stigmatizing shame ... casts its object into an underclass or even subclass that is irredeemable."[98] Sometimes a potentially productive shaming bursts through spectacularly, as in the Black Lives Matter protests or when Bernie Sanders won strong support for calling out the scandal of poverty-among-riches. But where the escape from shame is sold by the purveyors of right-wing populist politics, this essentially magical path has tended only to deepen the cycle of shame, to pass the shame to others, and to ignite an *additional* shaming of those who are backing these unrealistic and often cruel "solutions."

13

Shame and Mass Violence

WHILE SELF-INTEREST has often played a crucial role in driving mass violence in civil wars and genocides around the world, it would be unwise to overlook the very considerable role of emotion—not least the emotion of shame. A key problem in many disasters is the manipulation of shame to encourage violence. A second is the construction of shamelessness around a disaster.

While the discussions that follow are necessarily brief, I look first at the construction of shamelessness in civil war and global wars, drawing on the examples of Sri Lanka and Syria. Then I look more specifically at genocide, using the examples of Rwanda and Guatemala. After that, I examine the case of civil war and famine in Sudan, a case I followed particularly closely. Finally, I discuss some cases of mass violence and famine under communism, drawing on events in the Soviet Union, China, and Cambodia. In all of these discussions, we get a better idea of how shamelessness is constructed—and how shame and shamelessness can interact in highly destructive ways.

Shamelessness and Useful Enemies

In my experience, shamelessness has very frequently been constructed by pointing to a ruthless and vicious enemy who is held responsible for all the bad things that are happening. This tends to create damaging impunity for a range of *other actors*—particularly when they present themselves as confronting a vilified group such as "rebels," "terrorists," or "human smugglers." This in turn has tended to feed exploitation and political repression within some kind of "state of emergency" (either declared or not), while reproducing grievances and enemies in a way that lends legitimacy to a shameless and abusive system. Within such systems, the chosen enemy is likely to be both blamed and shamed. But shaming tends to add an extra level of emotional resonance to the identification of what I have called (in a book of the same title) "useful enemies."[1] Very often, blaming a party for specific actions tips over into demonizing them for their *inherent evil*, and this in turn adds to the impunity of those who claim to *oppose* this "evil." Something like the public humiliation of captured "enemies" can play into this collective shaming. All of this tends to narrow the space for a nuanced and critical public discussion. We should notice here an important phenomenon: shaming may be remarkably successful even when it doesn't actually induce shame. For example, it may consolidate group membership; it may help to win votes; and it may divert attention from one's own abuses. Shaming may "fail" in changing behavior for the better, and it may easily make this behavior worse. But this doesn't mean that the shamers have actually failed in their most important goals.

Often, the government in a conflict-affected country will make a show of cooperating with a global "war" of some kind, while perhaps pursuing its own program of violence and reaping the aid and impunity that come from ostensible cooperation in an international agenda.[2] Such "righteous" global wars have included a "war on communism," a "war on drugs," a "war on terror," and even a "fight against illegal migration."[3] Through a combination of blaming and shaming, a sense of self-righteousness has routinely been cultivated, largely sidelining any productive sense of shame.

Within such "wars," grave suffering has been facilitated and encouraged by a collective focus on high-profile enemies—and from the dangerous shamelessness that this fixation tends to induce. Where a group is demonized locally and internationally, the impunity is likely to be particularly intense; indeed, civilians risk losing the protection of national and international law through their association with a demonized group. Meanwhile, the causes of a rebellion tend to be obscured amid a joint condemnation of the rebels; in a combination of projection and amnesia, the faults of the society that "created" the rebels may be pushed aside in favor of a focus on the faults of the rebels.[4] Much the same goes for criminal gangs.[5] Meanwhile, as Nafeez Ahmed has shown very clearly, today's combination of energy, ecological, and economic crises tends to be conceptualized as profitable "security crises," reinforcing security structures and sidelining the underlying problems in the process.[6]

If we look briefly at the case of Sri Lanka, we can understand better how shamelessness is constructed around mass violence. When I was in Sri Lanka in 2009, I was able to investigate the government's attempts to create space for ruthless military tactics through intimidation and controlling information flows. As part of its public relations exercise, the democratically elected government of Mahinda Rajapaksa shamelessly insisted that not a single civilian was being killed by government forces in the course of what it called a "humanitarian rescue" mission for Tamil civilians in the north of the country. Such language not only inverted the truth with intimidating boldness; it was also a kind of humiliation—and a muzzling technique—for anyone (including aid workers) who did not contradict it. As part of this alleged "rescue," the government declared "safe areas" for civilians near the coast—a claim that was to be shockingly undermined by the government forces' mass shelling of civilians in these areas. The government also forcibly detained hundreds of thousands of Tamil civilians behind barbed-wire fences on the edge of the war zone. With the international community proving distinctly reticent in criticizing Colombo's human rights abuses, Tamil civilians in effect fell below the protection of national and international law. UN organizations also kept quiet. In fact, aid agencies—both within and outside the UN system—tended to sacrifice plain-speaking in the interests of access to the conflict zone—an access that largely failed to materialize.[7]

Looking to create political space for its ruthless "war ending," the Sri Lankan government positioned its military offensive as part of the *global* "war on terror," thereby instantly warding off a large measure of shame and blame. The Sri Lankan government also systematically intimidated journalists, aid workers, and anyone who started to reveal (or might have revealed) the extent of civilian suffering. When the Sri Lankan government ordered all non-rebels to evacuate rebel-held areas in 2009, it was able to label any critical information escaping the war zone as emanating from the rebels. By making outrageous statements and simultaneously intimidating people into silence, the Sri Lankan government managed to construct an "alternative reality" around the violence and to engineer a far-reaching collusion in its own lies.

As part of this, the Rajapaksa regime was continuously expanding its working definition of the enemy—from the Tamil Tiger terrorists to the Tamil population more generally, and on to international aid workers, journalists, and human rights workers, and eventually to many Muslims. In many ways, this was an effective system of repression since anyone who criticized President Rajapaksa, his war, or even his widening persecutions risked being labeled a terrorist sympathizer.[8] As in many other conflicts, criticism of government abuses was largely silenced through these means.

A remarkable aura of shamelessness around the atrocities was underlined in November 2019 when Mahinda Rajapaksa, having been defeated in the 2015 presidential elections, became Sri Lanka's prime minister; his brother and wartime defense minister, Gotobaya Rajapaksa, had recently become president.

The case of Syria can enhance our understanding of how shamelessness is constructed around large-scale abuse. Syria also offers another horrific example of how the global "war on terror" has been manipulated to deepen the shamelessness and impunity that facilitate mass violence. In Syria, a conspicuously legitimate political protest that attracted strong international approval was transformed into an armed rebellion—in large part through vicious counterinsurgency tactics that radicalized the protest. In turn, the rebels were quickly demonized as "terrorists," "criminals," and "fanatics" whose main priority was either beheading foreigners or looting. In interviews at the Turkey-Syria border, many Syrians told me that the Bashar al-Assad regime was pushing rebellion in directions that, paradoxically, were less threatening to him than peaceful protests.[9] In addition to attacking and radicalizing peaceful protesters, the Assad regime also fostered the image of a fanatical and illegitimate rebellion through other tactics: strategically releasing Islamist extremists from prison; faking "terrorist" attacks; cooperating economically with ISIS rebels and criminal elements; and focusing government attacks on *non-ISIS* rebels (which had the effect of incentivizing support for ISIS). As time passed, a conspicuous shaming and blaming of ISIS (including at the international level) helped solidify a damaging impunity for the Syrian government itself.

The rather systematic de-legitimization of protest and rebellion in Syria illustrated the importance of Arendt's "action as propaganda." As so often in wartime (not least in Sierra Leone), the condemnation of fanatical and greedy rebels tended to prevent acknowledgment of underlying grievances or government abuses. Meanwhile, areas with a significant rebel presence were deprived of aid—a government counterinsurgency tactic that was in effect exacerbated and legitimized by international fears that assistance would fall into the hands of "terrorists."[10] Among Syrian civilians, in turn, a sense of being deserted by the government and by the international community sometimes encouraged support for extreme jihadist groups that were offering their own (often violent) brand of protection and assistance.

Even as President Assad laid waste to the country, he was also able to present himself domestically as a guarantor of order and as a "lesser evil" in comparison to ISIS in particular. The tactic of fostering criminal and terrorist elements also bought Assad a little space in relation to the international community. Shortly before Boris Johnson became UK foreign minister, he stated explicitly that Assad was a "lesser evil" compared to ISIS. Significantly, the "war on terror" framework had served as a powerful incentive for Assad to nurture the "terrorist" element within the Syrian rebellion and to position himself as this "lesser evil."

We know that governments in Syria and Sri Lanka have by no means been the only ones to use the global "war on terror" as part of carving out impunity for the abuse of civilians. Other governments that have performed some version of this maneuver include those of Uganda, Somalia, Israel, Pakistan, Afghanistan, Russia, and China; the same goes for the Saudi/U.S./UK-backed faction in Yemen. In conflicts across the world, dissidents have routinely been relabeled as "terrorists" or "terrorist sympathizers."[11] These abusive systems have tended to have an inbuilt shame-proofing.

In addition to nurturing "useful enemies" and presenting oneself as a "lesser evil" and intimidating critics, techniques for maintaining shameless systems have included a widespread use of euphemism, a habit of bringing humanitarian "needs" into line with the favored or convenient response, and a tendency to redefine humanitarianism as the prevention of dangerous journeys by migrants and refugees. Another important technique has been redefining choices as unalterable circumstances—as, for example, when human-made famine is blamed on "the weather" or failure to relieve rebel areas is blamed on "security constraints" or when refugees' deaths in the Mediterranean are blamed on "the sea."

Genocide: Rwanda and Guatemala

Some 850,000 people were killed in the 1994 Rwandan genocide, and many of the more superficial explanations stressed "ancient ethnic hatreds." But political manipulations were crucial. The genocide followed a peace agreement, signed in 1993 at Arusha in Tanzania, which saw Tutsi rebels reaching an accommodation with a single-party Rwandan regime that was itself dominated by a small group of Hutus from the northwest of the country, the *Akazu* (or "little house"). When Hutu extremists organized and stirred up a genocide (against the Tutsi population and also some Hutu opposition members), key aims were disrupting the peace agreement, derailing the emerging democracy, and preserving power for this privileged group. Shame dynamics were also extremely important—on at least five levels.

First, mass killing in Rwanda was presented in extremist Hutu propaganda as a way of reversing past experiences of humiliation at the hands of the Tutsi ethnic group (notably under colonial rule and including public whippings), a subordination that was said to be on the verge of being reinstated.[12] In line with James Gilligan's theory about violent crime (but this time on a much wider scale), a sensitivity to threats in the present was greatly elevated by memories of past violence (whether these memories were direct, handed down from older generations, or stirred up by propaganda). When it comes to the past traumas that Hutu extremist propaganda was stirring and spotlighting, the propagandists served in effect as Sluzki's "hostile witnesses," ramping up past shame and the danger of its renewal and then proposing their own violence as the solution. An investigation by African Rights noted that a central feature of the cruelty during the genocide was humiliating Tutsis so as to "avenge" the wrongs of the past.[13] Some fleeing Tutsis said soldiers would beat them and then "insist that they clap their hands and thank them, with comments like 'Now we will make you feel what your great grandfathers did to us.'"[14] This was a combustible political context in which democratization and economic liberalization were pushed simultaneously and in great haste. Those with a vested interest in the established single-party rule were able to exploit these historical grievances, including the "memories" of shame, in an attempt to subvert reform through genocide.

A second element of shame infusing the violence was shame around "underdevelopment."[15] Part of this, as noted in chapter 12, was that "development" was often perceived as highly uneven and even humiliating, with many feeling shut out of the promised benefits of modernity. Before the 1994 genocide, there had been a growing pressure on land and a major problem of unemployment; yet, as African Rights noted, "Without land or employment, young men cannot advance in life; they cannot marry or achieve the social status of their parents."[16] Structural adjustment programs in the 1980s and early 1990s had reduced opportunities for government employment in particular. Yet underlying grievances, emotional discontents, and associated political dangers were largely excluded from the dominant international frameworks, and African Rights noted, "No sensitivity or concern was expressed [by the IMF or World Bank] as to the likely political and social repercussions of economic shock therapy," despite the fact that this was "a country on the brink of civil war." In fact, the World Bank team consciously excluded "non-economic variables" from their "simulations."[17] Such "variables" are often hard to measure and tend to get excluded from modeling that likes to present itself as "objective."

A third influential element of shame in Rwanda centered on the army, which was to play a key role in carrying out the 1994 genocide, along with the notorious *interahamwe* militias. Mahmood Mamdani notes that "as defeat disgraced it, the army exploded," turning away from the successful Rwandan Patriotic Front rebels and toward the civilian enemy within the country. The army was looking "to purify the nation and rid it of all impurities that detracted from its strength,"[18] and we can see here a variation of the jump from defeat to "betrayal" that was also damagingly influential in France after the Franco-Prussian War, in Germany after World War I, and in the United States after the Korean and Vietnam wars. In Rwanda, feelings of humiliation within the army had an economic dimension. Particularly given the shrinking opportunities within the state bureaucracy, joining the army had been one of the few feasible outlets for young men. But then major redundancies within the army were announced, partly as an economy measure and partly to accommodate rebels into the army.[19] As noted in chapter 12, the threat of a return to the "menial" labor of farming was not welcomed. Rapid DDR proved a major obstacle to peace, as was soon to be the case in Sierra Leone in 1996–97 and in Iraq from 2003.

A fourth important "shame" dynamic was that international shame around weak responses to the Rwandan genocide ended up feeding strongly into *subsequent* killing. With UN peacekeepers having been withdrawn from Rwanda in the midst of the killing, it very quickly became clear that the international community had essentially stood by and watched a genocide unfold. The main exception to this passivity was France, which had *actively encouraged* the genocide (notably by supplying arms even as the genocide raged) and had then helped perpetrators to escape via the "safe haven" that was set up under France's Opération Turquoise intervention.[20] In these circumstances, the Tutsi-dominated government that took over in Rwanda was granted a great deal of latitude within international circles, particularly when it came to its military intervention in neighboring DRC. Yet that intervention helped to trigger a devastating war in the DRC itself and to precipitate the massacre of hundreds of thousands of Hutu civilians inside the

DRC by forces with links to the new Rwandan government—effectively a second genocide.[21] Rwanda stressed that it was taking on the Hutu militias responsible for genocide, but its forces also quickly became involved in mining the DRC's valuable mineral resources.[22] Meanwhile, both Rwanda and Uganda were helped by their status as "favorites" in Washington and London (something that was eventually reflected in their participation in the so-called "coalition of the willing" supporting the invasion of Iraq and later in the selection of Rwanda as a destination for asylum seekers forcibly relocated from the UK). This complicated set of events illustrates the need to be aware of how shame around past inactions can feed into impunity in the present.

Shame fed into the evolving crisis in a fifth significant way, when various armed groups in the DRC (including the national army) became involved in large-scale violence against civilians, including widespread sexual violence. As the war within the DRC evolved, nonviolence was often portrayed as "unmanly" behavior, spurring young men into violence.[23] Rape was sometimes used a weapon of war, with humiliation being used to demoralize entire communities. As in Sierra Leone, fighters' abuses naturally attracted a growing chorus of condemnation, and this led in turn to a growing feeling among soldiers that civilians did not respect them. The widening rift between soldiers and civilians tended to intensify anti-civilian violence.[24] Such dynamics underline the need for sensitive security sector reforms that focus on national armies and get beyond the common focus on high-profile rebel groups.[25]

Turning to the civil war and genocide in Guatemala from 1960 (and the violent peace from 1996), one crucial element of shame was the humiliation dished out to indigenous Mayan communities who had been deprived of most of the best land through conquest and expropriation, forced to work on major landed estates, and systematically treated as less than human.[26] Since the 1996 peace process to a large extent ignored these underlying grievances, it was always going to be a violent and exploitative peace.

Within the civil war itself, shame was loaded onto victim communities as part of encouraging and cementing the violence. The underlying shame arising from exploitation was itself exploited when Mayan village patrols and their leaders (or *jefes*) were used in the counterinsurgency. In her fine study of the war and its aftermath, Judith Zur commented:

> the immediate power of a rifle and the ability to evoke fear in fellow villages is a more than satisfactory compensation for all the years of disrespect.... By casting his lot with the army, the *jefe* can see himself as "more" human than his fellow villagers.[27]

Moreover, government soldiers would encourage civil patrol leaders into atrocities against their own communities, driving a wedge between these *jefes* and the rest of the community and cementing the *jefes'* loyalty to the army.[28]

On top of this, government destruction of villages itself tended to propel men into the civil patrols. Once recruited the men often had to work far from home, losing touch with their old livelihoods—and being unable to provide for their families was an extra humiliation. Zur noted that the abusive civil patrols provided a space for the assertion of male identity and for what she calls a "suspect self-respect" for patrollers who now identified with the dominant military/Ladino group.[29] By encouraging and coercing cooperation from elements of the Mayan community, the government promoted division, distrust, confusion—and shame.[30] Shame among the victims of violence was further encouraged through the extremity of the violence itself, through official propaganda, and through purposefully isolating villages and victims from one another, so that many began to wonder why they had been specifically chosen as targets for retaliation. Zur notes that a common response was: "We must have committed a very bad sin. What sin could that be?"[31] Part of the oppression was shaming the victims of sexual violence into silence.[32] Meanwhile, the manipulation of violence and shame within the Mayan population was one way in which the Guatemalan government continuously constructed its own shamelessness, spreading responsibility for the suffering while also evading the charge of genocide.

In Guatemala, a kind of shamelessness around the violence was also encouraged by a national and international political context that positioned Communists, subversives, and drug criminals as intrinsically evil enemies whose defeat demanded a *mano dura* (or iron fist).

After outright war ended in 1996, shame also helped shape the violent peace that followed. A shifting ideological climate meant that soldiers who had been told they were heroes of an anti-Communist struggle were rapidly relabeled as dupes and abusers; the resulting resentments fed into various kinds of criminal activity. In Guatemala City in 2002, one source very close to the army told me:

> Those depending on the army came to see it as an obstacle—their repressive tactics were stopping markets in the United States and vacations in Miami and whatever. Now there's a huge protest in the officers' corps against the moneyed classes because they feel betrayed. They were doing their dirty work and then their backers decided they were no longer useful.

This sense of betrayal was compounded by the knowledge that the Guatemalan army had not suffered a decisive defeat at the hands of the rebels.[33] In these unpromising circumstances, many serving and former military officers nourished a symbiotic relationship with organized crime, participating in everything from drug-running to covert violence against human rights activists. In many ways, the international community played into their hands. Even as the "war on communism" faded, the 1990s saw the rise of a high-profile "war on crime/drugs." This new "war" helped legitimize large military budgets and provide cover for the security sector's collaboration with organized crime—underpinning the continuing shamelessness of a corrupt and violent system. Meanwhile, women were a particular target for postwar violence by civil patrol leaders: the shamelessness and impunity of these leaders were threatened by women's talk, by women's ridicule, and even by spiritual retribution. Zur brought out the threat of shame when she noted, "*jefes* (and men generally) are bewildered and offended by the women's laughter, their 'lack of respect', and wonder what they will do next."[34] Part of the practical problem was that official shamelessness was protected when the voices of Mayan civilians—and women in particular—were largely shut out of the peace process. This contributed to a continued silence around sexual and gender-based violence as well as around other forms of violence.[35]

Civil War and Famine: Sudan

In 1988, I was able to do some detailed research on the war and famine that were afflicting southern Sudanese in particular.[36] The primary cause of the famine was government-sponsored militia raiding against southern Sudanese groups that were said to be supporting the rebel SPLA (Sudan People's Liberation Army). Government definitions of the enemy expanded to allow the active starvation of the Dinka ethnic group. Meanwhile, the suffering inflicted on civilians by Khartoum tended to push people toward the rebels.[37] As in many other crises, there was also a kind of social construction of shamelessness, a process in which horrific events were repeatedly portrayed in ways that made them seem somewhat acceptable—whether to the immediate perpetrators of violence or to influential international actors. Again, it's important to understand how shame was warded off—and how it was perversely distributed.

Fears around the rebel SPLA gave an air of "legitimacy" to government tactics that were designed to weaken both the rebels and the populations that were said to be supporting them. The shamelessness of this cynical maneuver was underlined to me at Babanousa railway station, the key depot for dispatching relief trains to the south. Here, a railway worker willingly handed over to me damning statistics on the composition of these trains—in return for a smile and a tape of Michael Jackson songs. He saw no particular problem (or secret worth keeping) in the fact that the relief trains to the south, which were supposed to carry humanitarian aid, ended up carrying mostly commercial goods and military hardware for government garrison towns (a process that turned out to reflect, in part, the pressuring and bribing of railway officials by powerful commercial and military interests in northern Sudan).

In the face of a severe famine, international donor governments and the European Community cited "security constraints" and claimed that the numbers "in need and reachable" were limited to a few thousand. Yet these "constraints" themselves reflected the fact that rebels were sometimes attacking trains they knew to be used for military resupply. We can see here how abusive systems may generate and reproduce their own legitimacy, with action serving as a form of propaganda (in line with Arendt's concept of "action as propaganda") and shamelessness being continuously regenerated.

Shame and neglect were also an important part of the background story. Some of the northern pastoral groups recruited into militia violence had themselves been neglected in Sudan's economic development process. They were a political threat to Khartoum. Meanwhile, years of intermarriage between western Sudanese and southern groups had, according to Frances Deng (a Dinka intellectual who went on to become the UN's representative on internally displaced people), contributed to a desire among some of the militia groups to assert superiority over those to the south (sometimes dismissed as *abid* or slaves).[38] In the counterinsurgency, these northern groups were given status as part of the dominant elite (just as the *jefes* had been in Guatemala). Although having a relatively low status in relation to Sudan's central Nilotic elites, various Arab groups were given arms and impunity to allow the assertion of dominance over southern Sudanese—including through the ultimate degradation of famine.

In terms of international complicity, a key factor was the failure to supply significant amounts of international assistance to the famine areas. International relief operations were remarkably ineffective, and silence about human rights abuses was encouraged by the hope of getting permission for increased aid deliveries as well as by the felt need to keep the Sudan government "onside" as an ally of Western democracies—a buffer between the revolutionary regimes in neighboring Libya and Ethiopia. Meanwhile, at the tag end of the Cold War, the "Communist" label that was sometimes applied to the SPLA rebels helped create a remarkably shameless system in which slavery was being actively revived while a predatory counterinsurgency and a human-made famine unfolded under the watchful—and on the whole tolerant—eye of international diplomats. The northern Sudanese militias and their backers in Khartoum were largely exempt, for a long time, from international criticism. As part of this sotto voce system, the largest aid donors (the European Economic Community, USAID, and the UN) tended to focus on the *fact* that people had been displaced but not on *why* they had been displaced.

Exemplifying a much wider danger in humanitarian crises, even progressive-sounding doctrines could be harnessed to Khartoum's murderous endeavor. For example, the idea of targeting the poorest and neediest through providing relief to people in camps actually lent itself to the abandonment of all of those, many still in the south, who were *in the process of losing* their assets to the militias. Meanwhile, international aid donors tended to congratulate themselves on a prompt response to famine, a discourse that relied on defining famine as mass mortality and mass migration; yet in reality these phenomena were only the *final stages* in a long process of famine over several years, a process that involved state violence, cattle theft, and the use of violence to distort grain, livestock, and labor markets.[39] As earlier in the Vietnam War and later in the "war on terror," an image of success was rather consistently extracted from the reality of failure.

The international community remained largely mute on the government's blocking of relief aid. In practice, humanitarian aid was positioned on the edge of the oil-rich zone that the Sudan government wished to depopulate and monetize. The pattern of aid provision was tending to assist rather than counteract a process of ethnic cleansing and a process of famine creation. Meanwhile, the government was under pressure to repay mounting international debts, and oil revenue was one obvious way out of this bind.

This was a famine caused not so much by "market forces" as by what I call "forced markets," a process symbolized in the town of Abyei: a machine gun was pointed directly into the marketplace where Dinka people were surrendering their cattle for next to nothing.[40] One young man in the nearby famine camp at Meiram told me the Dinka victims of the famine were being treated "like dogs" and "had no rights." Apparently sophisticated U.S. satellite systems for predicting famine—comparing "lucky" green areas with more arid and browner areas—proved quite capable of giving precisely the wrong prediction, with green areas tending to attract violence (and hence famine) as a result of the impunity and desperation of people in brown areas. So this particular "science" did more to obscure the nature of the famine than to reveal it.

At the extreme, famine was actually being welcomed in the service of "development." In particular, livestock-rearing by those who became the victims of famine was sometimes presented by international donors as an anachronism, while "progress" and "agricultural development" were said to be served when southern famine migrants were forced to work for free or for very low wages on northern farms. Bizarrely, major donor organizations sometimes claimed that in *not delivering* substantial quantities of relief to famine victims, they had succeeded in *not creating* "*dependency*"—a variation of the colonial discourse that too much aid will only corrupt the recipients and make them lazy. As in many conflicts (and as we saw in a different way in the case of Guatemala), there was a shaming of the victims.

We should note, too, that while Sudan's democratic government was overthrown in 1989, many of the key dynamics unfolding in 1988 have persisted to the present. Susanne Jaspars's important long-term work in Darfur, western Sudan, brings out these continuities. In particular, a shameless manipulation of disaster has continued, while modern technology and an ostensibly progressive system of "remote management" have in many ways compounded the old tendency to blame and shame the victims of disaster. Again, government-sponsored violence has been downplayed. And as in 1988, the Sudan government has been able to launder its violence by holding out the hope of humanitarian access as an incentive for aid organizations—particularly within the UN—to keep quiet about underlying human rights abuses.

Illuminating the continuing construction of shamelessness around suffering, Jaspars shows how the representation of reality within the humanitarian system could diverge remarkably far from the truth. This echoed not only the distortions evident during the 1988 Sudanese famine but also the divergence highlighted by Arendt in the context of the Vietnam War.

Echoing dynamics in earlier famines, the Sudan government imposed tight restrictions on food aid to rebel areas (particularly from 2010), citing "insecurity"—a policy that the UN's World Food Program did not do much to challenge. Jaspars noted, "The actual effect of reducing food aid has been to help government counter-insurgency strategies and policies to empty the camps and bring IDP leaders over to the government side."[41] Meanwhile, in Jaspars's words, "International agencies have created a regime of truth in which malnutrition and food insecurity is due to people's own behaviors, in which conflict is invisible."[42] So a depoliticized, technical, and ostensibly highly scientific model of relief provision has facilitated a highly perverse distribution of shame around a failing system. Jaspars notes that in 2004, aid staff had often spoken about Darfur in terms of the urgent need for "protection," but less than a decade later the dominant discourse had come to center on "the risk of dependency," with those displaced on a long-term basis often portrayed as "cheats."[43]

While such shaming may do the "work" of responsibility-shifting even without instilling shame in those who suffer, the latter did in fact express shame for receiving food aid.[44] This was despite the very small amounts of food aid that had actually been received and despite the extreme difficulty of resuming normal livelihoods in the middle of a conflict. In both Sudan and Sierra Leone, I have myself seen how concern around "dependency" could hobble emergency relief,[45] and others like Barbara Harrell-Bond and Chris Dolan have documented the blaming and pathologizing of aid recipients.[46] More generally, as Mark Duffield notes in his excellent book *Post-humanitarianism*, the "end users" of aid have increasingly been blamed for "bad decisions."[47] "Resilience" has been the watchword, and the commonplace focus on women's behavior (good feeding practices, improved hygiene in the home, etc.) is part of a tendency to blame the victims.[48]

Drawing on Foucault's analysis of the various "regimes of truth" that are created by (and in turn legitimize) particular policy practices, Jaspars commented on aid organizations' discussions of modern-day Darfur:

> This regime of truth removes government responsibility for creating food insecurity and malnutrition through its war strategies and denial of access, and removes international responsibility for protecting civilians from large-scale loss of life at the hands of their own government.[49]

In recent years, the invisibility of conflict itself has been exacerbated by a growing fashion for providing aid "from a distance," relying increasingly on "remote management."[50] Such trends may bring their own threat of shame—the shame of having drifted so far from reality that one becomes a facilitator and apologist for abuse and for decisions increasingly made by machines. Yet this shame, too, can be warded off in the name of efficiency, "science," objectivity, and making decisions that are "fair" in respect to different crises around the world. To the extent that algorithms and machines are now making important decisions in humanitarian relief, the question of human shame—from one point of view—need hardly arise!

Disasters under Communism

The human capacity to construct "alternative realities" that stymie any productive shame can also be seen in several disasters under communism. Official shamelessness in relation to suffering around these disasters was fostered by a belief that they were somehow "necessary" for the economy, for development, or even (in the long term) for *famine prevention*. Meanwhile, preserving destructive "alternative realities" tended to encourage an expansion in the "enemy" category—if only so as to deter and police any criticism. Totalitarianism, whether Communist or fascist, was conducive to famine, and the decline of totalitarianism coincided with a significant decline in the incidence of famine.[51]

In 1932–33, as the Soviet Communist regime pushed for industrialization and for the collectivization of agriculture, nearly four million Ukrainians died not from crop failure but because they were deliberately deprived of food.[52] The Ukrainian famine and more generally the failure of collectivization played a part in generating Stalin's purges. The Russian poet and novelist Boris Pasternak noted in *Dr Zhivago*:

> Collectivization was an erroneous and unsuccessful measure and it was impossible to admit the error. To conceal the failure, people had to be cured, by every means of terrorism, of the habit of thinking and judging for themselves, and forced to see what didn't exist, to assert the very opposite of what their eyes told them.[53]

Saying what one knows to be untrue is profoundly shaming in itself. But as Sean Armstrong put it in a perceptive analysis, "The official 'party line' purported to explain everything and could not admit mistakes. The planned economy must succeed, so failures became interpreted in terms of conscious wrecking."[54] Within this mindset, "good, revolutionary wills had been thwarted by the operation of *evil* wills," with forced confessions helping to reveal the latter.[55] International actors also played their part in covering up or underplaying Stalin's terror—not least on the left. Sartre said it was "not our duty to write about Soviet labour camps,"[56] and more generally Anne Applebaum observed in her book *Gulag* that no one wanted to be told there was a darker side to the Allied victory "or that the camps of Stalin, our ally, expanded just as the camps of Hitler, our enemy, were liberated."[57]

Soviet "scientific" ideology confidently claimed that willpower could overcome all obstacles, that progress would be relentless, and that everything could be understood and predicted according to the laws of scientific Marxism. But when major obstacles were encountered, when famine emerged, when economic hardship proved enduring, and when opposition failed to disappear, official adherence to "science" fed into a "shadow side" of extremely "unscientific" behavior—violent blaming, irrational thinking, and ultimately Stalin's mass purges.[58] In this way, a process of keeping shame at bay fed into an escalating violence—and then an escalating threat of shame in a vicious circle.

The 1958–62 famine under Mao Zedong's "Great Leap Forward" claimed the lives of at least thirty million people. Coverage by Western journalists was extremely restricted.[59] As with the Ukraine famine, the principal cause of Mao's famine was forcible collectivization and excessive grain requisitioning by the state. A strong push for collectivization in the 1950s had seen peasants forced to pool their livestock, tools, grain, and labor; many farmers slaughtered their animals and got a much higher price for the meat than the collectives were paying for the animals. When famine came, Mao was remarkably shameless in his attitude to the deaths of so many millions, noting in 1957, "We are prepared to sacrifice 300 million Chinese for the victory of the world revolution," and telling the top echelon of the Chinese Communist Party in 1958,

"Deaths have benefits. They can fertilise the ground."[60] In this statement, famine-as-development had reached its logical conclusion. Many local cadres used food as a weapon to get rid of categories of people deemed dangerous or useless, including those too sick or too old to work.[61] State granaries were often full even as millions starved, and the party secretary in Xingyang, Henan province, one of the worst-affected areas, would shamelessly order twenty-four-course banquets in advance when he traveled to local communes.

Meanwhile, shame was instrumentalized to *promote* excessive requisitioning—and, in effect, to promote the famine. Class enemies were dragged onto stages and repeatedly humiliated. This was part of a political theater that turned the tables on those who were seen as historically dominant. Such theatrical humiliations also invited shame—and complicity—in the audience. Historian Frank Dikötter notes, "By implicating all the villagers in denunciation, beating and sometimes murder of a carefully targeted minority, all of them become permanently linked to the Party. . . . Everybody was to have blood on their hands."[62]

A second layer of shaming pertained to requisitioning. In his book *Hungry Ghosts*, Jasper Becker shows how districts would compete with each other to obtain the maximum grain requisitions, often greatly exaggerating the extent of the harvest. Prefectures organized competitions to see which local area could obtain the most grain. Under Mao, China developed a particularly murderous version of what modern democracies sometimes call "target culture," with shame and honor heaped on "bad" and "good" performance, respectively.[63] An upside-down morality involved the shaming of the victims but not the perpetrators. If you did not participate in the production of famine (by surrendering or requisitioning grain, for example), then you stood to be publicly shamed (and worse) as someone who was not meeting their targets for grain requisitioning, someone who was hiding grain, or someone who was drawing attention to facts that threatened the shamelessness of the Communist leadership. As in many other contexts,[64] the problem was not shame itself but the inhuman uses to which it was being put. Becker notes: "Huang Chuan county [in Henan province] urged its inhabitants to eat less for three days so that it could rise higher than ninth place, its leaders declaring that it was better to let a few hundred people starve to death than sacrifice their honour."[65] Becker notes the importance of maintaining a good image and impressing the authorities even as famine raged: "At each commune Mao visited, he was delighted to see electric irrigation pumps watering the fields, but they were always the same pumps, which had been taken from the last commune and which were then installed in the next while he slept."[66]

Following patterns in the Soviet Union, shame *arising from* the famine was accommodated through the selective blaming—and frequently shaming—of "counterrevolutionary" elements. If admitted at all, shortages were blamed on sabotage by former landlords and other wreckers. "Right opportunists" were blamed for hiding grain. Those who protested or were suspected of hiding grain were not just killed; many were tortured or publicly beaten. Some of those suspected of hiding grain or of insubordination were simply starved. Some had their noses pierced and wires inserted, before being forced to undergo the humiliation of pulling a plough like an ox. When the Chinese national army finally ordered distribution of grain from state granaries in 1961, the official version of the truth was that problems had been caused by landlords and rich peasants sneaking into revolutionary organizations and working against the interests of the majority of the peasantry.[67]

Many similar dynamics informed famine and mass killings under the Khmer Rouge in Cambodia. The process involved the mass shaming of city dwellers—forcing them into lower-status agricultural labor and subjecting them to life-or-death decisions by children. As with Soviet collectivization and as with China's "Great Leap Forward," practical problems caused by collectivization in Cambodia were a threat to the "scientific" thinking that allegedly underpinned the Khmer Rouge revolution. Such problems could not be officially acknowledged, and again this in turn fed into a widening search for scapegoats alongside an intensification of the allegedly scientific policies that were actually creating the suffering. Again, "science" morphed violently into magic.

In their revealing study of *Political Paranoia*, Robert Robins and Jerrold Post suggested that Pol Pot's Cambodia illustrated "the natural history of political paranoia." First, there was the promise of a new world after the destruction of a demonized group (in this case, everything non-Khmer or non-ethnic Cambodian). Second, policies based on these beliefs failed to bring happiness but actually increased misery and poverty. In the third stage of this process:

> The leader rationalizes the failure of these policies in terms of the continuation of demon-group values and conspiracies. The ideologically correct but discredited policies are therefore redoubled, and the hunt for the "conspirators" and "saboteurs" gains strength.[68]

Fourth and finally, Robins and Post observed, "In reaction to these policies, hostility and suspicion, then actual conspiracies and sabotage against the regime, begin to develop."[69] As in Russia and China, we can see how the attempt to ward off shame strongly inhibited any *lesson-learning* while also powerfully deepening the violence.

———

As part of an important book that shows the pressing need for accountability for mass starvation, Alex de Waal argues that for those who suffer a famine, the experience tends to be intensely shaming. This reflects many profound indignities (such as the sale of one's inheritance and the failure to perform basic rituals for the dead) as well as sometimes reflecting active participation in small acts of cruelty and exploitation. De Waal goes on to note:

> Too rarely are the political causes of mass starvation recognized for what they are: the transitivity of the verb "to starve" is forgotten. The survivors silently cry out for a "me, too" movement to liberate them from the shame that dogs their memories. . . . Conceiving of mass starvation as a crime, as a wrong inflicted by powerful men situated far away; as suffering for which blame should be directed outward, should be an act of emancipation. The message conveyed to the victims and survivors, by naming and memorializing famine as an atrocity, is elementary but compelling: *it wasn't your fault*.[70]

When we look more broadly at mass violence and related humanitarian disasters around the world, we can see how shamelessness is constructed—and we can see, again, the need to redistribute shame. In all of the cases of mass violence examined in this chapter, shame was kept at bay with a dangerous and escalating flight from reality, while shame and blame were routinely directed at victims rather than perpetrators. A failure to recognize the important part that shame has played in human disasters leads to lost opportunities for constructive interventions while playing into the hands of those who distribute shame in ways that greatly facilitate mass violence and suffering. Disasters have often been facilitated by a "big theory"—whether "political economy," ideas around "development," or the theory that one class or race will eventually triumph. Such theory has tended to be especially dangerous when it has urged short-term pain—usually *somebody else's pain*—for long-term gain.[71] When officials have seen themselves as "objective" or as following "reason" rather than emotion, they have tended to be especially dangerous.

In line with some of Hannah Arendt's work, we may say that the more the "official truth" departs from reality, the more the relevant authorities are likely to deem it necessary to resort to violence and intimidation in order to ward off shame and protect the relevant delusions. At the same time, such authorities are likely not simply to be protecting delusions but also to be nurturing the system of economic and political benefits that has grown up around—and helped drive—a particular disaster.

When we focus on the shamelessness of abusive systems, it is perhaps natural to assume that injecting more shame would be helpful. Reflecting the potentially positive effects of moral shame, shaming can be an important ally for those who want to challenge abusive systems. Amnesty and Human Rights Watch are among the influential organizations that routinely try to shame abusive parties into better behavior.

But when you try to inject shame into a shameless system, it may not go well. As noted in other contexts, shaming may or may not lead to shame—and any shame induced may or may not be helpful. As with Gilligan's criminals or the rebels in Sierra Leone, the shamed party may react not with productive shame and compliance but with a kind of fury, perhaps a righteous fury. A good deal is likely to depend on whether there is any "buy-in" to the values that the shamer is promoting. Much may also depend on whether the shamer is seen to have any moral authority. For example, in 2008–9 the Sri Lankan government exploited resentments at imperial or neo-imperial powers in insulating itself from criticism of human rights abuses—a case of "who are you to shame us?"

As things stand, a wide range of governments—for example, in Sudan, Serbia, and Sri Lanka—have reacted to international criticism by saying, in effect, "Look, the international community is just as domineering as we have been telling you!" In the Sri Lankan case, it was difficult for the United States and UK (the former colonial ruler) credibly to chastise the Mahinda Rajapaksa government for the indefinite detention—and torture—of Tamil civilians in 2009 when such things were being encouraged elsewhere as part of the global "war on terror."[72] Under the Trump administration, a related question arose for Americans engaged in diplomatic or human rights work: how are you going to export or encourage democracy when your president is importing significant elements of authoritarianism?

If shaming is problematic, keeping quiet about human rights abuses tends only to reinforce the shamelessness that has helped produce disaster in the first place. In these circumstances, the best approach is usually concrete practical pressure on abusive authorities alongside rigorous truth-telling. But condemnation should be informed by self-awareness and, crucially, it should not be allowed to squeeze out the task of *explaining* the violence (including perhaps *one's own role* in encouraging violence) or taking seriously the varied problems and perceptions of those who are contributing to violence. These problems, too, need addressing; and without this, shaming may simply be pouring fuel onto the fire. At the same time, the possible counterproductive effects of shaming may also be minimized when one gets one's own house in order—not least by prioritizing human rights in one's own domestic and foreign policy.

One senior Médecins Sans Frontières aid worker recalled of his time in Afghanistan: "I spoke with the Taliban and they told me, 'Don't talk to us about international law when the U.S. is breaking international law—for example, in relation to prisoners.' It was useless to talk international law with them."[73] Meanwhile, as Hugo Slim has argued, many warring parties may be inclined to respect human rights for (ideological and self-interested) reasons of their own:[74] finding some common ground, as the International Committee of the Red Cross has learned, may be better than crudely pointing the finger.

Selective shaming is also a major problem. Publicly trumpeted "villains" have often not been the principal sources of violence, and this process creates impunity for others. A process of naming-and-shaming that centers on one high-profile group, individual, or issue—Ugandan rebel Joseph Kony in the context of the "Kony 2012" campaign, for example, or conflict diamonds in the Democratic Republic of the Congo or indeed Sierra Leone's rebels—can easily obscure and reinforce other sources of abuse.[75]

14

Shame and the West

WHILE WE HAVE STRESSED the major role that shame played in Sierra Leone's civil war and a number of other civil conflicts around the world, it might be tempting to imagine that shame will play a lesser role in conflicts that involve countries in Europe and North America. Such an assumption would be in line, after all, with the view that shame and so-called "shame cultures" were somehow left behind as these richer countries "developed" and "modernized" and as "rational," "evidence-based" bureaucratic procedures came to the fore.

But shame, once again, is not so easily banished or "othered." In complex ways, shame and shamelessness have combined to drive and legitimize diverse forms of violence within and between Western countries. In this chapter, we first look at the rise of Nazism in Germany, then at Cold War tensions (with a focus on the Vietnam War and the nuclear standoff), and finally at the role of role of shame in the "war on terror."

In each case, the intention is not somehow to "weigh" the impact of shame against other causal factors. Nevertheless, we can see how—in each example—a highly perverse distribution of shame fed strongly into the violence that was either unfolding or being planned. And in all three cases, shame—rather than arising naturally or inevitably—was constructed in very particular (and often self-interested) ways.[1] As Catherine Lu has emphasized in relation to post–World War I Germany and post–World War II Japan, the construction of shame that prevails politically tends to have a major element of self-interest and to represent only one subset of many possible constructions of shame.

In each of the contexts discussed in this chapter, some of the most politically influential conceptions of shame centered on *weakness*, and this framing played a major role in encouraging and legitimizing violence. Part of the problem—at least with Nazism and the "war on terror"—was that a process of shaming for collective weakness tended to invite a proposal for "moral reform" that was itself extremely violent (and indeed immoral).

At the same time, much of the shame that we might expect to *arise from* large-scale violence was in each case warded off, and this was done through strategies that can, to a large extent, be identified. Again, Arendt's concept of "action as propaganda" proves particularly helpful. Another important strategy—which Arendt can once more help us to understand—has been constructing violence as a "lesser evil" in comparison to some greater catastrophe that "tough action" is said to prevent. Both "action as propaganda" and "choosing a lesser evil" have tended to take policymakers in the direction of a magical world of "alternative facts" in which their violence becomes not only a way of warding off the shame of weakness but a plausible (if often bogus and destructive) solution for complex real-world problems. Within such elaborate constructions, it is almost as if the possibility of shame has been abolished. A key move here has been the conscious setting aside of emotions, which have frequently been constructed as a form of weakness (as with Eichmann). Within this framework, the category of "unacceptable weakness" comes to embrace not only nonviolence but also shame around violence (which again may bring Eichmann to mind, as well as the rebels in Sierra Leone). In each of the three cases considered in this chapter, violence routinely led to an intensification of magical thinking as policymakers warded off shame through descending into an alternative reality that their violence was helping to create and helping to render plausible.

Shame and the Rise of Nazism

Of course, the rise of Nazism is an extremely complex phenomenon, with a huge literature discussing its many causes and effects. Significant elements of self-interest were at play, as well as a great variety of emotions from fear and anger to loneliness and bewilderment. But the role of shame is not to be underestimated.

Nazism and Nazi ideology played a major role in warding off shame around weakness, division, and immorality—a sense of shame that the Nazis were simultaneously promoting. In our earlier discussion of consumerism, we noted that advertisers often heighten the emotions—not least the emotion of shame—that they simultaneously promise to relieve. We've seen how Trump did this too. Of course, Nazi propaganda takes us a great distance from either Trump's political pitch or propaganda for soap. But it remains striking that the Nazis used propaganda to heighten emotions, including shame as well as fear, and that they were quick to offer simplistic and violent solutions for the painful feelings that they were helping stir up. Hitler, who in *Mein Kampf* actually compared propaganda to advertising soap, hyped up the shame of the 1919 Treaty of Versailles, which he presented as a "Diktat" and a crushing humiliation for the German people, and then immediately put himself forward as someone who would *erase* this shame by standing up to the cruelty of the Allies while simultaneously targeting an internal enemy on whom much of the stirred-up shame could be pinned.[2] Notoriously, the Nazis blamed the Jews not only for defeat in World War I but also for causing the war in the first place. Of course, the Nazi Holocaust itself involved a massive shaming—the yellow stars, forced street-cleaning, ghettos, concentration camps, the uniforms and numbers, the punishment of the innocent, the elements of enforced collaboration, and so on.

Nazi manipulations of shame should not be seen in isolation from more material interests. The 1917 Russian Revolution showed how drastically war could undermine elites' legitimacy.[3] And in a fevered atmosphere of hunger, inflation, and mass unemployment, Nazism promised to avert the threat of a Russia-style Communist revolution—not least by absorbing the energies and frustrations of angry and demobilized soldiers.[4] Nazism received significant backing from big business and helped derail class politics within Germany, effectively reorienting conflict along more "ethnic" or religious lines.[5] But even insofar as this was a self-interested political maneuver, it could not have been achieved without massive emotional manipulation.

In many ways, National Socialism succeeded in channeling discontent around the economy and capitalism in general into a much more focused discontent that targeted the Jews as the alleged embodiment of the nefarious banks and moneylenders who were said to have led Germany into a disastrous war; meanwhile, those parts of capitalism that were geared toward *production*, along with all the *non-Jewish* financiers, were largely let off the hook.[6] In his landmark 1939 analysis of the appeal of Hitler, Kenneth Burke made a perceptive observation (and one that perhaps anticipated the coexistence of "good markets" and "bad bankers" more recently):

> The middle class contains, within the mind of each member, a duality: its members simultaneously have a cult of money and a detestation of this cult.... Hence, there is "medicine" for the "Aryan" members of the middle class in the projective device of the scapegoat, whereby the "bad" features can be allocated to the "devil", and one can "respect himself" by a distinction between "good capitalism" and "bad capitalism", with those of a different lodge being the vessels of the "bad" capitalism.[7]

The Nazis hyped up not just the shame of Versailles but the "moral degeneracy" of Germany, and again presented themselves as a radical and cleansing force that would take this underlying shame away. Nazi propaganda denounced a "materialist" Germany, saying it had grown weak, divided, feminine, soft, and "bourgeois." Most of the first Nazi stormtroopers were German soldiers who portrayed certain groups— including Jews and women and often Jewish women—as bent on undermining the strength, masculinity, pride, and purity of Germany and thereby paving the way for the humiliation of the Versailles treaty itself.[8] A driving obsession among many stormtroopers was that a violent reassertion of masculinity was needed in order to defend against the "shame and betrayal, filth and misery," against the "red flood" of rebellious soldiers; the true soldier must not only suppress the effete coward lurking within himself but also prevent any mixing of races or of male and female.[9] The proto-Nazis had to find their own "wall" against chaos and shame: as Klaus Theweleit put it in a Freudian vein,

"The threat of the 'flood' may be combated with 'erections': towering cities, mountains, troops, stalwart men, weapons."[10]

As for Hitler himself, he urged the cultivation of the body—in particular the *male* body—as a countermeasure to this threatening corruption or "poisoning,"[11] and he wrote in *Mein Kampf* that the best place to achieve such a body was the army.[12] In the sphere of culture, Hitler observed, "The life of the people must be freed from the asphyxiating perfume of our modern eroticism." Hitler claimed art had been infected by what he called an "adults only" tendency,[13] and his own paintings were skillful and highly conventional depictions of landscapes and buildings.

Like many World War I veterans, Hitler was profoundly disturbed and disoriented, first, by the mass slaughter of his fellow soldiers and then by what he saw as the sudden, bewildering, and shameful surrender of the German authorities. Hitler was hospitalized in October 1918 with temporary blindness sustained as a result of mustard gas poisoning. While in hospital, he learned of the fall of the German monarchy and the loss of the war. In *Mein Kampf*, he described a "burning rage and shame" in which physical and psychological pain seem to have mixed together:

> During the night of October 13–14 [1918] the British began to throw gas-shells on to the southern front before Ypres [in Belgium]. . . . Towards morning I felt a pain which got worse with every quarter hour that passed, and at about seven o'clock I tottered rearwards with scorching eyes. . . . A few hours later my eyes had turned into burning coals, and it was all dark around me. I was sent to hospital . . . I was unable to read the newspapers. . . . Then one day the disaster came upon us suddenly and without warning. Sailors arrived in lorries and called on all to revolt, a few Jewish youths being the leaders. . . . Not one of them had ever been to the front. . . . The following days brought with them the worst realization of my life. . . . What I imagined to be a local affair was apparently a general revolution. In addition to all this, distressing news came back from the front. They wanted to capitulate. . . . So all had been in vain. In vain all the

sacrifices and privations, in vain the starvation and thirst for many endless months, in vain the hours we spent doing our duty, gripped by the fear of death, and in vain the death of two millions of men! ... Miserable depraved criminals! The more I tried in that hour to get clear ideas about that tremendous event, the more did I blush with burning rage and shame. What was all the pain of my eyes in comparison with this misery! ... In those nights my hatred arose against the originators of that act. ... With Jews there is no bargaining—there is merely the hard "Either—or". I resolved to become a politician.[14]

Later on in *Mein Kampf*, Hitler wrote that a million German lives lost at the war front could have been saved if "twelve to fifteen thousand of the Hebrew corrupters of the people had been held under poison gas."[15] Falsely alleging the under-representation of Jews in the German army,[16] he blamed defeat on "moral poisoning" perpetrated by Jews and Marxists.[17] Here, he was mirroring the murderous anti-Semitism of "White Russian" pro-tsarist forces, who were trying to explain away defeat and revolution through the idea that Jews had led noble soldiers astray. (Some White Russians fled to Munich, where Hitler was helping stir up Nazi sentiments, bringing with them *Protocols of the Learned Elders of Zion*, a tsarist forgery that the Nazis used to fuel anti-Semitism.)[18]

Pushing back against the "shame" of defeat, the Nazis generally accorded a great show of respect to veterans—and this became part of their political platform. In the weeks preceding the Reichstag elections of November 1933, members of the Nazi veterans' organization donned uniforms bedecked with flowers and paraded to polling stations bearing placards that read: "German, have you voted yet? If not, then my sacrifice was in vain."[19] (While using veterans' suffering to generate enthusiasm for further war, the Nazis actually had a very poor record in looking after the material and psychological needs of veterans, particularly those whose disability led to them being classified as "non-productive elements.")[20] The Nazis' loudly expressed reverence for soldierly values seemed to demand an ever-widening spiral of violence and humiliation directed at those who were deemed to be outside the community of past and future soldiers that the Nazis were idolizing. In recent years, many studies have addressed the problem of how to "reintegrate" soldiers into society, a process that ideally involves helping soldiers adjust to civilian life and helping them deal with the shame and trauma of wartime violence. In many ways, the Nazis turned this process on its head, dealing with shame around the war by attempting to transplant soldierly values from the army to the wider society. In this sense, "reintegration" was put into reverse.

Feeding into the Nazi project of internal "cleansing" was the idea that the finest elements in German society had been wiped out, while corrupt and criminal elements had come to the fore. In the wider society, the perceived need for "cleansing" also had a religious dimension. With defeat sometimes interpreted as a sign that God's favor had been temporarily removed from a "chosen people," chaplains in Germany played down the need for social reform while emphasizing the need to remobilize as a Volk, to protect Protestantism from secularism and revolution, and to remove elements of corruption that had weakened the moral fabric of Germany. More generally, the Weimar Republic was weakened significantly by an inability to establish a consensus on the war's meaning.[21]

Importantly, the idea of healing division by putting Germany on a war footing was not simply a Nazi idea; it had operated strongly *at the outset* of World War I. In 1889, Nietzsche had lauded war's "curative power,"[22] and both before and during World War I the hope was commonly expressed in Germany that war might heal troublesome internal divisions. Within this framework, war was not so much a source of shame as something that *removed* shame. And the relevant shame attached not so much to violence as to the weakness, impurity, and division that violence would allegedly remove. One German nationalist wrote in 1913: "Let us regard war as holy, like the purifying force of fate, for it will awaken in our people all that is great and ready for self-sacrifice, while it cleanses our soul of the mire of petty egotistical concerns."[23]

In his fascinating book *Hysterical Men*, Paul Lerner described how even the medical community was tainted by these ideas. Even as some two million young German men were mown down and killed by the other side:

> Medical writers ... reported that the war was improving the mental and nervous health of the civilian population. In these accounts war fostered feelings of communal solidarity that, many hoped, could overcome decades of division, continuing the Bismarckian strategy of using external conflict to forge domestic unity.[24]

Lerner noted that "rather than blaming the shocks and stresses of the battlefield for the onset of war neuroses, many [German] psychiatrists began to see war as a kind of cure, as a moral and psychological corrective to a civil society they deemed effeminate, degenerate and pathogenic."[25] Hysteria—a label carrying significant stigma and enduring feminine associations—became the officially favored diagnosis for tens of thousands of German soldiers who suffered psychologically during and after World War I. This amounted to a determined shaming of any "weakness": nervous soldiers were also frequently labeled as lazy, selfish, and unpatriotic—even sometimes as *"backstabbers"* undermining the war effort along with Jews and Marxists.[26] One psychiatrist suggested that neurotics' health actually *improved* at the front because of the comradeship and fighting spirit. After World War I, this route to "health" and "unity" was enthusiastically taken up, in a different way, by Hitler himself.

On top of the shame of weakness, of defeat and of the Versailles "Diktat," there was a more personal sense of shame among much of the general population. Hitler himself seems to have had a strong sense of *personal* shame, stemming in part from his experience as a struggling artist in Vienna, which he portrayed as dominated by Jews.[27] Of course, the process was immensely complicated, with multiple material and emotional factors involved. But a key element in the Nazis' success appears to have been the manipulation of shame: through offering an escape from these various kinds of shame, a malicious and fictitious ideology was able to make itself more attractive and more credible to large numbers of people.

One of the most insightful analysts of this process was Hannah Arendt, particularly in her book *The Origins of Totalitarianism* (the original proposal for which was called *The Three Pillars of Shame*). Arendt observed that at the point when the Nazis were making their pitch, large numbers of Germans had been disoriented and had been deprived of previous sources of recognition and respect by processes of modernization, industrialization, and mass migration to the cities. On top of all this came the mechanized destruction of World War I and the economic disasters of astronomical inflation, mass unemployment, and international sanctions and reparations. Arendt saw how an ideological belief that "everyone can make it" could easily turn into a habit of self-blame by those who had fallen on hard times: in the grip of this ideology, "The fact that with monotonous but abstract uniformity the same fate had befallen a mass of individuals did not prevent their judging themselves in terms of individual failure."[28]

In his book *Crowds and Power*, Elias Canetti drew on his experience of living in Austria in the 1920s and 1930s to throw light on the role of inflation—and its emotional fallout—in fueling anti-Semitism. In conditions of runaway inflation, Canetti noted:

> The wage-earner is hit equally with the rentier. Overnight a man can lose a large part, or all, of what he thought was safe in his bank. An inflation cancels out distinctions between men which had seemed eternal and brings together in the same *inflation crowd* people who before would scarcely have nodded at each other in the street. *No one ever forgets a sudden depreciation of himself,* for it is too painful. *Unless he can thrust it on to someone else,* he carries it with him for the rest of his life.... Something must be treated in such a way that it becomes worth less and less, as the unit of money did during the inflation. And this process must be continued until its object is reduced to a state of utter worthlessness. Then one can throw it away like paper, or repulp it.[29]

As for Arendt, she highlighted the disorientation accompanying rapid urbanization in particular, observing that "men in the midst of communal disintegration and social atomization wanted to belong at any price."[30] Part of what the Nazis offered was *an escape from the shame of insignificance*, a chance to become part of "something bigger," the opportunity to gain "access to history even at the price of destruction" (a phrase we invoked earlier in relation to the January 2021 Capitol invasion and in relation to Brexit).[31] When it came to the rise of Nazis, we can glimpse some of this motivation in the memoir of Melita Maschmann, who became a Nazi herself. Recalling the pomp of a 1933 Nazi torchlight procession that she'd witnessed as a teenager, Maschmann noted:

> I longed to hurl myself into this current, to be submerged and borne along by it. . . . At that age one finds a life which consists of school work, family outings and birthday invitations wretchedly and shamefully barren of significance. Nobody gives one credit for being interested in more than these derisory trivialities. Nobody says: "You are needed for something more important; come!" . . . I wanted to attach myself to something that was great and fundamental. This longing I shared with countless others of my contemporaries.[32]

Part of understanding extreme violence—as we saw in Sierra Leone—is understanding the self-righteousness of the violent; and we've seen that in shamelessness, shame is often being kept determinedly at bay. In Hitler himself, we certainly find a fanatically determined refusal to be shamed, which sat logically alongside his extreme sensitivity to personal and national shame.[33] He always seemed to *find a way to pass shame onto others*. Repeatedly, he insisted that those who were shaming him or shaming Germany were themselves exhibiting extremely shameful behavior. In these circumstances, shaming and perceived shaming—as embodied in the Versailles treaty, for example, or in democratic countries' criticisms of Hitler-in-power—did not prompt any kind of rethink, reform, or introspection; they just deepened the underlying fury.

Consider Hitler's speech to the Reichstag in January 1939. Noting that "democratic statesmen" were criticizing Germany's policies toward the Jews, Hitler observed:

> Today I can only assure these gentlemen that, thanks to the brutal education with which the democracies favored us for fifteen years,

we are completely hardened to all attacks of sentiment.... more than eight hundred thousand children of the nation had died of hunger and undernourishment at the close of the War....[34] We witnessed over one and a half million Germans being torn away from all that they possessed in the territories lying on our frontiers, and being whipped out with practically only what they wore on their backs.... For this reason, we ask to be spared all sentimental talk.[35]

In the same 1939 speech, Hitler turned the shame around in a different way. Railing at international criticism of the persecution of the Jews, Hitler expressed a sense of bewilderment that when democratic nations "are so enthusiastic about these 'splendid people', their settlement should suddenly be refused with every imaginable excuse."[36]

A clever propagandist will often lace a cocktail of lies with a little serum of truth. That makes everything so much more persuasive. Whether referring to something real or (more often) telling lies, Hitler showed a pretty consistent knack for turning shame around. He also turned shame around through his *actions*, reversing the shame of powerlessness through his atrocities and even using such "punishment" to imply a fault in his victims. Offering an escape from shame was a huge part of the appeal of the Nazis, whose murderous politics of scapegoating showed just how powerful and destructive the manipulation of shame can be.

Shame, Vietnam, and the Cold War

When it came to the Cold War, a key problem (as we've seen in many other contexts) was not so much shame itself as the type of shame that was operating, the things that people were and were not ashamed *about*. Again, shame around weakness was more influential than shame around suffering. More generally, emotion itself was routinely discouraged in favor of a self-conscious hyper-rationality among policymakers that played a significant part in warding off shame. Paradoxically, this purportedly "scientific" approach took key officials into a strangely magical world far removed from the realities of waging counterinsurgency or building up the capability and readiness to create a nuclear catastrophe.

As with Eichmann the belief that one can and *should* set emotions aside—especially shame around suffering that was being planned or inflicted—had the effect of disguising and ultimately legitimizing the massive violence that was being embraced or contemplated.

Yet the truth was that emotion—whether in Washington or the wider world—could not magically be wished away. For example, shame around weakness and concerns around "looking tough" drove much of the American response in Vietnam. President Nixon himself had a strong personal aversion to being seen as lacking in toughness, feeding his antipathy to withdrawal from Vietnam as well as his secret bombing of Cambodia.[37]

Destruction on the ground in Vietnam and Cambodia had predictable emotional consequences that essentially wrecked the carefully constructed models informing U.S. policy. Drawing on leaked official American documents that were published as "The Pentagon Papers," Arendt emphasized that senior American officials generally did not believe that bombing North Vietnam would be an effective military tactic that would defeat the Viet Cong. On the whole, bombing was recognized to be counterproductive—it was humiliating and enraging, and it hardened resolve.[38] Yet mass bombing was implemented in any case. And when (unsurprisingly) the mass destruction created additional enemies, this too was shamelessly put to use in justifying more violence.

Arendt showed how U.S. officials' overwhelming concern with "respect" and "image" helped induce and sustain the massive American bombing campaign in Vietnam. Many officials saw the bombing as a way to maintain America's image of strength and to demonstrate that *something* was being done. The overriding focus was on avoiding the impression of a humiliating defeat, on winning the next election rather than actually winning the war, and these priorities led even democratically elected officials to make a radical leap into a world of fantasy.[39] As Arendt put it, "The goal was the image itself, as is manifest in the very language of the problem-solvers, with their 'scenarios' and 'audiences,' borrowed from the theater."[40]

Part of the problem was a refusal to recognize that mass bombing by a foreign power could not resolve complex social grievances in a society with a fierce nationalist tradition. The prevailing American fantasy was that communism could be defeated by reducing (largely through killing) the supply of Viet Cong soldiers. But of course this ignored the *demand* for violence that arose from major social grievances as well as from the provocative and humiliating nature of the American attacks themselves.

One important technique for warding off shame and failure was that—as later in the "war on terror"—the expressed goals of policy were constantly being shifted.[41] As U.S. general William Corson commented in his remarkably frank and incisive book *The Betrayal*, "By leaping from one purpose to another the politician has, so far, not sat still long enough for the people to demand an accounting or a straight answer."[42]

As later in Afghanistan from 2001,[43] public relations involved an apparently endless supply of optimism, with each new step in the Vietnam War promising the success that the last step had unaccountably failed to deliver.[44] Numbers were a big "help" in constructing a kind of institutionalized shamelessness that systematically dismissed unwelcome evidence, with figures frequently used to obliterate both stories and suffering:

> It may be only natural for problem-solvers, trained in translating all factual contents into the language of numbers and percentages, where they can be calculated, to remain unaware of the untold misery that their "solutions"—pacification and relocation programs, defoliation, napalm, and anti-personnel bullets—held in store.[45]

Arendt noted, "It seems that no ivory tower of the scholars has ever better prepared the mind for wholly ignoring the facts of life than the various think tanks did for the problem-solvers."[46] The highly educated nature of the policy elite did not prevent what Arendt described as "the wilful, deliberate disregard of all facts, historical, political, geographical, for more than twenty-five years."[47] She highlighted a very basic lack of curiosity about Vietnamese society and the nature of "the enemy,"[48] so that, for example, "no one at the top knew or considered it important that the Vietnamese had been fighting foreign invaders for almost 2,000 years."[49] Commenting on Vietnam, Arendt noted that U.S.

officials were looking for formulas "expressed in a pseudo-mathematical language" that allowed predictions on the model of natural sciences, and that they "prided themselves on being 'rational', and they were indeed to a rather frightening degree above 'sentimentality' and in love with 'theory', the world of sheer mental effort."[50] Arendt showed that, as the Vietnam War escalated, U.S. policymakers drifted further and further from a reality that they had, on the whole, remarkably little interest in confronting. She saw, too, that wishing away evidence was inextricably linked with wishing away *people*. We know now that this double-maneuver was to be repeated in the "war on terror," and in both calamities a crucial result was the strengthening of the enemy and then the call for an intensified aggression to deal with this growing "threat."[51]

Another way of warding off shame over Vietnam was through turning on critics. Arendt observed that Washington's determination to wage war as it saw fit was feeding a systematic secrecy and a growing contempt for the legislative arm of the U.S. government as well as for the press. As so often with wars, the "enemy" category was in effect expanded so as to police dissent, while those who tried to shame the warmakers were themselves subjected to extreme shaming. Once violence had been embraced (as we saw in the very different contexts of Sierra Leone's civil wars and Gilligan's criminals), any productive shaming became extremely difficult and often in practice provoked some further, mutating violence.

Some of the shamelessness of American intervention in Vietnam and the strongly counterproductive actions also characterized the Cold War more broadly. Consider this hard-hitting analysis by Simon Clarke and Paul Hoggett in 2004:

> The massive overkill, the self-fulfilling nature of so many American interventions, the uncanny knack that American foreign policy has displayed of making its worst fears come true, the classic paranoid conviction that one is the misunderstood victim and never the perpetrator, the complete inability to perceive how one's own "defensive actions" are experienced by the other as provocation and threat—wherever we look, the "arms race" with the Soviet Union, the run-up

to the Cuban Missile Crisis, fear of communist contagion in S. E. Asia and Latin America, the current "war on terrorism" and "containment" of N. Korea, we see the same mixture of provocation, ineptness and misunderstanding.[52]

President Kennedy's nuclear brinkmanship during the 1962 Cuban Missile Crisis owed much to the desire to project an image of strength, something that had itself been fed by the failed attempt, in the notorious 1961 Bay of Pigs fiasco, to push Fidel Castro out of power.[53] Part of the background provocation here was the U.S. Air Force's proclamation that by 1962 it would have obtained a nuclear "first strike" capability, which it would seek to maintain. This kind of statement and the associated U.S. arms buildup helped push the Soviet Union, hardly seeking another war after the devastation it had suffered in World War II, into its own rapidly expanding nuclear weapons program.[54]

That brings us to Carol Cohn's work on the Cold War nuclear stand-off more generally, a stand-off that was based on a precarious system of hyperdestructive missiles that is still to a large extent in place. In Cohn's analysis, we get a sense of what was—and wasn't—considered shameful by American officials and think-tank professionals. Attitudes were broadly similar to those among officials dealing with Vietnam: again, shame around weakness was very much to the fore, while shame around the prospect of mass killing was remarkably scarce.

Notwithstanding the common idea that weapons were being built and destruction was being planned in the name of "deterrence," the language of America's Cold War strategists revealed an extraordinary shamelessness around mass destruction as well as demonstrating a shameless sexualization of destruction. In effect, shame centered largely around weakness (and at time impotence), inviting a competitive and heavily gendered escalation of nuclear "strength." Surveying the almost entirely male world of American nuclear experts, Cohn described how scientists and generals celebrated successful tests of the earlier atomic bombs with various versions of "It's a boy!" She also noted that

> lectures were filled with discussions of vertical erector launchers, thrust-to-weight rations, soft lay downs, deep penetration, and the

comparative advantages of protracted versus spasm attacks—or what one military adviser to the National Security Council has called "releasing 70 to 80 percent of our megatonnage in one orgasmic whump."[55]

Presented like this, the language becomes somewhat comical—until we remember (just as these experts appeared *not* to remember) that we are talking about a weapons system in which just one MX missile has the destructive power of 250–400 Hiroshimas.

In line with Arendt's portrait of security experts during the Vietnam War, Cohn showed how nuclear experts inhabited a world that was strangely and dangerously disconnected from the reality that they were mapping, planning, and shaping. The focus was on plotting scenarios that would allow an American "win." In scenario planning, "losing" was often equated with having fewer weapons at the end of the game, effectively ignoring the devastation that would have been inflicted on both sides by this point. Among these self-consciously rational individuals, an overriding "rational actor" model encouraged this kind of gaming, and the models themselves were almost entirely blind to the devastation being calmly contemplated. Cohn noted that "deterrence theory, and much of strategic doctrine altogether, was invented largely by mathematicians, economists, and a few political scientists." The pain, fear, terror, trauma, and desire for revenge that would come with a nuclear attack were routinely assumed away. So too was the psychological and strategic impact on "the enemy" of building up your own arsenal.

Helping to underpin the shamelessness of mass destruction (and alongside the sexual language) was a voracious use of technical and euphemistic language such as "first strikes," "peacekeeper" missiles, "counterforce exchanges," "limited nuclear war," "clean bombs," and even "surgically clean strikes." All of this disguised the horrific reality of bodies that would be incinerated, radiated, and torn apart in their billions—with some phrases even wrapping the destruction in the language of healing. Cohn suggested that if you learned the language of these experts, you would enter a new mode of thinking that loses sight of human beings, while "if we refuse to learn the language, we are virtually guaranteed that our voices will remain outside the 'politically relevant' spectrum of opinion."[56] In other words, to be recognized as a legitimate and realistic contributor, you had to sign up to a collective flight from reality. Cohn noted another paradox in all of this:

> What is striking about the men themselves is not, as the content of their conversations might suggest, their cold-bloodedness. Rather, it is that they are a group of men unusually endowed with charm, humor, intelligence, concern and decency. Reader, I liked them.[57]

One is reminded here that Eichmann—a gifted violin player, apparently attractive to women in his younger years, and psychologically astute when he wanted to be—could be charming enough. I have also had direct experience of international security experts at London's influential International Institute for Strategic Studies (IISS), an environment almost as male as the one described by Cohn. I could see the intelligence and sometimes a kind of well-dressed charm. But, reader, I actually *didn't* like them much. One problem was the weirdly emotionless reflex for "counting missiles" and the apparently overriding concern for how things looked from Washington or London. Another was the *internal* governance, which included a preference for military-style humiliation of new recruits. At one research retreat in a country house early in the fellowship, my fellow recruits and I had our research plans ruthlessly torn apart in a group meeting. My own drew the comment that "it reminds me of a proposal by a six-year-old boy" (which seems harsh, depending perhaps on the boy in question). The high-level assault on our various proposals prompted one of the new recruits, a mid-level Japanese diplomat, to observe drily, "Now I know the meaning of the word 'retreat.'"

Amid all the focus at IISS on missiles and threats from the Middle East, nobody talked about shame in international relations; but within the organization itself, there was rarely a shortage. As perhaps with any organization (and in line with Cohn's analysis), if you "learned the ropes" and "spoke the language," you could minimize the chance that shame—and incomprehension—would be channeled in your direction.

What also struck me at IISS in 1997 was that nobody was really questioning the need for NATO despite the Cold War having apparently come to a close with the fall of communism, the end of the Soviet Union, and the end of the Warsaw Pact. This book is hardly the place for a detailed analysis of why Putin invaded Ukraine—first in 2014 and then, even more destructively, in 2022. But any answer that neglected a notable sense of humiliation at Russia's loss of "great power" status (something we touched on in chapter 11) would be remarkably incomplete. Having essentially "lost" the Cold War, Russia found a U.S. government that was unashamedly proclaiming global predominance, going back on the commitment not to expand NATO eastward, bombing Yugoslavia without UN support, and declaring a willingness to rewrite the rules of international politics without significant input from Russia. President Yeltsin himself was furious, proclaiming that Russia was "not Haiti . . . and Russia will come back." And according to veteran Russian journalist Vladimir Pozner, there was a widespread "sense of losing this aura of greatness, or being told 'We don't care about you.' The reaction of the average Russian to that was one of 'You're insulting me, you don't respect me.'"[58]

Of course, at one level it makes no sense that anyone looking for respect and recognition would engage in actions (as in Ukraine) that, on any reasonable view of the matter, would quickly lead to a drastic reduction in respect. But one thing that emerges strongly from my own fieldwork in Sierra Leone (as well as from Gilligan's work with violent criminals in the United States) is that a drive for recognition and respect may, paradoxically, be quite consistent with behavior that, in practice, drastically *reduces* respect. To a large extent, this is because the desire for respect (for many people) centers primarily on notions of strength and recognition, with a corresponding sense of shame around weakness, invisibility, and any signs of disrespect. It would also appear that this psychological state is *historically conditioned* (in terms of either individual history or some wider history). The violent process that may be encouraged when respect is felt to be greatly lacking may become a particularly vicious circle. From this point of view, the idea that Putin has now stepped outside the bounds of humanity—and negotiation—is unlikely to be helpful.

Going back to the Cold War itself, the intention here is not to insist that emotions were somehow "more important" than material interests. The Cold War was profoundly shaped by a complex system of economic and political benefits that grew up around it—and proved remarkably hard to dismantle when the Cold War supposedly "ended." In the Vietnam War itself, incentives within the U.S. military were also conducive to the aggressive strategy that few senior officials seem to have believed would actually work. As David Hunt noted, "Promotions for artillery and air-unit commanders went to those who fired off the most rounds and launched the most bombing sorties."[59] Even the killing of civilians could be counted as part of the "score" or "body count" by which the performance of American soldiers was, in part, assessed.[60]

What is clear, though, is that shame-around-weakness has been a powerful driver of this violent system—and indeed has helped to structure and facilitate the extraction of material and political benefits on "either side." Winning votes and contracts through aggression will only work in any sustained way in circumstances where the accompanying conceptions of shame and honor are able to legitimize this process. Even when soldiers are encouraged to register a high "body count," there are perverse definitions of honor-as-killing that lie behind any material incentives.

Shame and the "War on Terror"

The shaming of the Taliban helped launch the "war on terror," and part of this was shaming the Taliban's "shame culture." In particular, the attack on Afghanistan was billed as liberating Afghan women from a society that was oppressing them through compulsory veiling, restricting access to education, and so on. This "shame culture" was also sometimes presented as a threat *to Americans*, as when the president's wife, Laura Bush, said, "Civilized people throughout the world are speaking out in horror—not only because our hearts break for the women and children in Afghanistan, but also because in Afghanistan, we see the world the terrorists would like to impose on the rest of us."[61]

Of course, the Taliban *did* mete out harsh punishments to many women who refused to cooperate with its rigid vision of a proper society. But the energetic shaming of the Taliban's "shame society" left several key facts out of the picture. First, the extreme challenges faced by women in Afghanistan did not simply begin with the Taliban, which had only taken power in 1995. Second, large-scale bombing and a prolonged civil war were not likely to improve the situation of women and girls any more than the situation of others in Afghanistan. Third, the United States had given major assistance to several of the more extreme jihadist groups over many years (notably with a view to using them against the Soviet occupation in the 1980s), so that Washington had actually played a huge role in nurturing the very group it was now attacking. (Indeed, the shaming of the Taliban may well have served some kind of function in protecting from the potential shame associated with this earlier nurturing.) Fourth, during its relatively brief spell in government the Taliban had actually succeeded in reining in the crime of rape (along with other crimes), and many of the warlords being supported by the United States against the Taliban actually had much worse records on this issue.[62] (Again, the shaming of the Taliban may have protected from the shame of being associated with these unsavory characters.)

As for the U.S.-led invasion of Iraq in 2003, the fierce debate around this intervention showed how easily shame could get marginalized in Americans' and Britons' discussions of *their own* countries and *their own* wars. Supporters of the military action in Iraq (many of them on the right) tended to present the intervention as a legitimate attempt to combat terrorism and a way of spreading freedom and democracy around the world. Meanwhile, left-wing critics tended to highlight elements of self-interest such as imperialist power politics, greed for oil, and the malign influence of the military-industrial complex. Of course, left/right distinctions were hardly definitive here—the UK's Labour prime minister Tony Blair, for example, was a key *supporter* of the invasion. Nor was the role of emotions ignored entirely. But on the whole the debate tended to underplay the emotional factors feeding into the invasion. In particular, the role of shame in shaping the "war on terror" was little remarked upon. American social psychologist Dov Cohen commented perceptively, "The prospect of fighting over honor or shame seemed too irrational for political discussion."[63] Crucially, the neglect of shame also extended to a failure to consider the shame—and the violence—that counterterror would almost inevitably *provoke*.

In reality shame does appear to have been a key driver of the U.S.-led violence. And as the "war on terror" evolved and shame threatened to intrude on an enterprise whose destructive and counterproductive effects were becoming increasingly pronounced, a range of identifiable techniques were used to keep shame at bay.

As a counterterrorist project, the 2003 attack on Iraq by the United States and its allies made very little sense. Notoriously, Iraq had no connection to the 9/11 attacks while Saddam's alleged "weapons of mass destruction" did not actually exist. On top of this, some observers had plausibly warned that the U.S.-led attacks on Iraq and Afghanistan would be *actively counterproductive*—and so it proved. Many Taliban fighters fled to Pakistan, helping to destabilize that country.[64] Inside Afghanistan, Western bombing and support for abusive warlords helped the Taliban get support. Globally, between 2000 and 2015, the number of terrorist attacks actually rose sharply from around 3,000 to around 29,000,[65] while the number of fighters in Islamist-inspired terrorist organizations also rose sharply.[66] Within the Middle East, the U.S.-led occupation of Iraq gave a huge boost to al Qaida in Iraq, which regularly resorted to acts of terrorism and which also proved to be a major seeding ground for ISIS (thereby contributing to war in Syria as well as in Iraq).[67]

Another counterproductive effect of the "war on terror" (generally under-recognized) is that it helped reproduce violence (including terrorism) in countries where governments *were not* overthrown, including Syria and Sri Lanka. Detailed research by a number of people (including myself) has shown that many abusive governments around the world have been able to manipulate the global "war on terror" so as to secure both aid and impunity even as they repress their own populations, often tarring rebels and dissidents with the brush of "terrorist." Like the military invasions of the "war on terror," this repression has itself been *provocative*, feeding violence in complex ways—and frequently reproducing "the terrorist."[68] Meanwhile, the process of shaming (and ostensibly counteracting) "terrorists" within these uninvaded countries has often encouraged a high degree of blindness to abuses by those (whether national government officials or international actors) who are doing the shaming.

Several important questions arise from this kind of analysis. Why, after the terror attacks of 9/11, would the U.S.-led alliance pick on a country (Iraq) with no logical connection to those attacks; and why would this alliance attack another country (Afghanistan) that was already ravaged by conflict and that itself had only a tenuous connection with 9/11? Why engage in violence that predictably reproduces terrorism? Why pursue wars that you are chronically unable to win? Why persist so long despite these evident failings? And why shore up abusive governments around the world with a global "war" that allows them to legitimize domestic repression and reinforce underlying grievances?

As a general rule, the adoption of a predictably counterproductive policy—and persisting with this policy despite observable failure—will strongly suggest that the "failing" enterprise has important hidden functions or purposes;[69] and we should certainly not neglect the political and economic functions of this "failing" enterprise, which were often very significant.[70]

In the case of the "war on terror," one significant windfall was the popularity boost that George W. Bush in particular obtained from his tough-talking and his policy of waging war. Al Qaida, prior to 9/11, had actually preoccupied Bush a good deal less than Al Gore, who got more votes than Bush in the 2000 presidential elections; after an initial surge on becoming president, moreover, Bush's ratings had fallen to around 50 percent. Yet within two days of 9/11, Bush's ratings were up to 82 percent. Slipping back over the next few months, they rose again with the 2003 invasion of Iraq.[71] In February 2005, Sidney Blumenthal commented, "The more terrorism dominates the media, the higher his [Bush's] ratings; and whenever terrorism declines, he begins to sink."[72]

In the wake of 9/11, President Bush suggestively ridiculed Bill Clinton's anti-terrorism strategies: "The antiseptic notion of launching a cruise missile into some guy's, you know, tent, really is a joke. I mean, people viewed that as the impotent America . . . a flaccid . . . not very tough country."[73] Bush said terrorists saw America as materialist and hedonistic and incapable of fighting back. Here, he was heightening the shame that he was promising to remedy, just as Trump (in a different way) was to do some fifteen years later. Oddly, Bush's "voice" here had moved rather close to the (imagined) voice of the terrorist, so that the terrorist's imagined critique of America was also, in a way, Bush's critique. American evangelist Jerry Falwell Sr. went further, portraying 9/11 as God's retribution for abortion, homosexuality, and secularization.[74] These passages recall Clifford Longley's analysis of the way a "Chosen People" may repeatedly discern in itself a dangerous drift to hedonism and unfaithfulness, seeking renewed favor and renewed protection from God through some kind of moral renewal.

We have seen how shame around "weakness" in foreign policy was later harnessed as part of the 2016 campaign to get Trump into the presidency, including by Sarah Palin when she accused President Obama of being a "weak-kneed capitulator-in-chief." Significantly, this process extended backward as well as forward: I was studying in America when Ronald Reagan's successful 1980 campaign for the presidency was greatly boosted by the media's hyping of America's shame over the holding of American hostages in Iran (sample on ABC News: "America held hostage—Day 443").

Apart from boosting Bush's ratings and image of toughness, the emerging "war on terror" helped sustain and legitimize the huge proportion of U.S. government spending that was still going to the military (along with all the associated private profits). Remarkably, the end of the Cold War only temporarily dented this proportion.[75] We know also that explicit plans to sustain this bonanza and to maintain U.S. "predominance" were made in advance of 9/11 and that key figures like Vice President Dick Cheney seized on the September 2001 attacks as a chance to implement these plans.[76]

A third element of self-interest that helped sustain and deepen the "war on terror" arose from the attempt by various governments around the world to "hijack" it for the purpose of repressing their own populations and legitimizing their own military institutions.[77]

As so often in politics, however, self-interest was far from being the whole story. Particularly for those initiating it, the psychological attractions of a "war on terror" were very significant. And even insofar as the "war on terror" served practical political functions in bolstering domestic political support and suppressing domestic dissent, these processes themselves depended on the psychological attractions of such a project—not least for the American public.

A key element in the psychological attraction of waging a "war on terror"—whether for politicians or the public—seems to have been the prospect of *an immediate reversal of shame*. While one could make a case that the "war on terror" was simply *retaliation* for 9/11, much of the *content* of retaliation appears to have been precisely this kind of reversal of shame. In line with our analysis of perverse and dangerous conceptions of shame in other chapters, much of the relevant shame *centered on feelings of weakness and powerlessness* that were naturally prompted, or at least greatly exacerbated, by the 9/11 attacks.

A major clue to the central role of humiliation in driving the (humiliating) response to 9/11 was the arbitrary choice of Iraq in particular as a target. Again, punishment without a crime is profoundly shaming and takes matters radically away from the world of guilt and the world of law. The recklessness and indiscriminate nature of the U.S.-led retaliation was itself a demonstration of power and control, and President Bush made explicit that desire to reassert control when he promised a response "in a way and at an hour of our choosing."[78]

The process of passing the shame—and its provocative effects—came out especially clearly in the horrific stories and images from Abu Ghraib. At the time of the U.S.-led intervention in Iraq, a U.S. Marine Corps manual noted:

> Do not shame or humiliate a man in public. Shaming a man will cause him and his family to be anti-Coalition. . . . Shame is given by placing hoods over a detainee's head. Avoid this practice. Placing a detainee on the ground or putting a foot on him implies you are God.[79]

Yet these were precisely some of the techniques used by American guards at the Abu Ghraib prison in Iraq, where such "cultural knowledge"—and indeed the photographing of abuses—was in effect used to *maximize* the shame that was being inflicted.[80] Revealingly, U.S. prisons in Iraq became a significant source of future terrorists, including those of ISIS.[81]

Bin Laden explicitly stated after 9/11 that "what America is tasting now is only a copy of what we have tasted. Our Islamic nation has been tasting the same for more than 80 years of humiliation and disgrace."[82] Since terrorism by Islamist jihadist groups was being fueled by experiences and collective memories of humiliation, the problems with waging humiliating wars in response to terrorism should have been obvious.[83] But again these important emotional factors tended to slip off Western governments' radar.

In his enlightening book *The Far Enemy*, Fawaz Gerges noted that the most effective strategy against many forms of terrorism has been to allow popular revulsion to take its course, without putting this benign process into reverse through a violent and ill-conceived retaliation;[84] yet al Qaida's terrorism was designed in part to push things in the *opposite* direction—by bringing out the true (violent) nature of "the enemy."[85] The "war on terror" fell foolishly into this trap—and the impetus to reverse shame and humiliation through imposing shame and humiliation was a central mechanism—on either side.

Of course, this is a cycle and so long as conflict remains in the mode of *pass the shame*, it is hard to see how it can end. The motivations for 9/11 were complex. But one American soldier who had attended high school in Egypt before serving in Iraq commented perceptively on the 9/11 attackers:

> They didn't choose a military target but a "soft" one, a target designed to drive home the idea that we cannot protect our women and children ... the terrorists were attacking the masculinity and image of our society ... trying to replicate some of the humiliation they felt themselves, by making America feel weak and helpless just as many of their home countries have felt weak and helpless against America in the past.[86]

Alongside the role of shame in generating the "war on terror" (and the role of the "war on terror" in generating shame), we need to understand how a sense of righteousness and shamelessness surrounding the destructive "war on terror" has been generated and sustained. Like other wars, the "war on terror" can usefully be seen as a war system that has involved a very particular—and very perverse—distribution of shame. Alongside a process of warding off the shame of weakness, of powerlessness, and of perceived immorality through violence, there has also been a sustained and often calculating process of warding off the shame of violence itself. The shame that has been defended against here is mostly shame around inflicting harm, though there has also been a threat of shame around stupidity (as in counterproductive tactics).

How then has the shame that one would normally associate with violence been kept at bay? And why (notwithstanding a turning away from outright invasions in favor of increased drone attacks under Obama) was failure not considered to be sufficiently shameful to abandon the "war on terror" itself?

A full assessment of how the "war on terror" has been legitimized would be very lengthy and would need to consider a wide range of techniques, including dehumanizing the enemy, deploying euphemisms, invoking the forces of "history," selling the project as virtually costless (in money or "American lives"), deploying secrecy, and neglecting proper evaluation. In chapter 2, we also saw how the peculiar mixture of shame and honor that has been directed at soldiers and veterans has helped legitimize the "war on terror." Another legitimizing technique lies in determining when history "starts": in particular, Western leaders have typically arrogated to themselves the power to define what is provocation and what is response; within this framework, history could be conveniently presented as beginning with the 9/11 attacks themselves and the likelihood of shame was significantly reduced.

A key factor that has been under-recognized is the way that violence itself has served to preempt the shame that violence might normally be expected to elicit—another disturbing example of Arendt's "action as propaganda." Bush's notorious statement that "Either you are with us or you are with the terrorists"[87] carried the strong and threatening implication that critics would be incorporated into a conveniently flexible "enemy" category. And in reproducing "the terrorist," the violence of the "war on terror" served in effect as powerful propaganda for itself—by "demonstrating" just how pervasive and dangerous the proclaimed enemy actually was. In this way, the greatest weakness of the enterprise—that it was reproducing the problem it claimed to be addressing—was magically turned into its greatest "strength."

Violence also legitimized itself when the war was imported into the "pre-war." On the very day that U.S., UK, and allied forces were to attack Iraq, Prime Minister Blair told the House of Commons: "This is a tough choice. But it is also a stark one: to stand British troops down and turn back; or to hold firm to the course we have set."[88] Even more startlingly, Secretary of State Colin Powell, on learning in mid-January 2003 that President Bush was committed to war, said walking away would have been disloyal to the president, to the U.S. military, and in particular to the several thousand soldiers who would be going to war.[89] Dov Cohen has noted:

> Very early on in the run-up to the war, the Bush administration seemed to understand the importance of "face" to the American public.... By the time some of the early weapons inspections reports came in, the United States had sent so many troops to the region and the administration had ratcheted up the rhetoric so much that the United States would have lost a tremendous amount of face by just turning around and going home.[90]

So here was another manipulation of shame. In some ways, this dynamic echoed one of the United States' earliest forays into foreign imperialism: the invasion of the Philippines in 1899. For by the time the policy on the Philippines could be affected by public discussion, U.S. forces had already battered the Spanish fleet and taken Manila, so that President William McKinley could say that the only relevant question was whether the United States should *leave* the islands it had already taken.[91]

That earlier war also showed how success could be used to generate an aura of "legitimacy." Bringing out the role of religious ideas around

Manifest Destiny in the Philippines invasion, Richard Hofstadter noted, "Misfortune is construed as Providential punishment, but success, as in the Calvinist scheme, is taken as an outward sign of an inward state of grace."[92] A more secular version of this was expressed in the wake of 9/11 when George W. Bush's close advisor Karl Rove said of the war on terrorism: "Everything will be measured by results. The victor is always right. History ascribes to the victor qualities that may not actually have been there. And similarly to the defeated."[93] In this way, successful action would serve as the best propaganda. (Incidentally, Hitler had his own version of this: "The victor will not be asked afterwards whether he told the truth or not. When starting and waging a war it is not right that matters, but victory.")[94]

Insofar as success could be claimed at all, it depended on highlighting a *series of successful wars* rather than acknowledging a single, failing one. When it came to Iraq, the message was first that Saddam's regime had been successfully dispatched; then there was the triumphant "defeat" of al Qaida in Iraq (after a "surge" in numbers of American troops); after that, ISIS was on many occasions said to be reeling from Western bombs and Western-backed militias. One thing that was habitually obscured in all these claims of "victory" was the considerable continuity of personnel (generally overlooked by a media that tended to be stuck in a "perpetual present") between these three enemies. Saddam's army— sacked en masse in 2003—actually provided a key core of skilled and armed men for al Qaida in Iraq and then ISIS. Indeed, the skills of Saddam's officers helped ISIS considerably, not least in its sophisticated use of surveillance and blackmail.[95] While the West trumpeted its military successes against Saddam and then al Qaida in Iraq, both al Qaida in Iraq and ISIS took advantage of the neglect of Sunni political, economic, and social grievances by a Western- and Iranian-backed regime in Baghdad,[96] another key reason for "the enemy" reproducing itself.

Bush and Blair shared a dangerous belief that they had understood the laws of history, that they could predict the future, and that those who stood in their way were simply a "force of reaction" that could be wished away, physically destroyed, or both. Bush declared that freedom was a "force of history," adding, "We can go forward with complete confidence in the eventual triumph of freedom.... History has an ebb and flow of justice, but history also has a visible direction, set by liberty and the Author of Liberty."[97] In a 2004 article, journalist Ron Suskind recounted that a George W. Bush advisor had accused him of being "in the reality-based community," and had added "that's not the way the world works anymore. We're an empire now, and when we act, we create our own reality."[98]

Blair lumped opponents of "modernity" into the same category as Islamist terrorists, invoking, for example, "the age-old battle between progress and reaction, between those who embrace the modern world and those who reject its existence." Blair also referred to a "false sense of grievance against the West."[99] Within this shared framework, the Bush/Blair team saw its task as accelerating historic processes that were happening in any case. In this weird world, "history" became both master and alibi—and again success would provide proof that this was indeed a righteous struggle, perhaps one that had God's approval.[100] But history does not always fall in line with those who think they can shape it. In foreign affairs as also domestically, those who have been dismissed as "reactionary" or "irrelevant" may end up refusing to disappear.

Much of the shamelessness of the attack on Iraq—and much of the humiliation that it imposed—can be better understood when we realize the many ways in which the enterprise resembled *a witch hunt*. These similarities underline just how far policy had departed from the "objective" and "scientific" status that it claimed, a claim that was rather fundamental to whatever aura of legitimacy it may have had. Strangely, this particular persecution came at a point where key Western governments were strongly committed, at least in theory, to "evidence-based policy." Moreover, the "war on terror" was launched with all the trappings of science like the latest weaponry and satellite photos that purported to show weapons of mass destruction. But, as often happens, this "science" cloaked a good deal of magic and strong elements of irrationality in what was actually an emotion-driven—and, to a large extent, a shame-driven—response. Intelligence work focussed not so much on assessing guilt as on establishing the inherently malevolent quality of the chosen target. The policy of preemptive attack by the United States and its allies meant, in effect, that Iraq was targeted for its presumed evil *intentions*, just as a witch might be. And of course it is very difficult to prove an *absence* of bad intentions. (Indeed, Rumsfeld's infamous comment on the weapons of mass destruction—"absence of evidence is not evidence of absence"—is a truism-cum-ruse that could apply equally to bad intentions.) On one plausible interpretation, Iraq was actually targeted based on its weakness (its *lack of* weapons of mass destruction), and a key factor here—as sometimes when elderly women in particular have been targeted as witches—was precisely the inability to strike back. It's that inability—as Girard emphasized—that qualifies the "scapegoat" for being attacked.[101]

On top of all this, the combination of toppling Saddam Hussein while undertaking very meager planning for the post-Saddam era implied the strangely magical view that removing one "evil" individual would somehow solve the problem. Significantly, confession played a key role in the drama too. Saddam was told that he could only prevent an attack by acknowledging the existence of weapons of mass destruction. But since these weapons did not actually exist, his only option for survival was to admit guilt for something he had not actually done. We might remember here the ancient practice of ducking a suspected witch: if you sank, you were innocent (but dead); if you floated, you were guilty (and might promptly be killed). When U.S. officials rejected the idea that Iraq could meet specified "benchmarks" to show compliance with weapons inspectors, Hans Blix said the U.S. position was: "The witches exist; you are appointed to deal with these witches; testing whether there are witches is only a dilution of the witch hunt."[102]

Very soon, when violence began to reproduce the terrorist, another kind of witch-hunt logic kicked in: since the original persecution was clearly not working, more witches had to be found! For the most part, this was a closed system that effectively insulated itself from criticism.[103] As in Arendt's analysis of totalitarianism, punishment had been largely divorced from crime, and the concept of guilt—so closely tied to the concept of legality—had been pushed aside by the violence itself. As also in Arendt's analysis of totalitarianism, the laws of "history" had been elevated above actual laws that held fast to the concept of guilt and prohibited this kind of attack. As policy departed further and further from its scientific and legal pretentions, potential shame around this irrationality, illegality, and indeed stupidity seems to have been warded off through further violence and further massaging of the truth.

Clearly, there are huge differences between the rise of Nazism, the Cold War, and the "war on terror," and each had enormously complex causes, consequences, and functions. But it's clear that shame and its manipulation played a major role in all three. Especially damaging was the preponderance of shame around weakness. From these cases, we can also learn something valuable about the techniques by which shamelessness has been generated and sustained. Whether through euphemism, through a perverse invocation of history's "laws," through "action as propaganda," through the rejection of emotion as weakness, through the invocation of certain kinds of "science," through the idea of "choosing the lesser evil," or through a magical belief in far-fetched solutions for shame and powerlessness, the planners and perpetrators of violence repeatedly freed themselves from the constraints of conscience and warded off the shame that might normally arise from inflicting harm; at the same time, they ensured that the voices of victims counted for little or nothing.

As the violence and suffering intensified, the need to ward off shame also intensified (particularly when the underlying project ran into major problems), and all this tended to encourage a widening in the definition of the enemy—and not least a shaming and persecution of *critics*. This in turn tended to deepen the violence as shaming was put to use in reinforcing the general shamelessness.

While self-interest may still be operating very strongly, understanding how shame is *harnessed* to self-interest is vital. In Western wars and mass violence—as we found also in our discussions of Eichmann, Trump, and Brexit—the manipulation of shame and shamelessness has frequently been linked to implicit ideas about masculinity (including masculinity-as-strength and masculinity-as-unemotional).

15

Conclusion

A SENSE OF SHAME surrounds the emotion of shame, and we urgently need to bring this shadowy emotion more into the open. While we often see shame as an individual problem or something deeply personal that we want to keep quiet, we need to recognize that shame is socially generated, produced by particular social and economic conditions, and instrumentalized for identifiable purposes. Without this kind of awareness, we are more susceptible to bogus and damaging "solutions" for shame, including a brand of right-wing populism that thrives on various kinds of escape from shame—not least through offloading shame onto others.

We need to recognize that shame is *what we have in common*.[1] Even the shameless often have some sense of underlying shame, as we've seen. Recognizing that we share a sense of shame can help us escape from what has been called the "prison" of shame:[2] by reducing our sense of isolation, it diminishes the feeling that we are somehow uniquely defective; by giving us a sense of humility, it reduces the urge to pile shame onto others; and by highlighting shame as a social and political problem, it gives us more and better ideas for tackling social issues (including problems that lie at the root of shame).

Rather than indulging in shaming or fleeing into delusions, in short, it would be more helpful to articulate our own sense of shame, to explore the ways in which society is constantly generating shame, and to highlight the various interested parties who benefit from this process (not least when they promise to *relieve* shame). Being frank about shame—its production, distribution, and manipulation—offers the prospect of loosening the grip that shame has on us all.

Impeding progress here—and exemplifying that process of pushing shame onto others—has been the common habit of portraying shame as an emotion that holds sway in societies *other than one's own*. This is something to which Western politicians and publics have frequently resorted, and we've seen how the shaming of "shame societies" has been a notable part of the "war on terror," for example. Challenging the manipulation of shame in global wars and the manipulation of shame *within* Western societies is made more difficult by the tendency to imagine that Western societies have somehow "outgrown" shame. They have not.

The book has queried the common view in the Global North that wars directly involving Western democracies are somehow rational and goal-directed while other wars are emotional and chaotic. We have seen that shame has played a key role in *many different kinds* of war around the world—often interacting with self-interest in complex ways as well as with a range of other emotions. Shame has played a significant role both in driving terrorism and in driving *responses to terrorism*.

The taboo on talking about shame is also an *opportunity*, and in this book I have tried to look shame squarely in the eye. Again, this means avoiding the temptation to "locate" shame in distant lands and distant eras. I have tried to put shame center-stage in the discussion of politics, drawing both on firsthand investigations and on a range of authors from diverse backgrounds and disciplines.

On the whole, I find that shame tends to put us precisely where some very powerful interests would like us to be. Part of the problem here is that when we operate within a framework of shame (rather than, say, anger), we tend to individualize major social issues. Another problem is that we remove responsibility from where it properly belongs. When it comes to global warming, we may load shame onto ourselves for not doing enough cycling or recycling, but at the same time we risk giving major commercial and political interests an excessively easy ride. With mental health, we also tend to individualize the problem, exacerbating an underlying shame that may itself be informing suffering and mental illness. In the UK, former head of mental health at the Ministry of

Education Natasha Devon has wisely stressed the dangers in telling schoolchildren to be more "resilient" even as mental health spending has been cut and even as the stress produced by exams and frequent testing is not sufficiently addressed.[3] Again, putting everything onto the individual can add a layer of shame to preexisting distress, while underlying social conditions are allowed to persist or even worsen.[4] Yet as psychologist Sanah Ahsan has noted in relation to a surge in mental health problems, "If a plant were wilting we wouldn't diagnose it with 'wilting-plant-syndrome'—we would change its conditions."[5]

On one reading, there has been increased attention to concepts like respect and recognition in recent years, reflecting in part a growing focus on the politics of identity.[6] Of course, it represents huge progress when groups that have been shamed and stigmatized can begin to escape this nightmare. But one significant risk is that concern with respect and recognition can squeeze out attention to more material factors—including the underlying socioeconomic conditions that often remain shockingly bad and that do so much to fuel people's feelings of not being respected and recognized.[7] Underlying conditions include social inequality and mass incarceration. Michelle Alexander has observed that even as the triumph of the civil rights movement was widely proclaimed, the U.S. prison population shot up from around 300,000 to over 2 million in less than thirty years.[8] The way forward is not to focus exclusively on respect or recognition or even on emotion more generally but to explore the complex role that shame is playing in fueling injustice and vice versa. I recognize the danger that, in a book about shame, somehow everything comes—magically!—to revolve around shame: in a project like this, the world is no doubt colored, to a significant degree, by one's "shame-colored spectacles." Nevertheless, there is an invitation here to consider a *wide range* of emotions (whether fear, desire/greed, hope, anxiety, or whatever) and to map their complex interactions not only with each other but with the more material and calculating side of political life.

Part of understanding the political and social role of shame is exploring how shame and shamelessness interact. We saw a complex interaction with Trump and Eichmann, both of whom tended to recoil from feelings of sympathy and to construct a sense of shame around lack of strength or success rather than lack of kindness. In the case of Sierra Leone's civil war, we saw various shameless *groups* surrounded by a threat of shame—a threat that they tended to ward off through further violence and through constructing shame itself as shameful.[9] From his work in U.S. prisons, Gilligan found that the most dangerous individual was a seemingly shameless person who was haunted by the threat of shame; with these individuals, even a mild shaming could produce an extremely violent reaction. In our discussion of the legacies of colonialism and the various political backlashes against attempts to highlight past and present violence, we have seen how a relatively shameless community may again react aggressively to the threat of shame—and how politicians can take advantage of this reflex. In such environments, attempts by previously stigmatized groups to shake off their shame (and assert pride in their identity) have sometimes been met with calls for "a revival of shame"—underlining the intensely political nature of battles around who should and shouldn't feel shame as well as the intensely political nature of battles around what people should feel shame *about*.

So a key problem tends to lie with the values behind a process of shaming. Here, the problem is not shame itself but the uses to which it is put. Flanagan makes this point very clearly: "Shame, the general purpose emotion, is not what is causing the problem. My proposal: Turn the tables. Attack the bad values as shameful."[10] In other words, the problem is the values that shame is "recruited to protect."[11] The same goes for pride: "Pride that one has gotten better at tennis is fine," Flanagan notes. "Pride that one is an exemplary neo-Nazi is not fine."[12]

While this makes a lot of sense, the provocative nature of a great deal of shaming still needs to be fully acknowledged and guarded against. We have noted that Flanagan—in his generally positive account of shame—observes that "when parents tell a child that they ought to feel ashamed because they lied, or hit their sibling, or behaved badly in school, they are not calling upon the child to think 'I am a failure.'"[13] We can perhaps accept this up to a point. But I think we always need to be conscious of when we or others are straying into an unnecessarily shaming discourse. The threat of demeaning someone's whole self is hovering around so many conversations, and subtle variations tend to make a big difference. Whether in everyday interactions or in political utterances, there is usually a choice between statements that involve significant shaming of the "target" person as a whole (or group as whole) and statements that don't. One could move from "You didn't empty the bin," for example, to "You always forget to empty the bin" to "You are completely irresponsible. It's like living with a small child!" Now it may be that the milder and more specific reprimand has had no appreciable effect and that therefore the shame is being strategically and even reasonably intensified. That might work. But if we go back to Retzinger's work on couples or any number of aspects of the politicization of shame considered within the current book, we should also be aware of how shaming can fuel cycles of anger and countershaming. Where shaming becomes intense, it can easily make the "target" dig in behind a sense of resentment or even self-righteousness. In politics, productive shame seems to depend on shared values; but in a highly polarized politics, shaming can easily drive different factions (perhaps different "moral communities") further apart.

I have argued in several books that there is more to war than winning. Moreover, when you fail to win (perhaps through targeting civilians in predictably counterproductive ways), you may be achieving other political and economic goals.[14] Somewhat analogously, while the ostensible aim of shaming is generally to induce better behavior, someone who fails to induce better behavior through shaming may nevertheless be quietly succeeding in other goals. Perhaps the shamers have diminished their own sense of shame, or vented their anger, or succeeded in looking good in front of others, or asserted their membership in a community, or distracted from their own bad behavior, or some combination of these—or something else. When behavior that is not "working" persists (and shaming today would seem to be a strong example of this), we have to rethink what its purposes actually are. We have to rethink what "working" actually means in this context.

At a more systemic level, understanding how dysfunctional political and economic systems function and how they sustain themselves means understanding the distribution of shame that these systems create and depend upon. A far-reaching manipulation and perverse distribution of shame has fueled and sustained violence of various kinds (whether this is war, humanitarian disasters, sexual violence, or other crimes). Such perverse distributions of shame tend to solidify and legitimize a wide range of abusive systems—not least through the idea that suffering is deserved and through the related idea that success or victory implies some kind of virtue or even Godly approval. Such ideas may seem self-evidently unhelpful when set out like this, but in practice there are thousands of ways to collude in perverse distributions of shame.

Importantly, those who can shape the distribution of risks within political and economic systems have usually been able to shape the distribution of honor and shame: we may notice, for example, that the heroism of soldiers has been used to legitimize war even as the risks to Western soldiers have been radically scaled down; when wars go wrong, soldiers often absorb much of the shame; when war is revived, soldiers are lauded again. In the financial world, the "risk-taking" of millionaires and billionaires has been used to legitimize the type of largely unregulated capitalism that provided their riches. Yet at the same time, big banks and corporations have skewed the markets by successfully lobbying for minimal regulation, low taxation, bank bailouts, minimal protection against oligopolies, and bankruptcy laws that favor big businesses over small businesses. Of course, the way I have interpreted these various systems reflects my own political views and biases. But all of us need critically to examine how shame and honor are being mobilized in our societies and with what kinds of purposes and effects.

In my view, shame has not only demoralized us; it has also helped produce a huge appetite for "magical" solutions, solutions that do not help in any practical sense and that are often actively damaging. Here we can usefully go back to Freud's insight that illusions are nurtured and sustained by the fulfillment of wishes, and we may observe that the wish to be free from shame seems to be one of the most powerful. That desire makes us extremely vulnerable to manipulation, however, and in this book we have seen how some of this manipulation works. The embrace of false solutions, meanwhile, has tended to produce a great deal of *additional* shame, including the shame of doing harm and the shame of getting things wrong. This mechanism seems to apply at both the individual and social level. So we get trapped in particularly vicious circles of shame.

When it comes to the individual, we know that addictions and even mental illnesses can offer some kind of escape from things that are too painful to face. In this sense, these scourges are not just problems but solutions. Some psychoanalysts have underlined this point by stressing that delusions can be protective and trying to reduce them too quickly can bring significant dangers.[15] At the same time, part of the problem created by these conditions is that they tend to prevent the pursuit of more realistic solutions for a person's problems.

Magical solutions serve identifiable functions not just for individuals who subscribe to them but also for a range of interest groups who are able to manipulate these various systems. We have explored this manipulation in quite a variety of contexts. The benefits of magical solutions are largely psychological: broadly, we think we have understood the world; we think we have a solution; and we think it's not our fault. There is a flight from the shame of incomprehension and personal responsibility. But such benefits are typically fleeting—not least because the magical solutions (more or less by definition) do not actually solve the problems they purport to address. At the same time, for those who "sell" these magical solutions, the benefits are often more tangible—victory at the polls, for example, or profits in the bank. Many of these benefits are quite enduring and survive even when the magical solution itself is unraveling. Of course, the sellers are not *simply* manipulators: they may be escaping the shame of ignorance and personal responsibility; they may believe (to a degree) in their own "solutions"; they may subscribe to the view that big problems are being solved with simple, tangible solutions—a wall perhaps, a bombing raid, or a consumer product advertised as magically bringing love, respect, or whatever. The sellers would probably not be very good salespeople if they did not, at some level, believe in their own snake oil.[16]

As at the individual level, a key problem lies in the way that magical thinking habitually impedes the search for more realistic solutions. Conversely, if we are going to think more clearly—and act more constructively—in relation to a range of severe and often life-threatening social problems, we need to get a much better sense of how shame and its manipulation have perpetuated these problems—not least by encouraging the embrace of magical solutions. We need to recognize the many problems *arising from* these solutions and the way this process in turn tends to feed shame and shaming in a vicious circle.

Shining a light on complex layers of underlying shame and on their manipulation can help the search for solutions that are less magical, less violent, and less counterproductive—a process of *disenchantment*.[17] Unless we become much better at recognizing and counteracting such manipulations, we will be left with political and economic systems that address many emotional needs in the short term while remaining (conveniently) blind to the factors *creating* these needs and (conveniently) indifferent to addressing these factors.

We have looked at the techniques of those who manipulate shame and sell magical solutions, highlighting some common elements. Rather central here has been the way shame has repeatedly been stirred and hyped by those who simultaneously promise to remove it—a kind of double game that recurs with remarkable frequency. Such actors do with shame what the mafia does with fear. A key "model" for this maneuver was highlighted in our discussion of shame and consumerism: routinely, commercial interests have both fostered and fed off a deep underlying shame about everything from our looks and our bodies to our houses and holidays. Within this sphere—and within the varied political systems and war systems we have examined—shame and shaming have played a key role.

The cycle of shame and promised escape tends to keep us working and spending (at least for those fortunate enough not to be discarded altogether), and it does so at a level of growth, waste, and resource consumption that the planet cannot tolerate. All too often, moreover, politicians take this ever-replenishing reservoir of shame and use it to release a torrent of abuse toward a variety of "outgroups" (as we have seen in the chapters on Trump in particular).

Drawing on the psychoanalytic tradition, we've noted a strong human tendency to flee from the shame and anxiety of powerlessness into some kind of fantasy of omnipotence[18]—a tendency that again appears to apply at a social as well as an individual level. We have seen the highly destructive consequences that can arise from trying to protect some kind of fantasy of omnipotence: denying defeat on the battlefield or at the polls; turning defeat into "betrayal" and persecution (as we saw in Germany and Rwanda);[19] turning on any critics; or simply fleeing from one war into another. These impulses, which many voters may *share* with their leaders, may go a long way toward explaining the fragility of democracy and, at the extreme, the slippery slope to mass murder.

One of the complications here is that condemning a flight into delusions can easily become another form of shaming, particularly when those who are embracing magical solutions (or solutions seen as magical) are denounced as, for example, "irrational" or "racist." The fact that shame played such a key role in the rise of Trump suggests notable dangers in the urge to denounce and shame his followers. On top of this, the regular and sometimes enjoyable denunciation of Trump and other prominent right-wing populists, while understandable in many ways, may end up obscuring—and ultimately feeding—the strange combination of complacency, selfishness, and magical thinking that elevated these figures in the first place. Such shamings may be, in part, a flight from one's own shame and complicity. Relevant here are the embrace of extreme inequality (including by many liberals), the magical belief in markets, and the belief that those who are not benefiting from "modernization" will magically melt away.

It is easy to be seduced by the idea that "all reasonable people" will agree on some basic policy fundamentals, and that those who do not are somehow beyond the pale. We've seen how an assumed "consensus" can feed a dangerously and profoundly shaming sense of nonexistence. Back in 2005, Chantal Mouffe noted that

> nowadays political antagonisms are being formulated in terms of moral categories ... when opponents are defined not in political but in moral terms, they cannot be envisaged as an "adversary" but only as an "enemy." ... Moreover, as they are often considered as the expression of some kind of "moral disease", one should not even try to provide an explanation for their emergence and success.[20]

Shortly after Trump became president, Nancy Fraser helpfully urged the importance of avoiding "a doubling down on progressive-neoliberalism's definition of 'us' (progressives) versus 'them' (Trump's 'deplorable' supporters)."[21] She also advocated the need to forge a common cause "among *all* whom his administration is set to betray: not just the immigrants, feminists and people of color who voted against him, but also the rust-belt and Southern working-class strata who voted for him."[22]

Meanwhile, one powerful person's sense that "history is on my side" can easily feed into other people's sense that history is passing them by—that they are redundant, disrespected, replaced, left behind, or simply invisible. Just as the shamed and "redundant" soldiers and officials of Saddam Hussein refused to disappear from history when these people were fired, so also it turned out that the many victims of globalization, automation, and official neglect within Western democracies and beyond were not ready to disappear as quickly or as quietly as the high priests of modernization perhaps predicted and preferred. In these circumstances, from Paris to London to Charlottesville, the (bogus) far-right message that there was a plan to "replace" white people with minorities acquired, for some, a ring of truth.

A major danger—and we saw it with Brexit too—is that when a political system has neglected and shamed large numbers of people (often shaming them not only through neglect and exploitation but also through an additional layer of verbal disparagement), many people may react in ways that precipitate a further round of shaming and scapegoating. This in turn may become a significant part of how a grossly unfair system renews and legitimizes itself. The mechanism seems very prominent today but is perhaps not so new if we think of the past shaming of the "criminal classes," for example.

We do not need to go to the other extreme, to live in fear of provocation or refuse to call a spade a spade. Nor should we succumb, in my view, to the fashionable idea—which would seem to mean the death of any semblance of free speech—that people have a right *not to be offended*. But we do need to be more aware of the many dangers that outright shaming brings in its wake. The act of shaming often covers a multitude of sins on the part of the shamer: it is frequently the enemy of *self*-awareness.

Moreover, the pleasurable righteousness of shaming others—which appears to have been strongly reinforced by the echo chambers and "you may also like" algorithms of the internet—is a remarkably ineffective way of solving problems but often a very effective way of making them worse.

Rational Actors and Magical Thinkers

The persistence of delusions is a striking phenomenon in the modern world, particularly given the increasing availability of information. Much of the discussion in this book underlines the limitations of the "rational actor" model.[23] When it comes to Freud's "scientific" age, we are in many ways *still waiting*. But rather than lurching to the other extreme and proclaiming that emotions have today somehow "taken over," we need to investigate the complex *interactions* between emotions and self-interest, whether in the Global North or the Global South and whether in today's politics or in earlier eras.

Academics and other analysts need to be more mindful of the critical role played by emotions in how politics plays out, not least in the context of war. We have seen how important it is to understand the relationship between emotions and delusions. Without this, we will continue to be confused and surprised when people somehow "fail" to act in their own interests—or at least in accordance with what we think they *should* value, which is not quite the same thing. Without an emotionally informed analysis, moreover, it is also too easy to be perpetually astonished by "mindless violence" and "irrational voting," with all the dangers of additional and provocative shaming that this brings. We also lose sight of the relatively powerful actors (perhaps including ourselves) whose actions and inactions have helped, perhaps over a long period, to create the "sudden madness" in the first place. That was certainly a lesson from Sierra Leone; it was also a lesson from the Rwandan genocide;[24] and it seems to be a lesson emerging from recent politics in Western democracies. Again, a better path than pointing the finger would be to explore one's own complicity in unfair systems that have been distributing both resources and shame in unfair ways, often generating magical thinking and violence in the process.

In terms of academic work, a hazard related to the sidelining of emotion *as an object of inquiry* is the sidelining of emotion *within the writing itself*. In learning to squeeze emotion from scholarly books and articles, academics may be succeeding in achieving a level of "dryness," abstraction, and borderline incomprehensibility that pleases university tenure committees but ends up facilitating a (politically convenient) marginalization of academic work. Arendt's own writing offers a valuable alternative "role model" here, in my view. For passion was always an integral part of her writing and she explicitly rejected as downright dangerous the setting aside of emotion and the habit of making "deductions" in isolation from one's own experience or from the experiences of others. This is one reason why (despite the passage of time and despite critiques of her work as insensitive on a number of fronts),[25] many people still look to Arendt for guidance today.

One of the conclusions to emerge from our explorations of shamelessness is how often abuse has been facilitated by an appeal to "science" and "objectivity"—and by the claim that we should resist more emotional responses. This last claim has been a persistent one and often a deeply gendered one too. A common phenomenon—exemplified by Eichmann but extending far beyond him and beyond the Nazi structures he inhabited—has been that those creating violence feel remarkably little shame around suffering they are inflicting and a great deal of shame around "weakness," around feelings of sympathy, and around "not doing their job." In general, rather than somehow "choosing" between the perils of shame and the perils of shamelessness, we would be better advised to explore, first, how they interact and, second, the values they reflect in particular contexts. How is shame constructed? What is it that is presented or seen as shameful and not shameful? Which are the types of shame that are most helpful and productive? And which are the most destructive? Such an inquiry will help us greatly when we try to understand when and why shamelessness is dangerous. A key moment of danger that this book has highlighted in many different contexts is when shame around weakness trumps shame around cruelty (and, yes, I am picking my verb carefully). Like other types of shame, shame around weakness has its cultural and familial conditions of existence, with heavily gendered constructions of shame often playing a key role.

Addressing Conspiracy Theory

In December 2020 (after Trump's defeat by Biden), an Ipsos poll found more than 1 in 3 Americans expressing the view that there was a deep state working to undermine President Trump, with fully 47 percent of respondents unable to identify the following statement as false: "A group of Satan-worshipping elites who run a child sex ring are trying to control our politics and media."[26] While comedians like Jon Stewart and Trevor Noah and filmmakers like Michael Moore have often been a welcome voice in what often feels like a crazy time and while humor can be a valuable weapon against extremism, nevertheless there is reason to believe that ridiculing and stereotyping entire groups of people tends to be counterproductive. It would seem, moreover, that the shaming of "magical" beliefs can sometimes help *entrench* these beliefs, so that conspiracy theories—for example—are not undermined but fortified. Here we can learn from the growing band of experts who now specialize in trying to get people out of the grip of conspiracy theories. Their techniques—highlighted for example in a December 2020 investigation by America's National Public Radio—throw interesting light on the relationship between shame and delusion.

Consider the insights of Diane Benscoter, who was herself extricated from the clutch of the Moonies (also known as the Unification Church) and has since the 1980s been trying to help people disengage from extremist ideologies while her nonprofit organization Antidote.com has also run recovery groups on the lines of Alcoholics Anonymous. Benscoter begins by noting that cultish groups offer "easy answers to life's hard questions." She stresses that cults tend to establish "this camaraderie and this feeling of righteousness and this cause for your life, and that feels very invigorating and almost addictive. You feel like you are fighting the battle for goodness, and all of a sudden you are the hero."

When engaging with someone who has fallen into the grip of a conspiracy theory, Benscoter says she is careful not to criticize. So a QAnon-style belief in a child sex ring would not be met with a flat contradiction but perhaps with a suggestion that the individual get involved in a nonprofit that fights human trafficking.[27] The idea here is that the person is not crazy but has had a good instinct misdirected by misinformation. Crucially, Benscoter will point to *her own* experience of being duped by the Moonies, to the way indoctrination tactics worked *on her*. She will also stress that such groups tend to paint views in the "world outside" as lies or as "evil." Other specialists urge the families of conspiracy theorists to resist the temptation to mock these beliefs. Also useful is helping believers "follow the crumbs" of research paths that may bring core beliefs into question (a tactic that offers more agency and respect than being told you are deluded, and that actually mirrors QAnon's encouragement to "do your research" and follow the crumbs that *they* favor).

Incidentally, I have myself had a brief experience of Moonie tactics as a young traveler in San Francisco. A friendly and good-looking young man and woman, saying they were from the Unification Church, invited me to a dinner, asked me to take off my shoes, and were soon impressing on me that I was afraid to love and afraid of a new adventure. They were with me the whole time and preventing me from comparing notes with others who'd come in off the streets: "Are these the Moonies?" I wanted to ask my fellow guests. When I made to leave, my hosts physically withheld my shoes. These individuals were stirring up a sense of shame in me and cutting me off from my usual reference points (not to mention my shoes)—and then offering a week on their "farm" as a solution. I remember conjuring up the (negative) views that absent friends and family would express in relation to the Moonies; without that, I think my own sense of shame and isolation would have led me to the farm; and once these techniques have worked once, they can presumably work again.

Shamelessness and Impunity

Even as we have explored the harm that shame and shaming can do, we have repeatedly been confronted by the problem of shamelessness. So while wishing shame away may be tempting, we should perhaps be careful what we wish for.

When we take seriously the many problems arising from shamelessness, it reminds us that shame can sometimes be helpful. This applies at least in the case of shame around choices. Particularly with an eye on contemporary politics, a convincing case can be made that we need shame as a moral emotion that rescues us from the perils of shamelessness.

However, even shame-for-choices has a distinctly mixed record. Such shaming may be ineffective. It may be counterproductive. And if it does lead to behavior that the shamer would like to see, then this outcome will only be helpful if the values embodied in the shaming are actually good ones.

We have stressed the need to consider the circumstances in which shaming is effective in changing behavior, and the circumstances in which it actually *reinforces or exacerbates* existing behavior. Key factors to examine here include whether the values behind the shaming are "bought into" by the recipient, whether the shamer is respected, what *type* of shame is being invoked, and whether the party being shamed has sufficient self-esteem to allow any productive shaming (as Gilligan's criminals clearly did not).

Whether we are talking about civil wars or global wars or humanitarian disasters or economic systems, *shameless systems* include wars and famines and peacetime economic and political systems that have rather glaring damaging consequences but that nevertheless retain significant legitimacy—at least in the eyes of those creating and sustaining them and perhaps also beyond these circles. These systems tend to depend on perverse distributions of shame that involve significant shaming of victims. At a societal as well as an individual level, shamelessness tends to be generated and sustained *through the shaming and blaming of others.*

A key mechanism here, in my view, is that highlighting a particular enemy tends to generate a damaging aura of shamelessness—and a sense of impunity—within the systems of repression and exploitation that grow up around this definition of the enemy. While blaming groups for specific bad behaviors plays a role here, shaming groups as *inherently evil*—which may include dehumanizing language and inflicting conspicuous shame on members who have been captured—tends to add a great deal of "theater" and a great deal of emotional power to the maneuver. Nothing generates shamelessness like a perverse and self-righteous distribution of shame.

When I was investigating Sierra Leone's 1990s civil war, it was common to blame rebels for all or virtually all of the atrocities. But one local saying noted, "When you point the finger, three of your fingers are pointing at yourself." (If you do it, you will see that it's true.) Some of the more thoughtful Sierra Leoneans—and many of those who had actually been attacked—emphasized that a great deal of suffering was being created by non-rebels, including those who claimed to be intervening helpfully such as local chiefs, government soldiers, civil defense fighters, West African peacekeepers, international financial organizations, and so on. Some of these groups had contributed to the outbreak of the war in the first place—and there were multiple hidden collaborations once war broke out. Again, what was particularly conducive to impunity here was that the rebels were not simply blamed but also shamed—sometimes for their inherently evil nature and sometimes for being "animals." In other words, they were demonized and dehumanized. These forms of shaming were hardly surprising given the rebels' atrocities and given that rebels had themselves engaged in humiliating violence. Significantly, a process of demonization feeds into shamelessness not only by distracting from the abuses of those who claim to confront the "demons" but also by justifying these other abuses (which can be presented as a kind of "lesser evil"). Revealingly, denunciation of rebels sometimes extended to academics who tried to *understand* the rebels.

Treating certain groups as *only bad* may quickly become, first, a provocation and, second, an alibi for the shamers and their allies. Where a conflict has an aura of legitimacy (at least at the time)—as in the global war on communism or the war on drugs or the war on terror or even the so-called fight against human smugglers and illegal migration[28]—the danger of creating an alibi for abuse tends to rise sharply. The aid agency Médecins Sans Frontières (MSF) has wisely drawn attention to those who are made to suffer, as the title of an incisive MSF book put it, *In the Shadow of "Just Wars."*[29]

In such cases, a sense of righteousness tends to send a potentially helpful sense of shame dangerously into hiding. After one of Arendt's students had written to her about his efforts to "be a very good person," she wrote back:

> You probably know the Talmudic story about the 36 righteous men for the sake of whom God does not destroy the world. No one knows who they are, least of all they themselves. Every kind of self-knowledge is here absolutely ruinous.[30]

We have seen also—for example, in the various disasters under communism as well as in the "war on terror"—that the threat of shame that naturally *arises from* violence has routinely been accommodated in ways that have actually intensified magical thinking and intensified the violence. These related processes tend to encourage a habitual and sometimes virulent blaming of those who question core magical beliefs—and a renewed stigmatizing of the victims.

Rather than shaming everything one doesn't like, it would be more constructive to consider the circumstances in which "shaming" produces improved behavior and the circumstances in which it makes things worse. When people feel that they have some basic security and respect and are not being belittled for their views or for their behavior or lifestyle, then they may be ready to take some kind of criticism. If they do not have that basic security or respect, they may simply reject the criticism—particularly if it comes from those they see as self-interested and hypocritical. Their own sense of righteousness is likely to be reinforced. If this is true of many voters, it is equally applicable to the shaming of those directly perpetrating violence. Whether within U.S. prisons or in a civil war like the one in Sierra Leone, perpetrators often exist within a state of shamelessness that may be difficult and dangerous to challenge head-on. Conversely, a sense of being respected (and a sense of humility on the part of the intervener) may allow some productive sense of shame.[31] There is some experimental evidence that when groups are encouraged to affirm their collective value, they become more ready to acknowledge collective guilt.[32]

Shaming can be particularly hazardous when recipients have built part of their identity around national or ethnic pride. On top of this, those who are invited to feel shame may feel they have *too much shame already* and cannot tolerate any more. Here, Arendt was again insightful. Notwithstanding her consistent insistence on individuals taking personal responsibility under any form of government, she observed that if citizens are held responsible for *everything* that their government does, then this "may lead us into an intolerable situation of global responsibility," perhaps prompting "political apathy, isolationist nationalism or desperate rebellion against all powers that be."[33]

Listening and Introspection

Around halfway through the Trump administration, I had a conversation with an American friend (a writer), and she expressed her sense of political and personal disorientation:

> Trump goes against everything I was taught to value. I was always taught to study hard, to know the facts, to consider others, to understand before proposing a solution. Here I see someone doing the exact opposite of everything I know to be true.

My friend also wanted to use this feeling as a way to understand and move forward:

> I feel personally rejected by what has happened. So I can actually imagine how other people feel when *they* are made to feel their views are wrong. It's about listening to each other. It's not about saying there are smart people and dumb people. It's not about convincing people to see it our way. With this identity politics we have now, only half the population can win and half will lose. The most important thing is governance—that's what needs fixing.

Somehow, we need to move toward more inclusive reflexes and a greater degree of curiosity about where other people are coming from. Here we might again follow Arendt's lead when she noted (in *Between Past and Future*), "I form an opinion by considering a given issue from different viewpoints, by making present to my mind the standpoints of those who are absent; that is, I represent them."[34] *Asking* them is even better. And while condemnation runs the grave risk of escalating a cycle of shaming, curiosity will usually serve us much better. If I may be allowed to quote British pop band Depeche Mode, "Before you come to any conclusions, try walking in my shoes." The curiosity that we need should include curiosity about the many functions of shame and the strategies of those who offer magical—and often self-interested—solutions for shame.

Getting a better understanding of the lives and perspectives of those with whom we disagree is a project that sits relatively naturally with another project that is urgently required. This is the task of turning our attention to our own "blind spots," including the various kinds of violence we encourage or endorse—not least through our own preferred brands of moral indignation.

Arendt referred to Eichmann's "authentic inability to think," notably to think from the other person's point of view;[35] conversely, the *ability* to think "may prevent catastrophes at least for myself, in the rare moments when the chips are down."[36] Arendt also linked thinking with skepticism and doubt, noting (as we've seen) that these often gave better protection against totalitarianism than "respectability" or "moral values."[37]

The pleasures and rewards of condemnation should in themselves alert us to its hazards. In July 2021, UK prime minister Johnson and home secretary Priti Patel expressed their "disgust" at those who had directed "appalling" racist comments at England footballers who had missed penalties in the 2021 European Championship.[38] Of course, the expressions of disgust were entirely merited, and the politicians' statements echoed the sentiments of millions. But these easy declarations also displayed (as many pointed out) a hypocritical shift toward condemning racism after these same politicians had done a great deal to incite it—not least in their immigration policies and in refusing to condemn spectators who had booed England players taking a knee in solidarity against racism. And alongside this sharp shift to condemning the racists, we may also observe a significant *continuity*: the habit of finding some group whose public denunciation—perhaps popular as well as pleasurable—may serve as a substitute for addressing complex problems to which one is simultaneously contributing. We have seen elements of the flight from reality in the denunciation of Trump himself.

The system of shamelessly producing and reproducing inequality—and massive violence abroad—long preceded Trump and helped produce him. We cannot understand either Trump's shamelessness or this wider shamelessness without a holistic assessment of the political, historical, and cultural forces that shaped them.

Also in 2021 in the UK, Boris Johnson proposed that offenders guilty of antisocial behavior be made to pay for their crimes in "fluorescent-jacketed chain gangs"—a humiliating (and racially loaded) "policy" that got a poor reception from police chiefs looking for less gimmicky approaches to tackling crime.[39] But Johnson and Patel displayed a keen sense of theater, and shame will always lend itself to political theatrics. The tactic of *passing the shame* is a kind of golden blinker—profitable politically *and* economically—that keeps our eyes shut when it comes to finding proper solutions for urgent problems.

The title of one of Brené Brown's books tries to capture the moment of liberation for an individual who finds relief from living with intense shame: *I thought it was just me!*[40] One implication of my own book is that if we can investigate and highlight the *social production* of shame (and the purposes this serves), then we may begin to think more clearly and to reduce the crippling levels of shame—and isolation—that we often tend to feel *as individuals*. We need to wake up to the nature and the extent of the manipulations that are going on around the economy, conflict, elections, and so on. If we are going to be more effective in challenging a wide range of social and political problems (from wars to massive inequality to migration crises), we need to look much more closely at the powerful role that shame and shaming have played—and continue to play—in cementing these systems. We also need to understand how shamelessness is created and sustained, and we need to keep in mind that certain kinds of shame can also be constructive if the circumstances are favorable. We need continuously to address the disjuncture between the distribution of shame and the distribution of responsibility.

Of course, none of this is easy—and the pitfalls are numerous. We have seen that in fleeing from shame we may easily find ourselves descending into a fantasy world that potentially brings more shame in its wake as "solutions" depart further and further from reality. It also seems to be the case that, even as we try to escape from the habit of *shaming*, we may quickly find ourselves falling into *new or modified* kinds of shaming. An interesting example—highlighted by the Slovenian philosopher Slavoj Žižek—is that in attributing a person's bad or criminal behavior to some individual or collective experience of deprivation, you may in effect be failing to give that category of people the compliment and basic respect that comes from recognizing a sense of agency.[41] I should also acknowledge—with more than a little shame of my own!—that the trap of fleeing from shaming into some new shaming is one that seems to hover uneasily over the current book. Notably, while I have stressed the dangers of simply condemning or shaming people, my strong interest in Hannah Arendt and in magical thinking perhaps risks leading me towards new kinds of shaming (shaming for being deluded, for example, or shaming for adopting elements of totalitarian thinking and practice).

What I have tried to do, however, is to hold this murky object of shame up to the light and to challenge, in a small way, the power that it exerts when it lurks in the dark. I have tried to examine this shadowy, powerful and elusive object: to twist it and turn it and find new angles, to do justice to shame's destructive power as well as its potentially helpful role, to challenge the idea that modern Western societies are no longer "shame societies", to document the many ways in which shame is imposed and instrumentalized, to investigate what it is that we are made to feel shame *about*, and to examine how shamelessness has been constructed and instrumentalized. Of course, such a project will not save us from the perils of either shame or shamelessness. But if we are more alert to the varied and damaging ways in which shame and shamelessness are put to use, then we will be in a better position to resist.

NOTES

Chapter 1

1. Wurmser (1994, 17) refers to "shame about shame."
2. Flood 2021.
3. Exceptions include: Weber 1976; Lasch 1979; Bourgois 1995; Andersson 2014; Akerlof and Shiller 2015; Hochschild 2018; Wolf 2011.
4. Keen and Andersson 2018.
5. Even Freud retreated from a reality of abuse toward emphasizing *fantasies* of abuse (Herman 1992).
6. Keen 2005.
7. On this impunity, see Keen 2012a.

Chapter 2

1. After 9/11, Bush said, "They want us to stop flying and they want us to stop buying, but this great nation will not be intimidated by the evildoers" (The White House/President George W. Bush 2001b).
2. Whipple 2012.
3. Whipple 2012.
4. Whipple 2012.
5. Whipple 2012.
6. Correll 2009.
7. See also Correll 2009.
8. Correll 2009.
9. Correll 2009; my interview.
10. Correll 2009.
11. This was in 2010 (De Leon 2015) and 2011 (Whipple 2012).
12. Whipple 2012.
13. Whipple 2012.
14. De Leon 2015, citing conversation with Rev. Nadia Bolz-Weber, pastor at the House for All Sinners and Saints in Denver.
15. Whipple 2012.
16. List from Wikipedia.
17. Keen 2012a.

18. Marin 1991, 43; interviews with IVAW veterans, Colorado.
19. O'Brien 1979, 100. See also MacPherson 1988.
20. On the latter point, see particularly Stiglitz and Bilmes 2008.
21. Ignatieff 2005.
22. Marvin and Ingle 1999, 2, 4.
23. The fear of being brutalized had helped to spur his political transformation.
24. Strandlof 2011.
25. Monroe 2020.

Chapter 3

1. Lewis 1971.
2. Dearing and Tangney 2011, 4.
3. Dearing and Tangney 2011.
4. http://www.yourdictionary.com/shame.
5. *Webster's New World Dictionary*; emphasis added.
6. Deonna and Teroni 2008, 69.
7. Cohen 2003, 1098; see also Deonna and Teroni 2008.
8. Cohen 2003, 1077.
9. E.g., Hirschkind and Mahmood 2002; Yaqoob 2008.
10. Yaqoob 2008.
11. See, e.g., Ahmed 2012.
12. Benedict 1974, 38.
13. Hinton 1998.
14. E.g., Gilligan 2003.
15. Gerodimos 2022, 43.
16. Pitt-Rivers 2017, 6.
17. Lindisfarne 1998, 254.
18. Fischer 2016, 835.
19. Cohen et al. 1996. "Southerners" were defined as those who had lived in the South for six years or more.
20. Cohen et al. 1996, 945.
21. Cohen and Nisbett 1997, 1193.
22. Hoggett 2017, 373.
23. Brown 2008, 5.
24. Nietzsche 2003a.
25. Brown 2008, 4.
26. Brown 2008, 23.
27. Brown 2008.
28. Brown 2008, xiii.
29. Bradshaw 1988, xvii.
30. Bradshaw 1988, 30.
31. Bradshaw 1988, xvii.

32. Bradshaw 1988, 40.
33. Dearing and Tangney 2011; Park 2016, 354.
34. Park 2016.
35. Cf. Brown 2008; cf. also Gilbert 1998, 22.
36. Thomason 2018, 26–27.
37. Talbot 1996, 11.
38. Andrews 1998, 179.
39. Park 2016, 357–58; Bradshaw 1988.
40. BBC, *The Making of Them*, 1994, YouTube, uploaded May 31, 2014.
41. Park 2016, 355.
42. Greenberg and Iwakabe 2011, 81–82.
43. E.g., Park 2016.
44. Sluzki 2013a.
45. Some therapists emphasize the importance of expressing anger at others—perhaps within the therapy room—rather than directing the anger inward.
46. Cohen 2001.
47. See also, e.g., International Alert 2004; Human Rights Watch 2003.
48. Fanon 2008, 139.
49. Fanon 2008, 9.
50. Fanon 2008, 47.
51. Fanon 2008, 71, citing Aimé Césaire.
52. Arendt 1968a, 446. Cf. also Bartov 2000.
53. Levi 1989, 54.
54. Levi 1989, 35.
55. Levi 1989, 38.
56. Aristotle 2020, 57.
57. Aristotle 2020.
58. Scheff 1994; cf. Retzinger 1991.
59. Scheff 2003, 239.
60. Thomason 2018, 11.
61. E.g., discussion in Bigliani 2013.
62. Hoggett 2017.
63. Teusch 2015, 196.
64. Freud 1974, 352.
65. Freud 1974, 352.
66. Freud 2005, 3.
67. Freud 2001b, 31.
68. Cameron 1943, 38; emphasis added.
69. Wurmser, 2015, 1619.
70. E.g., Longley 2003; Cohn 2007; Stearns 2009.
71. We might notice here, incidentally, that if shame later turns to rage, this may be reversing an earlier journey in the opposite direction.
72. Wurmser 2000, 400.

73. Freud 1960, 88.
74. E.g., Moguillansky 2013; Cameron 1943, 1959; Klein 1997; Stadter 2011.
75. E.g., Layton 2014, 167.
76. Cameron 1943, 1959.
77. E.g., Sandler 1960; Haapatalo 2019.
78. Lewis 1971, 419.
79. Lewis 1971, 428.
80. Gilbert 1998.
81. Stuewig et al. 2014. This was controlled for childhood economic circumstances and for measures of childhood aggression.
82. Stuewig et al. 2014, 225 (emphases added). Flanagan (2021) is critical of the measures used to ascertain the existence of shame. Dearing and Tangney (2011) also saw shame as weakening empathy and fueling aggression in part as a result.
83. Nietzsche 2003a.
84. Katz 1996.
85. Nietzsche 2003c, 102; emphasis original.
86. E.g., Skinner 1978.
87. Malthus 1798.
88. Longley 2003.
89. E.g., Deuteronomy, chapter 7, chapter 20.
90. Ruthven 2002, 134–35.
91. Lal 2005, 234.
92. Cf. Bartov 2000, on the Nazis and fear of the "inner Jew."
93. Lal 2005, 234.

Chapter 4

1. *OED*, 1635.
2. Plato 1997, book 9; see also Deonna and Teroni 2008.
3. Plato 1997, book 9.
4. Aquinas 1950, II-II, §144, Art. 4.
5. Flanagan 2021, 232.
6. Seok 2015, 24.
7. Putzel 2020.
8. Mendible 2016.
9. E.g., Bageant 2007.
10. Greenwald and Harder 1998.
11. Thomason 2018.
12. He's not mad keen on eye contact, so it's hard to be sure. Darwin observed behavior that suggested a sense of shame in his own dog Polly, observing that she—like him—was especially affectionate after an undiscovered offense (Darwin to F. P. Cobbe, November 28, 1972, https://www.darwinproject.ac.uk/letter/DCP-LETT-8652.xml).
13. Keltner and Harker 1998, 80.

NOTES TO CHAPTER 4

14. Keltner and Harker 1998.
15. Mendible 2016, 7.
16. Cf. also Pitt-Rivers 2017.
17. Cohen, Vandello, and Rantilla 1998; see also Bageant 2007.
18. Cohen, Vandello, and Rantilla 1998, 271.
19. Cohen, Vandello, and Rantilla 1998, 272.
20. Cohen et al. 1996.
21. Cohen et al. 1996, 957.
22. Freud 1991, 316.
23. Thomason 2018, 8; see also Flanagan 2021.
24. Thomason 2018, 1.
25. Thomason 2018, 12–13.
26. Thomason 2018, 151.
27. Thomason 2018, 164.
28. Flanagan 2021, 155.
29. Flanagan 2021, 251.
30. Flanagan 2021, 161.
31. Flanagan 2021, 254.
32. Flanagan 2021.
33. Flanagan 2021, 154.
34. Flanagan 2021, 133.
35. Deonna and Teroni 2008.
36. Deonna and Teroni 2008, 71.
37. Elias 2000, 163.
38. Cf. Freud 1991; Elias (2000) stressed Freud's influence; cf. also Foucault 1978.
39. On the latter, see Braithwaite 1993.
40. Malesevic and Ryan 2012.
41. Bauman 1991; Malesevic and Ryan 2012; Grossman 1995; Bourke 1999.
42. Thomason 2018.
43. Thomason 2018.
44. The case of choosing your gender does rather complicate matters since it would seem just as unjust to shame someone for choosing their gender as it would be to shame them for what they were born with.
45. Flanagan 2021, 221.
46. Flanagan 2021, 37.
47. Thomason 2018, 13.
48. Thomason 2018, 13.
49. Thomason 2018.
50. See, e.g., Fisher 1995.
51. Aristotle 2020, 67.
52. Ahmed 2012, 106; emphasis added. See also Moguillansky 2013.
53. Shakespeare 1967, 135.
54. Swinford 2022.

55. Jacquet 2015.
56. Gilbert 1998.
57. Arendt 2003a, 45.
58. Speirs 2013, 6.
59. Speirs 2013, 2.
60. Freud 1954, 42.
61. Freud 1954, 190.
62. Wurmser 1994, 260.
63. Wurmser 1994, 259.
64. Wurmser 1994, 263.
65. Lansky 2015, 128.
66. Cf. Mitton 2015.

Chapter 5

1. Gilligan 2003, 1154.
2. Gilligan 2003, 1151.
3. Gilligan 2003, 1149.
4. Gilligan 2003, 1149.
5. Gilligan 2003, 1150.
6. Gilligan 2000, 110.
7. Gilligan 2003.
8. Gilligan 2000, 77.
9. Gilligan 2000, 61.
10. Gilligan 2000, 65.
11. Drawing on Freud, Gilligan argued that "pain and punishment increase feelings of shame but decrease feelings of guilt" (2003, 1164).
12. Gilligan 2000, 113.
13. Compare also Martha Nussbaum's (2004) antipathy to *shaming punishments*.
14. Girard 1977, 2.
15. Cf. Scheff 1994; Retzinger 1991.
16. Gilligan 2016.
17. Gilligan 2003, 1165.
18. Luckenbill 1977. Unsettlingly, Luckenbill also suggested that victims were sometimes determined to "save face" too, a dynamic that he said often contributed to an escalation of violence.
19. Bourgois 1995.
20. Bourgois 1996, 414.
21. Anderson 1994, 1999.
22. Anderson 1994.
23. Anderson 1994.
24. Anderson 1994.
25. Braithwaite 1993, 1.

26. Braithwaite 1993, 2.
27. Pratt 2011.
28. Packer 2015.
29. Packer 2015, citing Farhad Khosrokhavar, *Radicalization: Why Some People Choose the Path of Violence* (New York: The New Press, 2017).
30. Conroy 2017; see also Kimmel 2019.

Chapter 6

1. I have changed his name.
2. Honneth 2004, 354.
3. Interview with Sierra Leonean human rights worker, Freetown, 1995.
4. Human Rights Watch 2003, 44.
5. Mitton 2015, 208.
6. Human Rights Watch 2003, 26.
7. *OED*, 502.
8. Mitton 2015, 185.
9. Human Rights Watch 1999, n.p.
10. Human Rights Watch 1999.
11. I have changed the name.
12. Fear was also a factor here. As Idriss put it, "They worry about betrayal to the army or the *kamajors*. There was a 'zero tolerance' law for civilians 'selling out'—that is, betraying them."
13. "Profiles" in Lord 2000.
14. Human Rights Watch 1999, n.p.
15. Human Rights Watch 1999, n.p.
16. Human Rights Watch 1999, n.p.
17. Keen 2012a.

Chapter 7

1. Arendt 1994a, 276.
2. Arendt 1994a, 150.
3. Arendt 1994a, 46.
4. Arendt 1994a, 47.
5. Stangneth 2014, 44.
6. Stangneth 2014, 267.
7. Stangneth 2014, 264.
8. Stangneth 2014, 15.
9. Arendt 1994a, 47.
10. Cesarani 2005, 6.
11. See, e.g., Maschmann 1964.
12. Arendt 1994a, 33.
13. Arendt 1994a.

14. See notably Browning 1992b.
15. Cesarani 2005, 98.
16. Lwow (also known as Lvov) is currently Lviv in Ukraine.
17. Arendt 1994a, 87.
18. Arendt 1994a, 87–88.
19. Cesarani 2005, 106.
20. Arendt 1994a, 88–89.
21. Cesarani 2005, 105.
22. Cesarani 2005, 116.
23. Cesarani 2005, 107.
24. Cesarani 2005, 116.
25. Cesarani 2005, 116.
26. Stangneth 2014, 278.
27. Stangneth 2014, 31.
28. Wurmser 1994, 263.
29. Cesarani 2005, 115.
30. Arendt 1994a, 105.
31. Arendt 1994a, 106.
32. Arendt 1994a, 105.
33. Arendt 1994a, 105.
34. Wildt 2005, 341.
35. Browning 1992a.
36. Cf. Nietzsche 2003a.
37. Wurmser 1994, 262.
38. Stangneth 2014, 304–5; emphasis added.
39. Stangneth 2014, 264.
40. Stangneth 2014, 265.
41. Arendt 1994a, 41–42.
42. On a wider view this shame was one illustration of the fact that emotion had not been set aside and rendered irrelevant.
43. Arendt 1994a, 137.
44. Arendt 1994a.
45. Stangneth 2014.
46. Stangneth 2014, 267.
47. Stangneth 2014, 303–4.
48. Cesarani 2005, 156.
49. Cesarani 2005, 157.
50. Bartov 1991, 2000; cf. also Hinton 1998.
51. Bartov 2000, 110.
52. Wildt 2005.
53. Stangneth 2014, 238–39.
54. Stangneth 2014, 364.
55. Stangneth 2014, 279.

56. Stangneth 2014, 279.
57. Stangneth 2014, 279.
58. Stangneth 2014, 280.
59. Stangneth 2014, 279.
60. Arendt 1994a, 52.
61. Arendt 1994a, 85.
62. Arendt 1994a, 96.
63. Arendt 1994a, 107–8.
64. Lehmann-Haupt 1989.
65. Arendt 1994a, 95–96.
66. Arendt 1994a, 96.
67. Wildt 2005, 345; Browning 1992b.
68. Arendt 1994a, 2003a.
69. Arendt 2003a, 37.
70. Hilberg 1980, 110.
71. Hilberg 1980.
72. Hilberg 1980, 104.
73. Hilberg 1980; Trunk 1981.
74. Arendt 1994a, 108.

Chapter 8

1. New York Times/CQ Transcriptswire 2016.
2. The *OED* (p. 571) defines embarrassment as "a feeling of self-consciousness, shame, or awkwardness."
3. This was a major distortion.
4. Haslett 2016.
5. Morrison 2011.
6. *New York Times* 2016b.
7. Buettner, Craig, and McIntire 2020.
8. *Los Angeles Times* 2016.
9. Wang 2016.
10. PBS/Frontline 2017.
11. PBS/Frontline 2017.
12. PBS/Frontline 2017.
13. Schwarz reports that he wrote most of it.
14. BBC Radio 4 2018a.
15. BBC Radio 4 2018a.
16. BBC Radio 4 2018a.
17. Sengupta 2019.
18. *Time* 2016.
19. Goldberg 2020.
20. Eder and Philipps 2016; cf. discussion of "chickenhawks" in Keen 2006.

21. Russian 2016.
22. E.g., Beauchamp 2016.
23. Guardian/AP 2016.
24. Eder and Philipps 2016.
25. Victor 2015.
26. *New York Times* 2016a; cf. Brown 2010.
27. *New York Times* 2016a.
28. Bartov 2000, 106; Bartov was writing about the fear, in Germany, of "the Jew within."
29. Blair 2016.
30. Hochschild 2018, 223.
31. *Los Angeles Times* 2016.
32. Scherer 2017.
33. Haberman 2015.
34. Chan 2017.
35. Scherer 2017.
36. Roundtree 2017.
37. Bilefsky and Barthelemy 2016.
38. Scherer 2017.
39. Arendt 1968a, 383.
40. Arendt 1968a.
41. Arendt 1968a, 348–49.
42. Arendt 1968a, 383.
43. Arendt 2006, 236.
44. See, e.g., Arendt 2006.
45. Durvasula 2018.
46. Bradshaw 1988.
47. D'Antonio 2016.

Chapter 9

1. Nuzzi 2016.
2. Reuters 2016.
3. Meixler 2018.
4. Guardian News/YouTube 2018.
5. Arendt 1968a, 190.
6. *OED*, 1528.
7. Davis 2021.
8. Kohut 1985, 56.
9. Kohut 1985, 57.
10. Trump's support among the *better-off* is often underestimated.
11. Public Religion Research Institute survey in Galston 2016.
12. Galston 2016.
13. Saul 2016.

14. Brown 2010.
15. Harkinson and Lee 2013.
16. See, e.g., Center for Strategic & International Studies 2020.
17. E.g., De Genova 2013.
18. Brown 2010; Freud 2001b.
19. See chapter 12.
20. Neate and Gambino 2016.
21. Factbase 2016.
22. Factbase 2016.
23. *New York Times* 2016a.
24. *Time* 2016.
25. Diamond 2018.
26. O'Toole 2020.
27. Bageant 2007, 31.
28. Bageant 2007, 8–9.
29. Channel 4 2016 (quoting Scott Huffman of Winthrop Poll Initiative).
30. Channel 4 2016 (quoting James Porter).
31. Hochschild 2016.
32. BBC2 2018; BBC Radio 4 2018b.
33. Hochschild 2016.
34. Hochschild 2018, 144.
35. Watkins 2018, 28.
36. Mayer 2020.
37. Snyder 2021.
38. Hochschild 2018.
39. Hochschild 2018, 145.
40. Williamson, Skocpol, and Coggin 2011, 34.
41. Hochschild 2018, 227; emphasis original.
42. Hochschild 2018.
43. Bageant 2007, 170.
44. Hochschild 2018, 225.
45. Hochschild 2018, 226.
46. Hochschild 2018, 227.
47. Locke 2019.
48. Nuzzi 2016.
49. Hochschild 2018, 228; emphasis original.
50. Wurmser 1994, 92.
51. Danner 2016.
52. Hochschild 2016.
53. Hochschild 2016.
54. Hochschild 2016.
55. Reich 2016.
56. Hochschild 2018, 226.

57. Hochschild 2016.
58. BBC Radio 4 2018b.
59. E.g., Jones 2017.
60. Levy 2016.
61. The plight of people that globalization and modernization left behind is also powerfully conveyed in Theroux 2015.
62. E.g., Bartels 2006.
63. Frank 2004a.
64. Akerlof and Shiller 2015.
65. Frank 2004a, 245.
66. Compare, e.g., Hickel 2015 on South Africa.
67. Bageant 2007, 4.
68. Bageant 2007, 34.
69. Bageant 2007, 83.
70. Wuthnow 2018, 2.
71. Cramer Walsh 2012.
72. Channel 4 2020.
73. Boyer 2020.
74. Mayer 2020.
75. Detrow 2016.
76. D. Smith 2017.
77. Liebovich 2020.
78. Lasch 1979, 82.
79. Cf. Hegel 1977; see also Taylor 1975, 153; Honneth 2004, 354.

Chapter 10

1. Stone 2016. I am grateful to Thomas Brodie for bringing the Farage example to my attention and for many enlightening conversations.
2. Arendt 1968a, 190.
3. O'Toole 2018, 93.
4. O'Toole 2018, 34.
5. O'Toole 2018, 35.
6. McCann 2018, Freedland 2022.
7. McCann 2018.
8. Behr 2017.
9. M. Smith 2017.
10. Booth, Travis, and Gentleman 2020.
11. O'Toole 2018, xvii.
12. O'Toole 2018, 136.
13. See, e.g., *Independent* 2000.
14. Lambert 1994.
15. Arendt 1973.

16. O'Toole 2018.
17. O'Toole 2018.
18. BBC Radio 4 2005.
19. O'Toole, 2018, 14.
20. E.g., Shrimsley 2018; cf. Jensen and Snaith 2016 on most businesses' preference for remaining.
21. O'Toole 2018.
22. O'Toole 2018, 190.
23. O'Toole 2018, 198.
24. Arendt 1968a, 211.
25. Harris and Domokos 2014.
26. Kuper 2019. At the time of writing, Oxford has supplied twenty-eight of fifty-five British prime ministers.
27. Kuper 2019.
28. Putzel (2020) includes an interesting discussion of the misogyny.
29. Elgot 2016.
30. O'Toole 2018, 68.
31. O'Toole 2018, 46.
32. O'Toole 2018, 30, 74.
33. O'Toole 2018, 17.
34. Keen 2021.
35. MacLeod and Jones 2018.
36. Cf. Keen and Andersson 2018.
37. Jones 2012, 233.
38. Jones 2012.
39. Jones 2012, 223.
40. Harris and Domokos 2019.
41. Mckenzie 2017, 275.
42. Jones 2012.
43. O'Hara 2014, 110–11.
44. Jones 2012, 223.
45. Rapley 2017.
46. Jones 2012, 225.
47. Mckenzie 2017, 266.
48. Jones 2012, 119.
49. Jones 2012, 248.
50. Mckenzie 2017, 274.
51. E.g., Keen 2007.
52. Fukuyama 2020.
53. Mouffe 2005, 30.
54. Arendt 1968a, 332.
55. Arendt 1968a, 332; emphasis added.
56. Arendt 1968a, 332.

57. Wright 2017, 191.
58. MacLeod and Jones 2018.
59. Eze 2017.
60. MacLeod and Jones 2018.
61. Jensen and Snaith 2016; see also Scott and Quaglia 2020.
62. O'Toole 2012, 132, 199.
63. O'Toole 2012, 173.
64. Mintchev 2021.
65. On this gulf and the referendum, e.g., see Koch 2016.
66. Mintchev 2021, 133.
67. See, e.g., Harris 2017.
68. See, e.g., Curtice 2019.
69. MacLeod and Jones 2018, 128.
70. Bullough 2019, 284.
71. Bullough 2019, 284.
72. *The Sun* 2018.
73. Hall 2019.
74. E.g., MacLeod and Jones 2018.
75. Cardiff University/YouGov 2019.

Chapter 11

1. See Klein 2007.
2. The concept popularized by DiAngelo (2018) in particular.
3. Caflisch 2020, 584. See also Davids 2020 on "micro-aggressions" and empire.
4. Fanon 2001, 2008; Kovel 1988.
5. Fanon 2008; Faludi 2007.
6. Grandin 2019, 266.
7. Alexander 2019.
8. Metzl 2020.
9. Metzl 2020.
10. Metzl 2020.
11. Hofstadter 2008, 133.
12. Hofstadter 2008.
13. Lembcke 1998, 50.
14. Belew 2018.
15. Shaw 2005; Tirman 2011.
16. Lal 2005, 231.
17. Said 2003.
18. Snyder 2021.
19. Arendt 1968a.
20. BBC Radio 4 2015.
21. See, notably, Cameron 2015.

22. Freud 1895.
23. Tremlett and Webster 2002.
24. Shatz 2021.
25. Keiger 2021.
26. Keiger 2021.
27. Vergès 2010, 102.
28. Vergès 2010, 95.
29. Vergès 2010, 104.
30. Vergès 2010, 103.
31. Vergès 2010, 103.
32. McAuley 2019.
33. Guilluy 2018.
34. McAuley 2019.
35. McAuley 2019.
36. McAuley 2019.
37. BBC Radio 4 2017; see also Louis 2017.
38. BBC Radio 4 2017.
39. BBC Radio 4 2017.
40. Irish Times/AFP 2001. Part of the context was anxiety among UK, Spanish, Portuguese, and Dutch officials around payment of reparations (Irish Times/AFP 2001).
41. Ahmed 2012, 118. Cf. also Fischer 2016 on the "national shame" of the Magdalen laundries in Ireland.
42. Beckett 2021.
43. Beckett 2021.
44. Beckett 2021.
45. Wolfe-Robinson 2021.
46. Stone 2021.
47. Mitchell 2021.
48. Petre 2017.
49. Gilroy 2004.
50. Kampfner 2003, 3.
51. Gilroy 2004, 49.
52. De Waal 2018a.
53. Gilroy 2004, 81.
54. O'Toole 2018, 91–92; emphasis added.
55. Yancy and Chomsky 2015.
56. Shatz 2021.
57. Lal 2005, 227.
58. On projecting everything "bad" to the outside, see particularly Brown 2010.
59. Taylor, Wintour, and Elgot 2015.
60. Thanks to Arjan Gjonca for making this point.
61. Bauman 1996, 15.
62. Amnesty International 2017a, 8.

63. E.g., author's research in Calais, France, 2016.
64. Gerodimos 2022, 43.
65. E.g., Castells 1998.
66. Wolf 2011, 126.

Chapter 12

1. Williams 2005, 189.
2. Williams 2005.
3. Binkley 2009.
4. Jackson Lears 2000, n.p.
5. Burkeman 2016, citing Ruth Cowan, *More Work for Mother* (New York: Basic Books, 1983).
6. E.g., Thomas 1978; Eire 1989.
7. Eire 1989, 25, citing Steven E. Ozment, *The Reformation in the Cities: The Appeal of Protestantism to Sixteenth-Century Germany and Switzerland* (New Haven: Yale University Press, 1975), 21–22.
8. Nietzsche 2003b, 149.
9. Weber 1976.
10. Cf. Lasch 1979.
11. E.g., Hoggett 2017.
12. Cf. Lasch 1979.
13. E.g., Lasch 1979.
14. Lasch 1979.
15. Mishra 2016; cf. Bauman 1996.
16. Chase and Walker 2012, 746.
17. Ray 2014.
18. Hegel 1977.
19. De Botton and Armstrong 2013, 62.
20. See Schor 1999.
21. Hughes 2020.
22. Morning News, WGN News, YouTube, March 22, 2022.
23. O'Neil 2022, 100.
24. Mendible 2016, 1.
25. Mendible 2016, 3.
26. Mendible 2016.
27. Nelson 2021.
28. D'Antonio 2016.
29. BBC's *Arena* once paid me a small fee to develop a program on advertising and nihilism; later, I found McIntosh (1996), who does it better.
30. Lasch 1979, 138.
31. Nietzsche 2003a, 2003c.
32. Honneth 2004; Houston is less sanguine.
33. Brennan and Pettit 2004, 24.
34. Brennan and Pettit 2004, 22.

35. E.g., Brennan and Pettit 2004, 93, 157.
36. Brennan and Pettit 2004, 157.
37. Brennan and Pettit 2004.
38. Cairns 2011, 27.
39. Cf. Richards 1996.
40. See also Hardin 1993.
41. Venugopal 2018.
42. Corson 1968, 141.
43. Richards 1996; Uvin 1998; Zur 1998; Wood 2001.
44. Uvin 2000, 173.
45. Uvin 1998, 116–17; cf. Wood 2001 on El Salvador and Zur 1998 on Guatemala.
46. E.g., Venugopal 2018.
47. Human Rights Watch/International Federation of Human Rights 1999, 60.
48. Sierra Leone Broadcasting Service 1997; emphasis added.
49. As in Collier 2000; see Keen 2012b.
50. Mkandawire 2001.
51. Saez and Zucman 2016.
52. Piketty 2016.
53. Piketty 2014.
54. Alston 2017; on drug addiction and rising mortality, see Case and Deaton 2015.
55. Frank 2016, 64.
56. Max Boot, "Trump Vowed Never to Forget the 'Forgotten Men and Women.' He Just Did," *Washington Post*, May 12, 2020.
57. E.g., Alston 2017.
58. Alston 2017.
59. Alston 2017.
60. Alston 2017.
61. E.g., Hochschild 2018.
62. E.g., Watkins 2018.
63. E.g., Alexander 2019.
64. E.g., Metzl 2020.
65. Alexander 2019, 34.
66. Alexander 2019, 13.
67. Jones 2012, 249.
68. Chase and Walker 2012, 746.
69. Chase and Walker 2012, 750.
70. E.g., Layton 2014.
71. Sandel 2016.
72. I am indebted to Ruben Andersson for his insights on distribution of risks within various systems, among many other matters. See particularly Andersson 2019.
73. Piketty 2014.
74. Krugman 2015.
75. Frank 2012, 41–42.

76. See, e.g., Glynos 2014.
77. Clarke and Newman 2012, 300.
78. Krugman 2015; Clarke and Newman 2012.
79. Clarke and Newman 2012, 307.
80. Frank 2012, 71–73.
81. Frank 2012.
82. Danner 2016.
83. Gillespie 2008.
84. Reich 2015.
85. Hoggett 2017, 368.
86. Peltz 2005; Layton 2010.
87. Hoggett 2017, 368.
88. Hoggett 2017, 368. The quote on "outliers" is from W. Espeland and M. Stevens, "A Sociology of Quantification," *European Journal of Sociology* 49, no. 3 (2008): 401–36.
89. Layton 2010.
90. Ball 2003, 220.
91. Cf. Bion 2013.
92. Layton 2010, 312.
93. Hoggett 2017, 369–70.
94. Hoggett 2017, 373.
95. E.g., Strathern 2000.
96. Duffield 2019; Arendt 1998.
97. Mendible 2016, 3.
98. Mendible 2016, 10.

Chapter 13

1. Keen 2012a.
2. Andersson 2014; Keen and Andersson 2018.
3. See particularly Andersson 2014; Keen and Andersson 2018; Keen 2012a.
4. Keen 2012a, 2012b.
5. On gangs, see, e.g., Mackey 2018.
6. Ahmed 2011.
7. Keen 2014.
8. Compare the widening of the Rwandan persecution to include Hutu "sympathizers" with the Tutsi (African Rights 1994).
9. Keen 2017.
10. E.g., Keen 2013.
11. Even as early as 2002, Ruthven (2002) noted this dynamic from Chechnya to Kashmir and Xinjiang.
12. E.g., Mamdani 2001.
13. African Rights 1994.
14. African Rights 1994, 40.

NOTES TO CHAPTER 13   303

15. Uvin 1998, 2000.
16. African Rights 1994, 20.
17. African Rights 1994, 21.
18. Mamdani 2001, 207.
19. African Rights 1994.
20. E.g., Cameron 2015.
21. Kisangani 2000.
22. UN Panel of Experts 2002.
23. Kelly 2010; Eriksson Baaz and Stern 2008.
24. Eriksson Baaz and Stern 2008.
25. Berdal 2018.
26. See Wood 2001, and Zur 1998, on discrimination experienced as shame in El Salvador and Guatemala.
27. Zur 1998, 107–8. Compare Deng 1986 on the Baggara Arabs and Dinka in Sudan.
28. Zur 1998.
29. Zur 1998, 103.
30. Compare Dolan 2009 on the Ugandan government turning members of the Acholi group against each other. Cf. also Levi 1989.
31. Human rights worker, Guatemala City, 2002.
32. Zur 1998; cf. Human Rights Watch 2003.
33. Compare Nazis; cf. also Gear 2002 on South Africa.
34. Zur 1998, 123.
35. Zur 1998.
36. Keen 1994.
37. Compare Kalyvas 2004.
38. Deng 1986.
39. Keen 1994; compare Rangasami 1985.
40. Ryle 1989.
41. Jaspars 2018, 152.
42. Jaspars 2018, 153.
43. Jaspars 2018, 166.
44. Jaspars 2018, 166.
45. Keen 1994, 2005.
46. Harrell-Bond 1986; Dolan 2009.
47. Duffield 2019.
48. Jaspars 2018, 165.
49. Jaspars 2018, 165.
50. Jaspars 2018.
51. De Waal 2018b.
52. Applebaum 2017.
53. Quoted in Becker 1996, 45.
54. Armstrong 2009, 231; see also Applebaum 2003.
55. Armstrong 2009, 233.

56. Applebaum 2003, 6.
57. Applebaum 2003, 8–9.
58. Armstrong 2009.
59. Becker 1996.
60. Chang and Halliday 2007, 535.
61. Dikötter 2015.
62. Dikötter 2015, 918.
63. Becker 1996.
64. Cf. also Flanagan 2021.
65. Becker 1996, 115.
66. Becker 1996, 122.
67. Becker 1996; Dikötter 2015.
68. Robins and Post 1997, 246.
69. Robins and Post 1997, 246.
70. De Waal 2022, 380.
71. Arendt 1968a, 1994c.
72. Keen 2014.
73. Personal communication, Amsterdam.
74. Slim 2007.
75. De Waal 2015; Autesserre 2012.

Chapter 14

1. Cf. Lu 2008.
2. E.g., Gilligan 2000.
3. See, particularly, Bartov 2000.
4. E.g., Bartov 2000.
5. This is a mechanism that has subsequently helped inform other genocides (including the 1994 Rwandan genocide) and racialized persecutions.
6. Adorno and Horkheimer 1997.
7. Burke 1974, 195–96.
8. Theweleit 1987.
9. Theweleit 1987, 398, 405.
10. Theweleit 1987, 402.
11. Hitler 1938, 105.
12. Hitler 1938, 193.
13. Hitler 1938, 113.
14. Hitler 1938, 91–92.
15. Kershaw 1998, 152.
16. E.g., Bartov 2000.
17. Hitler 1938, 105. See also Kershaw 1998.
18. Midlarsky 2005.
19. Diehl 1987.

20. Diehl 1987. This contradiction has been reinvented in different (and often less extreme) forms in many other societies from the United States and the UK to Iran.

21. Porter 2005.

22. Nietzsche 2003a, 31.

23. Lerner 2003, 48.

24. Lerner 2003, 48; see also Whalen 1984, 17.

25. Lerner 2003, 27.

26. Lerner 2003.

27. Kershaw 1998.

28. Arendt 1968a, 315; see also Bartov 2000.

29. Canetti 1973, 218–19; emphases added.

30. Arendt 1968a, 225.

31. Arendt 1968a, 332.

32. Maschmann 1964, 11–12.

33. On this sensitivity, see, e.g., Kershaw 1998.

34. De Waal gives a figure of 750,000 Germans dying from malnutrition, many of them after the Armistice when the British blockade was maintained for six months (see discussions in de Waal 2018a and 2018b).

35. Hitler 1939a.

36. Hitler 1939a; see also Wyman 1984.

37. E.g., Steinberg 1996.

38. Arendt 1973; Sheehan et al. 1971.

39. Arendt 1973. Even the South Vietnamese government had many important priorities other than winning the war (e.g., Corson 1968).

40. Arendt 1973, 20.

41. Arendt 1973.

42. Corson 1968, 81.

43. Whitlock, Shapiro, and Emamdjomeh 2019.

44. Arendt 1973.

45. Arendt 1973, 21.

46. Arendt 1973, 33.

47. Arendt 1973, 31.

48. Arendt 1973, 33; see also, e.g., Shultz 1978.

49. Arendt is quoting Ralph Stavins, Richard J. Barnet, and Marcus Raskin, *Washington Plans an Aggressive War* (New York: Random House, 1971), 246.

50. Arendt 1973, 15–16. On being "above sentimentality," compare also Allison on the Cuban Missile Crisis (Schaffer 1984).

51. See later in this chapter.

52. Clarke and Hoggett 2004, 94–95.

53. E.g., Lasch 1979.

54. Hossein-zadeh 2006; see also Segal 2003.

55. Cohn 1987, 693.

56. Cohn 1987, 714.

57. Cohn 1987, 690.
58. Vladimir Pozner, "How the United States Created Vladimir Putin," YouTube, Yale University, September 27, 2018.
59. Hunt 2010, 38.
60. See, notably, Faludi 1999, 331–32; see also Bourke 1999, 217.
61. Stout 2001.
62. Hirschkind and Mahmood 2002.
63. Cohen 2003, 1099.
64. Woodward 2010, 166. The increase in military action against the Taliban also displaced insurgents into other parts of Afghanistan, notably the north (Chaudhuri and Farrell 2011).
65. Global Terrorism Index 2015, 2016.
66. Goepner 2016, 113.
67. E.g., Gerges 2016.
68. E.g., Keen and Andersson 2018; Saferworld 2022.
69. Keen 2006.
70. Andersson and Keen, forthcoming.
71. Rampton and Stauber 2003, 143–44.
72. Blumenthal 2005.
73. Woodward 2002, 38–39. Compare also Theweleit 1987.
74. CNN.com 2001.
75. E.g., Hossein-zadeh 2006.
76. Hartung and Ciarrocca 2003; Klein 2007.
77. Keen 2006, 2012a.
78. Wren 2001.
79. Danner 2004.
80. E.g., Danner 2004.
81. E.g., Gerges 2016.
82. Gilligan 2003, 1162.
83. Gerges 2005; Keen 2006.
84. Gerges 2005.
85. Gerges 2005.
86. Creed 2009, 218–19.
87. The White House/President George W. Bush 2001a.
88. Guardian Unlimited 2003.
89. Woodward 2004, 270–71.
90. Cohen 2003, 1082.
91. Hofstadter 2008.
92. Hofstadter 2008, 175.
93. Woodward 2002, 338.
94. Hitler 1939b. I am grateful to Edward Balke for bringing this statement to my attention.
95. See, e.g., Reuter 2015.
96. See, e.g., Dodge and Wasser 2014.
97. US Government/White House 2004.

98. Suskind 2004.
99. Blair 2007.
100. E.g., Keen 2006.
101. Girard 1977.
102. Blix 2004, 202.
103. Compare also Foucault 1980 on Marxism and psychoanalysis.

Chapter 15

1. Haslett 2016; Hoggett 2017.
2. Brown 2008.
3. Aitkenhead 2016.
4. Cf. also Summerfield 1998.
5. Ahsan 2022.
6. Honneth 2004; Fraser 2017a, 2017b. Confronted about the very low pay of care workers in the UK, Prime Minister Rishi Sunak said there were many ways to increase the respect that these workers experience.
7. See Honneth 2004; also Fraser 2017a, 2017b.
8. Alexander 2019.
9. Keen 2005; Mitton 2015.
10. Flanagan 2021, 160.
11. Flanagan 2021, 185.
12. Flanagan 2021, 196.
13. Flanagan 2021, 251.
14. On war and "winning," see Keen 2012a.
15. Cameron 1943, 1959.
16. Compare Arendt 1973.
17. I am grateful to Thomas Brodie for suggesting this word.
18. E.g., Wurmser 1994; Lansky 2005.
19. On Germany, see also Schivelbusch 2001.
20. Mouffe 2005, 75.
21. Fraser 2017b.
22. Fraser 2017b.
23. Arendt 1994b, 1973.
24. Uvin, 1998, 2000.
25. E.g., Owens 2017.
26. NPR/Ipsos 2020.
27. Williams 2021.
28. Keen and Andersson 2018.
29. Weissman 2004.
30. Arendt 1975.
31. Compare Gilligan 2000.
32. Gunn and Wilson 2011.

33. Arendt 1968b, 83.
34. Arendt 2006, 237.
35. Arendt 2003b, 159.
36. Arendt 2003b, 189.
37. Arendt 2003a.
38. Merrick 2021.
39. Elgot 2021; Dodd and Elgot 2021.
40. Brown 2008.
41. Slavoj Žižek, "Full Address and Q and A, Oxford Union," YouTube, n.d., https://www.youtube.com/watch?v=S45x4EldHlg.

BIBLIOGRAPHY

Adorno, Theodor, and Max Horkheimer. 1997. *Dialectic of Enlightenment*. Trans. John Cumming. London: Verso (first published 1944).

African Rights. 1994. *Rwanda: Death, Despair and Defiance*. London: African Rights.

Ahmed, Nafeez. 2011. "The International Relations of Crisis and the Crisis of International Relations: From the Securitization of Scarcity to the Militarisation of Society." *Global Change, Peace and Security* 23, 3: 335–55.

Ahmed, Sara. 2012. *The Cultural Politics of Emotion*. New York: Routledge (first published 2004).

Ahonen, Pertti. 2018. "Europe and Refugees: 1938 and 2015–16." *Patterns of Prejudice* 52, 2–3: 135–48.

Ahsan, Sanah. 2022. "I'm a Psychologist—and I Believe We've Been Told Devastating Lies about Mental Health." *Guardian*, September 6.

Aitkenhead, Decca. 2016. "Sacked Children's Mental Health Tsar Natasha Devon: 'I Was Proper Angry.'" *Guardian*, May 13.

Akerlof, George, and Robert Shiller. 2015. *Phishing for Phools: The Economics of Manipulation and Deception*. Princeton: Princeton University Press.

Alexander, Michelle. 2019. *The New Jim Crow: Mass Incarceration in the Age of Colourblindness*. London: Penguin (first published 2010).

Allen, Chris. 2021. "Extremism in the UK: New Definitions Threaten Human and Civil Rights." *The Conversation*, March 29.

Alston, Philip. 2017. *Statement on Visit to the USA*. UN Special Rapporteur on Extreme Poverty and Human Rights. December 15. https://www.ohchr.org/en/statements/2017/12/statement-visit-usa-professor-philip-alston-united-nations-special-rapporteur.

Alweis, Lilian. 2003. "Collective Guilt and Responsibility: Some Reflections." *European Journal of Political Theory* 2, 3: 307–18.

Amnesty International. 2017a. *Facing Walls: USA and Mexico's Violations of the Rights of Asylum-Seekers*. June 15.

———. 2017b. *Libya's Dark Web of Collusion*. December 11.

Anderson, Elijah. 1994. "The Code of the Streets." *The Atlantic*, May. https://www.theatlantic.com/magazine/archive/1994/05/the-code-of-the-streets/306601/.

———. 1999. *Code of the Street: Decency, Violence and the Moral Life of the Inner City*. New York: W. W. Norton.

Andersson, Ruben. 2014. *Illegality Inc.: Clandestine Migration and the Business of Bordering Europe*. Oakland: University of California Press.

———. 2019. *No Go World: How Fear Is Redrawing Our Maps and Infecting Our Politics.* Oakland: University of California Press.

Andersson, Ruben, and David Keen. Forthcoming. *Wreckonomics: Why Failure Is the New Success.* New York: Oxford University Press.

Andrews, Bernice. 1998. "Shame and Childhood Abuse." In *Shame: Interpersonal Behavior, Psychopathology and Culture,* ed. Paul Gilbert and Bernice Andrews, 176–90. New York: Oxford University Press.

Applebaum, Anne. 2003. *Gulag: A History of the Soviet Camps.* London: Allen Lane/Penguin.

———. 2017. "How Stalin Hid Ukraine's Famine from the World." *The Atlantic,* October 13.

Aqoob, Salma. 2008. "Muslim Women and War on Terror." *Feminist Review* 88: 150–61.

Aquinas, Thomas. 1950. *Summa Theologica* (Complete). Library of Alexandria (written c. 1265–1274).

Arendt, Hannah. 1968a. *The Origins of Totalitarianism.* New York: Harvest/Harcourt (first published 1951).

———. 1968b. *Men in Dark Times.* New York: Harvest.

———. 1973. "Lying in Politics: Reflections on the Pentagon Papers." In Arendt, *Crises of the Republic.* Harmondsworth: Penguin (paper first published 1971).

———. 1975. Letter to Bill O'Grady, July 16, accessed via Hannah Arendt papers at the Library of Congress: http://memory.loc.gov/mss/mharendt_pub/04/041090/0044.jpg.

———. 1994a. *Eichmann in Jerusalem: A Report on the Banality of Evil.* London: Penguin (first published 1963).

———. 1994b. "Social Science Techniques and the Study of Concentration Camps." In *Essays in Understanding, 1930–1954,* ed. Jerome Kohn, 232–47. New York: Schocken Books.

———. 1994c. "The Eggs Speak Up." In Arendt, *Essays in Understanding, 1930–1954,* ed. Jerome Kohn, 270–84. New York: Schocken Books (paper written c. 1950).

———. 1994d. "Organized Guilt and Universal Responsibility." In Arendt, *Essays in Understanding, 1930–1954,* ed. Jerome Kohn, 121–32. New York: Schocken Books (paper first published 1945).

———. 1998. *The Human Condition.* Chicago: University of Chicago Press (first published 1958).

———. 2003a. "Personal Responsibility under Dictatorship." In *Responsibility and Judgement,* ed. Jerome Kern. New York: Schocken Books, 17–48 (first published 1964).

———. 2003b. "Thinking and Moral Considerations." In *Responsibility and Judgement,* ed. Jerome Kern, 159–89. New York: Schocken Books (first published 1975).

———. 2003c. "Home to Roost." In *Responsibility and Judgement,* ed. Jerome Kern, 257–75. New York: Schocken Books (first published 1975).

———. 2006. "Truth and Politics." In Arendt, *Between Past and Future,* 223–59. London: Penguin (first published 1967).

Aristotle. 2020. *Rhetoric.* Trans. W. Rhys Roberts. Digireads.

Armstrong, Sean. 2009. "Stalin's Witch-Hunt: Magical Thinking in the Great Terror." *Totalitarian Movements and Political Religions* 10, 3–4: 221–40.

Austesserre, Séverine. 2012. "Dangerous Tales: Dominant Narratives on the Congo and Their Unintended Consequences." *African Affairs* 111, 443: 202–22.

Bageant, Joe. 2007. *Deer Hunting with Jesus: Dispatches from America's Class War.* New York: Crown.

Baker, Kevin. 2006. "Stabbed in the Back! The Past and Future of a Right-Wing Myth." *Harper's Magazine*, June.

Baldo, Suliman. 2017. "Border Control from Hell: How the EU's Migration Partnership Legitimizes Sudan's 'Militia State.'" *Enough*, Washington, DC, April.

Ball, Stephen. 2003. "The Teacher's Soul and the Terrors of Performativity." *Journal of Education Policy* 18, 2: 215–28.

Barnett, Thomas, 2004. *The Pentagon's New Map: War and Peace in the Twenty-First Century*. London: Penguin.

Bartels, Larry. 2006. "What's the Matter with *What's the Matter with Kansas?*" *Quarterly Journal of Political Science* 1: 201–26.

Bartov, Omer. 1991. *Hitler's Army: Soldiers, Nazis and the War in the Third Reich*. Oxford: Oxford University Press.

———. 2000. *Mirrors of Destruction: War, Genocide and Modern Identity*. Oxford: Oxford University Press.

Baum, Dan. 2017. "Legalize It All: How to Win the War on Drugs." *Harper's Magazine*, April.

Bauman, Zygmunt. 1991. *Modernity and the Holocaust*. Cambridge: Polity.

———. 1996. *Tourists and Vagabonds: Heroes and Victims of Postmodernity*. Reihe Politikwissenschaft/Institut für Höhere Studien, Abt. Politikwissenschaft, 30. Wien: Institut für Höhere Studien (IHS). https://nbn-resolving.org/urn:nbn:de:0168-ssoar-266870.

BBC2. 2018. *Travels in Trumpland, with Ed Balls*. July.

BBC Radio 4. 2005. *Desert Island Discs*. Sue Lawley, October.

———. 2015. *Start the Week*. November 16.

———. 2017. *Stop the Week*. February 6.

———. 2018a. *PM* (Interview with Tony Schwarz). October 17.

———. 2018b. *Trump's Evangelicals*. October 19.

Beauchamp, Scott. 2016. "Donald Trump's Disrespect for the Military Is Appalling—and Unprecedented." *Guardian*, February 29.

Becker, Jasper. 1996. *Hungry Ghosts: China's Secret Famine*. London: John Murray.

Beckett, Andy. 2021. "Picking Fights Has Served Johnson's Tories Well—but It's a Strategy That May Backfire." *Guardian*, June 25.

Beckett, Margaret. 2018. "Civil Unrest? Violence on UK Streets? Let's Stop This Reckless Language." *Guardian*, February 3.

Behr, Rafael. 2017. "Divided Britain, Where the Brexit Alarm Is Sounded but No One Wants to Hear." *Guardian*, November 28.

Belew, Kathleen. 2018. *Bring the War Home: The White Power Movement and Paramilitary America*. Cambridge, MA: Harvard University Press.

Benedict, Ruth. 1974. *The Chrysanthemum and the Sword: Patterns of Japanese Culture*. New York: New American Library (first published 1946).

Bercovitch, Sacvan. 1975. *The Puritan Origins of the American Self*. New Haven: Yale University Press.

Berdal, Mats. 2018. "The State of UN Peacekeeping: Lessons from Congo." *Journal of Strategic Studies* 41, 5: 721–50.

Bigliani, Carlos Guillermo. 2013. "Humiliation and Shame: Dynamics and Destinies." In Carlos Guillermo Bigliani, Rodolfo Moguillansky, and Carlos Sluzki, *Shame and Humiliation:*

A Dialogue between Psychoanalytic and Systemic Approaches, 1–30. London: International Psychoanalytical Association/Karnac Books.

Bilefsky, Dan, and Claire Barthelemy. 2016. "Donald Trump Finds New City to Insult: Brussels." *New York Times*, January 27.

Binkley, Sam. 2009. "The Civilizing Brand: Shifting Shame Thresholds and the Dissemination of Consumer Lifestyles." *European Journal of Cultural Studies* 12, 1: 21–39.

Bion, Wilfred. 2013. "Attacks on Linking." *Psychoanalytic Quarterly* 82, 2: 285–300 (first published 1959).

Blair, Gwenda. 2016. "Inside the Mind of Donald Trump." *Guardian*, November 12.

Blair, Tony. 2007. "A Battle for Global Values." *Foreign Affairs*, January/February.

Blix, Hans. 2004. *Disarming Iraq: The Search for Weapons of Mass Destruction*. London: Bloomsbury.

Bluhm, Heinz. 1956. "Nietzsche's Final View of Luther and the Reformation." *PMLA* 71, 1: 75–83.

Blumenthal, Sidney. 2005. "Domestic Gibberish." *Guardian*, February 10.

Booth, Robert, Alan Travis, and Amelia Gentleman. 2020. "Leave Donor Plans New Party to Replace Ukip—Possibly without Farage in Charge." *Guardian*, June 29.

Bourgois, Philippe. 1995. *In Search of Respect: Selling Crack in El Barrio*. New York: Cambridge University Press.

———. 1996. "In Search of Masculinity: Violence, Respect and Sexuality among Puerto Rican Crack Dealers in East Harlem." *British Journal of Criminology* 36, 3: 412–27.

Bourke, Joanna. 1999. *An Intimate History of Killing: Face-to-Face Killing in Twentieth-Century Warfare*. London: Granta.

Boyer, Dave. 2020. "Donald Trump Reopens Campaign at Tulsa Rally, Declares Silent Majority 'Stronger than Ever.'" *Washington Times*, June 20.

Bradshaw, John. 1988. *Healing the Shame That Binds You*. Deerfield Beach: Health Communications.

Braithwaite, John. 1993. "Shame and Modernity." *British Journal of Criminology* 33, 1: 1–18.

Brennan, Geoffrey, and Philip Pettit. 2004. *The Economy of Esteem: An Essay on Civil and Political Society*. Oxford: Oxford University Press.

Brown, Brené. 2008. *I Thought It Was Just Me (But It Isn't)*. New York: Penguin Random House.

Brown, Wendy. 2010. *Walled States, Waning Sovereignty*. Brooklyn, NY: Zone Books.

Browning, Christopher. 1992a. *Ordinary Men: Reserve Police Battalion 101 and the Final Solution in Poland*. New York: HarperPerennial.

———. 1992b. *The Path to Genocide: Essays on Launching the Final Solution*. Cambridge: Cambridge University Press.

Buettner, Russ, Susanne Craig, and Mike McIntire. 2020. "The President's Taxes." *New York Times*, September 27.

Bullough, Oliver. 2019. *Moneyland: Why Thieves and Crooks Now Rule the World and How to Take It Back*. London: Profile.

Burck, C., and G. Hughes. 2018. "Challenges and Impossibilities of 'Standing Alongside' in an Intolerable Context." *Clinical Child Psychology* 23, 2: 223–37.

Burke, Kenneth. 1974. "The Rhetoric of Hitler's 'Battle.'" In Burke, *The Philosophy of Literary Form*. Berkeley: University of California Press (essay first published 1939).

Burkeman, Oliver. 2016. "Why Time Management Is Ruining Our Lives." *Guardian*, December 22.

Caflisch, Jane. 2020. "'When Reparation Is Felt to Be Impossible': Persecutory Guilt and Breakdowns in Thinking and Dialogue about Race." *Psychoanalytic Dialogues* 30: 578–94.

Cairns, Douglas. 2011. "Honour and Shame: Modern Controversies and Ancient Values." *Critical Quarterly* 53, 1: 23–41.

Cameron, Norman. 1943. "The Paranoid Pseudo-Community." *American Journal of Sociology* 49, 1: 32–38.

———. 1959. "The Paranoid Pseudo-Community Revisited." *American Journal of Sociology* 65, 1: 52–58.

Campbell, Lucy. 2020. "'I Was Shielded from My History': The Changes Young Black Britons Are Calling For." *Guardian*, July 30.

Canetti, Elias. 1973. *Crowds and Power*. London: Penguin (originally published in German 1960).

Cardiff University/YouGov. 2019. "Future of England Survey Reveals Public Attitudes towards Brexit and the Union." October 24. https://www.cardiff.ac.uk/news/view/1709008-future-of-england-survey-reveals-public-attitudes-towards-brexit-and-the-union.

Case, Anne, and Angus Deaton. 2015. "Rising Morbidity and Mortality in Midlife among White Non-Hispanic Americans in the 21st Century." *Proceedings of the National Academy of Sciences in the United States of America* 112, 49: 15078–83.

Castells, Manuel. 1998. *End of Millennium*. Malden, MA: Blackwell.

Center for Strategic & International Studies. 2020. *The Escalating Terrorism Problem in the United States*. CSIS Briefs. June 17.

Cesarani, David. 2005. *Eichmann: His Life and Crimes*. London: Vintage.

Chan, Sewell. 2017. "'Last Night in Sweden'? Trump's Remark Baffles a Nation." *New York Times*, February 19.

Chang, Jung, and Jon Halliday. 2007. *Mao: The Unknown Story*. London: Vintage.

Channel 4. 2016. *The Mad World of Donald Trump*. Aired January 26.

———. 2020. *Grayson Perry's Big American Road Trip*. Episode 3. Aired September 23.

Chase, Elaine, and Robert Walker. 2012. "The Co-construction of Shame in the Context of Poverty." *Sociology* 47, 4: 739–54.

Chaudhuri, Rudra, and Theo Farrell. 2011. "Campaign Disconnect: Operational Progress and Strategic Obstacles in Afghanistan, 2009–2011." *International Affairs* 87, 2: 271–96.

Chaudhury, Tufyal, and Helen Fenwick. 2011. *The Impact of Counter-terrorism Measures on Muslim Communities*. Project Report. Equality and Human Rights Commission, Manchester.

Clarke, John, and Janet Newman. 2012. "The Alchemy of Austerity." *Critical Social Policy* 32, 3: 299–319.

———. 2017. "'People in This Country Have Had Enough of Experts': Brexit and the Paradoxes of Populism." *Critical Policy Studies* 11, 1: 101–16.

Clarke, Simon, and Paul Hoggett. 2004. "The Empire of Fear: The American Political Psyche and the Culture of Paranoia." *Psychodynamic Practice* 10, 1: 89–106.

CNN.com. 2001. "Falwell Apologizes to Gays, Feminists, Lesbians." September 14. https://edition.cnn.com/2001/US/09/14/Falwell.apology/.

Cohen, D., J. Vandello, and A. Rantilla. 1998. "The Sacred and the Social: Cultures of Honor and Violence." In *Shame: Interpersonal Behavior, Psychopathology and Culture*, ed. Paul Gilbert and Bernice Andrews, 261–82. Oxford: Oxford University Press.

Cohen, Dov. 2003. "The American National Conversation about (Everything but) Shame." *Social Research* 70, 4: 1075–1108.

Cohen, Dov, Brian Bowdle, Richard Nisbett, and Norbert Schwarz. 1996. "Insult, Aggression, and the Southern Culture of Honor: An 'Experimental Ethnography.'" *Interpersonal Relations and Group Processes* 70, 5: 945–60.

Cohen, Dov, and Richard Nisbett. 1997. "Field Experiments Examining the Culture of Honor: The Role of Institutions in Perpetuating Norms about Violence." *Personality and Social Psychology Bulletin* 23, 11: 1188–99.

Cohen, Stanley. 2001. *States of Denial: Knowing about Atrocities and Suffering*. Cambridge: Polity.

Cohn, Carol. 1987. "Sex and Death in the Rational World of Defense Intellectuals." *Signs* 12, 4: 687–718.

Cohn, Samuel K. 2007. "The Black Death and the Burning of Jews." *Past & Present* 196, August: 3–36.

Collier, Paul. 2000. "Doing Well out of War: An Economic Perspective." In *Greed and Grievance: Economic Agendas in Civil Wars*, ed. Mats Berdal and David Malone. Boulder, CO: Lynne Rienner/International Peace Academy.

Conroy, J. Oliver. 2017. "'Angry White Men': The Sociologist Who Studied Trump's Base before Trump." *Guardian*, February 27.

Correll, DeeDee. 2009. "The Story of the Marine Who Wasn't." *Los Angeles Times*, July 8.

Corson, William. 1968. *The Betrayal*. New York: W. W. Norton.

Cramer Walsh, Katherine. 2012. "Putting Inequality in Its Place: Rural Consciousness and the Power of Perspective." *American Political Science Review* 106, 3: 517–32.

Creed, Pamela. 2009. "Myth, Memory and Militarism: The Evolution of an American War Narrative." PhD diss., George Mason University.

Curtice, John. 2019. "Have UK Voters Changed Their Minds on Brexit?" BBC News (bbc.co.uk), October 17.

D'Antonio, Michael. 2016. *The Truth about Trump*. New York: St. Martin's Press (first published 2015).

Danner, Mark. 2004. "The Logic of Torture." *New York Review of Books*, June 24.

———. 2016. "The Magic of Donald Trump." *New York Review of Books*, May 26.

Davids, M. Fakhry. 2020. "A Discussion of 'When Reparation Is Felt to Be Impossible.'" *Psychoanalytic Dialogues* 30, 5: 604–12.

Davies, Thom, Arshad Isakjee, and Surindar Dhesi. 2017. "Violent Inaction: The Necropolitical Experience of Refugees in Europe." *Antipode* 49, 5: 1263–84.

Davis, Mike. 2021. "Riot on the Hill." newleftreview.org, January 7.

de Botton, Alain, and John Armstrong. 2013. *Art as Therapy*. London: Phaidon.

De Genova, N. 2013. "Spectacles of Migrant 'Illegality': The Scene of Exclusion, the Obscene of Inclusion." *Ethnic and Racial Studies* 36, 7: 1180–98.

De Leon, Rev. Dan. 2015. "Come and See the Congregation of Samuels and Elis." Sermon, Friends Congregational Church, College Station, January 18.

de Waal, Alex. 1997. *Famine Crimes: Politics and the Disaster Relief Industry in Africa*. London: James Currey.

———, ed. 2015. *Advocacy in Conflict: Critical Perspectives on Transnational Activism*. London: Zed.

———. 2018a. "Commemorating Starvation in the 21st Century." Address given at Quinnipiac University, October 11, World Peace Foundation, Somerville.

———. 2018b. *Mass Starvation: The History and Future of Famine*. Cambridge: Polity.

———. 2022. "Truth, Memory and Starvation." In *Accountability for Mass Starvation: Testing the Limits of the Law*, ed. Bridget Conley, Alex de Waal, Catriona Murdoch, and Wayne Jordash, 379–93. Oxford: Oxford University Press.

Dearing, Ronda, and June Tangney. 2011. "Introduction: Putting Shame in Context." In *Shame in the Therapy Hour*, ed. Ronda Dearing and June Tangney, 3–19. Washington, DC: American Psychological Association.

Deng, Francis. 1986. *The Man Called Deng Majok: A Biography of Power, Polygyny and Change*. New Haven: Yale University Press.

Deonna, Julien, Raffaele Rodogno, and Fabrice Teroni. 2011. *In Defense of Shame: The Faces of an Emotion*. New York: Oxford University Press.

Deonna, Julien, and Fabrice Teroni. 2008. "Shame's Guilt Disproved." *Critical Quarterly* 50, 4: 65–72.

Detrow, Scott. 2016. "Trump Blasts Clinton's 'Deplorables' Comment in Asheville, N.C." NPR, September 12.

Diamond, Jeremy. 2018. "Trump Says US Will Impose Steel and Aluminum Tariffs." Cnn.com, March 1.

DiAngelo, Robin. 2018. *White Fragility: Why It's So Hard for White People to Talk about Racism*. London: Penguin/Allen Lane.

Diehl, James. 1987. "Victors or Victims? Disabled Veterans in the Third Reich." *Journal of Modern History* 59, 4: 705–36.

Dikötter, Frank. 2015. "Coping with Famine in Communist China (1949–62)." *European Review of History* 22, 6: 917–28.

Dodd, Vikram, and Jessica Elgot. 2021. "'Weird and Gimmicky': Police Chiefs Condemn Boris Johnson's Crime Plan." *Guardian*, July 27.

Dodd, Vikram, and Jamie Grierson. 2020. "Terrorism Police List Extinction Rebellion as Extremist Ideology." *Guardian*, January 10.

Dodge, Toby, and Becca Wasser. 2014. "The Crisis of the Iraqi State." *Adelphi Series* 54, 447–48: 13–38.

Dolan, Chris. 2009. *Social Torture: The Case of Northern Uganda, 1986–2006*. New York: Berghahn Books.

Duffield, Mark. 2007. *Development, Security and Unending War: Governing the World of Peoples*. Cambridge: Polity.

———. 2019. *Post-humanitarianism: Governing Precarity in the Digital World*. Cambridge: Polity.

Durvasula, Ramani. 2018. "These Are the Signs You're Dating a Narcissist." YouTube, June 25.

Eder, Steve, and Dave Philipps. 2016. "Donald Trump's Draft Deferments: Four for College, One for Bad Feet." *New York Times*, August 1.

Eire, Carlos. 1989. *War against the Idols: The Reformation of Worship from Erasmus to Calvin.* Cambridge: Cambridge University Press (first published 1986).
Elgot, Jessica. 2016. "Secret Boris Johnson Column Favoured UK Remaining in EU." *Guardian*, October 16.
———. 2021. "Johnson Proposes Hi-Vis Chain Gangs as Part of Crime Plan." *Guardian*, July 27.
Elias, Norbert. 2000. *The Civilizing Process.* Oxford: Blackwell (first published 1939).
Eriksson Baaz, Maria, and Maria Stern. 2008. "Making Sense of Violence: Voices of Soldiers in the Congo (DRC)." *Journal of Modern African Studies* 46, 1: 57–86.
Eze, Geoff. 2017. "What Are People in Stoke Really Thinking About? It's Not Brexit." *Guardian*, February 15.
Factbase. 2016. "Speech: Donald Trump in Henderson, NV—October 5, 2016." https://factba.se/transcript/donald-trump-speech-henderson-nv-october-5-2016.
Faludi, Susan. 1999. *Stiffed: The Betrayal of the Modern Man.* London: Chatto and Windus.
———. 2007. *The Terror Dream: Fear and Fantasy in Post-9/11 America.* New York: Metropolitan Books.
Fanon, Frantz. 2001. *The Wretched of the Earth.* Harmondsworth: Penguin 2001 (first published 1961).
———. 2008. *Black Skin, White Masks.* Trans. Charles Lam Markmann. London: Pluto (first published 1952).
Feuerbach, Ludwig. 2008. *The Essence of Christianity.* Mineola: Dover.
Fischer, Clara. 2016. "Gender, Nation, and the Politics of Shame: Magdalen Laundries and the Institutionalization of Feminine Transgression in Modern Ireland." *Signs: Journal of Women in Culture and Society* 41, 4: 821–43.
Fisher, Nick. 1995. "Review: Shame and Necessity." *Classical Review* 45, 1: 71–73.
Flanagan, Owen. 2021. *How to Do Things with Emotions: The Morality of Anger and Shame across Cultures.* Princeton: Princeton University Press.
Flood, Alison. 2021. "'It Is Obscene': Chimamanda Ngozi Adichie Pens Blistering Essay against Social Media Sanctimony." *Guardian*, June 16.
Foucault, Michel. 1977. *Discipline and Punish: The Birth of the Prison.* Trans. Alan Sheridan. London: Penguin.
———. 1978. *The History of Sexuality.* Trans. Robert Hurley. New York: Pantheon Books.
———. 1980. *Power/Knowledge: Selected Interviews and Other Writings.* Ed. C. Gordon. Brighton: Harvester Press (1972–77).
Frank, Thomas. 2004a. *What's the Matter with America? The Resistible Rise of the American Right.* London: Secker and Warburg.
———. 2004b. *What's the Matter with Kansas? How Conservatives Won the Heart of America.* New York: Henry Holt.
———. 2012. *Pity the Billionaire.* London: Harvill Secker.
———. 2016. *Listen, Liberal.* London: Scribe.
Fraser, Nancy. 2017a. "The End of Progressive Neoliberalism." *Dissent Online*, January 2.
———. 2017b. "Against Progressive Neoliberalism, a New Progressive Populism." *Dissent Online*, January 28.

Freud, Anna. 1954. *The Ego and the Mechanisms of Defence*. London: Hogarth Press/Institute of Psycho-analysis.

Freud, Sigmund. 1895. Letter to Wilhelm Fliess, in Freud Museum, London, exhibitions, Paranoia. https://www.freud.org.uk/exhibitions/paranoia/.

———. 1960. *Totem and Taboo*. Trans. James Strachey. London: Routledge (first published 1913).

———. 1974. "The Psychotherapy of Hysteria." In Sigmund Freud and Joseph Breuer, *Studies on Hysteria*, 337–93. Harmondsworth: Penguin (first published 1895).

———. 1991. "Civilization and Its Discontents." In Freud, *Civilization, Society and Religion*, 251–340. London: Penguin (first published 1930).

———. 2001a. "Remembering, Repeating and Working-Through." In *The Standard Edition of the Complete Psychological Works of Sigmund Freud*, vol. 12, ed. James Strachey. London: Vintage (paper first published 1914).

———. 2001b. "The Future of an Illusion." In *The Standard Edition of the Complete Psychological Works of Sigmund Freud*, vol. 21 (1927–31), 5–56. London: Vintage (first published 1927).

———. 2005. *The Unconscious*. Trans. Graham Frankland with an introduction by Mark Cousins. Penguin: London.

Fukuyama, Francis. 2020. *The End of History and the Last Man*. London: Penguin.

Gabbard, G. 1999. "Classic Article." *Journal of Psychotherapy Practice and Research* 8, 1: 64–65.

Galston, William. 2016. "Sex and the Citizens: Trump Edition; He Has Exposed Illusions—Mine Anyway—about Gender Relations in the U.S." *Wall Street Journal*, May 31.

Gear, Sasha. 2002. *Wishing Us Away: Challenges Facing Ex-combatants in the "New" South Africa*. Violence and Transition Series, vol. 8. Johannesburg: Centre for the Study of Violence and Reconciliation.

Gerges, Fawaz. 2005. *The Far Enemy: Why Jihad Went Global*. New York: Cambridge University Press.

———. 2016. *ISIS: A History*. Princeton: Princeton University Press.

Gerodimos, Roman. 2022. "Humiliation, Shame, and Violence: Honor, Trauma, and Political Extremism before and after the 2009 Crisis in Greece." *International Forum of Psychoanalysis* 31, 1: 34–45.

Gilbert, Paul. 1998. "What Is Shame?" In *Shame: Interpersonal Behavior, Psychopathology and Culture*, ed. Paul Gilbert and Bernice Andrews, 3–38. New York: Oxford University Press.

Gillespie, Paul. 2008. "'Free Enterprise for the Poor, Socialism for the Rich': Vidal's Claim Gains Leverage." *Irish Times*, September 20.

Gilligan, James. 2000. *Violence: Reflections on Our Deadliest Epidemic*. London: Jessica Kingsley.

———. 2003. "Shame, Guilt and Violence." *Social Research* 70, 4: 1149–80.

———. 2016. "Can Psychoanalysis Help Us to Understand the Causes and Prevention of Violence?" *Psychoanalytic Psychotherapy* 30, 2: 125–37.

Gilroy, Paul. 2004. *Postcolonial Melancholia*. New York: Columbia University Press (ebook version).

Girard, René. 1977. *Violence and the Sacred*. Trans. Patrick Gregory. 2nd ed. Baltimore: Johns Hopkins University Press.

Global Terrorism Index. 2015. *Measuring and Understanding the Impact of Terrorism*. Sydney Institute for Economics and Peace.

Global Terrorism Index. 2016. *Measuring and Understanding the Impact of Terrorism*. Sydney Institute for Economics and Peace.

Glynos, Jason. 2014. "Hating Government and Voting against One's Interests: Self-Transgression, Enjoyment, Critique." *Psychoanalysis, Culture & Society* 19, 2: 179–89.

Goepner, Erik. 2016. "Measuring the Effectiveness of America's War on Terror." *Parameters* 46, 1: 107–20.

Goffman, E. 1961. *Asylums*. New York: Doubleday Anchor.

Goldberg, Jeffrey. 2020. "Trump: Americans Who Died in War Are 'Losers' and 'Suckers.'" *The Atlantic*, September 3.

Grandin, Greg. 2019. *The End of the Myth: From the Frontier to the Border Wall in the Mind of America*. New York: Metropolitan Books.

Greenberg, Leslie, and Shigeru Iwakabe. 2011. "Emotion-Focused Therapy and Shame." In *Shame in the Therapy Hour*, ed. Ronda Dearing and June Tangney, 69–90. Washington, DC: American Psychological Association.

Greenwald, Deborah, and David Harder. 1998. "Domains of Shame: Evolutionary, Cultural and Psychotherapeutic Aspects." In *Shame: Interpersonal Behavior, Psychopathology and Culture*, ed. Paul Gilbert and Bernice Andrews, 225–45. New York: Oxford University Press.

Grossman, Dave. 1995. *On Killing: The Psychological Cost of Learning to Kill in War and Society*. Boston: Little, Brown.

Guardian/AP (Associated Press). 2016. "Father of Muslim American Soldier: 'Donald Trump, You Have Sacrificed Nothing.'" Video. July 29.

Guardian News/YouTube. 2018. "Laughter as Trump Lauds Politician's Body Slam of Guardian Journalist." October 19. https://www.youtube.com/watch?v=dW42IV3LExg.

Guardian Unlimited. 2003. "Full Text: Tony Blair's Speech." March 18. http://politics.guardian.co.uk/iraq/story/0,12956,916790,00.html.

Guilluy, Christophe. 2018. "France Is Deeply Fractured. Gilets Jaunes Are Just a Symptom." *Guardian*, December 2.

Gunn, Gregory, and Anne Wilson. 2011. "Acknowledging the Skeletons in Our Closet: The Effect of Group Affirmation on Collective Guilt, Collective Shame, and Reparatory Attitudes." *Personality and Social Psychology Bulletin* 31, 11: 1474–87.

Haapatalo, E. 2019. "On the Development of a Benign Superego: Thoughts Arising from Psychoanalytical Work with Children and Grownups." *Scandinavian Psychoanalytic Review*, September 17.

Haberman, Maggie. 2015. "Donald Trump Calls for Surveillance of 'Certain Mosques' and a Syrian Refugee Database." *New York Times*, November 21.

Hall, Macer. 2019. "Second Vote Will Lead to Civil Unrest: Brexit People's Vote Could 'Break up Britain.'" *Daily Express*, January 22.

Hardin, Kris L. 1993. *The Aesthetics of Action: Continuity and Change in a West African Town*. Washington, DC: Smithsonian Institution.

Harding, Celia. 2019. *Dissecting the Superego: Moralities under the Psychoanalytic Microscope*. London: Routledge.

Harkinson, Josh, and Jaeah Lee. 2013. "Charts: How Foreign Firms Flood America with Guns—and Get Rich Doing It." *Mother Jones*, April 4.

Harrell-Bond, B. E. 1986. *Imposing Aid: Emergency Assistance to Refugees*. Oxford: Oxford University Press.

Harris, John, and John Domokos. 2014. "UKIP's Rise in the East of England." Video. *Guardian*, September 15.

———. 2019. "We Spent 10 Years Talking to People. Here's What It Taught Us about Britain." *Guardian*, December 3.

Harris, Sarah. 2017. "Daily Mail's 'Crush the Saboteurs' Front Page Prompts Backlash." *HuffPost*, April 19.

Hartung, William, and Michelle Ciarrocca. 2003. "The Military Industrial Think Tank Complex: Corporate Think Tanks and the Doctrine of Aggressive Militarism." *Multinational Monitor* 24, 1–2: 17–20.

Haslett, Adam. 2016. "Donald Trump, Shamer in Chief." *The Nation*, October 24.

Hazard, Paul. 1969. "Freud's Teaching on Shame." *Laval théologique et philosophie* 25, 2: 235–67.

Hegel, Georg. 1977. *Phenomenology of Spirit*. Trans. A. V. Miller. Oxford: Oxford University Press (first published 1807).

Herman, Judith. 1992. *Trauma and Recovery: The Aftermath of Violence—from Domestic Abuse to Political Terror*. New York: Basic Books.

Hickel, Jason. 2015. *Democracy as Death: The Moral Order in Anti-Liberal Politics in South Africa*. Oakland: University of California Press.

Hilberg, Raul. 1980. "The Ghetto as a Form of Government." *Annals of the American Academy of Political and Social Science* 450: 98–112.

———. 1992. *Perpetrators, Victims, Bystanders: The Jewish Catastrophe, 1933–1945*. New York: HarperCollins.

Hilton, Alexander. 1996. "Agents of Death: Explaining the Cambodian Genocide in Terms of Psychosocial Dissonance." *American Anthropologist* 98, 4: 818–31.

Hilton, Boyd. 1986. *The Influence of Evangelicalism on Social and Economic Thought, 1795–1865*. Oxford: Clarendon/Oxford University Press.

Hinton, Alexander Laban. 1998. "A Head for an Eye: Revenge in the Cambodian Genocide." *American Ethnologist* 25, 3: 352–77.

Hirschkind, Charles, and Saba Mahmood. 2002. "Feminism, the Taliban, and Politics of Counter-Insurgency." *Anthropological Quarterly* 75, 2: 339–54.

Hitler, Adolf. 1938. *Mein Kampf (My Struggle)*. London: Hurst and Blackett (first published 1933).

———. 1939a. Reichstag speech, January 30. Shoah Resource Center, International School for Holocaust Studies.

———. 1939b. Speech to Wehrmacht commanders-in-chief. August 22. http://www.union.edu/PUBLIC/HSTDEPT/walker/OldNSChronology/3686Walker02.html.

Hochschild, Arlie Russell. 2016. "I Spent 5 Years with Some of Trump's Biggest Fans. Here's What They Won't Tell You." *Mother Jones*, September/October.

———. 2018. *Strangers in Their Own Land: Anger and Mourning on the American Right*. New York: New Press (first published 2016).

Hofstadter, Richard. 2008. *The Paranoid Style in American Politics and Other Essays*. New York: Vintage (first published 1965).

Hoggett, Paul. 2017. "Shame and Performativity: Thoughts on the Psychology of Neoliberalism." *Psychoanalysis, Culture & Society* 22, 4: 364–82.

Holland, Steve. 2020. "As Portland Pullout Proceeds, Trump Threatens More Force." Reuters, July 30.

Honneth, Axel. 2004. "Recognition and Justice: Outline of a Plural Theory of Justice." *Acta Sociologica* 47, 4: 351–64.

Hossein-zadeh, Ismael. 2006. *The Political Economy of U.S. Militarism*. Basingstoke: Palgrave Macmillan.

Hughes, Sali. 2020. "Trolls on 'Dragging' Sites Can Ruin Lives: It's Time They Answered for Their Actions." *Guardian*, October 5.

Human Rights Watch. 1999. "Sierra Leone: Getting Away with Murder, Mutilation, Rape." New York. https://www.hrw.org/reports/1999/sierra/.

———. 2003. "'We'll Kill You If You Cry': Sexual Violence in the Sierra Leone Conflict." New York. https://www.hrw.org/report/2003/01/16/well-kill-you-if-you-cry/sexual-violence-sierra-leone-conflict.

Human Rights Watch/International Federation of Human Rights. 1999. "Leave None to Tell the Story: Genocide in Rwanda." New York. https://www.hrw.org/sites/default/files/media_2020/12/rwanda-leave-none-to-tell-the-story.pdf.

Hunt, David. 2010. "Dirty Wars: Counterinsurgency in Vietnam and Today." *Politics & Society* 38, 1: 35–66.

Ignatieff, Michael. 2005. "Who Are Americans to Think That Freedom Is Theirs to Spread?" *New York Times Magazine*, June 26. http://www.ksg.harvard.edu/ksgnews/Features/opeds/062605_ignatieff.htm.

Independent. 2000. "Straight Bananas: How Euromyths Bend the Truth." April 25.

International Alert. 2004. *Women's Bodies as a Battleground: Sexual Violence against Women and Girls during the War in the Democratic Republic of Congo*. London. https://www.international-alert.org/wp-content/uploads/2021/10/womens-bodies-as-a-english.pdf.

Irish Times/AFP. 2001. "Britain Will Not Apologise for Slavery: PM's Office." *Irish Times*, September 3.

Jackson Lears, T. J. 2000. "From Salvation to Self-Realization: Advertising and the Therapeutic Roots of the Consumer Culture, 1880–1930." *Advertising and Society Review* 1, 1: n.p.

Jacquet, Jennifer. 2015. *Is Shame Necessary? New Uses for an Old Tool*. London: Allen Lane.

Jasanoff, Maya. 2020. "Misremembering the British Empire." *New Yorker*, October 26.

Jaspars, Susanne. 2018. *Food Aid in Sudan: A History of Power, Politics and Profit*. London: Zed Books.

Jaspars, Susanne, and Margie Buchanan-Smith. 2018. "Darfuri Migration from Sudan to Europe." *Overseas Development Institute*. London. September. https://www.jointdatacenter.org/literature_review/darfuri-migration-from-sudan-to-europe-from-displacement-to-despair/.

Jensen, Mads Dagnis, and Holly Snaith. 2016. "When Politics Prevails: The Political Economy of a Brexit." *Journal of European Public Policy* 23, 9: 1302–10.

Jones, Owen. 2012. *Chavs: The Demonization of the Working Class*. London: Verso (first published 2011).
Jones, Robert. 2017. "Trump Can't Reverse the Decline of White Christian America." *The Atlantic*, July 4.
Kalyvas, Stathis. 2004. "The Paradox of Terrorism in Civil War." *Journal of Ethics* 8, 1: 97–138.
Kampfner, John. 2003. *Blair's Wars*. London: Simon and Schuster.
Katz, Jack. 1996. "The Social Psychology of Adam and Eve." *Theory and Society* 25: 545–82.
Keen, David. 1994. *The Benefits of Famine: A Political Economy of Famine and Relief in Southwestern Sudan, 1983–1989*. Princeton: Princeton University Press.
———. 1998. *The Economic Functions of Violence in Civil Wars*. Adelphi paper 319. Oxford: Oxford University Press and International Institute for Strategic Studies.
———. 2005. *Conflict and Collusion in Sierra Leone*. Oxford: James Currey.
———. 2006. *Endless War: Hidden Functions of the War on Terror*. London: Pluto.
———. 2007. "Labour's Love's Lost." *Le Monde Diplomatique*, May.
———. 2008. *Complex Emergencies*. Cambridge: Polity.
———. 2009. "A Tale of Two Wars: Great Expectations, Hard Times." *Conflict, Security and Development* 9, 4: 515–34.
———. 2012a. *Useful Enemies: When Waging Wars Is More Important than Winning Them*. New Haven: Yale University Press.
———. 2012b. "Greed and Grievance in Civil War." *International Affairs* 88, 4: 757–77.
———. 2013. "When 'Do No Harm' Hurts." *New York Times*, November 6.
———. 2014. "'The Camp' and 'the Lesser Evil': Humanitarianism in Sri Lanka." *Conflict, Security and Development* 14, 1: 1–31.
———. 2017. *Syria: Playing into Their Hands*. London: Saferworld.
———. 2021. "The Functions and Legitimization of Suffering in Calais, France." *International Migration* 59, 3: 9–28.
Keen, David, and Ruben Andersson. 2018. "Double Games: Success, Failure and the Relocation of Risk in Fighting Terror, Drugs and Migration." *Political Geography* 67: 100–110.
Keiger, J. 2021. "France's Military Wages War on Macron's Values." *Spectator*, May 2.
Kelly, Jocelyn. 2010. "Rape in War: Motives of Militia in DRC." Special report, United States Institute of Peace, June 20, 1–15.
Keltner, Dacher, and Lee Anne Harker. 1998. "The Forms and Functions of the Nonverbal Signal of Shame." In *Shame: Interpersonal Behavior, Psychopathology and Culture*, ed. Paul Gilbert and Bernice Andrews, 78–98. New York: Oxford University Press.
Kershaw, Ian. 1998. *Hitler: 1889–1936 Hubris*. London: Penguin.
Kimmel, Michael. 2019. *Angry White Men: American Masculinity at the End of an Era*. New York: Bold Type Books (first published 2013).
King, John. 2002. "Bush Calls Saddam 'The Guy Who Tried to Kill My Dad.'" CNN, September 27.
Kisangani, Emizet. 2000. "The Massacre of Refugees in the Congo: A Case of UN Peacekeeping Failure and International Law." *Journal of Modern African Studies* 38, 3: 163–202.
Klein, Melanie. 1997. "On the Sense of Loneliness." In *Envy and Gratitude and Other Works 1946–1963*, 300–315. London: Vintage (paper first published 1963).

———. 1998. *Love, Guilt and Reparation, and Other Works, 1921–1945*. London: Vintage (first published 1975).

Klein, Naomi. 2007. *The Shock Doctrine: The Rise of Disaster Capitalism*. London: Penguin/Allen Lane.

Koch, Insa. 2016. "Bread-and-Butter Politics: Democratic Disenchantment and Everyday Politics on an English Council Estate." *American Ethnologist* 43, 2: 282–94.

Kohut, Heinz. 1985. *Self Psychology and the Humanities: Reflections on a New Psychoanalytic Approach*. New York: W. W. Norton.

Kovel, Joel. 1988. *White Racism: A Psychohistory*. London: Free Association Books (first published 1970).

Kreitner, Richard. 2014. "Hate to Say We Told You So." *The Nation*, September 8 (interview with Sherle Schwenninger).

Krugman, Paul. 2015. "The Case for Cuts Was a Lie. Why Does Britain Still Believe It? The Austerity Delusion." *Guardian*, April 29.

Kundnani, Arun. 2014. *The Muslims Are Coming: Islamophobia, Extremism and the Domestic War on Terror*. London: Verso.

Kuper, Simon. 2019. "How Oxford University Shaped Brexit—and Britain's Next Prime Minister." *Financial Times*, June 21.

Kuzmarov, Jeremy. 2008. "From Counter-Insurgency to Narco-Insurgency: Vietnam and the International War on Drugs." *Journal of Policy History* 20, 3: 344–78.

Lal, Vinay. 2005. "The Concentration Camp and Development: The Pasts and Future of Genocide." *Patterns of Prejudice* 39, 2: 220–43.

Lambert, Sarah. 1994. "Putting the Banana Story Straight." *Independent*, September 21.

Lansky, Melvin. 2005. "Hidden Shame." *Journal of the American Psychoanalytic Association* 53, 3: 865–90.

———. 2015. "'O, Coward Conscience, How Does Thou Afflict Me': Ruthlessness and the Struggle against Conscience in Richard III." *Psychoanalytic Inquiry* 35, 1: 117–35.

Lappin, Elena. 2002. "Atta in Hamburg." *Prospect*, September 20.

Lasch, Christopher. 1979. *The Culture of Narcissism: American Life in an Age of Diminishing Expectations*. New York: Warner Books.

Layton, Lynne. 2010. "Irrational Exuberance: Neoliberal Subjectivity and the Perversion of Truth." *Subjectivity* 3, 3: 303–22.

———. 2014. "Some Psychic Effects of Neoliberalism: Narcissism, Disavowal, Perversion." *Psychoanalysis, Culture & Society* 19: 161–78.

Lehmann-Haupt, Christopher. 1989. "Books of the Times; Aryan Archetype and His Date with a Grenade." *New York Times*, April 17.

Lembcke, Jerry. 1998. *The Spitting Image: Myth, Memory, and the Legacy of Vietnam*. New York: New York University Press.

Lemert, Edwin. 1962. "Paranoia and the Dynamics of Exclusion." *Sociometry* 25, 1: 2–20.

Lerner, Paul, 2003. *Hysterical Men: War, Psychiatry and the Politics of Trauma in Germany, 1890–1930*. Ithaca: Cornell University Press.

Levi, Primo. 1989. *The Drowned and the Saved*. London: Abacus.

Levy, Pema. 2016. "These Rust Belt Democrats Have the Toughest Job in America." *Mother Jones*, September/October.

Lewis, Helen. 1971. "Shame and Guilt in Neurosis." *Psychoanalytic Review* 58, 3: 419–38.

Lewis, Michael. 1998. "Shame and Stigma." In *Shame: Interpersonal Behavior, Psychopathology and Culture*, ed. Paul Gilbert and Bernice Andrews, 126–40. New York: Oxford University Press.

Liebovich, Mark. 2020. "Trump Has Called His Supporters 'Disgusting': Do They Care?" *New York Times*, October 10.

Lindisfarne, Nancy. 1998. "Gender, Shame and Culture: An Anthropological Perspective." In *Shame: Interpersonal Behavior, Psychopathology and Culture*, ed. Paul Gilbert and Bernice Andrews, 246–60. New York: Oxford University Press.

Locke, Jill. 2019. "Trump Is Not a Shameless Toddler: The Problems with Psychological Analyses of the 45th US President." *Krisis*, issue 1.

Longley, Clifford. 2003. *Chosen People: The Big Idea That Shaped England and America*. 2nd ed. London: Hodder and Stoughton.

Lord, David. 2000. Introduction to *Paying the Price: The Sierra Leone Peace Process*, ed. Lord. London: Conciliation Resources.

Los Angeles Times. 2016. "Transcript: The Most Important Exchanges of the Presidential Debate Annotated." September 26.

Louis, Édouard. 2017. *The End of Eddy*. Trans. Michael Lucey. London: Harvill Secker.

Lu, Catherine. 2008. "Shame, Guilt and Reconciliation after War." *European Journal of Social Theory* 11, 3: 367–83.

Luckenbill, David. 1977. "Criminal Homicide as a Situated Transaction." *Social Problems* 25, 2: 176–86.

Macdonald, James. 1998. "Disclosing Shame." In *Shame: Interpersonal Behavior, Psychopathology and Culture*, ed. Paul Gilbert and Bernice Andrews, 141–57. New York: Oxford University Press.

Mackey, Danielle. 2018. "El Salvador's 'Iron Fist' Crackdown on Gangs: A Lethal Policy with U.S. Origins." *World Politics Review*, February 6.

MacLeod, Gordon, and Martin Jones. 2018. "Explaining 'Brexit Capital': Uneven Development and the Austerity State." *Space and Polity* 22, 2: 111–36.

MacPherson, Myra. 1988. *Long Time Passing: Vietnam and the Haunted Generation*. London: Sceptre.

Malesevic, Sinisa, and Kevin Ryan. 2012. "Disfigured Ontology of Figurational Sociology: Norbert Elias and the Question of Violence." *Critical Sociology* 39, 2: 165–81.

Malik, Kenan. 2021. "If You Thought the Right to Protest Was Inalienable, Then Think Again." *Guardian*, March 14.

Malthus, Thomas. 1798. *An Essay on the Principle of Population*. London: J. Johnson/St. Paul's Church-Yard.

Mamdani, Mahmood. 2001. *When Victims Become Killers: Colonialism, Nativism, and the Genocide in Rwanda*. Princeton: Princeton University Press.

Manjoo, Farhad. 2008. *True Enough: Learning to Live in a Post-Fact Society*. Hoboken, NJ: John Wiley and Sons.

Mann, Michael. 2003. *Incoherent Empire*. London: Verso.

Mansfield, Edward, and Jack Snyder. 2005. *Electing to Fight: Why Emerging Democracies Go to War*. Cambridge, MA: MIT Press.

Marin, Peter. 1991. "Living in Moral Pain." In *The Vietnam Reader*, ed. Walter Capps, 43–53. New York: Routledge.

Marx, Karl. 1978. "German Ideology." In *The Marx-Engels Reader*, ed. R. Tucker. New York: W. W. Norton.

Maschmann, Melita. 1964. *Account Rendered: A Dossier on My Former Self*. London: Abelard Schuman.

Mayer, Jane. 2020. "How Mitch McConnell Became Trump's Enabler-in-Chief." *New Yorker*, April 12.

McAuley, James. 2019. "Low Visibility." *New York Review of Books*, March 21.

McCann, Philip. 2018. "The Trade, Geography and Regional Implications of Brexit." *Papers in Regional Science* 97: 3–8.

McIntosh, Alastair. 1996. "Eros to Thanatos: Cigarette Adverts." Blog. http://www.alastairmcintosh.com/articles/1996_eros_thanatos.htm.

Mckenzie, Lisa. 2017. "The Class Politics of Prejudice: Brexit and the Land of No-Hope and Glory." *British Journal of Sociology* 68, S1: 266–80.

Meixler, Eli. 2018. "President Trump Mocked Kavanaugh Accuser Christine Blasey Ford at a Mississippi Rally." *Time*, October 2.

Mendible, Myra. 2016. "American Shame and the Boundaries of Belonging." In *American Shame: Stigma and the Body Politic*, ed. Myra Mendible, 1–23. Bloomington: Indiana University Press.

Mendoca, Dina, and Susana Cadilha. 2019. "Bernard Williams and the Concept of Shame: What Makes an Emotion Moral?" *Labyrinth* 21, 1: 99–115.

Mennell, Stephen. 1990. "Decivilising Processes: Theoretical Significance and Some Lines of Research." *International Sociology* 5, 2: 205–23.

———. 2009. "An Exceptional Civilizing Process?" *Journal of Classical Sociology* 9, 1: 97–115.

Merrick, Robert. 2021. "'A Fire They Poured Petrol On.'" *Independent*, June 13.

Metzl, Jonathan. 2020. "The Politics of White Anxiety." *Boston Review*, October 23.

Midlarsky, Manus. 2005. *The Killing Trap*. Cambridge: Cambridge University Press.

Mika, Elizabeth, with Frederick Burkle. 2016. "The Unbearable Lightness of Being a Narcissist." Blog, March 31. https://medium.com/@Elamika/the-unbearable-lightness-of-being-a-narcissist-251ec901dae7.

Miller, Alice. 1987. *The Drama of Being a Child*. London: Virago.

Miller, Arthur. 1996. *The Crucible: Text and Criticism*. Ed. Gerald Weales. London: Penguin.

Mintchev, Nikolay. 2021. "The Cultural Politics of Racism in the Brexit Conjuncture." *International Journal of Cultural Studies* 24, 1: 123–40.

Mishra, Pankaj. 2016. "Welcome to the Age of Anger." *Guardian*, December 8.

Mitchell, David. 2021. "Being the Queen Sure Has Its Ups and Downs." *Guardian*, June 13.

Mitton, Kieran. 2015. *Rebels in a Rotten State: Understanding Atrocity in Sierra Leone*. London: Hurst & Company.

Mkandawire, Thandike. 2001. "Thinking about Developmental States in Africa." *Cambridge Journal of Economics* 25: 289–314.

Moguillansky. Rodolfo. 2013. "Shame, Humiliation, and the Hero." In Carlos Guillermo Bigliani, Rodolfo Moguillansky, and Carlos Sluzki, *Shame and Humiliation: A Dialogue between Psychoanalytic and Systemic Approaches*, 131–55. London: International Psychoanalytical Association/Karnac Books.

Monroe, Rachel. 2020. "How to Spot a Military Imposter." *New Yorker*, October 19.

Morrison, Andrew. 2011. "The Psychodynamics of Shame." In *Shame in the Therapy Hour*, ed. Ronda Dearing and June Tangney, 23–43. Washington, DC: American Psychological Association.

Mouffe, Chantal. 2005. *On the Political: Thinking in Action*. London: Routledge.

Nathan, Jack. 2019. "About the Analyst and Patient: The Superego in Borderline States of Mind." In *Dissecting the Superego: Moralities under the Psychoanalytic Microscope*, ed. Celia Harding, 110–25. London: Routledge.

Neate, Rupert, and Lauren Gambino. 2016. "Trump University 'Playbooks' Offer Glimpse of Ruthless Business Practices." *Guardian*, June 1.

Nelson, Laura. 2021. "California's Yoga, Wellness and Spirituality Community Has a QAnon Problem." *Los Angeles Times*, June 23.

New York Times. 2016a. "Transcript of Donald Trump's Immigration Speech." September 1.

———. 2016b. "Transcript: Donald Trump's Taped Comments about Women." October 8.

New York Times/CQ Transcriptswire. 2016. Transcript of the Second Debate, October 10.

Nietzsche, Friedrich. 2003a. *Twilight of the Idols* (first published 1889). In *Twilight of the Idols and The Anti-Christ*. London: Penguin.

———. 2003b. *The Anti-Christ* (first published 1895). In *Twilight of the Idols and The Anti-Christ*. London: Penguin.

———. 2003c. *The Genealogy of Morals*. Garden City, NY: Dover Publications (first published 1887).

NPR/Ipsos. 2020. "More than 1 in 3 Americans Believe a 'Deep State' Is Working to Undermine Trump." December 30.

Nussbaum, Martha. 2004. *Hiding from Humanity: Disgust, Shame and the Law*. Princeton: Princeton University Press.

Nuzzi, Olivia. 2016. "Draft Dodger Donald Trump Gets Hero's Welcome at Rolling Thunder." *Daily Beast*, May 29.

O'Brien, Tim. 1979. "The Violent Vet." *Esquire*, December: 96–104.

O'Carroll, Lisa. 2019. "More EU Citizens Are Seeking Help for Stress and Anxiety over Brexit." *Guardian*, June 2.

O'Hara, Mary. 2014. *Austerity Bites: A Journey to the Sharp End of Cuts in the UK*. Bristol: Policy Press.

O'Neil, Cathy. 2022. *The Shame Machine: Who Profits in the New Age of Humiliation*. London: Penguin/Allen Lane.

O'Toole, Fintan. 2018. *Heroic Failure: Brexit and the Politics of Pain*. London: Head of Zeus.

———. 2020. "Trump Has Unfinished Business; A Republic He Wants to Destroy Still Stands." *Irish Times*, December 26.

Owens, Patricia. 2017. "Racism in the Theory Canon: Hannah Arendt and 'the One Great Crime in Which America Was Never Involved.'" *Millennium* 45, 3: 403–24.

Packer, George. 2015. "The Other France: Are the Suburbs of France Incubators of Terrorism?" *New Yorker*, August 31. https://www.newyorker.com/magazine/2015/08/31/the-other-france.

Park, Christine J. 2016. "Chronic Shame: A Perspective Integrating Religion and Spirituality." *Journal of Religion and Spirituality in Social Work: Social Thought* 35, 4: 354–76.

PBS/Frontline. 2017. *President Trump*. Documentary, January 3.

Peltz, Rachael. 2005. "The Manic Society." *Psychoanalytic Dialogues* 15, 3: 347–66.

Petre, Jonathan. 2017. "They Kant Be Serious!" *Mail on Sunday/Daily Mail online*, July 27.

Piketty, Thomas. 2014. *Capital in the Twenty-First Century*. Cambridge, MA: Harvard University Press.

———. 2016. "Why Save the Bankers?" In Piketty, *Chronicles on Our Troubled Times*, 15–17. London: Penguin.

Pitt-Rivers, Julian. 2017. "Honor and Social Status in Andalusia." In *From Hospitality to Grace: A Julian Pitt-Rivers Omnibus*, ed. Giovanni da Col and Andrew Shryock, 3–34. Chicago: HAU Books (essay first published 1977).

Plato. 1997. *Republic*. Ware: Wordsworth.

Porter, Patrick. 2005. "Beyond Comfort: German and English Military Chaplains and the Memory of the Great War, 1919–1929." *Journal of Religious History* 29, 3: 258–89.

Pratt, John. 2011. "Norbert Elias, the Civilizing Process and Penal Development in Modern Society." *Sociological Review* 59, 1: 220–40.

Putzel, James. 2020. "The 'Populist' Right Challenge to Neoliberalism: Social Policy between a Rock and a Hard Place." *Development and Change* 51, 2: 418–41.

Rampton, Sheldon, and John Stauber. 2003. *Weapons of Mass Deception: The Uses of Propaganda in Bush's War on Iraq*. London: Constable and Robinson.

Rangasami, Amrita. 1985. "'Failure of Exchange Entitlements' Theory of Famine: A Response." *Economic and Political Weekly* 20, 41, October 12 (1747–51) and 20, 42, October 19 (1797–1800).

Rapley, John. 2017. "How Economics Became a Religion." *Guardian*, July 11.

Rawlinson, Kevin, and Peter Walker. 2021. "No. 10 Suggests Oxford Students Hit by Rhodes Boycott Should Be Compensated." *Guardian*, June 10.

Ray, Larry. 2014 "Shame and the City—'Looting,' Emotions and Social Structure." *Sociological Review* 62: 117–36.

Reich, Robert. 2015. *Saving Capitalism: For the Many, Not the Few*. New York: Knopf.

———. 2016. "Want to Reverse Sky-High Inequality? Bernie Sanders Is the Pragmatic Choice," *Guardian*, January 27.

Retzinger, Suzanne. 1991. "Shame, Anger, and Conflict: Case Study of Emotional Violence." *Journal of Family Violence* 6, 1: 37–59.

Reuter, Christoph. 2015. "The Terror Strategist: Secret Files Reveal the Structure of Islamic State." *Der Spiegel*, April 18. http://www.spiegel.de/international/world/islamic-state-files-show-structure-of-islamist-terror-group-a-1029274.html.

Reuters. 2016. "Donald Trump: 'I Could Shoot Somebody and I Wouldn't Lose Any Voters.'" *Guardian*, January 24.

Richards, Paul. 1996. *Fighting for the Rain Forest: War, Youth and Resources in Sierra Leone*. Oxford: James Currey.

Robins, Robert, and Jerrold Post. 1997. *Political Paranoia: The Psychopolitics of Hatred*. New Haven: Yale University Press.

Roundtree, Chayenne. 2017. "Was Trump Right about Sweden All Along?" *Daily Mail* (dailymail.com), April 7.

Roustang, Francois. 1987. "How Do You Make a Paranoiac Laugh?" *MLN* 102, 4: 707–18.

Russian, Ale. 2016. "Trump Boasted of Avoiding STDs while Dating." *People.com*, October 28.

Ruthven, Malise. 2002. *A Fury for God: The Islamist Attack on America*. London: Granta.

Ryle, John. 1989. "The Road to Abyei." *Granta* 26, spring: 41–104.

Saez, Emmanuel, and Gabriel Zucman. 2016. "Wealth Inequality in the United States since 1913: Evidence from Capitalized Income Tax Data." *Quarterly Journal of Economics* 131, 2: 519–78.

Saferworld. 2022. *Learning from Responses to Armed Conflicts Involving Proscribed Groups*. London, May.

Said, Edward. 2003. "A Window on the World." *Guardian*, August 2.

Sandel, Michael. 2016. "Do Those on Top Deserve Their Success?" BBC Radio 4, December 13.

Sandler, J. 1960. "On the Concept of the Superego." *Psychoanalytic Study of the Child* 15: 128–61.

Saul, Heather. 2016. "Sarah Palin's Speech Endorsing Donald Trump in Full." *Independent*, January 20.

Schafer, R. 1960. "The Loving and Beloved Superego in Freud's Structural Theory." *Psychoanalytic Study of the Child* 15: 163–88.

Schaffer, Bernard. 1984. "Towards Responsibility." In *Room for Manoeuvre: An Exploration of Public Policy in Agriculture and Rural Development*, ed. Edward Clay and Bernard Schaffer. London: Heinemann Educational Books.

Scheff, Thomas. 1994. *Bloody Revenge: Emotions, Nationalism and War*. Boulder, CO: Westview.

——. 2003. "Shame in Self and Society." *Symbolic Interaction* 26, 2: 239–62.

Scherer, Michael. 2017. "Read President Trump's Interview with TIME on Truth and Falsehoods." *Time*, March 23.

Schivelbusch, Wolfgang. 2001. *The Culture of Defeat: On National Trauma, Mourning, and Recovery*. London: Granta.

Schor, Juliet. 1999. *The Overspent American: Why We Want What We Don't Need*. New York: Basic Books.

Scott, James, and Lucia Quaglia. 2020. "Multi-level Financial Regulation and Domestic Political Economy." British Politics and Policy, LSE.

Segal, Hanna. 2003. "From Hiroshima to 11th September 2001 and After." *Psychodynamic Practice* 9, 3: 257–65.

Seibold, Birgit Susanne. 2011. *Emily Hobhouse and the Reports on the Concentration Camps during the Boer War, 1899–1902*. New York: Columbia University Press.

Sen, Amartya. 1984. *Poverty and Famines: An Essay on Entitlement and Deprivation*. Oxford: Clarendon (first published 1981).

Sen, Amartya, and Jean Dréze. 1991. *Hunger and Public Action*. Oxford: Clarendon.
Sengupta, Kim. 2019. "John McCain Will Win His Feud with Donald Trump from beyond the Grave." *Independent*, March 22.
Sennett, Richard. 1978. "Shame Is the Key." *New York Times*, March 12.
Seok, Bongrae. 2015. "Moral Psychology of Shame in Early Confucian Philosophy." *Frontiers of Philosophy in China* 10, 1: 21–57.
Severo, Richard, and Lewis Milford. 1990. *The Wages of War: When America's Soldiers Came Home—From Valley Forge to Vietnam*. New York: Simon and Schuster.
Shakespeare, William. 1967. *The Merchant of Venice*. Harmondsworth: Penguin.
Shatz, Adam. 2021. "Dynamo Current, Feet, Fists, Salt." Review of Raphaelle Branche, *Papa, Qu'as-tu fait en Algérie? London Review of Books*, February 18.
Shaw, Martin. 2005. *The New Western Way of War: Risk-Transfer War and Its Crisis in Iraq*. Cambridge: Polity.
Shaxson, Nicholas. 2018. *The Finance Curse: How Global Finance Is Making Us All Poorer*. London: Vintage.
Sheehan, Neil, Hendrick Smith, E. W. Kenworthy, and Fox Butterfield. 1971. *The Pentagon Papers*. New York: Bantam Books.
Shrimsley, Robert. 2018. "Boris Johnson's Brexit Explosion Ruins Tory Business Credentials." *Financial Times*, June 25.
Shultz, Richard. 1978. "Breaking the Will of the Enemy during the Vietnam War: The Operationalization of the Cost-Benefit Model of Counterinsurgency Warfare." *Journal of Peace Research* 2, 15: 109–29.
Sierra Leone Broadcasting Service. 1997. "RUF: Apology to the Nation." June 18.
Silberblatt, Irene. 2011. "Colonial Peru and the Inquisition: Race-Thinking, Torture, and the Making of the Modern World." *Transforming Anthropology* 19, 2: 132–38.
Singer, Peter. 1983. *Hegel*. Oxford: Oxford University Press.
Skinner, Quentin. 1978. *The Foundations of Modern Political Thought*. Vol. 2: *The Age of Reformation*. Cambridge: Cambridge University Press.
Skjelsbaek, Inger. 2006. "Victim and Survivor: Narrated Social Identities of Women Who Experienced Rape during the War in Bosnia-Herzegovina." *Feminism and Psychology* 16: 373.
Slim, Hugo. 2007. *Killing Civilians: Method, Madness and Morality in War*. London: Hurst & Company.
Sluzki, Carlos. 2013a. "Humiliation, Shame, and Associated Emotions." In Carlos Guillermo Bigliani, Rodolfo Moguillansky, and Carlos Sluzki, *Shame and Humiliation: A Dialogue between Psychoanalytic and Systemic Approaches*, 57–101. London: International Psychoanalytical Association/Karnac Books.
———. 2013b. "Comment II." In Carlos Guillermo Bigliani, Rodolfo Moguillansky, and Carlos Sluzki, *Shame and Humiliation: A Dialogue between Psychoanalytic and Systemic Approaches*, 49–55. London: International Psychoanalytical Association/Karnac Books.
Smith, David. 2017. "Trump Paints Himself as the Real Victim of Charlottesville in Angry Speech." *Guardian*, August 23.
Smith, Matthew. 2017. "The 'Extremists' on Both Sides of the Brexit Debate." *YouGov*, August 1.
Snyder, Timothy. 2019. *The Road to Unfreedom: Russia, Europe, America*. London: Vintage.

———. 2021. "The American Abyss." *New York Times*, January 9.

Sparrow, Andrew, and Toby Harndon. 2005. "History Will Forgive the War on Iraq, Blair Tells Us." *Daily Telegraph*, October 1.

Speirs, Ronald. 2013. "Nietzsche's 'Tier Mit Rothen Backen': The Birth of Culture out of the Spirit of Shame." *German Life and Letters* 66, 1: 1–21.

Spencer, Jonathan. 2008. "A Nationalism without Politics? The Illiberal Consequences of Liberal Institutions in Sri Lanka." *Third World Quarterly* 29, 3: 611–29.

Stadter, Michael. 2011. "The Inner World of Shaming and Ashamed: An Object Relations Perspective and Therapeutic Approach." In *Shame in the Therapy Hour*, ed. Ronda Dearing and June Tangney, 45–68. Washington, DC: American Psychological Association.

Stangneth, Bettina. 2014. *Eichmann before Jerusalem: The Unexamined Life of a Mass Murderer*. Trans. Ruth Martin. London: Vintage.

Stearns, Justin. 2009. "New Directions in the Study of Religious Responses to the Black Death." *History Compass* 7, 5: 1363–75.

Steinberg, Blema. 1996. *Shame and Humiliation: Presidential Decision Making on Vietnam*. Montreal: McGill-Queen's University Press.

Stern, Jessica. 2003. *Terror in the Name of God: Why Religious Militants Kill*. New York: HarperCollins.

Stiglitz, Joseph, and Linda Bilmes. 2008. *The Three Trillion Dollar War: The True Cost of the Iraq Conflict*. New York: W. W. Norton.

Stone, Jon. 2016. "Nigel Farage Delivers First Post-Brexit Speech to the European Parliament—in Full." *Independent*, June 28.

———. 2021. "Compensate Oxford Students for Rhodes Statue Academic Boycott, Downing Street Says." *Independent*, June 10.

Stout, David. 2001. "A Nation Challenged: The First Lady." *New York Times*, November 18.

Strandlof, Rick. 2011. "All Uphill from Here." *Sometimes Quickly, Sometimes Slowly* (blog), October 10.

Strathern, Marilyn. 2000. "The Tyranny of Transparency." *British Educational Research Journal* 26, 3: 309–21.

Stuewig, Jeffrey, June Tangney, Stephanie Kendal, Johanna Fold, Candace Meyer, and Ronda Dearing. 2014. "Children's Proneness to Shame and Guilt Predict Risky and Illegal Behaviors in Young Adulthood." *Child Psychiatry and Human Development* 46: 217–27.

Summerfield, Derek. 1998. "The Social Experience of War and Some Issues for the Humanitarian Field." In *Rethinking the Trauma of War*, ed. Patrick Bracken and Celia Petty. London: Save the Children/Free Association Books.

The Sun. 2018. "The Tories Must Prevent Remainer MPs from Stealing Brexit from the British People." December 6.

Suskind, Ron. 2004 ."Without a Doubt." *New York Times*, October 17.

Swinford, Steven. 2022. "Teachers Should Not Pander to Trans Pupils, Says Suella Braverman." *The Times*, May 27.

Talbot, Nancy. 1996. "Women Sexually Abused as Children: The Centrality of Shame Issues and Treatment Implications." *Psychotherapy: Theory, Research, Practice, Training* 33, 1: 11–18.

Taylor, Charles. 1975. *Hegel*. Cambridge: Cambridge University Press.

Taylor, M., P. Wintour, and J. Elgot. 2015. "Calais Crisis: Cameron Pledges to Deport More People." *Guardian*, July 30.

Teusch, R. K. 2015. "Sadomasochistic Relations between Ego and Superego in Anorexic Patients." *Psychoanalytic Psychology* 32, 1: 191–212.

Theroux, Paul. 2015. *Deep South*. London: Penguin Random House.

Theweleit, Klaus. 1987. *Male Fantasies*. Cambridge: Polity.

Thomas, Keith. 1978. *Religion and the Decline of Magic*. London: Penguin.

Thomason, Krista. 2018. *Naked: The Dark Side of Shame and Moral Life*. Oxford: Oxford University Press (Oxford Scholarship Online).

Time. 2016. "Read Donald Trump's Remarks to a Veterans Group." Time.com, October 3.

Times Online. 2004. "Blair Calls for New Law to Tackle Rogue States." March 5. www.timesonline.co.uk/article/0,,1-1027157,00.html.

Tirman, John. 2011. *The Deaths of Others: The Fate of Civilians in America's Wars*. Oxford: Oxford University Press.

Todenhofer, Jurgen. 2015. "I Know ISIS Fighters. Western Bombs Falling on Raqqa Will Fill Them with Joy." *Guardian*, November 27.

Tremlett, Giles, and Paul Webster. 2002. "Battle of Algiers Returns to Haunt Le Pen as Claims of Torture Focus on Far-Right Leader." *Guardian*, June 4.

Trump, Donald. 2016a. Campaign speech. Henderson, Nevada. October 15. https://www.youtube.com/watch?v=c5Byz9Qe8Ig.

———. 2016b. Interview with Barbara Walter. YouTube, May 3. Educational Channel. https://www.youtube.com/watch?v=vV42i0UyDCo.

Trunk, Isaiah. 1981. "Note: Why Was There No Armed Resistance against the Nazis in the Lodz Ghetto?" *Jewish Social Studies* 43, 3/4: 329–34.

UN Panel of Experts. 2002. *Final Report of the Panel of Experts on the Illegal Exploitation of Natural Resources and Other Forms of Wealth in the Democratic Republic of the Congo*. UN Security Council, October 16.

US Department of Veterans Affairs. 2020. *National Veteran Suicide Prevention Annual Report*. November.

US Government/White House. 2004. *President Sworn in to Second Term, The White House*. http://www.whitehouse.gov/news/releases/2005/01/20050120-1.html.

Uvin, Peter. 1998. *Aiding Violence: The Development Enterprise in Rwanda*. West Hartford, CT: Kumarian Press.

———. 2000. "Rwanda: The Social Roots of Genocide." In *War, Hunger, and Displacement: The Origins of Humanitarian Emergencies*, ed. E. Wayne Nafziger, Frances Stewart, and Raimo Väyrynen, 1:159–86. Oxford: WIDER/Oxford University Press.

Vance, J. D. 2017. *Hillbilly Elegy: A Memoir of a Family and Culture in Crisis*. London: William Collins.

Venugopal, Rajesh. 2018. *Nationalism, Development and Ethnic Conflict in Sri Lanka*. Cambridge: Cambridge University Press.

Vergès, Francoise. 2010. "'There Are No Blacks in France': Fanonian Discourse, 'the Dark Night of Slavery' and the French Civilizing Mission Reconsidered." *Theory, Culture and Society* 27, 7–8: 91–111.

Victor, Daniel. 2015. "Donald Trump's Lousy Week (Except for the Polling)." *New York Times*, July 2.

Voigtlander, Nico, and Hans Joachim Voth. 2012. "Persecution Perpetuated: The Medieval Origins of Anti-Semitic Violence in Nazi Germany." *Quarterly Journal of Economics* 127, 3: 1339–92.

Wang, Christine. 2016. "Trump: I Will 'Totally Accept' the Results of This Election 'If I Win.'" CNBC, October 20.

Watkins, Mary. 2018. "The Social and Political Life of Shame: The U.S. 2016 Presidential Election." *Psychoanalytic Perspectives* 15, 1: 25–37.

Weber, Max. 1976. *The Protestant Ethic and the Spirit of Capitalism*. London: George Allen and Unwin (first published 1930).

Weissman, Fabrice, ed. 2004. *In the Shadow of "Just Wars": Violence, Politics and Humanitarian Action*. London: Hurst & Company, with Médecins Sans Frontières.

Weiss-Klayman, Noa, Boaz Hameiri, and Eran Halperin. 2020. "Group-Based Guilt and Shame in the Context of Intergroup Conflict." *Journal of Applied Social Psychology* 50: 213–27.

Whalen, Robert. 1984. *Bitter Wounds: German Victims of the Great War, 1914–1939*. Ithaca: Cornell University Press.

Whipple, Kelsey. 2012. "Will the Real Rick Strandlof Please Stand Up?" *Westword*, July 26.

The White House/President George W. Bush. 2001a. "Address to a Joint Session of Congress and the American People." September 20. https://georgewbush-whitehouse.archives.gov/news/releases/2001/09/20010920-8.html.

———. 2001b. "President Outlines War Effort." October 17. https://georgewbush-whitehouse.archives.gov/news/releases/2001/10/20011017-15.html.

Whitlock, Craig, Leslie Shapiro, and Armand Emamdjomeh. 2019. "The Afghanistan Papers: A Secret History of the War." *Washington Post*, December 9.

Wildt, Michael. 2005. "The Spirit of the Reich Security Main Office (RSHA)." *Totalitarian Movements and Political Religions* 6, 3: 333–49.

Williams, Matt. 2021. "'Exit Counselors' Strain to Pull Americans out of a Web of False Conspiracies." NPR, March 3.

Williams, Raymond. 2005. "Advertising: The Magic System." In Raymond Williams, *Culture and Materialism*. London: Verso (paper first published 1961).

Williamson, Vanessa, Theda Skocpol, and John Coggin. 2011. "The Tea Party and the Remaking of Republican Conservatism." *Perspectives on Politics*, March: 25–43.

Winnicott, D. W. 1990. "The Concept of the False Self." In *Home Is Where We Start From: Essays by a Psychoanalyst*, 65–70. London: Penguin (first published 1986).

Wolf, Reinhard. 2011. "Respect and Disrespect in International Politics: The Significance of Status Recognition." *International Theory* 3, 1: 105–42.

Wolfe-Robinson, Maya. 2021. "UK Government Should Focus on Covid, Not Statues, Campaigners Say." *Guardian*, January 17.

Wood, Elisabeth. 2001. "The Emotional Benefits of Insurgency in El Salvador." In *Passionate Politics: Emotions and Social Movements*, ed. Jeff Goodwin, James Jasper, and Francesca Polletta, 267–302. Chicago: University of Chicago Press.

Woodland, Alex. 2020. "Trump Deployed 'Secret Police' to Portland to Provoke Violence for Campaign Ads, Oregon Senator Says." *Guardian*, August 5.

Woodward, Bob. 2002. *Bush at War*. London: Simon and Schuster.
———. 2004 *Plan of Attack*. London: Simon and Schuster.
———. 2010. *Obama's Wars*. London: Simon and Schuster.
Wren, Christopher. 2001. "Bush Leads Memorial Service for Victims of Terror Attack." *New York Times*, September 14.
Wright, Tony. 2017. "Democracy in Britain: Retrospect and Prospect." *Political Quarterly* 88, 2: 189–97.
Wurmser, Léon. 1994. *The Mask of Shame*. Northvale, NJ: Jason Aronson (first published 1981).
———. 2000. "Magic Transformation and Tragic Transformation: Splitting of Ego and Superego in Severely Traumatized Patients." *Clinical Social Work Journal* 28, 4: 385–402.
———. 2015. "Primary Shame, Mortal Wound and Tragic Circularity: Some New Reflections on Shame and Shame Conflicts." *International Journal of Psychoanalysis* 96: 1615–34.
Wuthnow, Robert. 2018. *The Left Behind: Decline and Rage in Rural America*. Princeton: Princeton University Press.
Wyman, David. 1984. *The Abandonment of the Jews: America and the Holocaust, 1941–1945*. New York: Pantheon.
Yancy, George, and Noam Chomsky. 2015. "Noam Chomsky on the Roots of American Racism." *New York Times*, March 18.
Yaqoob, Salma. 2008. "Muslim Women and War on Terror." *Feminist Review* 88: 150–61.
Young, Allan. 1995. *The Harmony of Illusions: Inventing Post-Traumatic Stress Disorder*. Princeton: Princeton University Press.
Younge, Gary. 2004. "'God Has a Plan: Bush Will Hold Back the Evil.'" *Guardian*, October 9.
YouTube. 2020 "'We Will Never Kneel to Our National Anthem or Our Great American Flag': Trump Says to NFL." June 21.
Zur, Judith. 1998. *Violent Memories: Mayan War Widows in Guatemala*. Boulder, CO: Westview Press.

INDEX

Page numbers in *italics* refer to figures.

Abd al-Wahhab, Muhammad ibn, Islamist reformer, 42
Abu Ghraib: "hicks with sticks" and, 15; stories and images from, 255–56
Access Hollywood (television show), 111–12
ActionAid, 88
Adichie, Chimamanda Ngozi, on shaming and in-group conformity, 1–2
advertising: cigarettes, 187–88; consumerism, 180–81
Afghanistan: military action against Taliban, 306n64; Taliban's shame culture, 250–51; U.S.-led attacks on, 252
African Rights, 214
age, person being shamed, 58–59
Agnew, Spiro, Vietnam War and, 167
Ahmed, Nafeez, on security crises, 210
Ahmed, Sara: on Blair's regret about slavery, 172–73; on feeling shame, 56
Ahsan, Sanah, on mental health problems, 265
Akerlof, George, on emotional issues, 140
Alcoholics Anonymous, 275
Alexander, Michelle: collective self-image, 198; mass incarceration in U.S., 166, 265; on segregation laws, 198
Algeria: France's loss of, 169; resettlement camps in, 176
"All Eyes on Me," Tupac, 87
al Qaeda, 42; defeat in Iraq, 259; terrorism, 253, 256

Alston, Philip: on poverty and human rights, 195–96; stereotypes of poor and race, 197–98; on welfare recipients, 197
American Dream, 129, 131–32, 138, 189, 206
American society: cost of war, 20; sacrifice of soldiers, 21–22
America's soldiers and veterans, shame and honor, 20
Amnesty International, 7, 177
Anderson, Elijah: on code of the street, 71; on competition for respect, 190; on prison and toughness, 71–72
anger: expression of, 287n45; as reaction to shame, 56
Antidote.com, 275
anti-Semitism, France, 169
anti-vaxxers, shaming of, 185
anxiety, 31
apology, shame signals, 47
Applebaum, Anne, on Soviet labor camps, 225
Apprentice, The (television show), 114, 130
Aquinas, Thomas, problem of shameless individuals, 45
Arendt, Hannah: on absolute power, 121–22; on action as propaganda, 34, 152, 212, 220, 233, 257–58; on alternative "role model," 274; on choosing a lesser evil, 110; on credibility of lies, 146; crime and punishment, 53–54; on Eichmann, 92, 95, 100, 102–4, 107–10, 281; on guilt and actions, 34;

333

Arendt, Hannah (*continued*)
on ideological belief, 240; interest in, 283; on law and laws, 261; on machines replacing all, 205; on official truth departing from reality, 229; on personal responsibility, 280; on political expressionism, 157; on respectable society, 59; on security experts during Vietnam War, 247; on sense of righteousness, 278–79; on totalitarian fantasies, 126; on totalitarian leader, 121; on U.S. policy on Vietnam, 243–45; on Vietnam War, 222

Argentina: Eichmann in, 94, 97, 99–100, 104; Eichmann on incompleteness of Holocaust, 102–3

Aristotle: on buy-in, 56; on emotion of shame, 36

Armstrong, John, on commercial images, 184

Armstrong, Sean, on official party line, 225

Art as Therapy (Botton and Armstrong), 184

Art of the Deal, The (Trump and Schwarz), 114

Assad, Bashar al-, Syria, 211–12

Atlantic, The (magazine), 115

Austerity Bites (O'Hara), 155

badge of honor, 8

Bageant, Joe: *Deer Hunting with Jesus*, 129; on his hometown, 140; on invisibility, 133, 156

Ball, Stephen, on education performance, 203

Banks, Aaron, Leave campaign, 145

Barczewinski, Stephanie, on English heroism, 151

Bartov, Omer: on enemy of self, 118; on Nazi atrocities, 105

Bauman, Zygmunt: on civilization and violence, 51; on tourists and vagabonds, 177

Bay of Pigs fiasco (1961), 246

Becker, Jasper, shaming and requisitioning, 226–27

Beckett, Andy, on culture wars, 173

Benedict, Ruth, on Japanese soldiers, 27

Benscoter, Diane, on falling into grip of conspiracy theory, 275–76

Betjeman, John, gloomy invitation of, 151

Betrayal, The (Corson), 244

Between Past and Future (Arendt), 280

Biden, Joe, victory of, 126

bin Laden, Osama, on 9/11 attacks, 256

bipolar disorder, diagnosis of, 18

Black Death, 38, 41

Black Lives Matter, 142, 166, 198, 207

Black Skin, White Masks (Fanon), 34

Blair, Tony: on conflicts, 173; on invasion of Iraq, 251, 258; on moderate middle ground in politics, 156–57; on nation's history, 174–75; on regrets about slavery, 172

Blix, Hans, on U.S. position, 261

Blood, J. J., murder by, 76

blood diamonds, 81

blood offering, veterans', 21–22

Blue Lives Matter, 166

Blumenthal, Sidney, on terrorism and ratings, 253

Bockarie, Sam, hunger for respect, 87

Born Naked Squad, Sierra Leone, 85

Boston Review (newspaper), 166

Botton, Alain de, on commercial images, 184

Bourgois, Philippe, on inner city Puerto Rican men, 71

Bradshaw, John: book on shame, 122; on feelings of shame, 35; on negative effects of shame, 31

Braithwaite, John, on reintegrative shaming, 72, 88

Braverman, Suella, on asylum seekers, 57

Brennan, Geoffrey, on economy of esteem, 189–90, 196, 199

Brexit, 5, 11; Calais as symbol for Brexiteers, 152; Cameron on, 149; consensus politics, 157; costs of, 159; as double game, 153; Farage on, 144; Johnson on, 144–45; Leave campaign, 145, 154, 158; Leavers, 149, 152, 159, 162; May on, 144, 148, 162;

Remain campaign, 145; Remainers, 161–62; residents views on, 154; shame and shamelessness, 152–53; shame of nonexistence, 153–59; shaming after vote, 159–62; shaming and scapegoating, 272; theater of shamelessness, 11, 147; Trump on, 119; Truss on, 158, 161
British Ceramic Confederation, 158
British National Party (BNP), 154, 155
Brown, Brené: defining shame, 30; self-flagellation, 30; on shame and responsibility, 282; on being trapped in shame, 30–31; understanding shame, 49
Brown, Wendy, fears around emasculated state, 127
Browning, Christopher, on Nazi massacres, 101
Buddhism, warrior heritage, 27
Bullingdon Club, 148
Bullough, Oliver, Leave campaign, 161
Burke, Kenneth, on coexistence of good markets and bad bankers, 235
Burn House Unit, Sierra Leone, 85
Bush, Billy, *Access Hollywood* tape, 112
Bush, George H. W., political campaign of, 166
Bush, George W.: on 9/11 attacks, 285n1; Blair and, 259–60; Powell and, 258; Rove and, 259; war on terror and, 253, 259
Bush, Laura, on Taliban's shame culture, 250

Caflisch, Jane, on white fragility, 165
Cairns, Douglas, on economy of esteem, 190
Calais: jungle camp at, 170–71; migrants/refugees in, 152
Cambodia, 208; communism in, 227–28; Hinton on, 27; U.S. policy on, 243
Cameron, David: on Brexit, 149; on conflicts, 173; on economic migrants, 177; resignation of, 148, 149
Cameron, Norman, on paranoia, 37, 38
Canetti, Elias, on inflation in Austria, 240

Capital in the Twenty-First Century (Piketty), 195
Carswell, Douglas, UK's Independence Party, 150
Castro, Fidel, Cuban Missile Crisis and, 246
Catholic Church, system of penances within, 182
Catholicism, Protestantism and, 182
Catholic Relief Services, 80
celebrities, idolization of, 184–85
Center for Rural Strategies, 141
Cesarani, David, study of Eichmann, 93, 95, 97–99
Chase, Elaine, on shame and poverty, 183, 198–99
Chavs (Jones), 153
Cheney, Dick, on September 2001 attacks, 254
China, 208; communism in, 225–27
China virus, Trump and, 127
Chinese Communist Party, 225
Chosen People (Longley), 41, 202
Christianity: guilt culture of, 28; Islam and, 41; Nietzsche's view of, 182, 189; Original Sin, 40; Roman Empire, 40; state of punishment and, 41
Chrysanthemum and the Sword, The (Benedict), 27
Churchill, Winston, Bengal famine (1943), 176
churning, soldier deployment, 20
cigarettes, advertising, 187–88
civilization, violence and, 51
Civilizing Process, The (Elias), 51
civil war(s), 7, 23, 197; Sierra Leone, 3, 10, 232; Sudan, 219–24
Clarke, Simon, on American foreign policy, 245–46
Clinton, Bill: Bush ridiculing, 254; nomination for 1992 presidency, 196; Trump on, 111
Clinton, Hillary: "basket of deplorables" comment, 8, 142, 159–60; on racism of police, 128; Trump on, 111, 113, 115

Coggin, John, Tea Party activists, 133
Cohen, Dov: on Bush administration, 258; on fighting over honor and shame, 252; North and South experiment, 29; on shame cultures, 26; social functions of shame, 48
Cohen, Stanley, on just world thinking, 33
Cohn, Carol: on deterrence theory, 247; on Cold War nuclear standoff, 246–48
Cold War, 12, 178, 220, 232; Cohn's work on, 246–48; Communists, 91; shame and, 242–50
colonialism: France, 168–72; reverse colonization, 175; shame and, 175–76; shame and shamelessness, 163; United Kingdom (UK), 172–75; United States, 163–68
Colston, Edward, statue of, 174
communism: Cambodia, 227–28; China, 225–27; disasters under, 208, 224–28; fall of, 178; Guatemala, 217–18; Soviet Union, 224–25
compulsions, 31
condemnation fueling abuses, 8; shaming and, 7–9
Conflict and Collusion in Sierra Leone (Keen), 74
conflict diamonds, Democratic Republic of the Congo, 231
conflict prevention, 47
Conservative party, 153; Johnson of, 147; May resigning, 150
conspiracy theory, addressing, 275–76
consumerism, 6, 180–88; idolization of celebrities, 184–85; shame and performance, 202–5; shame and the rich, 199–202; shame for poverty, 195–99; shame for underdevelopment, 191–95; solutions, 189; status symbols, 183
consumption, capitalism and, 183
Cooper, Anderson, interview with veteran, 17
Corrigan, Phil, on Brexit, 158
Corson, William on shifting policy goals, 244; on Vietnamese education system, 193

counter-pride movement, 46
Covid: shaming anti-vaxxers, 185; Trump and, 127; vaccine, 186; workers and heroes in, 205
Cox, Jo, murder of, 161, 162
criminals: guilt and punishment, 68–69; public fears of, 72; reintegrative shaming and, 72; shame as driving violence of criminals, 73; violent, in U.S. prisons, 65–67
criminal violence, Gilligan on extreme, 66–67
Crowds and Power (Canetti), 240
Cuban Missile Crisis, 246
culture wars, UK's, 173
Cut Hands Commando, Sierra Leone, 85
Cyrus, Miley, twerking of, 186

Daily Express (newspaper), 160, 162, 174
Daily Mail (UK newspaper), 120, 174
Daley, Janet, on Britain, 156
Danner, Mark, on Wall Street collapse (2008), 202
d'Antonio, Michael, on Trump, 113–14
Darwin, Charles, shame observation in dog, 288n12
Das Schwarze Korps (Heydrich), 101
Davis, Dee, on intonation of Washington, 141
Dearing, Ronda, on experience of shame, 25–26
demeaning, quality of being, 68
Democratic Party, 140; Clinton's 1992 nomination, 196
Democratic Republic of the Congo (DRC): conflict diamonds in, 231; Rwandan genocide and, 215–16
Deng, Frances, on militia groups in Sudan, 220
Deonna, Julien: anger as reaction to shame, 56; on bad press of shame, 50; on shame and humiliation, 68; on shame-prone individuals, 67

Depeche Mode, 281
depression, 17, 31
Desarthe, Agnès, on France and colonialism, 168–69
Devon, Natasha, on mental health of schoolchildren, 265
de Waal, Alex: on Britain creating famine, 175; shaming of famine, 228
diamond trading, 81
Dikötter, Frank, on shaming of villagers, 226
disenchantment, process of, 270
disgust, Mitton on shame and, 83–84
Dolan, Chris, on blaming of aid recipients, 223
DRC. *See* Democratic Republic of the Congo (DRC)
Dreyfus affair, 168–69
Dreyfus, Alfred, 168
Drowned and the Saved, The (Levi), 35
drug lord, 8
Doctor Zhivago (Pasternak), 224
Duffell, Nick, private school boarder, 32
Duffield, Mark, on end-user of aid, 223
"Duncan, Rick" (Captain): CNN interview of, 17; diagnoses of, 18; Iraq Veterans Against the War (IVAW), 14, 16–19, 23; PTSD (post-traumatic stress disorder), 14, 17–18; real name "Strandlof," 16–17; re-invention as Rick Gold, 18–19; shame and isolation, 24; shame dynamics, 9; war veterans and, 36
Durvasula, Ramani, on narcissists, 122
Dylan, Bob, on poverty, 198

eating disorders, 31
ECOMOG (West African military force), 74
economy: perverse distributions of shame, 188; shame and, 11. *See also* consumerism
Economy of Esteem, The (Brennan and Pettit), 189
education, performance and, 203
ego ideal: Freud, 48, 205; Freud's attitude, 36

Eichmann, Adolf, 73; Arendt on, 92, 95, 103–4, 107–10; in Argentina, 94, 97, 99–100; Cesarani on, 93, 95, 97–99; in Chelmno, 97; drawing the line, 107–8, 110; on emigration of Jews, 95–96; on incompleteness of Holocaust, 102–3; line of defense by, 107; as mass murder facilitator, 99; revulsion at atrocities, 96–99; role in Nazi Holocaust, 10–11; self-aggrandizement of, 93; setting aside emotions, 243; shamelessness of, 93–95, 112; Stangneth on, 93–94, 99; trial in Jerusalem, 96
Eichmann before Jerusalem (Stangneth), 93
Eichmann in Jerusalem (Arendt), 92
Elias, Norbert, on bourgeois notions of shame, 51
emigration of Jews, Eichmann on, 95–96
emotion, as object of inquiry, 274
End of Eddy, The (Louis), 172
End of the Myth, The (Grandin), 165
England footballers, reaction to missed penalties, 281
esteem, shame and, 188–91
Eurocrats, 145, 160, 173
Europhobia, 153
"Every Day Is Like Sunday," song (Morrissey), 151
Eze, Geoff, on Brexit, 158

Falwell, Jerry, Jr., on Trump, 139
Falwell, Jerry, Sr., on 9/11 as God's retribution, 254
family honor, honor killings and, 27
famine, 3; Cambodia, 227; China (1958–62), 225–27; prevention, 224; shame and, 228–29; Sudan, 208, 219–24; Ukrainian, 224
Fanon, Frantz: on colonialism, 165; on inferiority complex of colonized people, 34; on narcissism, 170; on shame around lack of recognition, 189
Farage, Nigel, on Brexit, 144
Far Enemy, The (Gerges), 256

fellow believers, shame-free community of, 83
Final Solution, Eichmann on, 103
Fischer, Clara, on women/girls in Magdalen laundries, 28
Flaherty, Mike, on veteran's avoidance of police, 17
Flanagan, Owen: positive account of shame, 49–50; on shame, 266–67; shame and pride, 266; on type of shaming, 53, 55
Floyd, George, death of, 166
Fondation Jean Jaurès, 171
Ford, Christine Blasey, Kavanaugh and, 125
Fox News, 23
fragiles, recruitment in prison, 73
France: colonialism, 168–72; national values of, 176; Opération Turquoise intervention, 215; resettlement camps in Algeria, 176; on yellow vest, 171
Franco-Prussian War, 168, 215
Frank, Thomas: on market populism in United States, 201; on outrage against bankers, 200–201; on right-wing policies, 139; on support of poorer people for Republicans, 140, 145
Fraser, Nancy, on 'us' versus 'them', 272
free market ideology, 201
French Revolution, 168
Freud, Anna: on defense mechanisms, 60; on reaction formation, 60; Wurmser drawing on, 102
Freud, Sigmund: on cigar as cigar, 146; ego ideal, 36, 48, 205; fantasies of abuse, 285n5; flights from reality, 37; on paranoia, 169; on primitives, 38; on projection, 38–39; scientific age, 273; stages of human history, 38; superego, 36; Wurmser drawing on, 102
Fukuyama, Francis, on liberal democracy, 157
Future of England survey, 162

Gardner, Robert, on Trump, 135
Gekko, Gordon, on greed, 202
gender, choosing, 289n44
genocides, 23; in Guatemala, 208, 216–18; in Rwanda, 208, 213–16, 273, 304n5
Gerges, Fawaz, on forms of terrorism, 256
Germany, 271; malnutrition, 305n34; moral degeneracy of, 235; Nazi project of internal "cleansing," 238. *See also* Nazism
Gerodimos, Roman: residual inferiority complex, 178; on restoring pride and honor, 28
Gianforte, Greg, Trump on, 125
Gilbert, Paul, shame driving emotions, 39
Gilligan, James: on cause of violent behavior, 65; evidence of shame around weakness, 63; on extreme criminal violence, 66–67; on loss of face, 66; on masculinity, 70–71; on mortification, 66; on shame along gendered lines, 146; on shame and violence, 69–70, 229; on violent crime, 213–14; on violent criminals in U.S. prisons, 10, 266
Gilroy, Paul, on war on terror, 175
Girard, René, on violence and victim, 69
Global North, 264, 273
Global South, 273
global warming, shadow of shame, 187
Gold, Rick, re-invention of Duncan, 18–19
Goldberg, Jeffrey, on Trump, 115
good behavior, 62
Good Housekeeping (journal), 181
Google Books, 4
Gore, Al, Bush and, 253
Grandin, Greg, on policing the U.S. southern border, 165
Great Depression, 195
Great Leap Forward, China's, 225, 227
Greenberg, Leslie, therapeutic interventions, 32
Grotius, Hugo, Arendt quoting, 121
Guardian (newspaper), 125, 154, 156, 169, 204
Guatemala, 3; genocide in, 208, 216–18
Guilluy, Christophe, on fear of replacement within Paris, 171

guilt: Christianity and culture of, 28; punishment and, 68–69; shame and, 39–40; shame vs., 25, 28
Gulag (Applebaum), 225

Hannan, Dan, on Brexit, 150
Harker, Lee Anne, on human interaction, 47
Harrell-Bond, Barbara, on blaming of aid recipients, 223
Harris, John, on resident perception on Brexit, 154
Haslett, Adam, on weaponizing shame, 112
Healing the Shame That Binds You (Bradshaw), 31
Heroic Failure (O'Toole), 145, 149
Heydrich, Reinhard: danger of being "too humane," 101; deathbed of, 108; orders to Eichmann, 96
Hilberg, Raul, on Jewish ghettos under Nazism, 109–10
Himmler, Heinrich: on children in mass slaughter, 105; Eichmann admiring words of, 100; speech of, 100–101
Hinduism, 42–43
Hindutva, fundamentalist movement, 42–43
Hinton, Alex: on politeness-turning-suddenly-to-violence in Cambodia, 48; on revenge in Cambodia, 27
Hitler, Adolf: January 1939 pronouncement on, 122; on Jewish problem, 122; personal shame of, 239; shame and rage, 236–37; speech to Reichstag (1939), 241–42
Hochschild, Arlie Russell: on American Dream, 130–32, 138; Louisiana study, 130, 133, 136; "makers" and "takers," 136
Hofstadter, Richard: on Philippines invasion, 259; on victories at America's expanding frontier, 166
Hoggett, Paul: on American foreign policy, 245–46; on moment of shame, 29–30; on performance, 202–5
Holocaust, 94, 108; Eichmann on incompleteness of, 102–3; Nazi atrocities, 105

Honneth, Axel: on mutual recognition, 75; on shame around lack of recognition, 189
honor killings, family honor and, 27
Höss, Rudolf, on Eichmann, 105
Housewives of Orange County, The (television show), 185
Huffman, Scott, on Trump supporters, 129–30
Hughes, Sali, on trolls and extreme distress, 185
humanitarian rescue mission, Sri Lanka, 210
human rights, self-righteousness and, 7–8
Human Rights Watch, 7, 83, 194, 229
human smuggler, 8
humiliation, 50; in definition of shame, 68; problem of, 69; trash TV, 59
Hungry Ghosts (Becker), 226
Hunt, David, on promotions for commanders, 250
Hussein, Saddam: soldiers and officials of, 272; weapons of mass destruction, 252, 261
hysteria, 239; study of, 36
Hysterical Men (Lerner), 238–39

Icahn, Carl, on Trump, 119
Ignatieff, Michael, on support for war, 21
IISS. *See* International Institute for Strategic Studies (IISS)
IMF (International Monetary Fund), 214
immigration, to United States from Latin America, 177–78
impunity, shamelessness and, 276–80
In Defense of Shame (Deonna, Rodogno and Teroni), 68
Independence Day, day of Brexit vote, 144
Industrial Revolution, 156
inferiority complex, Fanon on, 34
Ingle, David, on society's dependence on death of members, 21–22
In Search of Respect (Bourgois), 71
International Committee of the Red Cross, 231

international community, hostility of, 8
International Institute for Strategic Studies (IISS), 248–49
In the Shadow of "Just Wars" (MSF), 278
introspection, listening and, 280–83
inverted morality, Sierra Leone, 84–85
Iraq, 3; America's withdrawal from, 20; escalation of violence, 21; shamelessness of attack on, 260–61; U.S.-led alliance, 253; U.S.-led attacks on, 252, 255–56
Iraq Veterans Against the War, 13; "Captain Rick Duncan" and, 13–14, 16–19, 23
Ireland, Magdalen laundries, 28
Islam: Christianity and, 41; terrorism, 73; Wahhabist version of, 42
Islamophobia, war on terror and, 168
Israeli Defence Forces, 18
Is Shame Necessary? (Jacquet), 57
IVAW. See Iraq Veterans Against the War (IVAW)
Iwakabe, Shigeru, therapeutic interventions, 32

Jackson, Michael, tape of songs, 219
Jackson Lears, T. J., on advertising, 181
Jacobs, Ben, Gianforte's assault on, 125
Jacquet, Jennifer, on case of Antanas Mockus, 57–58
January 2021 Capitol invasion, 113, 126, 157, 241
Jaspars, Susanne, work on Darfur, 222–23
Jefferson, Thomas, freedom for all nations, 21
Jenrick, Robert on mobs erasing nation's history, 174
Jewish Councils, Nazism, 109
Jewish "problem," 109, 122
Johnson, Boris: on antisocial behavior, 282; on Assad as lesser evil, 212; on Brexit, 144–45; culture wars and, 173; on European markets and Brexit, 149; honesty as antidote to excessive political correctness, 147–48; on Leavers, 149; obsession matched in popular press, 146; on reaction to missed penalties of England footballers, 281; shame and shamelessness, 11
Jones, Martin, on failure on Brexit, 160
Jones, Owen: demonization of the working class, 198; working-class culture, 155–56; on working-class identity, 153–54
Jones, Robert, on "Make America Great Again" promise, 139
Jung, Carl, on "shadow side," 134
jungle camp, Calais, 152, 170–71
justice, 77, 79

Kamara, Charles, on lifestyle, 192
Kavanaugh, Brett, Blasey Ford's accusation against, 125
Keltner, Dacher, on human interaction, 47
Kennedy, John F., Cuban Missile Crisis, 246
Khan, Humayun, Trump and parents of, 116
Khan, Khizr, criticism of Trump, 116
Khmer Rouge, 27
Killing Eve (television series), 134
Kill Man No Blood, Sierra Leone, 85
Kimmel, Michael, on humiliation and shame, 73
Klein, Melanie, on superego, 39
Koffler, Keith, cultural destruction, 186
Kohut, Heinz, on power of gifted leader, 126
Kony, Joseph, campaign of, 231
Korean War, 215
Kormor, Gaskin, on education and lifestyle, 192
Kovel, Joel, on colonialism, 165
Kuper, Simon, on Johnson's shamelessness, 150–51

Labour Party, 160; Blair, 156–57
Lal, Vinay, analysis of Hindutva, 42–43
Lansky, Melvin, on Shakespeare's Richard III, 62–63
lapsing: Israelites, into idolatry, 41; religious, 43

INDEX   341

Lasch, Christopher: on alienation as commodity, 188; on narcissism, 151; on narcissistic personality, 143
Latin America, immigration to United States from, 177–78
Layton, Lynne, on shaming, 204
leaders, shamelessness of, 4
Le Monde (newspaper), 169
Le Pen, Jean-Marie, on loss of Algeria, 169
Le Pen, Marine: calling for "de-Islamization" of France, 172; National Front, 172
Lerner, Paul, on tainting of medical community in Germany, 238–39
Levi, Primo, *Sonderkommando*, 35
Levy, Pema, on Trump's promise, 139
Lewis, Helen, on shame in therapy, 39
Lindisfarne, Nancy, on Spanish women and men, 28
line counting, 14
listening, introspection and, 280–83
Locke, Jill: on Trump, 148; on Trump supporters, 134
London School of Economics (LSE), 203
London University, 203
Longley, Clifford: analysis of "Chosen People," 254; on Protestants' self-image, 41; Tea Party ideology, 202
Lord of the Flies style, 90
Los Angeles Times (newspaper), 186
Louis, Édouard, on factories of northern French village, 172
Lu, Catherine, on construction of shame, 232
Luckenbill, David, on shame in violent crime, 70
Lytton, Rick, Vietnam veteran on Trump, 124

McAuley, James, on yellow vest, 171
McCain, John, Trump on, 115, 134
McConnell, Mitch, Trump and, 132
Mckenzie, Lisa, on Brexit, 154, 156

McKinley, William, Philippines and, 258
MacLeod, Gordon, on failure on Brexit, 160
Macron, Emmanuel: on Algerian independence, 168; Station F inauguration, 171
mafia tactic, 6
Magdalen College, 174
Magdalen laundries, Ireland, 28
magical solutions, shame, 268–71
magical thinkers, rational actors and, 273–74
Make America Great Again, promise, 138–39
Making of Them, The (BBC documentary), 32
Malesevic, Sinisa, on human inhibitions around violence, 51
Malthus, Thomas, on disasters and population, 41
Mamdani, Mahmood, Rwandan genocide, 215
Mandelson, Peter, on Brexiteers, 160
Manigault, Omarosa, Trump and, 114
Mao Zedong, Great Leap Forward, 225, 227
market populism, Frank on, 201
Markle, Meghan, press campaign against, 185
Marvin, Carolyn, on society's dependence on death of members, 21–22
Maschmann, Melita, memoir of, 241
masculine dignity, 71
masculinity, conception of, 70
Mask of Shame, The (Wurmser), 135
mass violence: Guatemalan genocide, 216–18; Rwandan genocide, 213–16; shame and, 11–12; shamelessness and useful enemies, 208–13; war and famine in Sudan, 219–24. *See also* violence
May, Theresa: on Brexit, 144, 148, 162; resignation of, 150
Médecins Sans Frontières (MSF), 230, 278
media, shame and shaming, 23
Mein Kampf (Hitler), 234, 236–37
Meloni, Giorgia, on being ashamed of one's identity, 45
Mencius, on shamefulness, 45

Mendible, Myra: on national decline, 47; on shaming, 185–86, 206–7
mental illness: PTSD (post-traumatic stress disorder), 18; signs of, 18
Merchant of Venice, The (Shakespeare), 56–57, 84
Metzl, Jonathan, on white anxiety, 166
Mexican American War (1846–48), 165
Mexican immigrants, Trump on, 117
military coup, Sierra Leone, 85
Mitton, Kieran, on shame and disgust in Sierra Leone, 83–84
Mockus, Antanas, Jacquet on case of, 57–58
modernity, lifestyle and, 192
Modernity and the Holocaust (Bauman), 51
Momoh, Joseph, loyalty to, 81
Moneyland (Bullough), 161
Moonies, Benscoter on, 275–76
Moore, Michael, as comedic voice, 275
morality, collective inversion of, 102
moral pain of veterans, as pathology, 20
moral shame, concept of, 52
Morrison, Andrew, on narcissism and shame, 112
Morrissey's song "Every Day Is Like Sunday," 151
mortification, 66
Mother Jones (newspaper), 130
Mouffe, Chantal: on consensus politics, 157; on moral disease, 271
Müller, Heinrich, Eichmann on, 97
Muslim Brotherhood, 42
Muslim terrorists, Trump and, 127
Muslim war hero, Trump and, 116
MX missile, 247

Naked (Thomason), 36
narcissism, 31; shame and, 112
Nation, The (magazine), 112
National Football League, 142
National Front, Le Pen as head, 172
National Public Radio, 275
National Rally party, 170

National Security Council, 247
Native Americans, treatment of, 164
NATO (North Atlantic Treaty Organization), 249
Nazism, 233, 262; Churchill standing up to, Eichmann and, 10–11; Germany, 232; hierarchy, 96; Holocaust, 10–11, 51, 234; ideology, 101, 234; internal "cleansing" of Germany, 238; Jewish Councils, 109; *Mein Kampf* (Hitler), 234, 236–37; propaganda use, 234; rise of, and shame, 233–42; victims of, 35
New Deal, 195
New Jim Crow, The (Alexander), 166
New Yorker, The (magazine), 23
New York Review of Books, The (Danner), 202
New York Times The (newspaper), 21, 116
Nietzsche, Friedrich: curative power of war, 238; on shamelessness, 59–60; view of Christianity, 182, 189
Nixon, Richard: political campaign of, 166; Vietnam and, 167, 243
Noah, Trevor, using humor, 275

Obama, Barack: global apology for United States, 142; national debt under, 128; Trump accusation of wiretapping, 120; Trump and, 114; Trump on, 111; Trump on birth certificate of, 113
O'Brien, Tim, Hollywood obsession with deranged veterans, 20
obsessions, 31
Occupy Denver, 19
Occupy Wall Street, 19
O'Hara, Mary, on austerity of UK, 155
Old Testament, Israelites, 41
omnipotence, fantasy of, 270–71
O'Neil, Cathy, on shaming anti-vaxxers, 185
On the Political (Mouffe), 157
Opération Turquoise, France's, 215
opportunity, talking about shame as, 264
Oriel College, 174
Original Sin, Adam and Eve, 40

Origins of Totalitarianism, The (Arendt), 34, 121, 149, 240
Orwell, George, on *The Charge of the Light Brigade*, 151
O'Toole, Fintan: on Brexit campaign, 158–59; on imaginary oppression, 145; occupying England's own streets, 175; on self-harm, 151–52; on upper-class arrogance, 149
Oxford English Dictionary, 44, 55, 68, 83
Oxford Myth (Kuper), 150
Oxford Union, culture in, 150
Oxford University, 148

Packer, George, on violent jihadism, 73
Palin, Sarah: in campaigning for Trump, 127; on weakness of foreign policy, 254
Paranoid Style in American Politics, The (Hofstadter), 166
Park, Christine, on self-blame of children who have been abused, 32
passing the shame, tactic of, 282
Pasternak, Boris, on collectivization, 224
Patel, Priti: on political theatrics, 282; on reaction to missed penalties of England footballers, 281
Pearl Harbor, Japanese Americans and, 167
Perry, Grayson, on Wisconsin, 141
personality disorder, war trauma relabeled as, 20
Pettit, Philip, on economy of esteem, 189–90, 196, 199
Philippines: McKinley and, 258; Manifest Destiny in invasion, 259
Phishing for Phools (Akerlof and Shiller), 140
Piketty, Thomas: on risk-taking, 200; on world capital, 195
Pitt-Rivers, Julian, on Spanish women, 28
Plato, warning on shamelessness, 44, 63
political correctness, Johnson and, 147–48
political economy, of shame, 191
Political Paranoia (Robins and Post), 227–28
political processes, role of shame in, 4–5

political psychology, 5
Pol Pot, 227–28
Porter, James, on Trump supporters, 130
Post, Jerrold, Pol Pot's Cambodia, 227–28
Post-humanitarianism (Duffield), 223
post-traumatic stress disorder (PTSD), 14, 17, 18, 31
poverty: American Dream and, 189; shame and poor in richer countries, 195–99; stereotypes of poor and race, 197–98
Powell, Colin, on Bush's commitment to war, 258
Pozner, Vladimir, on Russia losing aura of greatness, 249
Pratt, John, on public fearing criminals and prisoners, 72
prediction, Trump on, 119
prison of shame, escape from, 263–64
projection, Freud's idea of, 38–39
projective identification, 38
Protestantism, 41, 42, 183; Catholicism and, 182
Protocols of the Learned Elders of Zion, 237
PTSD. *See* post-traumatic stress disorder (PTSD)
punishment, shame and, 68–69
Purple Heart, 16
Putin, Vladimir: shame and, 179; Ukraine invasion, 249

QAnon, 186, 275–76
Quarterly Journal of Economics (journal), 195
Qutb, Sayyid, Muslim Brotherhood, 42

Rajapaksa, Gotobaya, Sri Lanka, 211
Rajapaksa, Mahinda: abuse of Tamil civilians, 230; Sri Lanka, 210–11
Rapley, John, on meritocratic society, 156
rational actors: magical thinkers and, 273–74; model, 4–5
Reagan, Ronald: campaign (1980) for presidency, 254; election of, 132; on free market, 202; inequality under, 196

reality TV, 6c
Rebels in a Rotten State (Mitton), 84
Rees-Mogg, Jacob: on Brexit, 150; costs of Brexit, 159
Reformation, 182, 184, 187
Reich, Robert: on book tour in America's heartlands, 138; on use of lobbying, 202
Reich Security Main Office, 96, 98
reintegrative shaming, Braithwaite on, 72, 88
religion, shame, violence and, 40–43
Reppenhagen, Garett: idea of a just war, 22; on process of brutalization, 22
Republican Party, 126, 139
re-shaming, 11
respect: shame and, 56–58; violence and, 71
Retzinger, Suzanne, on anger and shame, 36, 267
revenge: fantasy of planning, 39; fear of replacement and, 175
reverse colonization, 175
Revolutionary United Front (RUF) rebels, Sierra Leone, 81–82, 84
Rhodes, Cecil, statues of, 174
right-wing populism, solutions of, 189
risk-takers, shame and, 200
Robins, Robert, Pol Pot's Cambodia, 227–28
Rodogno, Raffaele, on shame and humiliation, 68
Roman Empire, Christianity, 40
Roosevelt, Theodore, on benefits of expansion, 176
Rove, Karl, on war on terrorism, 259
Russian Revolution (1917), 234
Ruthven, Malise, Islam and Protestantism, 42
Rwanda, 271; Democratic Republic of the Congo (DRC) and, 215–16; genocide in, 208, 213–16, 273, 304n5; Uvin's study of, 193–94
Rwandan Patriotic Front rebels, 215
Ryan, Kevin, on human inhibitions around violence, 51

sacrifice, veterans', 21–22
Said, Edward, on America and the Middle East, 167
Saltzman, Rebecca, on PTSD among veterans, 19
Sandel, Michael, on shamelessness of rich, 199
Sanders, Bernie: on scandal of poverty-among-riches, 207; support for, 138
Sassen, Willem, 104; Eichmann and, 105–6; Nazi sympathies of, 94
Scheff, Thomas, on anger and shame, 36
schizophrenia, 19; diagnosis of, 18
Schwarz, Tony, Trump and, 114
Secret Service, 115
Segal, Hanna, symbolic language, 67
self-flagellation, 30
self-injury, 31
self-loathing, 49
self-reform, shame prompting, 50
self-righteousness, human rights and, 7–8
self-worth, recipient of shame, 58
Seok, Bongrae, Confucian tradition of shame, 45
Serbia, 3, 230
Shakespeare, William: shameless character Richard III, 62–63; shaming in *The Merchant of Venice*, 56–57, 84
shame: consumerism, 180–88; damage of, 25; distribution of, 188–94; double game, 6; dysfunctional, 3; escape from, 45, 263–64, 270; esteem and, 188–91; flight from, 35–40; good and bad, 52–54; guilt and, 39–40; guilt vs., 25; instrumentalized, 3; isolation and, 24; magical solutions for, 268–71; manipulation of, 3; moral, 52–53; of nonexistence, 153–59; performance and, 202–5; perverse distributions of, 6–7, 33–35, 267–68; political economy of, 191; poor in richer countries, 195–99; positive aspects of, 46–52; religion, violence and, 40–43; rise of Nazism and, 233–42; shamelessness and, 64;

shamelessness and underlying, 59–63; shaming and, 54–59, 63; trapped in, 29–33; trends in use of word, 2; type of, 58; underdevelopment and, 191–95; Vietnam, Cold War and, 242–50; war on terror, 250–62

Shame and Guilt in Neurosis (Lewis), 39

shame and shamelessness: Brexit, 152–53; colonialism, 163; interaction of, 265–66

shame and shaming, 2–3, 6, 54–59; media and, 23; negative aspects of, 9–10; positive aspects of, 10

shame culture(s), 3, 232; aura of backwardness, 26; condemning, 26–27; guilt culture vs., 28; Taliban, 250

shameless: definition, 44; trends in use of word, 4

shameless leader, celebration of, 46

shamelessness, 4, 6; Brexit and, 147; dangerous, 46; of Eichmann, 93–95; impunity and, 276–80; perils of, 45; role in Sierra Leone, 88–90; science and objectivity, 274; shame and, 64; Sierra Leone and, 90–91; theater of, 45, 147, 277; underlying shame and, 59–63; Wurmser on cultures of, 101–2

shameless systems, 277

Shame Machine, The (O'Neil), 185

shame of war, Abu Ghraib and, 15

shame-proneness, 31, 40, 50

shame societies, 283; concept of, 2

shaming: age of person being shamed, 58–59; blaming and, 9; blindness to abuses of shamers, 8–9; buy-in, 56; condemnation and, 7–9; fueling abuses, 8; intentional act of, 55; people having respect for source of, 56–58; sense of self-worth in recipient of, 58; shame and, 54–59, 63; theater of, 45; type of shame, 58

Shiller, Robert, on emotional issues, 140

Sierra Leone, 273; atrocities, 85; atrocities in war, 75; civil war in, 3, 10, 74–91, 232, 266, 278; counterinsurgency, 81–82; dependency and emergency relief, 223; education and poverty, 193; Foday (captured peace worker) in, 86, 89; inverted morality in, 84–85; perverse definitions of shame, 58; rebel court in, 77; rebel initiations in, 79–80; rebels in, 229; recognition and respect, 75; Revolutionary United Front (RUF) rebels in, 81–82, 84, 192, 194; role of shamelessness in, 88–90; Sam Bockarie (rebel commander), 87; shame and shamelessness, 61; shame undercurrents in, 82–83; Smythe on atrocities in war, 191–92; student Idriss in, 74–80; war in, 72; war system of, 90–91; West Side Boys fighters, 86–87, 89; young fighters in, 67

Skocpol, Theda, Tea Party activists, 133

Slim, Hugo, on respecting human rights, 231

Sluzki, Carlos: on hostile vs. friendly witnesses, 32–33; Hutu propagandists as hostile witnesses, 214

Smythe, Amy, on atrocities of war, 191–92

Snyder, Timothy: on "gamers" and "breakers," 132; on shame of defeat, 168

Social Darwinism, 108

social glue, shame as, 48

social media, 1; narcissist and, 122

Social Mobility Commission (UK), 145

social transgression, shame signaling apology for, 47

soldiers: churning of, 20–21; honor, 24; sacrifice of, 21–22

Somerset Capital Management, 159

Sonderkommando, Levi on, 35

Soviet Union, 208; communism in, 224–25; selective blaming, 227

Speirs, Ronald, on Nietzsche and shamelessness, 59

spiral of shame, 2

Sri Lanka, 3, 230; human rights abuses, 230; Rajapaksa government, 210–11, 230; Tamil civilians, 210–11; Tamil Tiger terrorists, 211; war in, 252

Stangneth, Bettina, studies of Eichmann, 93–94, 99, 105–6
state of punishment, Nietzsche and, 41
States of Denial (Cohen), 33
status symbols, products as, 183
Stephanopoulos, George, on Trump, 119
Stern, Howard, Trump and, 116
Stewart, Jon, using humor, 275
Stolen Valor Act (2005), 17
Stone, Roger, on Trump, 113
Strandlof, Rick, 16–17; background of, 18. *See also* "Duncan, Rick" (Captain)
Strangers in Their Own Land (Hochschild), 130
Strasser, Valentine, Sierra Leone, 87
substance abuse, 31
Sudan, 3, 230; civil war and famine in, 208, 219–24; dependency and emergency relief, 223; Dinka ethnic group, 219–21; Jaspars's work on Darfur, 222–23; SPLA (Sudan People's Liberation Army), 219–20
suicide, 31
Summa Theologica (Aquinas), 45
Sun, The (newspaper), 146, 162
Sunak, Rishi: on respect for care workers, 307n6; Truss and, 174
superego: Freud's attitude, 36; Klein and Freud, 39
Suskind, Ron, on Bush advisor "reality-based" accusation, 260
symbolic language, action as, 67
Syria: al-Assad regime, 211–12; war in, 252

Talbot, Nancy, on shame and sexually abused women, 32
Taliban, shame culture/society, 250, 251
Tangney, June, on experience of shame, 25–26
Tea Party, 132, 201; activists, 133; ideology, 202
Tennyson's *The Charge of the Light Brigade*, 151
Teroni, Fabrice: anger as reaction to shame, 56; on bad press of shame, 50; on shame and humiliation, 68; on shame-prone individuals, 67
terrorist attack of 9/11: United States, 176–77; U.S.-led alliance, 253
Thatcher, Margaret: on Britain's "nanny state," 147; on unions and working class, 156
theater of shamelessness, 147, 277; Brexit, 11
Theweleit, Klaus, on chaos and shame, 235–36
This Fickle Heart (Desarthe), 168
Thomason, Krista: on feelings of shame, 36; looking back on moments of shame, 31–32; on moral shame, 52–54; on shame's painful qualities, 49
Three Pillars of Shame, The (Arendt), 240
Time (magazine), 119–20
Times (newspaper), 156
Tory Party, 147
totalitarianism, 34, 59, 121, 126, 149–50, 224, 240–42, 261, 281, 283
Totem and Taboo (Freud), 38
transformation, Trump's promise of, 118
trash TV, 59–60
Treaty of Versailles (1919), 234, 241
Troye, Olivia, on Trump and Covid pandemic, 143
Trump, Donald, 73; *Access Hollywood* tape, 111–12; anti-Muslim ban, 168; behavior as presidential candidate, 124–26; binaries, 115–18; Clinton on supporters of, 8; consensus politics, 157; election of, 124; extreme shamelessness of, 11; on fear of being wrong, 119–23; framing of shame, 123; promised wall of, 127; as protector of American women, 117–18; public condemnation, 1; shame and supporters of, 129–43; shame definition, 112; on shame of defeat, 168; South Korea and, 128; supporters and "deplorable" label, 57; support of, 5, 138; Twin Towers attack (9/11), 119–20; Vietnam of, 116; as winner in business, 113

Trumpelstiltskin, 126
Trumpism, 146, 153, 162
Trump University, 128
Truss, Liz: on Brexit, 158; Sunak and, 174; tax cuts of, 161
Truth about Trump, The (d'Antonio), 113
Tupac: Sierra Leone rebels favoring song by, 88; song "All Eyez on Me," 87
Turkey/Syria border, 3; Assad regime, 211

Uganda, 212, 216, 231, 303n30
UK Independence Party (UKIP), 154, 155; on Brexit, 144, 150
Unconscious, The (Freud), 37
underdevelopment, shame and, 191–95
Unification Church (Moonies), Benscoter on, 275–76
United Kingdom (UK): Blair on history of, 174–75; colonialism, 172–75; national values of, 176. *See also* Brexit
United States: immigration from Latin America, 177–78; mass incarceration in, 165–66; national values of, 176; shame and backlash, 163–68
University of Illinois, 26
UN's World Food Program, 222
USAID, 220
Uvin, Peter, on Rwandan genocide, 193–94

Vacuum Oil Company, Eichmann and, 95
Venugopal, Rajesh, education and employment, 193
Vergès, Francoise, on modern-day France, 170
Versailles treaty (1919), 234, 241
veterans: neglect of welfare, 21; sacrifice of, 21–22
victims, saving face, 290n18
Vidal, Gore: on poor and rich, 202; on value of product, 183
Vietnam: shame, Cold War and, 242–50; U.S. policy on, 243–45; Vietnam War, 116, 167, 215, 221–22, 232, 245

violence: civilization and, 51; shame, religion and, 40–43; task of explaining, 230. *See also* mass violence

Wahhabism, 42
Walker, Robert, on shame and poverty, 183, 199
Wall Street, 200–201; crash of 1929, 195
Wall Street (movie), 202
Walsh, Katherine Cramer, on Wisconsin, 141
war(s): on communism, 178, 209; on drugs, 178, 209; shamelessness and useful enemies, 208–13; Sierra Leone, 90–91; trauma as personality disorder, 20
war on terror, 12, 23, 27, 73, 175, 209, 221, 233; fundamentalists and, 41; Gilroy on, 175; global, 211, 212, 252; Iraq Veterans Against the War (IVAW) and, 16; Islamophobia and, 168; pain of veterans, 20; role of shame in generating, 257; shame and, 250–62; on threat of shame from violence, 279
Watkins, Mary, on American Dream, 132
weak soldiers, Trump on, 115–16
"weapons of mass destruction," Saddam's, 252, 261
Weber, Max, on Protestant ethic, 182
Weimar Republic, 238
Western democracies, 28
Western societies, 264, 283; policymaking of, 27
West Side Boys fighters, Sierra Leone, 86–87, 89
What's the Matter with Kansas (Frank), 139
white fragility, Caflisch on, 165
White Lives Matter, 166
Wildt, Michael, on insecurities of Nazis, 105
Williams, Raymond: on advertising, 180; magic system, 180, 187

Williamson, Gavin, on censoring history, 174
Williamson, Vanessa, Tea Party activists, 133
Wolf, Reinhard, on foreign policy, 179
working-class identity: depiction as lazy, 155; Jones on, 153–54
World Bank, 214
World War I, 12, 51, 105, 215, 234, 236, 238
World War II, 93, 115, 164
Wright, Tony, on Brexit, 157–58
Wurmser, Léon: on core experience of shame, 135; on cultures of shamelessness, 101–2; on omnipotence of responsibility, 37–38; on shamelessness and shame, 61–62
Wuthnow, Robert, on Washington and big corporations, 141

yellow vest, France, 171
YouTube, 23

zero tolerance law, civilians, 291n12
Žižek, Slavoj, on criminal behavior, 283
Zur, Judith, on war in Guatemala and its aftermath, 217–18

A NOTE ON THE TYPE

This book has been composed in Arno, an Old-style serif typeface in the classic Venetian tradition, designed by Robert Slimbach at Adobe.